D1563223

IN THE SHADOW OF THE DICTATORS

The British Left in the 1930s

PAUL CORTHORN

Tauris Academic Studies
LONDON • NEW YORK

For my parents

JN
1121
.C67
2006

Published in 2006 by Tauris Academic Studies, an imprint of I.B.Tauris & Co Ltd
6 Salem Road, London W2 4BU
175 Fifth Avenue, New York NY 10010
www.ibtauris.com

In the United States of America and Canada distributed by
Palgrave Macmillan a division of St. Martin's Press
175 Fifth Avenue, New York NY 10010

International Library of Political Studies 11

ISBN-10: 1 85043 843 9
ISBN-13: 978 1 85043 843 4

A full CIP record for this book is available from the British Library
A full CIP record for this book is available from the Library of Congress

Library of Congress catalog card: available

Printed and bound in India by Replika Press Pvt. Ltd
camera-ready copy edited and supplied by the author

CONTENTS

Acknowledgements   iv

Conventions and Abbreviations   v

Introduction   1

1. The Aftermath of 1931: August 1931 to October 1934   9

2. The Sanctions Crisis: October 1934 to October 1935   40

3. The Fascist Advance: October 1935 to July 1936   60

4. The Outbreak of the Spanish Civil War: July 1936 to October 1936   86

5. The Forging of a United Front: October 1936 to January 1937   106

6. The Unravelling of the Unity Campaign: January 1937 to May 1937   129

7. The Final Shattering of Unity: May 1937 to March 1938   159

8. The Approach of War: March 1938 to August 1939   179

Conclusion   212

Notes   217

Bibliography   271

Index   277

ACKNOWLEDGEMENTS

My thanks are due, first of all, to Peter Clarke who provided invaluable guidance as he supervised the Ph.D. on which part of this book is based. He also allowed me access to the Stafford Cripps papers which – with the kind permission of the Cripps family – were under his custodianship. More recently, he read and scrupulously commented on a draft of my book. Martin Brett and Deborah Thom offered much needed advice as I first considered the possibility of postgraduate research. Philip Williamson supervised my MA dissertation which opened up many subsequent lines of inquiry. Eugenio Biagini and the late Ben Pimlott acted as my Ph.D. examiners, very usefully suggesting how I could expand my work. Eugenio Biagini also commented on a penultimate draft of my book. David Dutton and Rohan McWilliam did likewise, making suggestions which have strengthened the final version. Richard Toye has provided a constant flow of stimulating ideas and rigorous criticism.

Archivists and librarians in locations listed in the bibliography have provided much valuable assistance. The wholehearted support given by Stephen Bird, Janette Martin and Darren Treadwell at the Labour History Archive and Study Centre in Manchester has always made working there a genuine pleasure.

At I.B.Tauris I am grateful to Lester Crook for his long-standing enthusiasm for the project, and to Elizabeth Munns for guiding me through the production process.

Many friends have helped along the way. Katherine Borthwick has provided unfailing support. My parents, Madeline and Patrick Corthorn, have always encouraged my career. I am very proud indeed to be able to dedicate this book to them.

CONVENTIONS AND ABBREVIATIONS

All places of publication are London unless otherwise stated.

AEU	Amalgamated Engineering Union
BLPES	British Library of Political and Economic Science
BUF	British Union of Fascists
CI	Communist International
CPA	Communist Party Archive
CPGB	Communist Party of Great Britain
DLP	Divisional Labour Party
HCLA	Home Counties Labour Association
IFTU	International Federation of Trade Unions
ILP	Independent Labour Party
ISP	Independent Socialist Party
LCC	London County Council
LHASC	Labour History Archive and Study Centre
LPA	Labour Party Archive
LPACR	*Labour Party Annual Conference Reports*
LRC	Labour Representation Committee
LSI	Labour and Socialist International
MFGB	Miners' Federation of Great Britain
NAC	National Administrative Council
NCL	National Council of Labour
NEC	National Executive Committee
NFRB	New Fabian Research Bureau
NJC	National Joint Council
NUDAW	National Union of Distributive and Allied Workers
NUR	National Union of Railwaymen
NUWM	National Unemployed Workers' Movement
PLP	Parliamentary Labour Party
POUM	Partido Obrero de Unificacion Marxista; Workers' Party of Marxist Unity

PPU   Peace Pledge Union
RPC   Revolutionary Policy Committee
SSIP   Society for Socialist Inquiry and Propaganda
TGWU   Transport and General Workers' Union
TUC   Trades Union Congress
TUCAR   *Trades Union Congress Annual Reports*
UAB   Unemployment Assistance Board
ULF   University Labour Federation
5 HC Debs *House of Commons Debates*, 5th series

INTRODUCTION

Left v. Labour Party (moderates)

During the 1930s British politics were increasingly dominated by the rise of the fascist dictators. The Left offered a series of radical responses, which put it very publicly at odds with the Labour party's moderate majorities and provoked frequent arguments and extended debate. Yet it was the failure rather than the success of the Left which had an abiding impact. By the end of the decade the Left's hopes of mobilising a significant body of domestic opinion against the British government had undoubtedly been thwarted. In one sense what had happened was clear: the Left had been checked institutionally by the power and established authority of the Labour party. At another level, however, the Left had itself failed, both tactically and ideologically, through its inability to present a coherent alternative. Time and again divisions emerged as it faced developments such as Mussolini's invasion of Abyssinia, Franco's uprising in Spain and Hitler's drive for territorial expansion. Significantly, these divisions correlated with the Left's constantly changing, and often conflicting, views of another dictatorship: the Soviet Union under Stalin. This had wider implications for the Left's own shifting identity – in ways that remain understudied and that still want convincing explanation.

In the Shadow of the Dictators considers the non-Communist Left largely in organisational terms. The Labour left took the form of the Socialist League between 1932 and 1937 and then became more loosely grouped around the *Tribune* newspaper. It retained a symbiotic relationship with the Independent Labour Party (ILP) which had disaffiliated from the Labour party in 1932. In numerical terms these organisations were not large. The Socialist League had no more than 3,000 members for most of its existence. Following its disaffiliation from the Labour party, the ILP's membership had quickly dwindled from more than 16,000 to about 4,500 by 1935 and thereafter continued to decline, though at a much slower rate. Nevertheless, neither the League nor the ILP could be ignored.

The Socialist League was particularly notable for its high-profile members. Its chairman and chief financial backer was Sir Stafford Cripps, a leading member of the Parliamentary Labour Party (PLP) who was widely regarded as a future leader of the party. Indeed, he became a cabinet minister in 1942 and went on to play a pivotal role in the post-war Labour governments, not least as chancellor of the exchequer. Among its other active members the League counted William Mellor, the former guild socialist; Charles Trevelyan, the former cabinet minister; the young Barbara Betts, who, as Barbara Castle, later achieved prominence in the Labour governments of the 1960s and 1970s; and Ellen Wilkinson, the hunger march activist. The fiery Welsh miners' MP, Aneurin Bevan, who challenged for the Labour party leadership in the 1950s, was also closely linked with the Socialist League. Moreover, the League had heavyweight intellectual support from Harold Laski, professor of political science at the London School of Economics, from H. N. Brailsford, the distinguished socialist writer, and, for some time at least, from G. D. H. Cole, the prolific Oxford don.

The ILP, though its leadership was admittedly less illustrious, punched above its weight in political terms. Throughout the 1930s it never had less than three representatives in Parliament. For most of this period its chairman was the Clydesider, James Maxton, who enjoyed a considerable reputation in the Labour movement, and its secretary was the prolific journalist Fenner Brockway who edited the ILP's paper – the *New Leader*. Furthermore, in 1938 George Orwell, who was steadily gaining a literary and political reputation, also joined the ILP. The profile of the organisational Left was further boosted by its loose, but sometimes fraught, association with Kingsley Martin's influential weekly journal the *New Statesman and Nation* throughout the decade and with Victor Gollancz's famous Left Book Club from 1936.

Although the Labour party has been dominated throughout its history by moderate social democratic elements, this does not mean that the Left has been unimportant. In particular, the Left has often been able to exert a degree of influence during periods – such as the 1950s and the 1980s as well as the 1930s – when the Labour party has been in opposition and undergoing a significant reappraisal of policy.

The Left has never been a homogenous entity but in the 1930s it was markedly more cohesive than at other times in the twentieth century. Often the Left has been held together only by a loosely defined Marxist interpretation of an economically-based class struggle and an immediate desire to push the Labour party in a more truly 'socialist' direction. In the 1930s, however, the Left possessed an institutional identity – or rather two of them – of a kind which was subsequently lacking in later decades. While the Bevanites in the 1950s were grouped loosely under Aneurin Bevan, and in the 1980s the two foremost members of the so-called 'hard left' – Tony Benn and Eric Heffer – had no formal links with each other, the leading members of both the Socialist League and the ILP met at least once a month (albeit not with each other) to discuss their policy positions and orchestrate their actions. This was one of the reasons why the dissolution of the Socialist League in 1937 represented a major defeat for the Left.

Even more important, the Left in the 1930s was united by its tightly defined political philosophy. Both the Labour left and the ILP shared a distinctive analysis of 'capitalist-imperialism', which, as David Blaazer has shown, led them to see domestic and foreign policy as interconnected.[1] This political philosophy had considerable intellectual pedigree. In his classic 1903 work on *Imperialism* the radical Liberal J. A. Hobson presented under-consumption as 'the taproot of imperialism'. He argued that in advanced industrialised countries the growth in productive power exceeded the growth in domestic consumption. Capitalists found themselves with more goods than they could sell profitably in the domestic market and with spare capital for which they could not find remunerative investment at home. They sought out opportunities abroad, and then relied on their national armed forces to protect their interests. It was, however, Brailsford who first followed these arguments through to socialist conclusions. Hobson had insisted that the excessive accumulation of capital that gave rise to imperialism was not an inherent feature of capitalism, but an anomaly that could be corrected through social reform. However, in his *The War of Steel and Gold* in 1913, Brailsford added the powerful socialist indictment that the whole process was 'a necessary inevitable accompaniment of capitalistic civilisation'. Largely through the efforts of Brailsford, the Hobsonian analysis had begun to exert a considerable influence over the ILP in the 1920s, which continued into the next decade.[2] Indeed, in the 1930s it underpinned the Left's whole response to the rise of fascism, which it interpreted as an extreme form of 'capitalist-imperialism'.[3] Above all, this analysis explains the Socialist League and the ILP's fundamental unwillingness to trust the National government in international affairs; they argued that not only would it necessarily act in its own 'capitalist' and 'imperialist' interests, but sensationally contended that it was even on the point of adopting a very English form of 'gentlemanly' fascism.

The Left's arguments always had a certain emotional appeal in a Labour party nominally committed to socialism, but in the political context of the 1930s their arguments had a particular resonance. Following prime minister Ramsay MacDonald's defection from the Labour party and his formation of the National government in 1931, the Labour party had swung to the left, envisaging a future struggle between socialism and capitalism. The party began to adopt a more moderate stance by 1934, but – even as the rise of fascism became the principal political issue after 1935 – it retained some of its earlier anti-capitalist views. This was why the Left's opposition to National government rearmament on account of its 'capitalist' and 'imperialist' tendencies could not be easily dismissed. Indeed, the Labour party as a whole opposed rearmament on broadly this basis until 1937. It is against this background, therefore, that the question of why the Left's policies were so decisively rejected becomes important.

Part of the explanation has been clearly elucidated: the more moderate figures controlling Labour's National Executive Committee (NEC) and the Trades Union Congress (TUC) General Council were working very closely to ensure their own supremacy and to defuse the threat from the Left. This interpretation – with various emphases and addressed either explicitly or implicitly – has been brought out by a number of different historians. In his influential survey *A Short History of the Labour Party* Henry Pelling argued that in the years immediately after 1931 crisis the TUC General Council, under the control of Ernest Bevin and Walter Citrine, 'moved in to take the helm' of the movement. For the remainder of the 1930s, Pelling contended, they worked through the National Joint Council (NJC), which was renamed the National Council of Labour (NCL) in 1934, and began to dominate the movement through control of policy.[4] More recent, and more detailed, work has argued that it is more accurate to consider that the NEC, and particularly Hugh Dalton and Herbert Morrison, dominated the Labour movement in the 1930s but, in doing so, worked closely with the TUC General Council which did exert its influence on certain issues. Ben Pimlott's *Labour and the Left* stressed that the NJC 'was never out of step with the majority view on the NEC', while his distinguished biography of Dalton further elucidated the importance of his subject arguing emphatically that 'the Labour party that entered the 1940 Coalition and formed a majority government five years later had an unmistakeably Daltonian stamp'.[5] So far as economic policy is concerned this appears to be the case.[6] On the other hand, the TUC General Council did take a larger role through the NCL in shaping foreign policy as, for example, Tom Buchanan's study *The Spanish Civil War and the British Labour Movement* makes clear.[7]

The NEC-TUC grouping – backed by block votes at the party conference – was obviously well placed to control the Labour party. But this does not adequately explain the scale of the Left's defeat. In 1937 the Left's proposal for a united front of working-class parties – the Labour party, the ILP and the Communist Party of Great Britain (CPGB) – as an alliance against the National government was rejected at the Labour party conference by a large majority that included more than just trade union votes. In 1939 the Labour left's advocacy of a popular front – a broader coalition including Liberals as well as working-class parties – met a similar fate.

In this sense it is Pimlott's *Labour and the Left* which has most shaped interpretations of the Left in this period by considering how its own actions contributed to its defeat. Thinking mainly in terms of the Labour left, Pimlott argued that it was 'consistently wrong on tactics'.[8] He identifies these as 'the tactics of direct confrontation' which meant that the Crippsite left 'engaged in factional fight after factional fight whose main effects were to alienate Labour opinion, and taint its own proposals'.[9] This theme ties in with the main argument of Pimlott's book, which is that the Labour party's best opportunity for influencing British politics in the 1930s was to lead a broad opposition, involving the dissident Conservatives – Winston Churchill, Leo Amery and Anthony Eden – as well as Liberals such as Archibald Sinclair, against Neville Chamberlain's foreign policy of appeasement. Pimlott argued that the very loose association, which Labour tentatively began to forge with these factions after Munich in autumn 1938, could have been made into an actual alliance. However, he contended that at this stage the party leadership was vigorously opposed to any kind of popular front because its most enthusiastic supporters within the party were Cripps and some of his former Socialist League colleagues. The previous year the NEC had severely reprimanded them for their advocacy of a united front, which it had perceived as a Communist attempt to infiltrate the Labour party, and now it rejected the idea of a wider alliance as simply another Communist plot.[10]

In addition to Pimlott's work, other contributions have added to a understanding of how the Left was operating in the 1930s, charting the Labour left's factional power struggle with the NEC-TUC grouping and establishing the contours of its response to the economic depression and then to the rise of fascism.[11] James Jupp's *The Radical Left* has done the same for the ILP, detailing its relations with the Labour party and the CPGB.[12] Even so, a full appreciation of the reasons underlying the failure of the Left has not been given. It is clear that after 1934 the Labour left adopted a similar approach in many respects to the ILP and sought to attract wider left-wing opinion to its policies rather than trying directly to influence the Labour party.[13] Yet, as it did so, the Left experienced a series of internal ruptures, which seriously undermined its position. Some of these differences have been noted but many of them – particularly those within the ILP and the Labour left rather than between them – have not been fully analysed.

In the Shadow of the Dictators investigates these divisions, examining in detail the policies the Left advocated at different points in response to the rise of fascism and providing a full account of the internal politics of the

Labour left and the ILP. In doing so, it benefits from the extensive range of
institutional and private paper sources – in addition, of course, to newspaper
sources – now available.

Above all, the book advances a new interpretation by arguing that, in a
variety of different ways, it was conflicting views of the Soviet Union which
were at the heart of the Left's inability to put forward a coherent political
position. In general terms, of course, the centrality of the Soviet Union to
the Left has been established. Indeed, David Howell has recently noted that
by the early 1920s in the Labour party 'the earlier Left varieties had become
more homogeneous, with identity centred increasingly around support for
the Soviet Union'.[14] This remained the case at least until the early 1930s, as
Andrew J. Williams's study of the years between 1924 and 1934 has
emphasised.[15] Both the ILP and the Socialist League viewed the Soviet
Union as the central point of reference not just in their domestic economic
policies but also in their foreign policies, where they placed a great deal of
faith in it as an ideological ally against international fascism in 1933 and
1934. The next few years, however, were enormously dislocating for the Left
– they saw the Soviet Union's entry into the League of Nations in 1934, the
purges and Show Trials between 1936 and 1938, and its contentious tactics
in the Spanish Civil War.

Yet the various views that the Left as a whole adopted towards the Soviet
Union during this time have either received only cursory attention,[16] or have
been interpreted in terms of debates between Trotskyists and fellow-
travelling Stalinists, thus distorting the stance of the bulk of the Left which
did not adhere to either of those positions.[17] The emphasis subsequently
placed on Orwell's experiences – particularly his time serving with the ILP
contingent in the Spanish Civil War which entrenched his suspicions of the
Soviet Union and was memorably described in *Homage to Catalonia* – has also
prevented an appreciation of the intricate range of responses to these events
on the non-Communist Left.

The ways in which reactions to developments in the Soviet Union fed into,
and undermined, the Left's response to fascism is then the central theme of this
book, and their collective impact on the Left's identity is its underlying
current. Under the impetus of the deepening international crisis, the Left's
ideology underwent a significant evolution. In a hesitant and, at times,
contradictory manner an anti-Stalinist critique developed across much of the
Left.[18] This involved an explicit comparison with Hitler's regime for its
methods of intimidation, its abuse of political and civil liberties, and its
disregard for judicial procedure – all of which was broadened out into an attack
on 'dictatorship'. Examining the core characteristics of dictatorship in this way
increasingly preoccupied the Left, ironically at the same time as the Labour

party repeatedly chastised the Left for its own supposed links with the Soviet dictatorship. Dictators and dictatorships thus shaped the intellectual and rhetorical frameworks within which the Left worked in the 1930s.

The book is divided into eight chapters, which proceed chronologically. The first chapter draws on existing work to illuminate the institutional dynamics of the Labour party after 1931. It chronicles the ILP's movement towards disaffiliation and the formation of the Socialist League. It shows that by 1934 the ILP was involved in an uneasy united front with the CPGB, and that the Socialist League was engaged in an intra-party struggle with the NEC-TUC grouping, increasingly over issues of foreign policy. The chapter seeks to emphasise the different ways in which the pro-Soviet identity of the ILP and the Socialist League was apparent in these years.

Chapter Two considers October 1934 to October 1935 as the Socialist League and the ILP responded to Mussolini's impending invasion of Abyssinia. Both organisations argued against support for League of Nations sanctions, instead advocating 'mass resistance' in order to depose the 'capitalist' and 'imperialist' National government. However, in summer 1935 a serious split emerged within the Socialist League as a sizeable minority decided to support collective security now that the Soviet Union was an active member of the League of Nations. This polarised debate and forced the Socialist League leaders to criticise Soviet foreign policy in the way that the ILP had already adumbrated over the course of the previous year.

Chapter Three covers the period between October 1935 and July 1936 and analyses the ILP's divisions over sanctions. The initial ILP line had been to call for 'working-class sanctions' against Italy: the refusal to produce or handle goods bound for Italy. Now, however, the influential ILP Parliamentary Group began to argue that it was wrong for British workers to take sides between Mussolini's regime and that of the Abyssinian Emperor. Meanwhile, both the ILP and the Socialist League campaigned against National government rearmament, and the Socialist League announced its support for CPGB membership of the Labour party.

Chapter Four examines the initial responses to the outbreak of the Spanish Civil War between July and October 1936. The Socialist League became a principal critic of the NCL's acceptance of the National government's non-intervention and helped to build up wider Labour enthusiasm in favour of support for the Republican side. The Spanish Civil War also brought to a head divisions within the Socialist League between those who supported its official policy of a united front and those who advocated a popular front as a more effective means of checking fascism. Like the Socialist League, the ILP opposed British non-intervention, but at the same time became critical of the Soviet Union's failure to help the

Republicans. The chapter also argues that the first round of Show Trials in Moscow prompted a distinctly anti-Stalinist critique to emerge from the ILP and from some of those in the Socialist League.

Chapter Five analyses the tense negotiations for a united front between the Socialist League, the ILP and the CPGB which took place between October 1936 and January 1937. It examines how hostile views of the Soviet Union's domestic regime plagued the discussions. The chapter shows that, for the time being at least, such differences could be overcome in light of the Soviet Union's popular decision to intervene in Spain.

Chapter Six is concerned with the actual Unity Campaign between January and May 1937. It analyses the developing opposition to the campaign by parts of the Socialist League, as well as by the ILP. The Soviet Union's suppression of the Workers' Party of Marxist Unity (POUM) in Spain, with which the ILP in particular had close links, together with a further round of Show Trials in Moscow, meant that anti-Stalinist criticisms were never very far from the surface. The chapter considers in detail why the Socialist League National Council decided to disband once it had been disaffiliated by the NEC and membership of it had been declared incompatible with membership of the Labour party.

Chapter Seven covers the period between May 1937 and March 1938 and explains how, after its dissolution, the former leaders of the Socialist League tried to continue the Unity Campaign, albeit to no avail. It shows that – amid further purges in the Soviet Union and Communist attacks on the POUM in Spain – the united front completely broke down. The ILP's anti-Stalinist criticism now intensified to unprecedented levels, and – with unity shattered – some important figures on the Labour left became more openly critical of the Soviet Union.

Chapter Eight analyses the period between March 1938 and August 1939 as the likelihood of war increased and the Soviet Union became markedly less central to the Left's outlook. Many on the Labour left now became willing to form a broader popular front and began to advocate an immediate strategic alliance with the Soviet Union in order to defend distinctly British values; they no longer publicly championed the Soviet Union as an ideological ally. Meanwhile, the ILP remained committed to working-class action, but significantly abandoned its long-term commitment to defend the Soviet Union. The ILP's foremost debates in these years concerned its relationship to the pacifist movement and re-affiliation to the Labour party, which it decided to pursue in August 1939. Together with the defeat of Cripps's final popular front initiative, this closed a period in the institutional history of the Left, just before the announcement of the Nazi-Soviet Pact.

1

THE AFTERMATH OF 1931

August 1931 to October 1934

The crisis of 1931, and its aftermath, shaped the organisational relationships of the Left for much of the coming decade. The minority Labour government under MacDonald had proved unable to devise a strategy to meet the economic crisis and the prime minister had instead formed a National government, supported by the Conservatives and many Liberals – but not by the mass of his own party. The Labour party now swung dramatically to the Left, yet by 1932 the more moderate elements dominating the NEC and the TUC General Council began to assert their influence. In this context the majority of the ILP moved steadily towards disaffiliation, distancing itself from the Labour party in a number of ways and significantly justifying its position – at least in part – with reference to its extremely favourable views of the Soviet Union. At the same time the left-wing think-tank the Society for Socialist Inquiry and Propaganda (SSIP) and that part of the ILP which wanted to remain inside the Labour party increasingly converged and subsequently formed the Socialist League – which was named after William Morris's left-wing body of the 1880s. During the course of 1933 and 1934 the ILP engaged in a turbulent united front agreement with the CPGB, setting itself further apart from the Labour party which had firmly rejected the idea. The Socialist League did not express support for the united front at this stage but nevertheless found itself embroiled in its first public disputes with the NEC-TUC grouping. The arguments were nominally over both domestic and foreign policy but, with the rise of Hitler prompting the Socialist League to demand a more wholehearted commitment to socialism, they were, in effect, as much about the League's greater affinity with the Soviet Union.

I

During the 1920s the Labour party established its position as the main opposition party and formed a minority government, under MacDonald, for the first time in 1924.[1] At the same time the Labour party became increasingly associated with the political philosophy of gradualism. MacDonald's ideas about the organic development of socialism from a vibrant capitalism had fused with a belief in the 'inevitability of gradualness' originally associated with the veteran Fabians Sidney and Beatrice Webb. MacDonald frequently portrayed socialism as a national and classless philosophy contrasting strongly with class-based capitalism. Labour's 1928 programme, *Labour and the Nation*, was characteristic of this whole approach. It demanded limited nationalisation, an increase in direct taxation and a strengthening of the League of Nations, but emphatically avoided priorities and timetables. However, during the second minority Labour government of 1929–31 gradualism began to appear increasingly bankrupt as the government was steadily undermined by a deepening economic depression. Throughout the 1920s the number of insured unemployed had never fallen below a million. The one definite short-term commitment in the Labour party's 1929 election manifesto was to deal immediately with this problem. However, unemployment began to rise following the Wall Street Crash in October 1929 and climbed to an unprecedented 2.5 million by December 1930.

Although dissatisfaction with MacDonald and his regime only became widespread within the Labour movement after 1930, parts of the ILP had been adopting an increasingly critical posture for a number of years.[2] Until the end of the Great War the ILP had been the individual members' section of the Labour party. However, Arthur Henderson's reforms in 1918 had set up ward and constituency (divisional) Labour parties with provision for direct individual membership. The nature of the ILP's relationship with the Labour party now became ambiguous; it was no longer the main way into the party for non-trade unionists, but it still counted party heavyweights such as MacDonald and Philip Snowden as well as rising parliamentary figures including Clement Attlee, the future party leader, among its members. Gradually, however, the ILP became increasingly factional, attracting those who were openly dissatisfied with the policies of the Labour party. Many in the ILP had felt a sense of disappointment with the 1924 minority Labour government, arguing that it had placed parliamentary expediency before its commitment to socialism. From 1926 the ILP veered even more sharply to the left as it strove to become a powerhouse of socialist ideas. Maxton, Brockway, John Wheatley, Fred Jowett and the economist Frank Wise became the prime movers in the ILP and produced *The Living Wage*, which was endorsed by the ILP annual conference in 1926. This policy statement was shaped by its co-author Hobson and based squarely on his theory of 'underconsumption'– the proposition that the maldistribution of income led to over-saving and, in turn, to economic slump and unemployment. *The Living Wage* therefore advocated increased direct taxation, a 'living wage' and family allowances as well as comprehensive nationalisation and planning. Above all it was an immediate programme, which would be introduced at once by the next Labour government even if it were in a minority. Inevitably, the ILP now began to lose much of its moderate support. Attlee had his candidature transferred from the ILP to the Divisional Labour Parties in December 1926, and Snowden resigned the following year.

The ILP took an increasingly confrontational stance towards the Labour government between 1929 and 1931.[3] Partly, differing views of the Soviet Union were at stake as Williams has recognised. With the ILP's long-standing affinities with the Soviet Union, it was not surprising that Brailsford, Brockway, Maxton and Wise had been some of the sharpest critics of MacDonald's 'non-respecting' of the 1929 election pledge to bind Britain and Russia more closely together.[4] However, the more specific cause of the deterioration of relations between the ILP and the government came over economic policy. As the depression worsened and capitalism really seemed to be in crisis, they attacked Snowden's unwillingness, as Chancellor of the Exchequer, even to consider their economic remedies. During 1930, these tensions fed into existing anxieties about the status of the ILP Parliamentary Group. This group – led by Maxton – objected to the rigidity of party discipline and argued that it was unreasonable to ask MPs, through the party's standing orders, to vote for Bills which had not been approved by the PLP or the party conference. It was indeed significant that MacDonald resigned his own membership of the ILP in 1930.

In contrast to the ILP's long-running tradition of dissent, the formation of the SSIP in June 1931 was a direct manifestation of the disillusionment that many Labour intellectuals felt with the Labour government.[5] During winter 1930–1 a number of them had begun meeting at Easton Lodge, the home of the Countess of Warwick, under the guidance of G. D. H. Cole, the former guild socialist.[6] They soon decided that an institutional identity was essential and constituted the SSIP as a 'new unofficial organisation' within the party.[7] The barrister D. N. Pritt, the economist E. A. Radice and the sketch cartoonist Frank Horrabin were, together with Attlee, Cripps and Mellor, the SSIP's most prominent members.[8] Significantly, Cole managed to persuade the trade unionist Bevin to act as chairman of this body. However, given Bevin's administrative duties as general secretary of the Transport and General Workers' Union (TGWU) he had little time to devote to the SSIP and Cole remained its central figure.[9] The SSIP was determined not to become a political faction like the ILP and did not seek affiliation to the Labour party, or to sponsor electoral candidates: its members were known as 'loyal grousers'. Nevertheless, through conferences and weekend schools, it sought to offer constructive criticism of the government from a socialist standpoint, as well as to develop detailed alternative policies.[10]

II

The events of August 1931, when the Labour government was overwhelmed by a sterling and budget crisis, completely discredited the political philosophy of gradualism.[11] The collapse of the main Austrian bank in May 1931 had precipitated the financial crisis. This had led to the freezing of assets across Europe, which in turn meant that London became subject to large withdrawals of gold, threatening Britain's position on the gold standard. MacDonald accepted the reasoning of Snowden who forcefully asserted that only a policy of retrenchment would restore confidence and set recovery in process. He accepted the verdict of the May Committee, which on 31 July 1931 recommended a £97 million cut in burgeoning government expenditure, of which two thirds would come from cutting unemployment benefit, raising contributions and imposing a means test. When foreign holders of sterling then became convinced of Britain's insolvency and started to sell, the Bank of England borrowed heavily from the United States and France in order to maintain the pound's parity on the gold standard. However, a £350 million loan proved insufficient and the New York Federal Reserve only agreed to provide a further £80 million if the government demonstrated its willingness to implement the May Committee proposals. Initially it appeared that the Cabinet would comply, but by 23 August it had reached deadlock. MacDonald and Snowden, along with 12 other ministers, were willing to accept a ten per cent cut in unemployment benefit, but another nine refused. MacDonald offered the government's resignation, but announced the following day that the King was to invite 'certain individuals, as individuals, to take upon their shoulders the burden of government' and that he was to remain as prime minister. In the event, however, Snowden, J. H. Thomas and Lord Sankey were the only Cabinet ministers who joined the new and largely Conservative National government.

The Labour movement responded to these dramatic developments by adopting a more stridently socialist viewpoint – the kind that the ILP and the SSIP had previously advocated.[12] Henderson, who had been elected party leader, was personally inclined towards a restrained approach and even held hopes that MacDonald would soon return to the party.[13] However, the TUC General Council was determined that the Labour movement should offer unwavering opposition to the National government. Significantly, it was able to dominate at this crucial juncture because it had definite ideas about the nature of the crisis and some sense of how the movement should proceed. Before 1926 the Council's concerns had been almost wholly industrial. But in the aftermath of the General Strike the TUC General Council, and Bevin in particular, had begun to take great interest in general economic policies, even monetary policies.[14] The General Council had been aggrieved with what it saw as the PLP's lack of consultation during the second Labour government and seized the opportunity to play an important role in convincing many in the Cabinet to resist any cuts.[15] Bevin and Citrine argued that the sterling crisis was a conscious ploy by international capitalism to defeat the Labour government.[16] As a result by the end of August Labour's three Executives (the NEC, the PLP Executive and the TUC General Council) had declared 'vigorous opposition' to the National government and published a manifesto, which called for resistance to 'international and national financial interests' and defence of the working class through 'determined opposition' to all cuts in incomes, social services and public works.[17] It was clear that the Labour party was readily following the TUC lead. Indeed, George Lansbury, the veteran pacifist and feminist, and Christopher Addison, a medical doctor and a former Liberal who had joined the Labour party in the 1920s, had always been more steadfast than many of their colleagues in their opposition to cuts in unemployment benefit. In late August they even began to argue that a 'bankers' ramp' had brought about the fall of the Labour government.[18] Now many others in the party started to see distinct advantages in explaining the crisis in this way. It provided a means of putting the blame on MacDonald and Snowden rather than on the party and enabled former Cabinet members to gloss over their earlier support for the benefit cuts. For example, Morrison, who had possibly considered even joining MacDonald in the National government,[19] now asserted that 'Labour must move to the left – the real socialist Left'.[20]

This impassioned socialist rhetoric soon developed into apocalyptic claims about the imminent collapse of capitalism even by those on the moderate wing of the party such as Dalton and Morrison.[21] Moreover, at this point a Finance and Trade Committee was set up in order to devise the party's new socialist programme.[22] Despite initially devoting much of its time to considering Britain's commitment to the Gold Standard (work which became less relevant once the National government itself took Britain off the Gold Standard on 20 September), the committee proposed in outline bold measures of socialisation that marked a significant departure from MacDonaldite moderation and which were subsequently overwhelmingly endorsed at the party conference.[23] Besides the reversal of the unemployment and social service cuts, the Labour party was now committed to public ownership of the 'banking and credit system', the coal, power, transport, and iron and steel industries, the creation of National Investment, Import and Export Boards, and the participation of workers in the management of socialised industries.[24]

The SSIP now fell in line behind the Labour party, readily sanctioning its affirmation of socialist tenets. The crisis had convinced Cole – like many others – that capitalism was 'tottering and ready to fall'. He was now perfectly willing to approve the party's resolve to 'fight the working-class battle henceforth on the plain issue of capitalism versus socialism, and on the basis of an immediate socialist policy'.[25] Cripps took the same attitude, and this had important implications for his role on the Labour left for the rest of the 1930s. Cripps had previously professed a less thoroughgoing socialism than many others in the SSIP. He was a successful KC who had only joined the Labour party in 1929. Cripps did, however, come from a political family. His father, Lord Parmoor, had been a Conservative who transferred his allegiance to the Labour party and became Lord President of the Council in both the 1924 and 1929–31 Labour governments. Cripps was also the nephew of Beatrice Webb, whose husband Sidney was a significant Labour politician and had been (as Lord Passfield) Colonial Secretary in the 1929–31 Labour government. MacDonald appointed Cripps as Solicitor General in October 1930, giving him the customary knighthood and then arranging for him to contest the East Bristol constituency in January 1931.[26] MacDonald also invited Cripps to remain as Solicitor General in the National government in late August 1931.[27] However, Cripps not only refused but in the next few weeks moved rapidly to the left. In his view it was now 'absolutely necessary to throw off once and for all the attitude of compromise – and to come out boldly with a slap-up Socialistic policy'.[28] Indeed, Cripps undoubtedly captured the mood of the Labour party conference in October 1931 when he insisted that the 'one thing that is not inevitable now is gradualness'.[29]

A significant minority in the ILP, led by Wise and including Brailsford and Trevelyan, also endorsed the Labour party's new left-wing stance. In June 1931 the ILP had indicated the course it would take in August by declaring its outright opposition to the interim majority report of the Unemployment Insurance Commission. The ILP strongly opposed its recommendations of a reduction in benefit payments, a shorter period of benefit entitlement, increased contributions and a means test on transitional benefit claimants.[30] Brailsford now welcomed the Labour party's willingness to engage capitalism in 'the struggle for economic power'.[31] Similarly, at the party conference Wise spoke approvingly of how the imminent collapse of capitalism had prompted the Labour party to rediscover its 'socialist faith'.[32]

At the same time many in the ILP followed Maxton and Brockway who remained keen to keep their distance from the Labour party and now began to question its commitment to the ambitious socialist goals it had adopted.[33] Like many in the Labour movement Maxton and Brockway argued that capitalism was collapsing, and that the crisis had been precipitated by a bankers' plot to maintain it.[34] Yet they differed from the rest of the movement in the extent of their reaction. They argued that nothing short of a 'revolutionary situation' was 'rapidly approaching'.[35] They hinted strongly that extra-parliamentary methods might have to be adopted if the working class was to win control of the economic and financial system and made a point of establishing contact with the Communist-dominated National Unemployed Workers' Movement (NUWM).[36] The split in the ILP ranks at this juncture was of great significance; it paved the way for the formation of the Socialist League when the Wise group of 'loyal' ILPers and the SSIP would join together before attempting to impress their radical programme on an increasingly moderate party.

However, at this stage the SSIP and the Wise group of the ILP found themselves not merely sharing the prevailing mood of the Labour movement, but also involved in its policy-making. Attlee, Cripps, Wise, Radice and Addison were prominent members of the all-important Trade and Finance Committee.[37] And, after the National government announced in early October that it would contest a General Election with MacDonald as its leader, Laski was given overall responsibility for drafting the party's election manifesto.[38]

III

The campaign preceding the general election – which was held on 27 October – sealed the divisions between the Labour party and MacDonald's National Labour Group, and its outcome then saw a dramatic reduction of the Labour party's parliamentary representation, with important consequences. Labour's seats in parliament fell from 288 to just 46, compared to the National government's 554 seats of which 470 were Conservative.[39] Crucially, this loss of seats was so severe that it changed the institutional balance within the Labour movement.[40] It shifted the centre of power away from the PLP, where both the Wise group and the SSIP were strongly represented, and towards the NEC and the TUC General Council. The parliamentary party had effectively controlled the movement for the previous decade by dominating the NEC, the key decision-making body in the

Labour party between annual conferences. By 1924 MPs counted for nearly half of the NEC. After 1929 this proportion increased to two thirds, with an average of ten members of the government on the 24 seat Executive. However, the electoral debacle of 1931 broke the close link between the PLP and the NEC because most of the parliamentary leaders – including Henderson, Morrison, Dalton and Arthur Greenwood – lost their seats. Indeed, Lansbury was the only former Cabinet minister and member of the NEC to hold his seat. Exactly half of the PLP were representatives of the Miners' Federation of Great Britain (MFGB) and its composition was not unlike that of the pre-war party or even the Labour Representation Committee (LRC) as which the Labour party had started life in 1900. The average parliamentary membership of the NEC fell from over 16 in 1929–31 to just three between 1931 and 1935. Although Henderson remained overall party leader, Lansbury was duly elected as PLP leader in November 1931. With the relatively junior Attlee as his deputy, and the inexperienced Cripps as the other leading member of the PLP, Lansbury led the small band of parliamentarians that was now overshadowed by the NEC as the voice of the political wing of the movement.[41]

Following the loss of their parliamentary seats, Dalton and Morrison began to use the NEC as their power base and found themselves increasingly allied with Bevin and Citrine on the TUC General Council. The TUC leaders were seriously disillusioned with the entire parliamentary party, and began to assert forcefully that the Labour party was just the political wing of the TUC. In November 1931 they seized the opportunity to formalise their position of increased influence within the movement: the moribund NJC was reconstituted with an inbuilt majority of members from the General Council over those from the NEC and the PLP, and at the same time was given an extended jurisdiction to 'consider all questions affecting the Labour movement as a whole'.[42]

In December the NEC – with the full support of the General Council – set up a Policy Committee, a restructured version of the body set up in September, to construct the new and comprehensive Labour programme. It had standing sub-committees on industrial organisation, finance and trade, local government and social services, and constitutional matters.[43] Significantly, prominent members of the SSIP such as Attlee and Cripps as well as loyal ILPers like Wise, who had been influential on the earlier Trade and Finance Committee, were now sidelined as Morrison and Dalton controlled the most important sub-committees. Dalton and Morrison resented the way in which Cripps and Attlee had been promoted to front bench status in the House of Commons simply because they had held their seats.[44] Now Morrison dominated the Industrial Organisation Sub-committee, where he developed the public corporation model for nationalised industries based on the one he had formulated for the London Passenger Transport Board while Minister of Transport between 1929 and 1931.[45] And Dalton chaired the Finance and Trade Sub-committee, which counted the young Labour economists Evan Durbin, Hugh Gaitskell and Douglas Jay among its members, and worked closely with the XYZ Club, an anonymous body of Labour sympathisers in the City.[46]

IV

The majority in the ILP now moved closer to disaffiliation. Maxton and the ILP Parliamentary Group had been denied official Labour party endorsement for the General Election.[47] However, at a meeting of the National Administrative Council (NAC) – the ILP's decision-making body – on 7 November 1931 Brockway, as ILP chairman, and Maxton were actually against immediate disaffiliation. John Paton, the party secretary, also sided with them and stressed the dangers of disaffiliation from an organisational point of view.[48] As a result the meeting took the decision to cancel a Special Conference planned for the end of November which was to have discussed disaffiliation.[49] Perhaps the fact that five ILP MPs – the Clydesiders Maxton, John McGovern, George Buchanan and David Kirkwood as well as Richard Wallhead who represented Merthyr Tydfil – had been returned in the 1931 General Election gave Maxton and others hope that they would be able to assert a greater influence over the numerically diminished PLP.[50] Indeed, after the election Maxton had even been offered a place on the Labour Front Bench by Henderson and Lansbury.[51] However, the momentum pushing the ILP towards disaffiliation continued to build. Overall, the divisional conferences held in January and February 1932 voted by two to one in favour of remaining inside the Labour Party. Yet it did become clear at this juncture just how far support for disaffiliation was growing in the London area: its divisional conference endorsed the idea by 41 votes to 28.[52] Accordingly, when the NAC considered these results on 20 and 21 February, it decided to allow the ILP national conference to debate disaffiliation. At the same time though, the NAC declined to make any recommendation to the conference on the issue.[53]

To some extent what had happened was that the ILP branches, and particularly those in London, had been able to influence its overall direction in ways that become more explicable through an understanding of the ILP's structure. R. E. Dowse comments that throughout the ILP's history the NAC was 'weak . . . with little power of initiative in policy matters'.[54] The NAC comprised a representative from each of the nine regional divisions together with four national members, a chairman and a treasurer. However, the branches enjoyed considerable autonomy – being able to send their own chairmen, *ex officio*, as members of the NAC. Only the four national members, and the chairman and treasurer, were actually elected by the conference. Now, in March 1932, before the national conference met, an organised London-based body moved to prominence within the ILP: the Revolutionary Policy Committee (RPC) which had been formed in 1930, had the Poplar health inspector C. K. Cullen as its chairman and contained the solicitor Jack Gaster among its foremost members.[55] The RPC argued more strongly even than Brockway and Maxton that a revolutionary situation was imminent. Its central concern was to ensure that the ILP moved further away from the Labour party and closer to the CPGB in order to prepare for the imminent collapse of capitalism. Crucially, given the NAC's relative weakness, the RPC was able to push the ILP further towards disaffiliation.[56] At the ILP conference in Blackpool it was Cullen who moved a resolution in favour of disaffiliation. In the event this was rejected by 183 votes to 144. It was, however, perhaps more indicative of the hardening mood in favour of disaffiliation that a resolution for continued unconditional affiliation was rejected by 214 votes to just 98. In the end though, the conference simply resolved that the NAC should continue to negotiate with the Labour party for the satisfactory revision of the Standing Orders.[57]

These ensuing talks proved unsuccessful and, as the more moderate figures re-asserted control over the Labour party, Brockway – with the support of Paton – increasingly spoke of the need for the ILP to 'become revolutionary instead of reformist'.[58] Maxton did likewise, strongly invoking the example of the Soviet Union and proudly comparing the dispute between the ILP and the Labour party to that between the Bolsheviks and Mensheviks.[59] This change of stance as much as pressure from the RPC explains why – following unsuccessful discussions with the Labour party – the NAC decided at its meeting on 4 June to advise the proposed Special Conference to vote in favour of disaffiliation. On this occasion only Pat Dollan, the Scottish representative on the NAC, had voted against this recommendation.[60] When the Special Conference met on 30 July, the ILP duly voted by 241 to 142 in favour of disaffiliation and a revolutionary policy. This course had been strongly endorsed not just by the RPC but also by Maxton and Brockway, the latter speaking of the 'explosive effect' of the Soviet example and the ways in which it might inspire the workers to revolution.[61] The arguments made by Dollan and Wise – in favour of continued affiliation on the basis that the ILP would otherwise lose considerable support – had been rejected.[62]

V

While the majority of the ILP chose to leave the Labour party, the NEC's attempt to monopolise its policy-making processes prompted the SSIP, together with the loyal ILPers, to make renewed attempts to shape the Labour party's programme. The Wise group and those in SSIP still held some hopes of influencing the Labour party.[63] However, they increasingly recognised that their aspirations were likely to be thwarted if the Labour party's right wing was allowed to re-assert itself and develop a more measured approach to socialism.[64]

Cripps resented the NEC's domination of the party machine and felt that the PLP was deprived of appropriate influence over its policy-making.[65] Yet the SSIP now proved an inadequate vehicle through which he, Attlee, Cole, Laski and others could oppose the NEC because its role was too highly circumscribed. For instance, an official statement of objectives issued in November 1931 stressed that it aimed 'not at providing a new and rival policy, but at working out more fully and clearly the policy already endorsed by the Labour party and the TUC'.[66] This was the basis on which Bevin, with his ambivalence towards 'intellectuals', continued to support the SSIP.[67] However, the constraints that made Bevin amenable to involvement in the SSIP led many of its most prominent members to form the House of Commons Group at Easton Lodge on 16–17 April 1932. It had a much more ambitious character than the SSIP and sought in a more explicit way to shape the Labour party's policies.[68] Its membership included G. D. H. Cole, his wife Margaret Cole, Lansbury, Addison, Cripps, Horrabin, Mellor, Laski, Attlee and Pritt as well as the barrister G. R. 'Dick' Mitchison and the influential Labour intellectual R. H. Tawney. Dalton was also a member but significantly Bevin was not.[69] Indeed, Bevin's attitude towards the House of Commons Group demonstrated that it was a different kind of body to the SSIP. Less than a month after the Group's formation he was complaining to Cole about the 'patronising air' taken by its members towards the unions.[70] By July he had rejected Cole's suggestion that he chair a special meeting of the House of Commons Group at the TUC in a way that made it absolutely clear he wanted nothing to do with the Group.[71]

Before long, signs of the antipathy that would later epitomise relations between the Socialist League and the NEC-TUC grouping became apparent. One of the issues at conflict was the extent and scope of the emergency powers that a future Labour government would have to introduce in order to overcome capitalist obstruction. Cole and his former guild socialist associate, Mellor, were clear that these were likely to be substantial. Dalton, however, strongly disagreed.[72] Another point of dispute arose over the nationalisation of the joint-stock banks. While Cole was convinced of their pivotal importance, Dalton was not.[73] It was clear that Morrison was aligning with Dalton. He had politely refused Cole's initial invitations to attend the meetings of the House of Commons Group.[74] However, in May he informed Cole that his attendance was frankly 'undesirable' and that he would feel 'rather awkward', because he was involved with the NEC's committees which were dealing with 'the same matters'.[75]

The discord between the moderate and radical wings of the Labour party soon further intensified. By the end of May 1932 the House of Commons Group had produced a 'Programme of Action', outlining its core policy proposals,[76] which Dalton inevitably refused to sign.[77] The programme was sent to the NEC Policy Committee,[78] but the National Executive acted quickly to ensure that it was shelved.[79] Cole and Wise both now made personal approaches to Dalton, asking him to consider seriously the nationalisation of the joint-stock banks[80] but found him determined that he 'must not yield to these people'.[81] The Finance and Trade Sub-committee's own conference resolutions that were published in July reflected this attitude. They proposed the nationalisation of the Bank of England and accepted the possible need for some emergency powers, but they made no mention at all of the nationalisation of the joint-stock banks.[82]

VI

The SSIP and the ILP Affiliation Committee now saw the sense in joining together to pursue their common objectives. In early July 1932 Cole had been confident that he would be able to induce those in the ILP who decided against disaffiliation from the Labour party to join a re-shaped SSIP. In a memorandum to the SSIP Executive Committee he argued that they must pre-empt the formation of a new affiliationist body by openly appealing to the loyalists to join the SSIP. He was willing to accept major changes to the SSIP that would see it become a 'far more formal type of organisation', with new and larger branches incorporating the old SSIP branches as research centres, more regular meetings, a national organiser and systematic fund-raising. He also recognised that the SSIP would have to consider affiliating to the Labour party at the local and national level – a course that it had previously rejected. His only reservation was that the reformed SSIP must not participate in electoral politics by promoting candidates in either parliamentary or local elections.[83]

However, the momentum shifted to the Wise group later in July after the ILP special conference decided to disaffiliate from the Labour party. Wise and his followers now set up the ILP Affiliation Committee because they continued to regard the Labour party as 'the one organisation which, whatever its imperfections, has any chance of achieving socialism in our time'.[84] Wise then arranged for his extended article on the need for an affiliated Socialist body to be published on 13 August 1932 to coincide with the announcement of a conference of the National Affiliation Committee to be held in London on 20 August.[85] Moreover, in the week before the conference a number of loyal ILP branches in the south formed the London and southern counties ILP Affiliation Committee. This committee included Horrabin and Brailsford and became the organising centre of the national affiliation movement. One of its first decisions was to hold a regional conference in London in September.[86] The meeting of the National Affiliation Committee in London on 20 August then heard details of further regional conferences to be held in Lancashire, Yorkshire, South Wales and the Midlands. It was indicative of the growing confidence of the affiliationists that the committee agreed to put forward nominees for adoption by the Labour party as candidates in the November municipal elections.[87]

Cole had made a serious miscalculation in thinking that he could outmanoeuvre the affiliationists. As Wise was aware, they were in a strong position with the backing of sections of the ILP throughout England, Wales and Scotland and virtual control of the regional organisations in Lancashire, the North East and Scotland outside Glasgow. Wise speculated that they might have as many as 10,000 potential supporters in these branches whereas the SSIP had only 300 members. The affiliationists were, therefore, prepared 'to go ahead and try to form a Socialist organisation inside the Labour party'.[88]

When Cole realised there was a possibility that the SSIP might be completely eclipsed unless it merged with the ILP Affiliation Committee, he let Wise know that the SSIP would be prepared to make concessions. He told George Catlin, who was in touch with Wise, that he would 'not necessarily rule out under all circumstances the nomination of candidates by such a body'.[89] On this basis Wise agreed to meet the SSIP, as well as the New Fabian Research Bureau (NFRB), with a view to incorporating them into the new organisation. The NFRB was another think tank whose membership included Cole, Attlee, Mitchison and Laski, as well as Gaitskell and Durbin. Apparently due to Dalton's misgivings over Cole, at this point the NFRB was not in a position to influence the NEC Policy Sub-committee.[90] During summer 1932 the NFRB had also been considering the possible need for emergency powers and the question of the nationalisation of the joint-stock banks.[91] In any case, the SSIP executive met on 16 September before meeting Wise the following day, and gave wide support to Cole's position that they should not 'be confronted with an accomplished fact in the new Socialist League'.[92]

Nevertheless, the Affiliation Committee was particularly successful in managing 'to preserve the nucleus of its own organisation'.[93] It was indeed doubtful that they saw 'the fusion as a real amalgamation and not a mere absorption'.[94] First of all the NFRB left the discussions because they felt Wise was forcing the pace so that the new body could affiliate to the Labour party at its annual conference in October. Horrabin – who was in a rather anomalous position as a member of the SSIP, but an Affiliation Committee representative at the negotiations – admitted that he was 'rather acutely ashamed of the bargaining-grudging spirit of "my side"'.[95] This approach clearly paid dividends. After 'much difficulty and several near-ruptures', the affiliationists secured Wise as chairman over the SSIP's choice of Bevin. They also largely had their way in the disputes over the composition of the 20-seat executive. Ten of these were to be elected on a national basis, and the other ten from the regions – an arrangement bound to benefit the affiliationists who retained the loyalty of many ILP branches around the country. The SSIP demanded five of the national seats and the right to nominate to the regional seats. The Wise group was reluctant to concede more than three, but eventually agreed to four.[96]

The SSIP had been overwhelmed in the negotiations. Bevin refused to join the executive of the new Socialist League.[97] Cole had been consistently opposed to the Socialist League's involvement with electoral politics, but had finally been unable to insert any effective guarantees into its constitution.[98] Cole told Cripps who had been 'specially concerned about the possibility of Wise and his friends wanting to make the Socialist League the nucleus for a political party with the possible danger of a row with the Labour party at a later stage' that he had 'impressed upon the Wise group the fact that we are only amalgamating on condition that the new show will not be primarily electoral, and have found a substantial agreement with this view on the part of certain of Wise's leading supporters, notably Brailsford and Horrabin'.[99]

Nevertheless, when the SSIP executive met on 26 September it concurred with the decision made by the National Affiliation Committee the previous day and agreed to the formation of the Socialist League.[100] At this stage Cole himself voted against the amalgamation. In 1948 he wrote that this was because he 'regarded it as indispensable to carry Bevin into the new body' so that it would have a link with the trade unions. Reluctantly he agreed to follow the majority, but was 'soon to repent'.[101] However, this retrospective reflection obscures the fundamental agreement between the ILP affiliationists and the members of SSIP over questions of policy and tactics, notwithstanding their disagreement over the fielding of electoral candidates. After all, many prominent members of the SSIP had been involved with the House of Commons Group and, in early July, Cole had been willing to change radically the constitution of the SSIP in order to incorporate the Wise group. Moreover, the rules of the Socialist League did not allow the National Council to promote or run electoral candidates; a compromise reached at the inaugural meeting of the Socialist League simply left open the possibility that the branches of the Socialist League could make nominations to the divisional Labour parties to which they were affiliated but that any 'Socialist League' candidate whose nomination was accepted would have to run as a divisional Labour party candidate either for a local authority or for Parliament.[102] Before the negotiations had even begun Wise had actually stressed that he was keen 'to avoid the causes which landed the ILP in its present mess . . . partly by abstaining from putting forward our own candidates for municipal and national purposes except through the Labour parties'.[103] Perhaps Cole's later attitude was inspired more by personal bitterness towards Wise, who had increasingly seized the initiative during the negotiations, than through genuine misapprehension at the shape that the League was taking.[104] Cole himself admitted that the negotiations had been 'greatly complicated by rival personal ambitions among would-be leaders'.[105] Moreover, Bevin hardly drew any distinction between those in the SSIP such as Cripps and Mellor and the loyal ILPers. He lamented that he did 'not believe the Socialist League will change very much from the old ILP attitude, whoever is in the Executive'.[106] Bevin may well have been slighted by Cole's inability to secure his chairmanship, but he did nevertheless offer the Socialist League space in the *New Clarion* – which the TUC General Council had recently helped to launch – for publicity.[107]

The inaugural conference of the Socialist League was held on 2 October 1932 at which its constitution was approved pending final adoption by the League's annual conference which was scheduled for Whitsun the following year. Wise was confirmed as chairman, and Brailsford, Cole, Cripps, Horrabin, Kirkwood, Mellor and Trevelyan elected on to the National Council, where they were joined by Frederick Pethick-Lawrence, who had been deeply involved the female suffrage movement, Arthur Pugh, the trade unionist, and Alfred Salter, the pacifist.[108] Dollan's Scottish Socialist Party, which had been formed in the summer after the decision of the majority of the ILP to disaffiliate, was invited to co-operate with the Socialist League 'upon a basis yet to be determined',[109] but in fact never did so.

VII

The Socialist League's first ten months of existence set the scene for its coming struggle with the NEC-TUC grouping. As early as the first week in October – at the Labour party conference – Dalton and Bevin faced opposition from Wise and Cripps who demanded that the joint-stocks should be nationalised in addition to the Bank of England.[110] In the end, the actual vote showed the Socialist Leaguers had narrowly prevailed – even if the NEC was subsequently able to gloss over the inconclusive result and assert that Wise and Cripps were only seeking 'a reaffirmation of the policy of our Party'.[111] Trevelyan then put another resolution to the conference which asked that when Labour next took office 'with or without power, definite socialist legislation must be immediately promulgated, and that the Party shall stand or fall in the House of Commons on the principles in which it has faith'.[112] Henderson opposed the resolution but was continuously interrupted and heckled by the delegates.[113] Attlee then spoke in support of the resolution, which was put to the conference and carried.[114] Together, these events represented a significant early success for the Socialist League, reflecting the strength of the lingering left-wing feeling in the Labour movement.

Dalton noted that in the aftermath of the party conference there was 'much suspicion of this new body in outside circles, at T[rans]p[or]t House and on the N[ational] E[xecutive]'.[115] Nevertheless, at this stage the Socialist League professed its firm loyalty to the Labour party. When the Socialist League formally applied for affiliation to the Labour party on 10 October, it enclosed its rules and constitution. These blandly committed the Socialist League 'to make Socialists, and to further by propaganda and investigation the adoption by the working-class movement of an advanced programme and a socialist outlook', at the same time as affirming its commitment to the class struggle.[116] Henderson was in Geneva at this point but the National Agent wrote to him about the application giving his opinion that the Socialist League's constitution did 'not conflict with the Labour party constitution in such a way as to raise doubts about affiliation'.[117] On 18 October Henderson resigned as party leader and so Lansbury, the leader of the PLP, became overall party leader. However, Henderson remained party secretary and, as such, agreed that the Socialist League constitution contained 'nothing inconsistent with the position of an organisation affiliated to the Labour party'.[118] After consideration by the NEC the Socialist League's application for affiliation was then accepted on 26 October 1932.[119]

Crucially, the next few months determined the Socialist League's pattern of membership as well as that of the disaffiliated ILP. This period saw the Socialist League's most rapid organisational growth. By January 1933 it claimed to have over 70 branches.[120] Area Conferences, which were held in the North East in December 1932, in South Wales in January 1933, and in Yorkshire and Lancashire in February 1933, were also obvious signs of

Socialist League growth.[121] There was no systematic attempt on behalf of the National Council to build up its branches. The Socialist League's Secretary was Radice, the economist who had been secretary of SSIP but who had so many other commitments that he had little time left for Socialist League duties.[122] What was happening was that many ILP branches were transferring their loyalty to the Socialist League. The ILP lost 203 of its 653 branches between July and November 1932. It lost 128 branches in Scotland alone, though it retained a strong presence around Glasgow, and in Yorkshire lost 23 branches out of 63.[123] As Paton memorably put it, 'the clean break [with the Labour party] seemed to be making a clean sweep of the party members'.[124] However, it is important to note that the ILP only lost one branch in London where the RPC was particularly strong, and this determined the ILP's internal dynamics for the coming years, giving it a notable London bias.[125]

Gateshead branch in the North East is a good example of how ILP branches defected to the League. Gateshead ILP had been an active branch with five members on the County Borough Council. Significantly, four of these joined the League at its inaugural meeting.[126] The minutes of the Gateshead branch, which were taken by its secretary Ruth Dodds – one of the Borough Councillors who had transferred their allegiance to the Socialist League – have survived and this makes it possible to trace the broader membership trends in this particular case. The branch had nearly 80 members by the end of 1932 and this figure did not change markedly for the next four years.[127]

Further Socialist League branches were formed in early 1933 largely through the efforts of Glyn Evans who was appointed as national organiser in early January.[128] In the period from January to June, Evans visited Yorkshire, Lancashire, the North East, the Midlands, South Wales and the South West. Altogether, he added 26 branches but only seven of these became active. Others were either never formally confirmed, or confirmed but reported no further activity.[129] Nevertheless, by summer 1933 the Socialist League claimed to have 2,000 members.[130] By this point the central patterns of the Socialist League's branch organisation for the rest of its existence had been established. More than half of its branches were concentrated in London while, on the strength of Cripps's high profile, the branch in his Bristol constituency was actually the largest in the country.[131]

Meanwhile, in the first half of 1933 the Socialist League developed policies which it set against those that the NEC was concurrently formulating. After its formation, the Socialist League National Council had initially encouraged its branches to concentrate on propaganda and local research into municipal government, housing, local industry and unemployment.[132] Accordingly, by the end of the year the Gateshead branch was holding fortnightly 'propaganda meetings'[133] and had set up a research group to consider the scope for the development of housing and social services.[134] In the New Year the Gateshead branch's Executive Committee welcomed the Head Office's suggestion of 'Doomsday' books detailing local conditions.[135] However, as the year progressed the Socialist League put itself at odds with the NEC Policy Sub-committee and particularly the Finance and Trade Sub-committee which – under Dalton's guidance – were drawing closely on the ideas of the NFRB, as they were to do for the rest of the 1930s.[136] By July the NEC had produced a policy document entitled *Socialism and the Condition of the People*. At the same time the Socialist League adumbrated many of its own policies in a series of 'Forum Lectures' that were given by its prominent figures at Transport Hall in London between January and March 1933.[137] The Socialist League's programme was then endorsed at its first annual conference at Derby on 4 and 5 June 1933.

It is important not to overstate the differences between the economic policies of the NEC and the Socialist League. Above all, they both envisaged a planned socialist economy based on the public ownership of industry.[138] For example, a central part of the NEC's *Socialism and the Condition of the People* was its commitment to a National Investment Board to co-ordinate investment programmes and overall planning. The Socialist League likewise stressed how it sought the creation of new planning machinery, again most notably a National Investment Board.[139] Moreover, in constructing their ideas about a planned socialist economy both the NEC and the Socialist League drew on the example of the Soviet Union which had been unaffected by the worldwide economic depression and was undergoing rapid industrialisation through the Five Year Plan.[140]

Nevertheless, the Socialist League's programme differed in emphasis from that of the NEC in a number of ways, which tended to be exaggerated in the course of political argument. While the NEC anticipated the possible use of some emergency powers[141], the Socialist League annual conference endorsed an Emergency Powers Act 'giving it authority . . . to put into force any measures that the situation may require for the immediate control or socialisation of industry'.[142] The Socialist League also disagreed with the NEC over the nature of the nationalisation that should take place. The NEC envisaged a 'public corporation' model of nationalisation and extensive compensation to private stockholders in the industries that were nationalised.[143] On the other hand, the Socialist League sought more workers' control under the influence of Cole and Mellor, the former Guild Socialists, and also argued that there should be a strict limit to the time period for which compensation was paid to stakeholders.[144] Similarly, while the NEC accepted that some reform of the House of Lords was desirable as soon as possible and that parliamentary procedure should be speeded up in order to ensure the effective introduction of socialism, the Socialist League wanted more far-reaching changes including the immediate abolition of the House of Lords and the acceptance of a more executive form of government.[145]

VIII

From March 1933 the mounting call for a united front not only hardened the divisions between the Socialist League and Labour's moderate majorities, but also those between the ILP and the Labour party. The ILP was deeply involved with what soon became known as the International Bureau for Revolutionary Socialist Unity, often simply referred to as the International Bureau.[146] This sought to be an alternative to both the Labour and Socialist International (LSI), to which the Labour party was affiliated, and the Communist International (CI) or Comintern. Crucially, at this juncture, the International Bureau responded quickly to the growing power of Hitler's Nazi Party in Germany and sent a telegram to both the LSI and the Comintern from its Paris conference of 4 February 1933, calling for a joint meeting to 'establish a plan of action to assist the workers who are now opposed by fascism in its various forms and to break the power of the counterrevolution everywhere'.[147] This was followed by a declaration from the LSI on 19 February which stressed the imperative of joint action between the German social democrats and the Communists to defeat Hitler, adding that the LSI 'has always been ready to negotiate with the CI with a view to common action as soon as this body is also ready'.[148] The Comintern reply, however, was the significant departure. While professing to lack faith in the LSI statement, it nonetheless called on national Communist parties to try to affiliate to social democratic parties in an attempt to provide greater resistance – a 'united front' – against fascism.

The CPGB had already performed a number of twists and turns in policy, which – in different ways – had left a legacy of ill-feeling in the Labour party.[149] It had been formed in 1920 and for the first years of its existence had sought to infiltrate local Labour parties with the ultimate aim of taking over the whole party. As a result the Labour leadership persuaded the party conference to reject Communist affiliation in 1922; to make CPGB members ineligible for endorsement as candidates in 1924; to prohibit them from joining the individual sections of local Labour parties in 1925; and to prevent them from attending Labour party conferences even as trade union delegates in 1928. However from 1928 the CPGB, in response to the new

Comintern line, changed its strategy to one of 'Class against Class'. This meant that all social democratic parties, such as the British Labour party, were treated as dismissively as other capitalist parties and indeed labelled as 'social fascists'. This period in Communist history, however, ended in 1933 and the CPGB contacted the Labour party, the Socialist League and the ILP with a united front proposal on 9 March.

The ILP was the most receptive. On 5 March the NAC had already decided 'immediately to approach with concrete proposals' the Labour party, the TUC, the Socialist League, the CPGB and the Co-operative party.[150] Now it responded to the CPGB initiative and the two parties then met on 17 March and agreed to hold a series of joint meetings drawing attention to the fascist danger.[151] Following the Labour party's rejection of the united front – which was in line with the advice of the LSI not to collaborate with national Communist parties until the Comintern had more clearly defined its position – the CPGB and the ILP then wrote a joint letter to the Labour party asking it to reconsider its attitude.[152] Through its association with the Communists, the ILP had clearly put further distance between itself and the Labour party.

The ILP was particularly keen to secure the Socialist League's participation in the united front. The prospects initially looked hopeful. Cole and Wise were attracted to the idea and eventually decided, together with Tawney, to write to the Labour party – as individuals – advocating a united front.[153] Cole later recalled that while he recognised that the Communists were 'dangerously disruptive', he considered that they 'would be led to modify their tactics if they were working inside the Labour Party', and that 'their sincerity and vigour, if it could be rightly directed, would be invaluable in raising the level of individual effort and zeal among the active Labour workers'.[154] Brockway also took up the issue of the united front personally with Cripps, who was becoming increasingly important in the League. Cripps, however, was opposed on the grounds that it would diminish his individual influence in the Labour party. In April 1933 he told Brockway that: 'I want to make my influence within the party as effective as possible and I feel that I can best do this by refraining from taking any such step as you suggest'.[155] Perhaps in part for this reason, and also because it was reluctant openly to defy the Labour party, the Socialist League decided to refrain from participation in the united front – a decision which was later endorsed at its annual conference.[156] Nevertheless, its relations with the moderate grouping within the Labour party also significantly soured during this period.

The NJC had rejected the Communist proposal for a united front on 21 March, producing a document entitled *Democracy versus Dictatorship* three days later. This condemned fascism and communism as reflexes of each other and both as antithetical to democracy.[157] Crucially, this was widely interpreted as a rebuke to the Socialist League's recent policy proposals, and in particular to Cripps who had emphasised the need for far-reaching emergency powers during the transition to socialism in his Forum Lecture, which was later published with the provocative title 'Can Socialism Come by Constitutional Methods?'[158] Significantly, the Socialist League's response made clear the extent to which it possessed a pro-Soviet identity. The Socialist League criticised the tendency 'to regard the fascist attack upon democratic freedom as akin in character to the attack which has been made upon it in Russia'. Indeed, to the Socialist League the differences between Russian communism on the one hand and Italian and German fascism on the other mirrored the differences between socialist executive government and capitalist executive government. The Socialist League argued that both systems were illiberal and authoritarian. But it argued that in the Soviet Union the revolutionary dictatorship was a temporary expedient which aimed to consolidate the workers' control of economic power in the interim period before the democratic classless society could be created. In contrast it held that the ruling elites in the fascist states sought the permanent suppression of liberty and parliamentary government.[159]

The Socialist League further argued that the defence of democracy was not in itself a sufficient safeguard against fascism. Wise famously asserted that 'free speech, a so-called free press are no more parts of the eternal verities than is free trade'.[160] Dalton and Citrine privately dismissed Wise's article as 'Communism without the courage of its convictions'.[161] The June 1933 edition of *Labour Magazine* then published the first of Citrine's three-part analysis of the factors – social, economic and political – that led to continental fascism with the intention of showing that Britain was not likely to follow the same path. Nevertheless, in the light of the seizure of power by the Nazis in Germany Citrine still felt it was 'necessary to criticise and oppose tendencies towards dictatorship' such as those he perceived to come from Wise and Cripps. He insisted that the basic freedoms, which he considered the Socialist League wanted to abrogate, were essential to the survival of organised Labour.[162] Cripps replied at the Socialist League annual conference in June 1933, stating emphatically that 'the proper body to decide policy is the annual conference, and not the general secretary of the TUC'.[163]

The immediate lesson the Socialist League had drawn from the rise of Hitler was the need for more thoroughgoing socialism. Cripps argued that Hitler had 'pounced upon and eaten the Social Democrats in Germany'. It was in this context that he asserted the Socialist League was 'prepared, if capitalism attempts to suppress the working-class movement in this country, to take all such steps as at this time seem necessary to try and exert the power of the working class'.[164] The debate continued into the summer.[165] In July Citrine confronted the Socialist League leaders privately about the matter.[166] At the same time Dalton's exasperation with the Socialist League also reached new levels. He wrote in his diary of their 'silly bogey-mongering publicity and vote-scaring hysterics about "Dictatorship"'.[167]

IX

By summer 1933 the Socialist League had become a more tightly-knit organisation. Partly this occurred as a result of the changed membership of the National Council, which gave it a more cohesive left-wing stance.[168] Pugh – the relatively moderate trade unionist – had resigned in January. At the Socialist League annual conference in June Pethick-Lawrence, who had only joined the Socialist League 'on the strength' of Cripps's signature and had been at odds with it over the joint-stock banks, did not stand for re-election for the National Council.[169] Salter and Kirkwood did likewise. They were replaced on the National Council by Constance Borrett and Donald Barber, who would both go on to play important roles in the rest of the Socialist League's development.[170] Cole was actually re-elected but he then decided to resign in July – at the same time as the secretary Radice – allowing Lionel Elvin, the young educationalist based at Trinity Hall, Cambridge, to take his place. From this point Cole was increasingly uninvolved with the League as an organisation, though he did remain broadly supportive of it. A further significant change occurred at the first National Council meeting after the conference. Cripps, who had become increasingly prominent in the League, was now elected as its chairman, replacing Wise who became vice-chairman.[171]

At the same time the Socialist League also assumed a much more developed organisational structure. As late as December 1932 Cripps had envisaged the Socialist League remaining 'loosely directed' so that it could play 'a most useful part' in the Labour party's reconsideration of policy.[172] However, by June 1933 the National Council had formed a number of committees. The main one was the General Purposes Committee consisting of Cripps, Wise, Barber, Borrett, Brailsford, Horrabin and Mellor.[173] This later became known as the Executive Committee and was appointed by the National Council from its own membership 'to deal with matters arising between National Council meetings and matters delegated to it by the National Council'.[174] It was usually made up of those National Council members who lived in the Greater London Area and could therefore easily attend weekly meetings. The National Council also set up a number of other committees, which were to meet several times in the year. There was a Finance Committee, an Organisation and Propaganda Committee, a Publications and Publicity Committee, and a Research Committee chaired by Brailsford. In June 1933 the Socialist League also moved from its offices in Abingdon Street to larger ones at 3 Victoria Street, SW1 and appointed a General Secretary, F. C. Henry, to work at Head Office together with Margaret McCarthy, the assistant general secretary, and a junior assistant.[175]

Furthermore, at the Socialist League annual conference the National Council gained acceptance of its plans to extend the role of the Area Committees which had recently been set up in Cardiff, Swansea, London, Manchester, Sheffield, Leeds, Bishop Auckland and Newcastle-upon-Tyne. In addition to acting as intermediaries between the branches and Head Office, the Area Committees were now empowered to co-ordinate 'branch activities by holding aggregate conferences of members, supplying speakers to local Labour Parties, Trade Union branches and Co-operative Guilds, and arranging a series of Forum Lectures'.[176] In August the National Council announced plans for area conferences in September and October to foster greater regional co-operation and area secretaries, such as the former Communist J. T. Murphy in London, Barbara Betts in Manchester and Ruth Dodds in the North East, were now elected to direct this activity.[177]

In spite of these structural developments, at this stage the Socialist League was determined to remain loyal to the Labour party. The League contended that its members were playing a full part in the discussion of the major issues facing the movement because they used the League for 'common thinking' directed not to strengthening their own organisation but to making the movement more effective.[178] This was consistent with the attitude that the Socialist League adopted at the Labour party conference in October 1933 when Greenwood introduced the NEC's policy document – *Socialism and the Condition of the People* – and stressed that this was an indication of the direction in which it was moving rather than a detailed policy programme.[179] Cripps had been due to move references back on behalf of the Bristol East Divisional Labour Party (DLP), which embodied some of the main planks of Socialist League policy: abolition of the House of Lords, reform of parliamentary procedure, and far-reaching emergency powers. However, he did not do so and instead, as a very visible act of concession, applauded the start which the NEC had made to its reconsideration of policy, and said he looked forward to a 'fuller discussion' of details at the next party conference.[180] The conference agreed that the matters raised by Cripps 'be relegated to the National Executive for consideration and report'.[181] In recognition of his stance, Cripps was even given a place on the NEC's Policy Sub-committee on constitutional and parliamentary reform.[182]

X

During the course of 1933, as the potential threat from Hitler became clearer, significant differences began to emerge between the NEC and the Socialist League over foreign policy for the first time. Since the end of the Great War the Labour party had based its foreign policy on support for the League of Nations.[183] However, it was only in the 1930s as the international situation began to deteriorate, firstly with the Japanese attack on Manchuria in 1931 and then the rise of Nazism in 1933, that the party became concerned with the way in which the League of Nations collective security system would actually operate. Article XVI of its Covenant described the range of sanctions – 'moral', economic and military – that the League of Nations might use against an aggressor nation, but did not define the circumstances in which each might be invoked. In summer 1933 the NEC, strongly under the influence of Henderson, began to argue that it might be necessary to place a physical restraint in the way of fascist aggression. They were fearful of the consequences for international peace if the League of Nations acquiesced again in the face of explicit aggression as it had in the case of Manchuria. Moreover, although the true extent of the threat from Hitler had of course yet to be fully perceived, the overt militarism of Nazism certainly brought the danger worryingly close to home. Now, ahead of the 1933 party conference, Henderson produced a pamphlet – *Labour's Foreign Policy* – which for the first time argued for the creation of an international police force as the basis of the League of Nations pooled security.[184]

These proposals were anathema to the Socialist League, which was deeply distrustful of the states that controlled the League of Nations, including the British National government. At its conference in June 1933 it outlined the two strands of its foreign policy. One concerned the way that the Labour movement should react if the National government attempted to involve the country in war, the other the actual policy that a future Labour government should pursue. The Socialist League agreed that if a war developed out of 'the necessities of capitalism and imperialism', the members of the Socialist League should pledge themselves 'neither to fight nor in any way actively to help' the National government to wage war, even if this meant a general strike.[185] The adoption of this policy reinforced the Socialist League's position as heir to a particular left-wing tradition. Resistance to involvement in a 'capitalist' war, including a general strike, had been a popular cry on the Labour left since the end of the Great War. Brailsford, and a number of others in the ILP, had been particularly prominent advocates throughout the 1920s.[186] The Socialist League conference also agreed that while a future Labour government should maintain nominal membership of the League of

Nations, its overriding loyalty would be to the international working class. The linchpin of its foreign policy was therefore to be the 'establishment of close economic and political relations' with the Soviet Union.[187] In this respect, the Socialist League's pro-Soviet stance went beyond that of the NEC.[188]

Nevertheless, at this stage the opposing views held by the NEC and the Socialist League did not precipitate a dispute. At the Labour party conference in October 1933 Trevelyan moved a war resistance resolution, which explicitly provided for the use of a general strike against the National government.[189] However, on this occasion the NEC simply accepted the resolution.[190] It seems that while there was still some hope of success at the World Disarmament Conference, which was being chaired by Henderson, the NEC did not want to risk a potentially embarrassing debate.[191]

XI

During these on-going policy disputes within the Labour party, the ILP continued to co-operate with the Communist party, albeit in an uneasy alliance. Brockway later wrote that the ILP had 'slipped into a united front with the Communist Party . . . without considered intention'.[192] Certainly at one level Brockway and Maxton had drifted towards the CPGB because they were increasingly concerned that the ILP was becoming isolated from the organised working-class movement and they knew the Communists had firm links with the unemployed through the NUWM.[193] At another level, however, the ILP's support for the united front owed much to the RPC. As early as October 1932 – after Gaster secured election to the important London Divisional Council and its executive – the NAC had been openly concerned about the RPC's increasing tendency to act as a party within a party.[194] Now the RPC was moving increasingly towards support for a united Communist party.[195] Indeed, at the ILP national conference in March 1933 the RPC ensured that a resolution was passed by 83 votes to 79, which instructed the ILP – against the wishes of the NAC – 'to approach the CI with a view to ascertaining in what way the ILP may assist in the work of the International'.[196] The NAC duly did this and, following extended correspondence, received a statement from the Comintern on 30 April expressing its willingness to begin negotiations.[197] Meanwhile, the NAC meeting on 14 April voted to continue and expand the united front, having received assurances from Harry Pollitt, the CPGB General Secretary, that any Communist attacks on it would cease.[198] The ILP NAC stressed that 'the ordinary work of the ILP as a distinct organisation should not be neglected',[199] but this nonetheless ushered in a period of 'co-operation in "day-to-day" activities in practically every sphere' between the CPGB and the ILP with, for instance, speakers from both parties sharing a platform at the 1933 May Day demonstrations.[200]

Before long, however, the ILP's collaboration with the CPGB became highly contentious, provoking serious opposition from different groups within its ranks. The ILP MPs McGovern and Wallhead were strongly opposed, with Wallhead soon resigning over the issue. The party secretary, Paton, was also hostile to the whole idea, and now began to work closely with Elijah Sandham, the Lancashire representative on the NAC, who in July defied the NAC to circulate material to his local ILP parties urging them to oppose the united front.[201] Brockway and Maxton continued to champion the united front but they themselves found relations with the Comintern – which they felt was trying to impose a 'role of tutelage' – increasingly difficult.[202]

By the end of 1933 relations with the Comintern had deteriorated further. To some extent this was because of Brockway's criticism of both the German Communist party and recent Soviet foreign policy. Brockway had visited Germany in 1931 and, since then, had been deeply critical of the Communists' dismissal of other working-class parties as 'social fascists'.[203] He was now also disappointed that the Comintern would not take seriously his suggestion of an organised refusal by the international working class to make or handle goods destined for Germany. When the Soviet Union then renewed its earlier Trade Agreement with Germany, his criticism mounted.[204] The more serious problems with the united front, however, were domestic ones. In December Paton decided to resign from the party. This served to polarise opinion on the issue and highlighted the differences among the leadership, not least because it prompted Brockway's resignation as chairman in order to assume the full-time secretarial responsibilities while Maxton took over at the helm.[205] The NAC had already begun to receive letters from individual members throughout the country criticising its policy. Indeed, Brockway later recalled that it 'was locally . . . that the united front broke down most seriously' because of a growing feeling that the 'Communist party was proving untrustworthy by exploiting the united activities for its own sectarian advantage'.[206]

As a result of these different pressures the NAC decided to undertake a survey of branch opinion. This showed that a 'majority of branches were in favour of co-operation . . . on a specific basis' but that there was a 'small majority against co-operation in general activity' and a 'definite majority' which 'desired a certain amount of local autonomy' on the issue. When the NAC considered these findings at its meeting on 10 and 11 February 1934, it recommended – after some debate – that the united front should assume a more limited form, simply involving 'common working-class action . . . on specific objects agreed by representatives of the two parties from time to time'.[207] The ILP national conference held at York over Easter then formally endorsed this change of stance, as well as rejecting – by 98 votes to 51 – a resolution in favour of immediate 'sympathetic affiliation' to the Communist International proposed by the aptly named Comintern Affiliation Committee, a small group that was even more favourable to links with the Communists than was the RPC. Signifying its change of position since the previous year, the conference also rejected the RPC's resolution calling for a delegation to be sent at once to Moscow to resolve any 'outstanding difficulties'.[208]

The RPC's strength had clearly been checked but relations with the CPGB continued to be a source of division within the ILP. Shortly after the national conference the RPC, in order to strengthen its position, amalgamated with the Comintern Affiliation Committee, effectively subsuming it.[209] Meanwhile, in May Sandham resigned from the ILP, together with a majority of the Lancashire ILP branches, and formed the Independent Socialist Party (ISP).[210] At the national conference the Lancashire division had been publicly censured for circulating its branches with literature hostile to the united front. After this, even the ILP's modified stance was seemingly not enough to pacify it.

As its relations with the Communists proved problematic, the ILP made efforts to establish closer relations with the Labour party or the Socialist League, albeit to no avail. The NAC had become increasingly concerned about the advance of fascism in early 1934, as news emerged of the suppression of political opposition in Austria under the regime of Chancellor Dollfuss. On 13 February the NAC wrote to the Labour party, the TUC, the Co-operative party and the CPGB asking for 'an immediate consultation between representatives of all sections of the working class so that we may plan common action'.[211] The following day, Maxton and Brockway met Henderson who made it clear that the Labour party would not contemplate working with the CPGB.[212] The ILP continued to court the Socialist League but – despite its own growing distance from the NEC – in June it 'cancelled arrangements made for a private consultation with representatives of the NAC'.[213]

XII

During the first half of 1934 the Socialist League sensationally began to argue that the National government was not merely 'capitalist' and 'imperialist', but was also leaning towards fascism.[214] Laski had sketched out the arguments about the National government's 'fascist' tendencies in 1933.[215] Now Cripps advanced them publicly on 6 January 1934 in his so-called 'Buckingham Palace' speech, which attracted much contemporary criticism for its apparently Republican tone. Indeed, Cripps claimed the Socialist League's proposed economic and constitutional reforms – including the abolition of the House of Lords – were so fundamental that it would be necessary 'to overcome opposition from Buckingham Palace'. Just as significantly Cripps suggested such a radical programme was necessary in order to stave off fascism. He argued that capitalism was an inherently unworkable system and presented fascism as its 'last stage' into which it was inexorably driven by pressure to sustain its economy and to suppress the working class. Provocatively, Cripps then argued that the National government itself was on the verge of adopting a very English form of fascism. He contended that 'there are a number, especially of the younger people, in the National government who would willingly have . . . a country gentleman type of fascism'.[216]

The NEC and the TUC General Council responded quickly to Cripps's comments. At the Constitutional Sub-committee on 19 January 1934 Dalton and Citrine criticised Cripps not just for his reference to the monarchy but for his advocacy of a general strike, emergency powers bill, prolonging Parliament, and nationalisation without compensation. Dalton made 'a violent – perhaps too violent – speech' claiming that the Conservatives regarded Cripps as their greatest electoral asset and that Cripps was unable to see that he was 'damaging the party electorally'. Attlee and Laski defended Cripps but the sub-committee eventually drafted a resolution distancing it from the comments without actually naming anyone.[217] When the NEC met on 24 January Henderson opposed issuing any statement at all. He feared it would simply further sour the atmosphere by provoking 'counter attacks including perhaps one from Lansbury'.[218] Beatrice Webb noted in her diary that while Henderson did not favour Cripps's policy of 'all or nothing', his main concern was to bring the party together and heal the rift between the PLP and the Socialist League on the one hand, and the NEC and the TUC on the other.[219] Even so, the statement was eventually accepted by 18 votes to 4. It re-affirmed the position in *Democracy versus Dictatorship* and repudiated statements by party members at odds with declared policy 'so far as there were any'.[220]

Despite the NEC's efforts at restraint, detail was soon added to the Socialist League's analysis of the burgeoning fascism of the National government. J. T. Murphy, who had joined the Socialist League in 1933 after leaving the CPGB the previous year and was now the secretary of the London Area Committee, wrote an influential pamphlet entitled *Fascism: The Socialist Answer* in early 1934.[221] The National Council now drew on this to draft the

THE AFTERMATH OF 1931

preface to *Forward to Socialism* – their policy statement which was submitted to the 1934 Socialist League annual conference. It boldly stated that 'fascism is growing rapidly in our midst, not in the number of people wearing black shirts, but in the minds and actions of the ruling class and of the government itself'. The Socialist League presented the Trades Disputes Act of 1927, which forbade civil service trade unions from affiliating to the Labour party or the TUC, as a first tentative step towards fascism. It also held that 1931 had been a definite triumph for fascism in the way that the National government had effectively overridden political parties with its spurious 'national' cry. Now the Socialist League claimed that parliament was being by-passed with the considerable increase in ministerial legislation. Specifically it asserted that with the creation of a police college, Lord Trenchard's police force was 'being rapidly militarised and placed in the hands of "property-class-conscious" leaders'. And it likened the government's reforms in agriculture under Walter Elliot to those in Mussolini's fascist corporate state. Through the use of subsidies the government was said to be 'guaranteeing interest and profit to the private owners at the expense of the farm workers and the consumers'.[222]

XIII

The Socialist League now prepared for a showdown with the NEC at the 1934 Labour party conference. By this juncture, the Cripps-Mellor axis, which underpinned the Socialist League for the remainder of its existence, had been firmly established. Wise had died suddenly in November 1933 and Cole had, of course, resigned from the National Council in the previous July. Together Cripps and Mellor – who was confirmed as the new vice-chairman in June 1934 – had drawn up the Socialist League's new programme, *Forward to Socialism*. The most significant way in which this differed from earlier Socialist League statements was by developing a timetable for its programme of wholesale socialisation. With a conscious nod towards the Soviet Union, a 'Five-Year Plan of Socialisation' was unveiled which would take place under emergency powers with very limited compensation and some measure of workers' control. Internationally, the Socialist League once again argued that a Socialist government 'should work in unison with the Soviet Union, whether in regard to economic agreements, the League of Nations, disarmament or peace'.[223] This programme was then accepted at the Socialist League annual conference by 51 votes to 13, when it met at Leeds on 20 and 21 May 1934.[224]

This was firmly at odds with the NEC's *For Socialism and Peace*, which was published in July 1934. For a start, *For Socialism and Peace* advocated nationalisation on the public corporation model with rights of compensation to stake-holders. The foreign policy section of the NEC's report was entitled *War and Peace* and had been shaped by Henderson, who dominated a joint sub-committee set up in February 1934 to define more clearly the party's stance.[225] *War and Peace* maintained that Labour's long-term foreign policy aims were disarmament and the creation of an international police force. However, it argued that in the more immediate term 'there might be circumstances under which the government of Great Britain might have to use its military and naval forces in support of the League [of Nations] in restraining an aggressor nation'. *War and Peace* nominally reconciled this policy with war resistance of the type advocated by the Socialist League but in such a way that this resistance would only operate in certain very limited conditions.[226]

With these rival programmes published, the tension between the Socialist League and the NEC increased to an unprecedented extent. The Socialist League submitted 75 amendments to *For Socialism and Peace*, though these were later reduced significantly in number by the Conference Arrangements Committee.[227] Through its new monthly journal – *The Socialist Leaguer* – which was edited by Horrabin, the Socialist League now pitted its programme directly against the NEC's *For Socialism and Peace*. In a context where the threat from Hitler was becoming increasingly apparent after Germany left the Disarmament Conference and the League of Nations in October 1933, Horrabin made the standard Socialist League argument that the rise of fascism made it more important than ever to commit the Labour party to thoroughgoing socialism at home. He contended that the Labour party 'must learn the lesson of Germany and Austria – the lesson that compromise and subordination of socialist purpose and practice to electoral and tactical calculations end in defeat'.[228] Anticipating the TUC's endorsement of *War and Peace* at its meeting in early September, Murphy criticised the 'contemptuous rejection of the weapon of the General Strike . . . in the fight against fascism and capitalist war' which involved the 'surrender [of] the workers completely to capitalism'.[229] Furthermore, in the month before the party conference Area Committees organised meetings to discuss the Socialist League amendments.[230]

At the Labour party conference itself Cripps accepted the section of *For Socialism and Peace* outlining its policy towards reform of the House of Lords and parliamentary procedure.[231] These were clearly not the most contested issues,[232] and the Socialist League then put forward an amendment, which embodied the crux of its programme and stressed the need for a future Labour government to 'secure at once . . . economic power sufficient to enable it to proceed unhampered with the Socialist reorganisation of our industrial and social system'.[233] Dalton easily dismissed the Socialist League's proposals, arguing that it was 'a skeleton statement . . . not developed in any detail'.[234] The Socialist League's amendment was rejected by 2,146,000 to 206,000.[235] A resolution put forward by Mitchison which called for compensation to be limited to a period of years,[236] was then rejected by an even larger majority after being strongly refuted by Morrison.[237] Henderson introduced *War and Peace* and drew attention in particular to the Soviet Union's entry into the League of Nations in September 1934. The NJC had first urged the National government to encourage Soviet entry in May 1934, and the NEC had proposed a resolution to this effect at the conference although by this point the Soviet Union had already joined.[238] Now Henderson – receiving important support from Attlee who had completely distanced himself from the Socialist League[239] – powerfully argued that even the Soviet Union recognised 'it may sometimes be necessary to co-operate with capitalist states for the preservation of peace'.[240] This really did undermine Mellor's opposition when he argued instead that a future Labour government should base its foreign policy on an alliance with the Soviet Union. It was little surprise that the Socialist League's amendments to *War and Peace*, which also called for resistance to capitalist wars, were then rejected by 1,519,000 to 673,000.[241] This was a very serious defeat, which would lead the Socialist League to rethink its strategy. It would do so, however, in new and deeply unsettling circumstances, as the Soviet Union's response to the rise of international fascism increasingly differed both from its own and from that of the ILP.

2

THE SANCTIONS CRISIS

October 1934 to October 1935

The decisive rejection of its programme at the Labour party conference in 1934 brought to an end the first phase of the Socialist League's existence. Thereafter instead of simply trying to win support for its policies at the party conferences, the Socialist League began to operate in a similar way to the ILP, attempting to mobilise support within the wider Labour movement. Now, as the rise of international fascism clearly became the foremost political issue of the day, the Socialist League and the ILP both developed policies which called for 'mass resistance' to any 'capitalist-imperialist' war and, as such, were strongly opposed to the Labour party's support for the League of Nations. There were, however, significant differences in approach between the ILP and the Socialist League. While the ILP readily grappled with the fact that the Soviet Union had now joined the League of Nations, becoming cautiously critical, the Socialist League initially preferred to gloss over the matter. Nevertheless, in summer 1935, as Mussolini threatened to invade Abyssinia (present-day Ethiopia) and the difficult dilemmas of anti-fascism had to be faced in practice, far-reaching divisions emerged within the Socialist League. A sizeable minority now argued that there were definite 'socialist' reasons for supporting sanctions which were endorsed by the Soviet Union. This, in turn, forced others in the Socialist League to begin to criticise Soviet foreign policy in order to justify their own position.

I

Following its overwhelming defeat at the Labour party conference in October 1934 the Socialist League reconsidered its line of attack on official Labour party policy. Even before the conference had formally ended, the 50 members of the Socialist League in attendance met to discuss the future direction that the League would take. They recognised that the Socialist

League now had little chance of directly winning over the Labour party –
dominated by the NEC and buttressed by the affiliated trade union votes at
the Labour party conferences – to its own more radical stance, and agreed to
hold a special national conference in November to reconsider its strategy.[1]
Before then, the direction that the Socialist League leadership was taking
became clear. In an important article for *The Socialist Leaguer* in October,
Mellor criticised the trade union block but directed as much of his resent-
ment at the NEC for undermining the Socialist League's arguments through
its control of the Conference Arrangements Committee, which had reduced
Socialist League's 75 amendments to *For Socialism and Peace* down to 12. The
lesson he drew from this was that whereas the Socialist League had
previously concentrated on developing its policies and 'getting them
discussed within the party' particularly at the annual conference, now the
League's propaganda 'must be extended' and directed towards winning over
'the wider Labour movement and Trade Union movement'. Mellor argued
that there were sizeable minorities within the various trade unions which
broadly supported the Socialist League line. To mobilise these people Mellor
urged the Socialist League branches and Area Committees to organise
conferences involving local Labour parties, trades councils and youth
movements so as to draw them into the Socialist League's sphere. He also
urged an expansion of branches and members and called for existing
branches to act 'more consistently together'. Finally, Mellor suggested that
the Socialist League should concentrate on the more immediate issues facing
the Labour movement rather than the shape of a future Labour government.[2]
    When the Socialist League's special conference met on 24 and 25
November 1934 at the Caxton Hall in London, it declared emphatically that
the League had 'passed out of the realm of programme-making into the
realm of action'. It also adopted the slogan 'The Will To Power' and
generally endorsed the type of changes set out by Mellor. As part of the
attempt to broaden the League's appeal, the conference also decided that it
was no longer necessary to be an existing member of the Labour party to join
the Socialist League; it was now only required that new Socialist League
members should join the Labour party within two months. The National
Council was also given increased authority to co-ordinate Area Committee
and branch activity.[3]
    Over the next few months the Socialist League National Council acted on
these conference decisions. Cripps formally launched the Socialist League's
membership campaign at a well-publicised meeting at the Caxton Hall on
21 December.[4] This prompted the Cambridge branch to decide 'to engage
during the immediate future in an extensive membership campaign . . . to
attach more definitely to ourselves a large body of supporters in the Trade

Union Movement'. Like many Socialist League branches, while having a good relationship with the local Labour party, Cambridge had only six members who were trade unionists.[5] Membership campaign meetings were then held by branches in London and the provinces in January and February 1935.[6] In January the National Council appointed Murphy, who had experience in building up CPGB rank and file membership, as the League's General Secretary with responsibility for overseeing its membership drive. The National Council meeting on 3 February decided to ask the Area Committees, in consultation with branches, to draw up 'three month plans of activity'.[7] During February there were area conferences in Durham, Hull and Cardiff, which all sought to increase membership. In March Mellor addressed a conference in London on the new function of the Socialist League.[8] By May 1935 Murphy claimed that in terms of new branches and members he could 'emphatically report progress'. There had indeed been 20 new Socialist League branches formed since the beginning of the year.[9] However, the Socialist League must have had a high turnover of branches and members because in summer 1935 it paid affiliation fees to the Labour party for a membership of 3,000[10] – the same number as in the previous year and the level at which it would remain until the Socialist League's final months of existence.

Significantly, the NEC and the TUC General Council felt threatened by the Socialist League's new stance. They had secured their hold over Labour party policy by 1934. However, with a general election expected before 1936, the NEC and the TUC General Council still wanted firmly to establish their ideological supremacy by discrediting the Socialist League which claimed to offer a more genuinely socialist policy.[11] Dalton, for instance, recorded in his diary summary of 1934 that he continued to be exasperated with Cripps's behaviour, and the way that he considered that 'he alone, and his little SL clique, is of the true faith'.[12]

II

During the first few months of 1935 the Socialist League and the ILP developed foreign policies which directly opposed that of the NEC and the TUC General Council. By this stage there were developing concerns that Hitler's regime might pose a threat to other countries, which grew further after March 1935 when Hitler publicly announced that, in contravention of the Treaty of Versailles, a German air force now existed and military conscription was being introduced. Primarily with Germany in mind, the Socialist League now devoted more and more of its attention to emphasising how it advocated 'mass resistance' to involvement in any capitalist war and warned that the NEC and TUC General Council's support for the League of Nations was antithetical to the 'class' interests of the workers.[13] This policy, including a general strike, had been recently endorsed at its special conference in November 1934[14] and given a central place in its propaganda.[15] Ominously, however, at this juncture the Socialist League chose to ignore the fact that the Soviet Union was now in the League of Nations.

The ILP's position had many similarities with that of the Socialist League. In exactly the same way it too claimed that the National government was 'moving towards fascism' through, for instance, the militarisation of the police force and agricultural reconstruction under Elliot. It was also deeply critical of the Labour party's willingness to support a League of Nations dominated by 'capitalist-imperialist' governments.[16] Unlike the Socialist League, however, the ILP dealt directly with 'the changed foreign policy of the Soviet Union and its implications'.[17] Ahead of its Easter annual conference, the NAC drafted a resolution which – while asserting that the 'prevention of an attack upon the Soviet Union is of first importance to the working class of the world' – nonetheless argued that the 'participation of the Soviet Union in the League of Nations . . . must not deter revolutionary socialists from exposing the capitalist-imperialist character of the League'. The resolution also made it explicit that if the Soviet Union and the capitalist governments were 'part of one bloc in a future war, it will still be the duty of the working class to refuse to collaborate with the capitalist governments in prosecuting war and to concentrate on the objective of overthrowing the government by a social revolution'.[18]

Predictably the NAC's policy towards Soviet foreign policy heightened the existing factional tension within the ILP. Gaster of the RPC was so strongly opposed to it that in late March he wrote an article expounding a much more favourable view of Soviet foreign policy. When A. H. Hawkins, a former Communist and now chairman of the London Divisional Council, then sent the piece to Brockway, insisting that it be published in the *New Leader*, this then precipitated a major row within the party. Brockway refused to publish it, asserting the established principle that internal debates were not published in the party's national newspaper.[19] Gaster, however, was not prepared to concede easily, raising the issue of Brockway's intransigence at the NAC meeting on 19 April. He was unable to have the decision not to publish his article overturned but he did make the powerful argument that since the conference had not yet endorsed the NAC's more sceptical view of Soviet foreign policy, it was in fact Brockway – and not he – who was at odds with official party policy.[20]

The outcome of the ILP conference itself represented a considerable defeat for the RPC in policy terms. The NAC's resolution, which was moved by

Jennie Lee, who had been the MP for North Lanark between 1929 and 1931 and who had recently married Bevan, won endorsement from the delegates. There could have been no doubt what was at stake. Lee began by making it clear that 'mass resistance' against war included a general strike and stressed that – in spite of any sympathy with their international counterparts – the workers should not involve themselves in a League of Nations war even against Germany. Most of her speech, however, dealt with the position of the Soviet Union. She was keen to refute the view that 'the ILP did not support Russia'. Yet, she emphatically maintained that 'if Great Britain were supporting Russia in one bloc of capitalist states against another', it would be important for the workers to oppose the war and concentrate on 'establishing a workers government in this country'.[21] Events at the conference also made it clear that the RPC's position was under threat in a broader sense: a resolution was endorsed which declared that unofficial groups – like the RPC – were 'bad in principle'.[22]

The ILP's new attitude to the Soviet Union's foreign policy had already fed into its relations with the Communists. Brockway in particular had been criticised by the CPGB and the Comintern after suggesting that the Soviet Union was departing from the truly revolutionary path by joining the League of Nations which had been dismissed by Lenin as a 'thieves' kitchen'.[23] Nevertheless, at this stage the ILP maintained the same overall position towards the CPGB as it had held for the past year. It continued to reject the united Communist party proposals of the RPC, claiming that 'any attempt to combine the ILP and the Communist Party would have divisive rather than unifying effects'.[24] Instead, both Maxton and Brockway pushed for a 'new working-class party' including the Labour party.[25] Similarly, a NAC resolution passed at the conference called for unity between the International Bureau and both the Comintern and the LSI.[26]

III

Despite earlier tensions it was only as Italy threatened to violate the Covenant of the League of Nations by invading Abyssinia that matters came to a head between the Socialist League and the NEC on foreign policy. Italy and Abyssinia were both members of the League of Nations, and so the other member-states were pledged to act under its Article X which committed them to preserve the territorial integrity of all members of the League of Nations against external aggression. Mussolini had been building up his forces in East Africa since late 1934, but it was only in June that the League of Nations Council seriously turned its attention to the dispute. Crucially, by this point the influence of Henderson within the Labour party was well

in decline. He was in his seventies and suffering from almost constant ill
heath. Accordingly, in summer 1935 it fell to Dalton, Attlee, Bevin and
Citrine to advance the case for a collective check on Mussolini through the
League of Nations. Significantly, the announcement of the results of the
Peace Ballot provided a context in which they felt able to demand a firm
commitment to League of Nations sanctions. The Ballot of nearly 12 million
people demonstrated, as its leading organisers on the League of Nations
Union had hoped, massive support for collective security. A clear majority
was even prepared to endorse the use of military sanctions against an
aggressor.[27]

However, the National government also responded to the Peace Ballot in
a way that greatly shaped the subsequent debate within the Labour party.
Stanley Baldwin, who had succeeded MacDonald as prime minister in June
1935, now replaced the government's earlier ambivalence with much more
explicit support for collective security in an attempt to win over this 'League
of Nations' vote ahead of the general election.[28] This meant that Dalton and
his allies were now effectively asking the party tacitly to endorse the foreign
policy of the National government. Indeed, Labour's three Executives (the
NEC, the TUC General Council and the PLP) met on 3 and 4 September
1935 and, influenced by Dalton, Attlee, Bevin and Citrine, drafted a
resolution demanding that the League of Nations should 'use all the
necessary measures provided by the covenant' against Mussolini.[29] And,
following a powerful speech by Citrine explicitly stressing the likely need
for 'military' sanctions, the TUC meeting at Margate on 5 September
endorsed the resolution by 2,962,000 votes to 102,000.[30] Yet this was just
six days before Samuel Hoare, the foreign secretary, announced the National
government's commitment to 'collective resistance to all acts of unprovoked
aggression' at the League of Nations Council meeting.[31]

These events prompted the resistance of the small pacifist section of the
Labour party, which significantly included the party leader, the
septuagenarian Lansbury, as well as the leader of the Labour party in the
House of Lords, Arthur Ponsonby. Since the end of the Great War, and
particularly in the peaceful international climate of the mid and late 1920s,
pacifism – the belief that all war is wrong – had fitted comfortably within
the more loosely pacifistic Labour party. During these years Labour had
consciously viewed itself as a party of peace with its overriding foreign-
policy objective being the achievement of disarmament.[32] However, since
1933 the NEC and the TUC General Council had been increasingly willing
to endorse the use of collective force. In the 1920s Ponsonby believed he had
discovered a new and truly objective form of pacifism, dubbed 'humanitarian' or 'utilitarian' by Martin Ceadel. This did not fall back on prior

religious or political assumptions but instead made the simple calculation
that the unhappiness and destruction caused by war would always outweigh
its benefits. After 1933 he began to oppose the Labour party's emerging
foreign policy on these grounds. He had spoken against the tentative
endorsement of collective force in *War and Peace* at the 1934 Labour party
conference. Now, as the Labour party looked likely to commit itself to
sanctions against Italy, he resigned from leadership in the House of Lords on
17 September.[33] Lansbury's Christian pacifism also inspired serious
reservations about the nature of the policy in *War and Peace*. As the sanctions
crisis developed in summer 1935 Lansbury, as party leader, voiced the official
party line but increasingly made known his personal objections and support
for unilateral disarmament.[34] Inevitably, rumours now abounded that he too
would resign.[35]

This was the wider context in which the Socialist League also announced
its opposition to support for League of Nations sanctions.[36] Before the
Socialist League's annual conference on 9 and 10 June 1935 its leaders began
to muster support for a policy of resistance to National government
participation in any attempt by the League of Nations to restrain Mussolini.
Horrabin's editorial in *The Socialist Leaguer* in May 1935 called for
'immediate action' in the form of a general strike.[37] Moreover, the influential
Brailsford was called on to contribute, and argued forthrightly that the
'policy of mass resistance to any capitalist war was still the right one'.[38]

At the Socialist League conference itself, Cripps introduced the mass
resistance resolution. He warned 'the workers not to be misled into support of
a war . . . in the name of the League of Nations', because 'if war comes before
the workers in Great Britain have won power, that war will be . . . in the
interests of British imperialism'. He again repeated the danger of fascism
emerging in an 'English country gentleman' form, and stressed that the
'primary duty of Socialists in every country is to wage the struggle against
their own capitalism'. He also made it clear that the Socialist League envisaged
the local trades councils taking a leading role in organising a general strike in
the event of a 'capitalist' war.[39] However, at the conference divisions between
the leaders of the Socialist League were revealed for the first time. Cripps,
Mellor and Mitchison were confronted by Murphy, the Socialist League's
general secretary, who spoke strongly in favour of collective security.

Significantly, Murphy based his arguments squarely on the Soviet Union's
changed stance since the previous year, which stated that despite the
fundamental differences between itself and the capitalist states there was
now a need for them to work together through the League of Nations to keep
the more 'immediate challenge' from fascism in check.[40] The arguments
advanced by the Soviet Union and the Comintern had considerable appeal

to Murphy. He had actually been involved with the formation of the Comintern in 1920, and in 1926–7 had spent 18 months working at its headquarters in Moscow. He was acquainted with, and impressed by, the leaders of the Soviet Union – particularly Lenin and Stalin. He had also been a prominent member of the CPGB from its formation until 1932, when he left mainly because of a personal disagreement with Pollitt over how best to expand the CPGB's mass base. Murphy had then joined the Socialist League in April 1933, which he believed was going to help move the Labour party in a left-wing direction compatible with his 'revolutionary Marxist' out-look.[41] In any case, by arguing in favour of sanctions at the conference, Murphy forced the pro-Soviet Socialist League – at least momentarily – to think about its hitherto unstated dilemma: how could it justify a 'socialist' opposition to collective security when the Soviet Union was now an active member of the League of Nations? For Murphy the answer was clearly that it could not. For the rest of the Socialist League, however, the issue was left unresolved. The mass resistance resolution was passed. Murphy recorded that while he had some sympathy, Mellor and particularly Cripps 'swept the conference'.[42] Nevertheless, they had not grappled with the contradiction now inherent in their approach. Indeed, the conference once again carried a resolution committing a future socialist government to close co-operation with the Soviet Union as the very 'keynote' of its policy.[43]

IV

After this point the tension between the Socialist League and the NEC and the TUC General Council quickly mounted. The Socialist League's new stance of seeking to gain support from the wider Labour movement meant that it now not only submitted its conference resolutions for consideration at the party conference, but also began to make extensive plans to win support for its policy.[44] In July it arranged for a large number of conferences to be held across the country in mid-September.[45] The NEC was clearly very concerned. The absence of Henderson from the NEC – not just because of his ill health but also because he had been replaced as party secretary by Jim Middleton in December 1934[46] – meant that he could no longer act to restrain the NEC's determination to discredit the Socialist League. Now the NEC tried, to no avail, to avert the challenge from the Socialist League. It told the Socialist League sharply that 'affiliated societies can properly look to the annual conference . . . for the formulation of party policy', and that there was, therefore, 'no necessity' for the conferences.[47]

In early September, at the crucial meeting of Labour's three Executives, Cripps registered dissent from the majority view favouring the use of sanctions for what he regarded as an 'imperialist war' against Italy. Perhaps it was because his views were so irreconcilable with those of Dalton, Attlee, Bevin and Citrine that he did not even attend the second day of discussions when the vote was taken on the draft resolution.[48] In any case, the TUC General Council soon hit back. The London Trades Council made it clear that it did not wish to be associated 'in any way' with the conference planned for Memorial Hall on 14 September.[49] 'Transport House has been on the move', Murphy informed Cripps. Earlier in the summer when the Socialist League proposed its series of conferences the London Trades Council had declared itself in favour of an anti-war stance and agreed to sponsor the Socialist League conference. Now, however, it reversed its position as a result of direct pressure from Bevin and Citrine.[50]

As the National government increasingly committed itself to League of Nations sanctions, the Socialist League produced a more detailed statement of its position. Under Mellor's editorship the front page of *The Socialist* in September pitted the issue bluntly in terms of 'War or Socialism'. In his capacity as general secretary, Murphy informed the branches of the Socialist League that this was to be 'regarded by all speakers at the Anti-war Conferences as their guide'.[51] Stressing the wider significance of the imminent Italian attack on Abyssinia, Mellor portrayed it as 'the signal for a large-scale imperialist drive . . . by the economically hard-pressed capitalist powers', notably Germany. Yet he also sharply dismissed talk of preserving the political independence of Abyssinia through the League of Nations as mere 'window-dressing behind which the forces of international capitalism fight for economic mastery'. Indeed, he asserted that the British and French governments were only motivated to act in this case because their own interests in the Sudan and Egypt, as well as their relative strategic positions *vis-à-vis* Italy, were directly threatened. Mellor now introduced 'working-class sanctions' as a possible means of restraining Mussolini. However, these only applied to the 'hypothetical situation' in which British capitalists were involved in supplying war materials to both Italy and Abyssinia. Then, he argued, the workers should refuse to produce them for Italy. Mellor's central point was that mass resistance to war was needed so as to create a domestic crisis leading to the defeat of 'capitalist imperialism' and precipitating the formation of a socialist government.[52]

V

Momentarily it appeared that the Socialist League was advancing a united challenge to the NEC-TUC line. Its two dominating personalities, Cripps and Mellor, were in agreement on tactics and policy.[53] They could also count on the firm support of a majority of those on the Socialist League's National Council and its Executive Committee, including Mitchison, Horrabin, Elvin, Dodds and Ellen Wilkinson.[54] Barbara Betts, who was by this point involved in a passionate affair with the married Mellor[55], was very strongly in favour of 'mass resistance' as she made clear in a long letter published in the *New Statesman*.[56] Laski was also publicly backing 'revolutionary resistance to war'.[57] Others in the Socialist League held more strictly pacifist objections to support for sanctions but supported its general line. Constance Borrett, a member of the National Council since June 1933, argued that the Socialist League policy was 'absolutely correct both from the socialist and pacifist standpoint' even though she herself was a supporter of Lansbury.[58] Similarly Naomi Mitchison, the writer and wife of G. R. Mitchison, supported the Socialist League but regretted that it 'didn't quite . . . emphasise the real pacifist position'.[59] The Socialist League's policy was, of course, not pacifist because it did not oppose all war but simply capitalist ones. At the same time, however, pacifists continued to be welcomed within the Socialist League ranks.[60]

However, others in the Socialist League now became increasingly uneasy about endorsing mass resistance. The threat from Mussolini was becoming increasingly clear as he refused to accept any of the attempts at conciliation made by the Council of the League of Nations throughout September. Moreover, the Soviet Union was standing firmly for collective security. Litvinov, the Soviet foreign minister, registered his full support for the imposition of sanctions against Italy at the League of Nations Council on 6 September 1935 and the CPGB fell in line with this policy, renouncing its own earlier support of mass resistance. Together, these factors prompted serious divisions to emerge within the Socialist League, which went on to destroy the momentum of its campaign.

As general secretary Murphy found it increasingly hard to follow a policy he had so vigorously opposed at the Socialist League's annual conference.[61] On 17 September he wrote a critical nine-page letter to Cripps, which – apparently for the sake of Socialist League unity – he decided not to post until after the party conference. The growing likelihood of aggression from Mussolini now made him more convinced than ever of the correctness of the line taken by the Soviet Union. He made it clear that he considered Cripps and Mellor naïve for taking an 'isolationist' view and not realising that with fascism internationally 'on the offensive' and 'intent on war . . . our enemy is not only in our own country'. Murphy followed the Soviet argument that fascism was a far more menacing and directly threatening type of regime than standard capitalist imperialism. Accordingly, he argued that 'the defeat of the fascist powers' was the foremost priority and that to talk of 'mass resistance' aimed at turning out the National government was actually 'to dodge over our immediate responsibilities because . . . even if there were an election tomorrow we could not get a majority'.[62]

A number of other prominent figures in the Socialist League also announced their inability to follow the official Socialist League line in the weeks before the party conference. One of these was Trevelyan, who had ironically been responsible for introducing the war resistance resolution at the 1933 party conference. Significantly, however, the primary motivation for his earlier advocacy of mass resistance seems to have been a fear that the British government would become involved in a war against Russia.[63] Trevelyan had moved from the Liberal party to the Labour party after the Great War and had continued to move leftwards. He was now undoubtedly entering his most overtly pro-Soviet phase as the sympathetic tone of his 1935 book, *Soviet Russia: A Description for British Workers*, demonstrates.[64] He had not attended the Socialist League conference in June 1935, interestingly because he was in Moscow at the time.[65] Now, however, he told Cripps that he did not 'feel inclined to oppose the application of sanctions, even at the risk of Italy biting in every direction like a mad dog', provided that France and the Soviet Union were also committed to action.[66] He was supposed to move a mass resistance resolution at the Socialist League conference at Gateshead, but withdrew saying that he was now 'diametrically opposed' to such a policy. In clear contrast to the Cripps-Mellor position, he held that if 'Mussolini is stopped it will in fact be the worst blow to expansionist imperialism that could be given'.[67] So great was his allegiance to the Soviet Union he argued that 'if Russia will act too, I think it our socialist . . . duty to approve sanctions'.[68]

Similarly, D. N. Pritt, the KC who had been elected on to the Socialist League's National Council in June, now also made clear his opposition to the policy of mass resistance.[69] Significantly, he too was favourably disposed to the Soviet Union. He had been greatly impressed by the socialist experiment during his visit to the Soviet Union in 1932, and in his autobiography described how the visit represented a 'big jolt forward in my political thought'.[70] Thereafter he became increasingly forthright in his endorsement of the Soviet system. In 1934 he became chairman of the Society for Cultural Relations between the people of Britain and the Soviet Union. He was on good terms with the Soviet Ambassador to Britain at this time, Ivan Maisky, and claimed to have 'learnt a great deal from him'.[71]

Some other leaders of the Socialist League, who were not fellow travellers, were nevertheless ambivalent in their support of the Cripps-Mellor stance in a deteriorating international environment. Bevan was certainly apprehensive. Mellor informed Cripps that Bevan was 'somewhat critical' of their position and indeed Bevan even planned to raise his objections with Cripps in person.[72] Bevan's first major biographer, Michael Foot, who was personally close to his subject, also acknowledged that he may have 'had doubts about the line to which the Left had committed itself'.[73] To a large extent Bevan's reservations surely reflected his longer-term concerns about the role of the Socialist League. When the Socialist League had been formed in 1932 Bevan, despite his obvious affinity to its outlook, had not wanted to become too deeply involved. He feared that, like the ILP, it would involve him in 'those obligations arising out of associations which tend to obscure one's vision and limit one's freedom of decision'.[74] Whatever his reservations Bevan remained loyal to the Socialist League, at least in public. He spoke in support of mass resistance at the Socialist League conference in Birmingham on 21 September, emphasising his distrust of the British and French governments.[75] He also reiterated his opposition to Labour's official policy in his own constituency of Ebbw Vale on 28 September.[76]

Brailsford's position was particularly ambiguous. He retained his left-wing suspicion of the British and French governments, and doubted that they would take any effective action against Italy through the League of Nations.[77] Nevertheless, as an expert in foreign affairs, he was well aware of the seriousness of the situation, and became prepared to test the apparent sincerity of the British government.[78] This led him to argue against the official Socialist League line that it would be 'a mistake to oppose or resist sanctions'.[79] Above all, he seems to have been unclear in his own mind as to the correct course to take at this time. He wrote that the Labour party 'ought not to call for sanctions', though it should not 'oppose them actively', because 'one cannot trust such a government to administer them, or after the conflict to make a salutary peace'. He had not even completely abandoned thoughts of mass resistance. He argued that 'if it comes to . . . a duel between British and Italian imperialism, then the duty of opposition should be clear to every honest Socialist'.[80] Brailsford had been the British Left's most prominent critic of the Versailles settlement, arguing that one of its most serious flaws was that it unjustly took territory off Germany, and then used the League of Nations to maintain this status-quo.[81] After 1933 Brailsford had argued that treaty revision was more necessary than ever to remove the causes of Germany's grievances and to undermine support for Hitler.[82] These deeply-held views had underlain his earlier support for the Socialist League policy of war resistance. Now, however, Mussolini's attack on Abyssinia had prompted Brailsford to begin to reconsider his standpoint as the extent of the danger from fascist aggression became apparent.[83]

Kingsley Martin, the editor of the *New Statesman* who had been a conscientious objector during the First World War, also moved in the same

direction as Brailsford at this point. He had previously used his position at
the helm of an influential left-wing journal to support the Socialist League.[84]
Now, however, he began to suggest the need to oppose the fascist powers
with some form of collective force and to consider that on this occasion it
might be possible to trust the National government.[85] On 14 September
Martin took the unprecedented step of directly criticising the Socialist
League in the *New Statesman*. He argued that the Socialist League held 'a
doctrinaire attitude we find hard to understand' because it was 'not necessary
to pretend that the National government's policy is inspired by idealism',
but simply to recognise that 'its present aim was to check fascist aggression'.[86] This was a significant change on Martin's part and he wrote to Cripps
explaining his evolving views.[87] Martin might have thought that the
Socialist League stance, particularly as expressed by Cripps, 'was hopelessly
ill-judging and academic', but he nonetheless came to this conclusion
hesitantly. Even after announcing his views in the *New Statesman,* he reflected
on events at the League of Nations headquarters in Geneva, in an anguished
late-night letter to Konni Zilliacus, a resident League of Nations official.
Martin did not think the proceedings there had 'anything to do with the
ideals of the League or collective security or the preservation of Abyssinian
independence'. Instead he considered that the National government was
keen 'to persuade Mussolini to share Abyssinia with us'. In these circumstances he still wondered whether the Labour Party 'ought in fact to oppose
the National Government with might and main'.[88] Overall though, Martin
'thought it a legitimate gamble that . . . we could get a real League victory'.[89]

The divisions between the leaders of the Socialist League were also
reflected among its rank and file. It is, of course, rather more difficult to
discern the precise misgivings felt by the ordinary Socialist League members.
Like the population at large, they were perhaps beginning to perceive Italian
and German fascism as a real threat to the peace of Europe. Moreover, it
seems likely that the Socialist League's continued commitment to a close
alliance with the Soviet Union in the future, but its opposition to the foreign
policy currently being pursued by that country, may have confused many.

The Socialist League conference held at the Memorial Hall in London on
14 September, at which Cripps was the main speaker, was deeply divided.
Cripps forcefully advocated mass resistance, and also made it clear for the
first time that he was opposed to economic, as well as military sanctions,
arguing that the one would probably lead to the other. However, the
arguments put forward in favour of collective security by the delegate from
the London Communist Party were also well received. The war resistance
resolution was eventually carried by 265 to 171, but the counting was
contentious. It seems possible that the Socialist League leadership had

already tried to ensure a favourable result by allocating seats in the Hall to their most 'loyal' members. The overflow meeting, which was not allowed to participate in the actual vote, was overwhelmingly against the resolution and, by implication, in favour of sanctions.[90] Martin, who had attended the conference, was clear – despite his own uncertainties on the issue – that the 'discussion showed a confusion of mind which was appalling'.[91]

The Socialist League conferences in the provinces also struck an irresolute note, as Murphy reported to Cripps. On the one hand, the Manchester conference chaired by Mitchison and addressed by Mellor had recorded 'very good support' for the Socialist League approach. On the other, the Reading conference had been vigorously opposed, and the local branch had even refused to sell *The Socialist*. More typical was the Cardiff conference where 'there was some opposition and some support for the sanctions policy'. Similarly, at Swansea, where Murphy spoke, the resolution was carried, but he sensed that 'they were not quite convinced that we were right'. After the Leeds conference Elvin had said that 'there would have to be some change in the method of getting our policy across'. The Durham conference was particularly confused – the resolution was carried but 'without the con- ference feeling quite clear as to whether the sanctions policy was in opposition to our resolution'.[92] Significantly, it seems that Murphy may have played some role in fomenting this uncertainty within the Socialist League. At the Newcastle conference the chairman, Alderman Adams, had divulged that Murphy felt there should have been a special conference of the Socialist League before the policy was advanced – a claim Murphy now strongly denied to Cripps.[93] Overall though, there was no doubt that, as the leading Communist Rajani Palme Dutt subsequently told the CPGB Central Committee, the position of the Socialist League leadership had 'thrown confusion into the "Left"'.[94]

VI

Against this backdrop Cripps tried to clarify and strengthen the Socialist League's position before the party conference. He now explicitly made the powerful link between the Socialist League's opposition to the use of sanctions by the National government and the opposition that the PLP had voiced against the National government's rearmament programme since its introduction in July 1934. Both policies, he argued, were based on the same intense distrust of the 'capitalist' National government.[95] On 15 September Cripps also decided to resign from the NEC, to which he had been elected the previous year, in an attempt to show people 'where I stood' and to 'disassociate' himself formally from the Executive's foreign policy.[96] To some extent, this boosted the Socialist League's campaign. Cripps's resignation attracted considerable media attention, as it was debated by the NEC on the 19th, and as Cripps was then called upon subsequently to explain his decision.[97] Moreover, after a meeting of the Socialist League Executive Committee on 19 September, Wilkinson and Elvin also decided to withdraw their candidatures for election to the NEC as a gesture of support for the official Socialist League line.[98]

The Socialist League National Council met on 22 September. It approved the line taken by the Executive Committee and in *The Socialist* and tried to clarify it further. In a circular subsequently distributed to its branches, it argued that Socialist League members 'must not flinch from declaring that the immediate needs of the Soviet Union *vis-à-vis* France and Germany do not constitute valid grounds for mobilising the workers of this country in support of the "sanctions" policy of the "National" government or of the League of Nations'. In an attempt to shift attention away from the fact that it still wanted a future Labour government to align with the Soviet Union, the National Council urged that its members 'must not be led aside by speculation as to what a Socialist Government would or would not do'. Moreover, with a great deal of public attention focussing on the position of Lansbury, it stressed that it was 'as a Socialist and not as a pacifist organisation that the Socialist League declares its policy against war'.[99]

Cripps also now thought seriously for the first time about how to explain the Socialist League's opposition to sanctions at a time when they were being strongly advocated by the Soviet Union. In early September he had had a lengthy discussion about the Soviet Union's stance with Maisky when he stayed at Cripps's home at Goodfellows.[100] Furthermore, a 20,000 word unpublished manuscript in the Cripps archive shows how the Abyssinian crisis prompted Cripps to think in depth about the international situation and how to justify the Socialist League's position. Significantly, after grappling with this dilemma Cripps argued that 'the position of a working-class party . . . in opposition to a government of its class enemies, is vitally different to that of a working-class government which can itself control foreign policy'.[101] Whereas the British Labour party had no influence at all over foreign affairs, the Soviet Union could 'withdraw or refuse to act' if it changed 'its view of the sanctions war'.[102] Cripps went on to argue that the Soviet Union was acting in an 'opportunist' manner, and pursuing a policy that was, as he told Trevelyan, 'extremely dangerous' to the working class in other countries.[103] The following month Betts made a forceful statement of this new argument in *The Socialist*. She argued that the Soviet Union's primary concern was its own security and that it was effectively adopting a policy of *realpolitik*. It was 'striving above all things to keep the League intact for use against Hitler' because it knew 'that only military sanctions will suffice against Germany'. Moreover, she argued that there was a definite hypocrisy in the Soviet Union's stance because if 'military sanctions are applied against Italy, the Soviet Union . . . knows the war will be an imperialist war'.[104] To some extent this vindicated the official Socialist League position but also served to polarise opinions within it.

VII

From mid-September the ILP also experienced divisions as it grappled, much more directly than the Socialist League, with differing interpretations of its war resistance policy. As tension had mounted in East Africa, the ILP argued that the League of Nations would do 'nothing to stop Italy's intentions',[105] and reiterated its plans for 'overthrowing any war-making capitalist Government'.[106] The ILP, however, soon went further than this and – under the influence of Brockway – advocated 'working-class sanctions' in a much more explicit way than the Socialist League. On the basis that there was 'no doubt' that Italy was 'the aggressor', Brockway called on the British workers to 'take the initiative against the aggression of Italy' and 'refuse to make, handle, or transport war materials for Italy – whether finished armaments or materials which can be made into armaments'.[107]

Significantly, this policy received full endorsement from the International Bureau, when its enlarged executive met during the ILP summer school at Letchworth on 10–11 August. With Brockway presiding and Campbell Stephen acting as the other ILP delegate, a resolution was drawn up which condemned the attitudes of the LSI and the Comintern which were both, of course, supporting sanctions. In contrast the International Bureau called on the workers to resist involvement in a capitalist war. Crucially, it also made it clear that it considered the crisis 'a clear case of an imperialist outrage upon "democracy"' and stated that it 'unconditionally takes the side of suppressed peoples against imperialist rulers, and declares openly that it wishes for the defeat of Italian imperialism and the victory of the Abyssinian people'. To do this it sought an 'international working-class boycott of imperialist Italy and its allies', the 'preservation of the boycott of armaments and munitions to Italy or Italian territories', and the 'prevention of the transport of troops to Africa'.[108]

Over the next month this policy became central to the ILP position. It was 'accepted without opposition by the National Council of the Party',[109] and expounded time and again in the New Leader.[110] At the same time Brockway intensified his criticism of Soviet foreign policy. He argued that it sought 'to reverse the revolutionary analysis of fascism as a natural and inevitable development of capitalism under certain economic, national and psychological conditions', and showed that for the Soviet Union capitalist democracy had now become 'worthy of defence in time of war in unity with the capitalist class against fascism'.[111] Brockway was also personally critical of Litvinov for not publicly denouncing Italy or supporting Abyssinia,[112] while McGovern attacked the Soviet Union for joining the League of Nations in the first place.[113] This, of course, worsened relations with the RPC, but it did not cause the major cleavage in the ILP.

Brockway had thought that the call for working-class sanctions was being 'received with enthusiasm by the party'.[114] However, in mid September Maxton requested a meeting of the ILP's Inner Executive.[115] This body, which had been formed as a result of the move towards centralisation in the ILP after 1934, comprised Brockway in addition to the three ILP MPs (McGovern and Buchanan as well as Maxton). It met more regularly than both the NAC and the Executive Committee, which had been formed at the same time as the Inner Executive but was slightly larger.[116] In any case, according to Brockway, at the meeting of the Inner Executive 'Maxton carried his Parliamentary colleagues with him when he urged that "working-class sanctions" could not be distinguished publicly from League sanctions and would help to create a psychology for war against Italy'. This was a very important change but Brockway apparently felt duty-bound as secretary to accept this policy until the party conference.[117]

The ILP did not publicly admit that its stance had changed. However, whereas in the past the ILP had made clear its loyalty to Abyssinia, a resolution adopted by the Inner Executive now argued that 'the difference between the two rival dictators [Mussolini and the Abyssinian Emperor Haile Selassie] and the interests behind them are not worth the loss of a single British life'. At the same time, of course, the Inner Executive continued to emphasise the uncontroversial aspects of its policy and urged the workers 'to offer the maximum opposition by holding mass demonstrations in their area, [and] by refusing to bear arms'.[118]

Interestingly, however, and perhaps because of the theoretical nature of the debate, this division of opinion did not split the ILP at this juncture. Brockway had not signed the Inner Executive's resolution, but he now spoke alongside Maxton at the demonstration arranged by the London ILP at the Memorial Hall on 26 September. Brockway also undoubtedly threw himself behind the ILP's war resistance campaign, addressing meetings – for instance that in Norwich on 27–29 September. Other ILP meetings – in Lancashire and the North East – were seemingly free from dispute.[119] And on 27 September the New Leader published a letter signed jointly by Maxton and Brockway, which called on all working-class organisations to communicate with the ILP 'so that the fullest cooperation can take place in planning resistance to war'.[120]

Moreover, the *New Leader* – despite its own recent deviation in policy – was able to criticise the Socialist League on the grounds that it 'analyses the present position on lines similar to the analysis of the ILP, but it gives no immediate lead to the workers in action'.[121] From the ILP's point of view, the Socialist League meeting in London 'failed in its purpose to show how mass resistance to war can be put into operation'. Similarly, when Mellor spoke at the Manchester conference, the *New Leader* condemned his failure 'to give a lead in action'.[122]

VIII

By the time the Labour party conference met at the Dome in Brighton on 30 September the Socialist League was deeply divided. The pacifists had also failed to win much support, and so, with the trade unions holding two million block votes, the outcome of the debate on 'Italy and Abyssinia' had apparently already been secured.[123] Nevertheless, in a context where news of Italy's attack on Abyssinia was expected at any time (and indeed came on 3 October) the key figures on the NEC and TUC General Council were concerned that the Socialist League and the pacifists could still make an impression on the conference as well as on wider Labour opinion. Accordingly, they set out to discredit not just Lansbury but also Cripps. Indeed, Dalton regarded it as a particular imperative that Cripps 'be argued with and answered'.[124]

At the party conference it was Dalton who moved the resolution favouring the use of military, alongside economic and financial, sanctions. He argued that it was possible to support the National government in imposing sanctions because it was, in effect, now following an established Labour policy as it responded to the popular mandate of the Peace Ballot. He then accused Cripps, as well as Lansbury, of inconsistency. Cripps's dual role as front bencher and chairman of the Socialist League left him particularly vulnerable to such charges. Now Dalton readily recalled how Cripps had spoken in favour of collective security 'by armaments if necessary' in the House of Commons as recently as March 1935.[125] Beatrice Webb, who attended the conference, described the direction that it was taking in her diary: 'Transport House was set on steam rolling Stafford and his group and put up Dalton to do it with the help of the trade union officials'.[126]

Cripps followed Dalton and launched directly into a criticism of the resolution. He repeated his argument that the NEC and the TUC were wrong to place any trust in the 'capitalist' and 'imperialist' National government. He stressed that the 'central factor in our decision must turn, not so much upon what we as a country should, or should not do, but upon who is in control of our actions'. Sensationally, he claimed the League of Nations was an 'International Burglars Union' with which, he prophetically warned, Mussolini was likely to 'drive a satisfactory bargain . . . even though they have momentarily turned policemen'. Despite his passing reference to 'working-class sanctions', Cripps was clear that 'the British workers cannot at this moment be effective in the international political field'. Instead he asked the movement to devote its whole energies 'to the defeat of . . . capitalism and imperialism . . . in this country'.[127]

Whatever the appeal of such emotive socialist rhetoric, the Socialist League case was soon considerably weakened, as the conference was made aware of the divisions that had become pronounced within the Socialist League during the past month. Trevelyan, who was remembered by the conference as the mover of the 1933 anti-war resolution, now felt that it was his 'duty' to say that he supported the League of Nations 'in applying all kinds of sanctions against Italy if she goes to war'.[128] He made it clear that his apparent *volte-face* had been prompted by the Soviet Union's active involvement in the League of Nations. He dismissed Cripps's arguments claiming that it would be difficult for the National government to pursue imperialist aims through the League of Nations with the 'great Russian government controlled by the workers' there to check it.[129]

Mellor subsequently spoke in support of Cripps's arguments asking the conference to remember that 'the positive action of fighting your enemy at home is greater in value than the negative disaster of defending your home enemy abroad'. However, the impact of the split within the Socialist League in weakening its position was now seen vividly as Mellor was forced to pay as much attention to refuting the arguments of Trevelyan as those advanced by Dalton. He now repeated Cripps's earlier argument that too much significance should not be made of the Soviet Union's involvement with the League of Nations. It was merely acting pragmatically to ensure its own security amid rising international tension.[130]

Finally, any sympathy that the Socialist League might still have elicited from the conference was dispelled by Bevin's speech. Most of his efforts were, of course, directed towards discrediting Lansbury who had been well-received by the conference delegates and had gone on to elucidate passionately his Christian pacifist beliefs and his consequent opposition to any use of force in international affairs.[131] Although Lansbury had expressed his willingness to resign, the power-broking trade unionist Bevin made a bullying speech in which he accused Lansbury of betraying the movement by his inability to follow its agreed policy. Famously, Bevin raged at

Lansbury that it was 'absolutely wrong' to be 'hawking your conscience round from body to body'.[132] Significantly, in his dramatic speech Bevin also accused Cripps as well as Lansbury of disloyalty to party decisions. He argued that Cripps had not made his case sufficiently clear at the previous party conference or at the critical meeting in early September before the TUC meeting. He again made his attack decidedly personal, revealing his dislike of middle-class 'intellectuals'. Powerfully, Bevin ended his speech by comparing the actions of Lansbury and Cripps with those of MacDonald in 1931 whose 'great crime . . . was that he never called in his party'.[133] The subsequent passage of the three Executives' resolution by 2,168,000 to 177,000 was a conclusive endorsement of a sanctionist League of Nations policy.[134] A considerably smaller number of dissenting votes had been cast than in the previous year when 673,000 had opposed the NEC's *War and Peace*. Both the Socialist League case and the pacifist one had been conclusively defeated. The impact of the sanctions crisis, however, was far from over. Indeed, during the next six months the ILP's own divisions over the issue would come to the fore.

3

THE FASCIST ADVANCE

October 1935 to July 1936

In the aftermath of the Labour party conference the Socialist League played down its opposition to sanctions which, to an extent, eased its relations with the NEC and the TUC General Council. Early in 1936, however, it found itself once again at the centre of intra-party struggle as – in defiance of the NEC – it announced its support for CPGB affiliation to the Labour party. Meanwhile the ILP continued to wrestle with its own divisions over sanctions. The ILP annual conference in April 1936 saw a bitter dispute between those – such as Brockway – who advocated 'working-class sanctions' and those – such as Maxton and the Parliamentary Group – who insisted that the British workers should not involve themselves directly in the struggle. The issue was eventually resolved in favour of the Parliamentary Group's position but only after it had fully exploited its power within the party in a controversial manner. As the fascist dictators gained ground the Socialist League and the ILP campaigned together against National government rearmament and refined their support for a united front. For the ILP the rejection of a broader popular front was unproblematic but for the Socialist League this was an altogether more delicate matter.

I

Following the dramatic confrontation at the Labour party conference a good deal of tension remained between the Socialist League and the NEC-TUC grouping as well as within the Socialist League itself, which had experienced its first major rupture. Trevelyan wrote with exasperation to his wife that 'Cripps did not amount to more than saying that we must wait till we had a Labour government before using the League powers'.[1] On 8 October Murphy posted the letter to Cripps which he had written before the party conference and that revealed the full extent of his opposition to mass resistance.[2] He claimed subsequently that he 'felt more and more that the growing power of Nazism in Germany was a threat not merely to socialism but to all civilisation as we knew it' and was 'convinced that we were heading towards war'.[3] Pritt also made his considerable unease with the official Socialist League line known to Cripps.[4] At the same time Brailsford continued to move more decisively in favour of support for collective security.[5] There was also continued disquiet from the Socialist League rank and file. In mid-October Joseph Needham, the biochemist who was chairman of the Cambridge branch, endorsed a resolution in favour of collective security as chairman of a combined meeting of the Cambridge University Socialist Society and Labour Club.[6]

On 6 October 1935 the Socialist League National Council met and decided – despite the attack on, and the defeat of, their policies at the Labour party conference – to remain inside the Labour party. The National Council recognised that this was an important decision which it advised all its branches to discuss.[7] Anticipating the announcement of the general election, the National Council issued a circular on 11 October which called upon the Socialist League to 'concentrate its energy in the country upon a sustained drive for the return of a Labour government'. Significantly, it stressed that 'at such a time the area of difference within the Labour party should be kept as small as possible'.[8] There was obviously a pressing need for the Labour party to pull together at this point. Lansbury resigned as party leader on 8 October, and Attlee was appointed as an interim leader. As expected Baldwin then acted quickly and on 19 October called a general election for three weeks' time in an attempt to exploit Labour's divisions.[9] The Labour party now sought, above all, to overcome its appearance of disarray and was helped by the actions of the Socialist League. Murphy later described how the Socialist League 'trimmed its sails'. While it maintained 'its adherence to the Bristol conference decision about opposing a capitalist war, it now refrained from any active campaign against the party's decision to support sanctions against Italy'.[10] Cripps made it clear in *The Socialist* that the immediate necessity was to 'minimise to the best of our ability any area of difference within the ranks of the Labour movement, so that our united attack upon our class opponents in the class struggle may be the more effective'. Accordingly, the Socialist League was committed not to 'conduct any oppositional campaign in the constituencies against the Party's decision on the immediate issue of sanctions'.[11] Indeed, during the election campaign – and only a month after their bitter confrontation at Brighton – Bevin and Cripps even appeared on the same platform in Bristol.[12]

The general election on 14 November saw the Labour party stage a moderate recovery. It gained more than a hundred seats to take its total to 154 seats but the National government retained a large majority with 429

MPs of whom 387 were Conservatives. With the Labour party's endorsement of sanctions, there had in fact been little to distinguish its policy on the central issue of the day from that of the National government. As C. L. Mowat perceptively put it, Baldwin 'had stolen their [the Labour party's] clothes, and they could only protest that he would never wear them'.[13] Attlee was then elected as Labour party leader after a three-way contest against Morrison and Greenwood on 26 November.[14]

However, in mid December the discussions between the British and French foreign ministers – Hoare and Laval – came to light. There was considerable public outrage as it seemed that through the Hoare-Laval Pact the National government planned to cede more than half of Abyssinia to Italy. Baldwin disassociated the Government from the statement, reaffirmed its commitment to collective security and Hoare resigned as foreign secretary to be replaced by Anthony Eden. Cripps stressed how he had predicted in September that such a bargain would be made.[15] In the House of Commons, he attacked the Hoare-Laval pact as an 'imperialist deal' making a mockery of the National government's supposed 'liberal sentiments' and support for the League of Nations and revealing its 'double dealing and deceit'.[16]

Nevertheless, even now the Socialist League did not pit its own stance against that of the NEC. The likes of Dalton had also criticised the National government for temporarily abandoning collective security, but now maintained their broad support for its sanctions policy and actually pushed the National government to apply more stringent economic, particularly oil, sanctions against Italy during the ongoing Abyssinian war. Perhaps Cripps and other Socialist League leaders such as Mellor were aware that by further developing their opposition to the Labour party's support for sanctions at this stage they would be liable to re-open an issue that could divide the Socialist League itself. Even though the Socialist League played down its opposition to sanctions, albeit without retreating from its original stance, the divisions within the Socialist League did not disappear altogether – suggesting that a more thoroughgoing opposition may well have fatally fractured it. As it was, some of those within the Socialist League who had supported sanctions in September now called for oil sanctions. In the first draft of his autobiography Pritt explained how this caused difficulties. He recalled that at about this time:

> Cripps and J. T. Murphy had advertised me to address a big meeting . . . and expected me to oppose the extension of sanctions to petrol. I refused to follow this line, and offered either to make a speech in which I said nothing about it, or to fall victim to an attack of influenza! They chose the latter offer.[17]

Brailsford took the same stance as Pritt. In early 1936 he argued publicly in favour of the introduction of oil sanctions. Recognising that oil was 'the one economic sanction that can have a prompt effect on the military operations' given its use in tanks and aeroplanes, he was even prepared to accept that this might increase the danger of an Italian attack on the British fleet. Brailsford regarded this course of action as imperative arguing that 'if the League recoils before this threat, any conception of it as a judicial body wielding police powers is at an end'. He argued that it would become 'the League of the Hoare-Laval plan', which would abandon 'all pretence of covenanted justice' and simply 'play a minor part in compounding felonies and rounding off the ragged edges of conquests'.[18]

The ILP's trajectory at this point differed from that of the Socialist League in not retreating from opposing sanctions. Immediately after the Labour party conference the ILP further developed its critique of the Labour party's foreign policy, powerfully linking it with arguments about rearmament. Stressing the more widely accepted proposition that if 'money is to be spent on armaments it will not be available for social purposes', the New Leader argued that if the Labour party was 'prepared to support the National Government in a policy which involves war, it cannot refuse to the National government the armaments necessary for war'.[19] This important point was reiterated by Lee in her open letter to Bevin,[20] and in subsequent New Leader editorials.[21]

As speculation mounted that the National government would fight a General Election on a central plank of collective security and rearmament, the ILP National Council called for a National War Crisis Congress comprising all sections of the working class opposed to military sanctions and war. The National Council sought the creation of 'Committees of Action' in each district to mobilise support and plan resistance, but envisaged the Congress assuming a role of national co-ordination. Crucially, as it announced its initiative, the National Council reiterated the danger of involvement in 'a war of rival imperialisms in Africa', showing that – for now – the ILP's divisions on this issue were at least publicly concealed.[22] The ILP's formal election manifesto then pledged 'relentlessly [to] resist any proposals for rearmament' and the foreign policy which necessitated it. In contrast to the Socialist League, its stance was firmly pitted against the Labour party which it contended had 'seriously compromised its opposition' to rearmament.[23]

The ILP's approach, however, soon became more ambiguous, reflecting an awareness of its inability to win wider support for its policies. In early December the ILP National Council instructed the Inner Executive 'to watch the political situation carefully and to summon the Congress immediately circumstances justify such action'.[24] After the revelations of the Hoare-Laval pact, the ILP reiterated its line of asking the British workers 'to challenge British imperialism' as 'the best contribution we can make to save the African workers from becoming the slaves of African imperialism'.[25] However, Brockway's editorial informed the *New Leader* readers that there was a need to 'take a realistic view' – recognising that even if 'war threatens there may not be sufficient working-class support to apply the policy of the General Strike'.[26]

II

In early 1936 the Socialist League gave public endorsement to a united front for the first time, putting itself once again at odds with the NEC. The events at the Comintern Congress held in Moscow in July and August 1935 were greatly significant in this development. While the CPGB had still retained a critical posture towards the Labour party, Dimitrov, the Comintern general secretary, now gave an emphatic endorsement to CPGB efforts to create a united front. In response, Pollitt made a speech pledging to renew the CPGB application for Labour party affiliation.[27] The application was not to be made until after the Labour party conference and was then delayed further by the calling of the general election. Nevertheless, the Communist party manifesto called for the election of a Labour government and in a considerable number of constituencies Communists actively supported Labour candidates.[28] The CPGB then formally applied for affiliation on 25 November 1935 citing 'the most dangerous war situation' as the crucial factor. Since fascist Italy had attacked Abyssinia, and Germany was 'preparing to attack the Soviet Union and to plunge the whole world into war', it argued that there was a need for working-class action to defeat the National government and fascism. While the CPGB maintained its 'revolutionary standpoint', it insisted that this was not 'a manoeuvre or for any concealed aims' and that it was 'willing to accept the Labour party as the federal organisation of a united working class'.[29]

Until this point the Socialist League had, of course, been reluctant to associate with the CPGB or the ILP. Nevertheless, the idea was keenly discussed in Socialist League circles. It was a topic of debate at the Socialist League annual conferences in 1934 and 1935 as well as at an aggregate meeting of the London Area Committee on 6 April 1935.[30] Cripps's personal opposition to any kind of united front – on the basis that it would diminish his influence in the Labour party – had continued. In October 1934 he turned down an offer from the Communist sympathiser, John Strachey, for co-operation between 'a small group of persons whose opinion in the Labour movement cannot be disregarded'. Cripps argued that: 'I still feel convinced that the only effective thing we can do is to try to stir up the party from inside, and it is quite idle to hope that a great mass of the party will ever combine with outside left-wing organisations'.[31] However, others on the Socialist League National Council and its Executive Committee, including Mellor, looked more favourably on the idea of a united front and had, for example, been willing to enter discussions with Strachey.[32] Without Cripps's agreement there were unofficial discussions between members of the Socialist League, the ILP and the CPGB in November 1934.[33] Moreover, as recently as April and May 1935 Mellor had instigated further discussions between himself, Mitchison and Elvin and the ILP about the creation of a 'united platform' on certain issues.[34] These meetings had inspired heated correspondence between the NEC and the Socialist League during summer 1935 which only came to an end when Mellor and then the Socialist League Executive Committee insisted that Mellor, Mitchison and Elvin had been at the meetings in their private capacities rather than to represent the Socialist League.[35]

Nevertheless, by the end of 1935 the Socialist League, and importantly Cripps, had become more openly supportive of a united front. The change of Comintern approach in August 1935, the Socialist League's defeat at the party conference in October and the outcome of the general election in November – which returned moderates such as Dalton to Parliament – were the crucial factors in this decision. The Socialist League leaders now realised that the Socialist League alone would not be able to wield much influence in a party dominated by the NEC and the TUC General Council. The Socialist League, therefore, began to move closer to both the CPGB and the ILP. A letter from Cripps to his father, Parmoor, shows this line of thinking and how, with Labour support for National government sanctions against Italy, he feared that 'we are moving towards a capitalist concentration of power in this country which is likely to draw the Trades Union and Labour elements with it'.[36] It seems that Cripps had changed his mind and now advocated Communist affiliation in order to counterbalance what he saw as an increasingly reactionary Labour leadership.

The Socialist League Executive Committee responded positively, but privately, to the CPGB affiliation proposal in January 1936. On the 15th it conveyed its views officially to the Labour party in a letter to Middleton. The Socialist League based its support on the perceived existence of rank and file backing for working-class unity within the wider Labour movement, and on its conviction that the Labour party was 'the party in which all sections of the socialist and working-class movement, whatever their differences of attitude and outlook, should unite'. The Socialist League Executive

Committee wanted the Labour party to meet the Communist Party and 'frankly discuss their application' and then 'state clearly and publicly the terms, if any, upon which their application would be acceptable'.[37] It was clear that this was a developing point of dispute between the Socialist League and the NEC even though the NEC had yet to make its formal response to the CPGB. The NEC planned to discuss the Socialist League's letter the following week when it debated Communist affiliation but warned that the 'terms upon which organisations can affiliate to the Party have been clearly laid down by our Annual Conferences in our Party Constitution and Standing Orders'.[38] The oppositional campaign run by the Socialist League against the NEC's policy of League of Nations sanctions had only increased its antipathy towards the Socialist League and made a sharp response to the League's support for CPGB affiliation likely. Bevin – in close alliance with Dalton over foreign policy – revealed the extent of his ill-feeling in a letter to Cole. Bevin was completely exasperated with irresponsible 'intellectuals' and considered that 'the latest and most ghastly thing was the Cripps upset'.[39]

On 27 January 1936 the NEC met to determine its line. It decided that 'no circumstances have arisen to justify any departure from the decision registered by the annual conference . . . in 1922' which rejected affiliation because 'the fundamental difference between the democratic policy and practice of the Labour party and the policy of dictatorship which the Communist party had been created to promote was irreconcilable'. The NEC also argued that 'the victories of the Fascist dictatorships were in part facilitated by the campaigns for Communist dictatorship that preceded the campaigns – which effectively split the working class movement and rendered their overthrow possible'. Above all, the NEC considered that the application was only a 'deviation in the tactics' of the Comintern and that the CPGB sought 'to utilise party facilities on the platform, in public conference and in the party press, to displace their essential democratic and Socialist character and substitute a policy and programme based upon Communist Party principles'.[40] Now the Socialist League pitted its views directly against those of the NEC. The National Council of the Socialist League met on 2 February and 'decided unanimously' to support affiliation. It urged that, at the very least, the Executive of the Labour party meet CPGB representatives as they had suggested, putting 'difficulties and differences which have accrued over a number of years . . . into proper perspective' and overlooking 'theoretical differences . . . between the Communist Party and the Labour party'.[41] The NEC's curt reply – that 'fundamental' differences of policy presented 'a very practical consideration', again hinted at the developing cleavage between the Socialist League and the NEC on this matter.[42]

Prominent members of the Socialist League now began to speak forthrightly in favour of a united front with the CPGB at League meetings throughout the country during February. They often emphasised the energy that both the CPGB and the ILP brought to the workers' cause and the CPGB's genuine change of policy – involving a complete end to their oppositional tactics and willingness to operate within the Labour party.[43] To an extent the NEC and the TUC General Council now chose to deal with the Socialist League by ignoring it: for the first time the *Daily Herald* gave only scant coverage to the activities of the Socialist League as Beatrice Webb perceptively noted in her diary.[44] The *Daily Herald* was owned jointly by Odhams press and the TUC, and was firmly under the editorial control of the TUC General Council. Indeed Bevin, who was chairman of the *Daily Herald* board, often referred to it as 'my paper'.[45]

For the time being, the Socialist League refrained from joint activities with the Communist party – action which would have meant defying the NEC. Hitler's remilitarisation of the Rhineland in March 1936, in contravention of the Treaty of Versailles, prompted further CPGB demands for united action. The CPGB wrote in identical terms to the NEC and the TUC General Council suggesting 'a common plan of campaign against the war aggressive policy of Hitler' by all working-class organisations.[46] The CPGB also wrote to Murphy enclosing their letter to the Labour party and affirming their 'willingness to co-operate with the Socialist League in any measures which you may put forward for action in the present serious and critical situation'.[47] The Executive Committee of the Socialist League made a cautious response. At one level this concerned its views of Soviet foreign policy. Just as before the sanctions crisis, the Socialist League still insisted that a future Labour government should ally with the Soviet Union. However, the Socialist League was opposed to the Soviet line of 'collective security in the present situation' – with Mellor again dismissing the Soviet Union's foreign policy as a matter of expedience.[48] The Socialist League's coolness towards the CPGB proposal was, moreover, also underpinned by its awareness that it was treading a fine line in the Labour party. Its reply to the CPGB emphasised the necessity of observing the Labour party constitution while still reiterating its support for Communist affiliation.[49] Even so, the Socialist League was actually drawing closer to the CPGB all the time. Mellor warned that what he saw as the Labour party's increasing tendency for 'open collaboration with capitalism' meant that soon it might have 'neither the right nor the authority to condemn joint activity against capitalism with the Communists by the League or by any affiliated organisation'.[50]

While the Socialist League had made it clear that it sought the involvement of the ILP in a united front, by early 1936 the ILP had become less enthusiastic about the idea. This was largely as a result of its recent deterioration in relations with the CPGB during the General Election and its own opposition to Labour party affiliation. Given the relatively small number of ILP candidates – just 20 – the NAC had advised its members 'to support those Labour candidates who are prepared definitely to pledge themselves against military sanctions and war'.[51] Its overall strategy was laid out by Maxton who argued that 'if a Labour government is returned to power, we will help to keep it in power as long as it is not acting against the interests of the workers'.[52] It came as a tremendous shock, however, that the CPGB planned to support official Labour party candidates against ILP ones except in the ILP's three existing seats: Maxton's in Bridgeton, McGovern's in Shettleston, and Buchanan's in Gorbals. In practice this meant it campaigned against Lee in North Lanark, Campbell Stephen in Kilmarnock and Brockway in Norwich.[53] In the event, the ILP actually gained an MP – Stephen – but ILP-CPGB relations sank to their lowest point since 1933.

The distance between the ILP and the CPGB was also increased at this juncture as the pro-Communist RPC resigned from the party. In a high-profile split, Gaster and Cullen, together with between 50 and 60 supporters from the London Division, now joined the CPGB.[54] Publicly, they explained their secession by citing both their disappointment that John Aplin had been elected as chairman of the London Division and their objection to ILP criticism of the pro-collective security line of the CPGB.[55] The reality was not so straightforward: the RPC had actually discredited itself within the ILP by the inability of its leaders to agree a line on the Abyssinian crisis. The RPC's official position, voiced by its chairman Cullen, was of course to follow the Soviet Union (and the CPGB) in supporting sanctions.[56] This clearly put it at odds with the ILP, and especially with those dominating the Inner Executive who were most strongly opposed to assisting Abyssinia in any way.[57] Gaster, however, was in favour of Brockway's original policy of 'working-class sanctions', arguing for 'direct working-class action against Italy's war plans [which] would entirely alter the relations of forces internationally'.[58] It was against this background of internal division, therefore, that the RPC decided to disband itself on 29 October.[59] In any case, it was clear that the mood within the ILP had now turned more decisively than ever against the RPC. Aplin, who had worked hard to reduce the RPC's influence over the London Division, now took Gaster's seat on the NAC in January 1936.[60] Furthermore, in early February 1936 the London ILP conference instructed the NAC 'to dissolve all unofficial groups within the party'.[61]

Altogether these factors meant that the ILP responded coolly to the CPGB proposal for Labour party affiliation. Emphasising in particular its differences with the Labour party over foreign policy, it instead developed calls for a united front of the working class on a 'federal basis'[62] arguing that it would not be possible to work through 'one rigid organisation'.[63] The implication that the ILP did not want to re-affiliate to the Labour party was already clear, even before it was made explicit in a NAC resolution passed at the Easter conference.[64] The ILP, however, went further – criticising not only the CPGB's recent electoral tactics but also the Soviet Union's foreign policy. For these reasons the *New Leader* argued that Communist Parties were 'more and more becoming organisations in defence of political democracy rather than organisations of Revolutionary Socialism', creating considerable difficulties for the successful operation of a united front.[65]

III

At this juncture, the ILP's attention was deflected pending the debate at its party conference over the application of its war resistance policy to the Abyssinian crisis. Until this point the different views had been largely held in check but now, as the delegates met at Keighley in Yorkshire on 11 April 1936, they came prominently to the fore. Brockway's view – that the war was 'an act of imperialist aggression by Italy on a backward people' and that the working-class movement should have been urged 'to stop materials going to Italy' – was pitted directly against that of Maxton and the Parliamentary Group, and now sponsored by the NAC, which argued that both Italy and Abyssinia were 'governed by dictators' and that accordingly 'the workers should not take action one side or the other, but should concentrate on their struggle at home against British capitalism and imperialism'.[66]

The most forceful supporter of Brockway's line was C. L. R. James. James was a West Indian-born political activist and writer who, after moving to Britain in the early 1930s had joined the ILP where he had increasingly adopted a Trotskyist stance – that is to say one that was not only critical of the Stalinist regime in the Soviet Union but also explicitly supportive of Trotsky who had lost out in the power struggle that had followed Lenin's death.[67] Trotsky was forced into exile in 1929, and began to argue that Stalin's bureaucratic regime was politically conservative and had destroyed the revolutionary purpose of the Comintern. He further argued that a truly revolutionary party should be formed in the Soviet Union whose prospects of success would depend on the progress made by revolutionaries elsewhere in Europe. These were arguments which James largely reiterated in his 1937 book *World Revolution*. Trotskyists had only formed a very small part of the ILP before October 1934 when they formed the Marxist Group. Even after this point, moreover, they only slowly gained ground, doing so mainly in the London ILP.[68] Now, however, the group found itself represented at the 1936 ILP conference by James.

Significantly indicating the lack of resonance of strictly Trotskyist arguments within the wider ILP, James pitched his arguments in much broader terms. Amid a 'tense atmosphere',[69] he began by making reference to the fact that the revised NAC stance was at odds with the resolution agreed by the International Bureau in mid-August 1935 and accepted by the ILP at that point. The crux of James's argument, however, was that the ILP 'in its obligations to the Colonial people, must assist them in their struggle against Italian fascism'. This was a point which chimed with the ILP's broader stance on imperialism. Earlier the conference had overwhelmingly endorsed a resolution instructing the NAC 'to devise means of taking further action in support of the Nationalist and Revolutionary movements within the Empire, and of developing sympathetic contact with them'.[70] Furthermore, Brockway noted in his memoirs that James 'appealed as a black worker for help for the black population of Abyssinia' which had 'an emotional effect'.[71] Attempting in some ways to reply to the NAC's insistence that there was a need to concentrate on the domestic struggle against the National government, James further added that 'if the workers here had taken such independent action they would immediately have come into conflict with the Government here, and the situation of "fighting your own government" would have become a real issue'.[72]

James's arguments were supported by C. A. Smith – the editor of *Controversy*, the internal discussion organ established in 1933 – who objected explicitly to the control of the Inner Executive by the Parliamentary Group, and by Jones, of the Lancashire Divisional Council, who charged the National Council with political expediency for changing its line as the General Election approached. Much of the subsequent debate, however, turned on the practicality of 'working-class sanctions'. Brockway's arguments that they could indeed have been put into practice were countered by James Carmichael, the Scottish organiser, as well as the MPs McGovern and Buchanan, who argued it was simply naïve to consider that the trade union rank and file could be mobilised for some kind of working-class action given their reformist leadership.[73] According to Brockway, there was no doubt that McGovern's arguments 'carried weight'.[74] Before the debate closed, however, the Lancashire Division advanced a resolution supporting Brockway's initial line and frankly stating its opinion that the subsequent action of the NAC was 'in direct conflict with declared party policy and a contradiction of party discipline'. In the fraught atmosphere of the conference this was eventually carried by 70 votes to 57.[75]

The most dramatic events, however, were yet to come. According to Brockway, as soon as the result was announced 'Maxton remarked calmly that the Parliamentary Group would have to reconsider its position'. Brockway feared 'at once from his demeanour that a serious party crisis would follow'.[76] Following a meeting of the Parliamentary Group,[77] a special meeting of the NAC was called for that evening at which Maxton tendered his resignation as its chairman, informing the meeting that McGovern and Stephen would resign with him. He argued frankly that the Parliamentary Group was unable to carry out the policy endorsed by the conference and proposed that it would act independently on this issue while attempting to follow agreed ILP policy elsewhere.[78] Brockway recalled that Maxton's comments had fallen 'like a bombshell' but was convinced that they would seriously split the party if they were repeated to the conference. Brockway's particular concern was that 'faced by the prospect of losing Maxton and the Parliamentary Group, the majority would rally to them, leaving those who took my view a futile and isolated section'. Brockway therefore 'decided on compromise and when James Carmichael proposed a ballot of the membership . . . agreed at once, though without any illusions about the result': he thought it 'inevitable that the vote would be influenced more by the desire to retain Maxton and his colleagues than by the political issue'. In any case, Brockway himself then drafted the compromise resolution.[79]

This resolution, which was moved the following day by Maxton, acknowledged the differing views within the party and the inability of three members of the Inner Executive to follow the agreed policy. Given the narrowness of the vote, it called for a ballot of the party membership on the issue – the results of which would be revealed in early July. In the meantime it advocated 'liberty for the expression of differing views'. Unsurprisingly, this was not well received by the London delegates who argued that it 'was a flouting of party decisions properly debated and carried through conference'. Brockway countered that it would be 'a bad blow' for the party to lose Maxton and that there was an overriding need to compromise 'for the sake of the maintenance of the ILP and its work'. The resolution was duly passed by 93 votes to 39, but this left the delegates 'stunned',[80] and led some of Brockway's supporters to claim that he had 'ratted'.[81] A report given to the Politburo about the ILP conference noted the 'absolute lack of any enthusiasm, the complete confusion, the manoeuvres of the NAC to sink the desires of the delegates who wish to contest their line in regard to the war in Abyssinia'.[82] Notwithstanding the CPGB's obvious political differences with the ILP, this was not that far wide of the mark.

After the conference, Brockway tried to put a favourable gloss on the situation in the *New Leader* by arguing that the intensity of the debate had obscured the fact that the ILP was absolutely united in its determination to resist war under a capitalist government in all circumstances.[83] Large differences did, however, remain. The party published a pamphlet entitled *Should Workers take Sides*, containing three articles arguing that they should, and three arguing that they should not.[84] Those endorsing the former view included Brockway, James and Bob Edwards, the Lancashire NAC representative who had been suspended from the party in 1934 for his involvement with the Comintern Affiliation Committee but had since adopted a more mainstream position within the ILP.[85] Those advocating the latter course were Maxton, McGovern and Joseph Southall. McGovern also attacked his opponents' case in *Controversy*, contending that it was deeply problematic for socialists to fight for the Abyssinian Emperor.[86] In response, Smith asserted that had he been in Abyssinia 'only conflicting duties or sheer cowardice would have prevented my fighting against the fascist invaders'.[87] James readily joined this debate, revealing that early in 1935 he had contacted the Abyssinian Embassy in London and offered to serve the Emperor even in a military capacity. He agreed that British imperialism had to be challenged but asserted that Italian capitalism was 'the same enemy, only a little further removed'.[88]

In early July 1936 the outcome of the membership ballot was announced: it showed a majority in favour of 'refusal to back either Italy or Abyssinia and of opposition to the sending of materials to either side'.[89] The *New Leader* did not reveal the actual voting statistics, but they were 809 to 554 in favour of the Parliamentary Group's position.[90] This result no doubt reflected a widespread desire not to lose the ILP MPs at a time when interest in Abyssinia was waning as the Italian army secured control. It was also, of course, firm evidence of the Parliamentary Group's power within the ILP. In any case, the NAC now tried to be conciliatory. It stressed that it did 'not regard the vote of the party on the Italo-Abyssinian War as laying down a policy to be applied under all circumstances', and asked the Executive Committee to prepare a statement on the issue for eventual discussion at the next annual conference.[91] Significantly, while reiterating the central need for 'the development of working-class determination to meet the threat of war by organised mass resistance' with the aim of overthrowing the government, the ILP National Council accepted the 'special duty of defending the Soviet Union' through 'organised working-class refusal of war materials to any other capitalist Government attacking the Soviet Union'.[92] This was clearly the one case in which the policy of direct involvement in international affairs did apply. In spite of the Soviet Union's changed foreign policy, this had been accepted without argument at the ILP conference in April,[93] testifying to the ILP's enduring pro-Soviet identity.

IV

Meanwhile from March 1936 the Socialist League had devoted much of its energy to attacking the National government's rearmament programme. Significantly, by opposing rearmament the Socialist League was not disagreeing with official Labour party policy but it was nevertheless setting itself up against Dalton, Bevin and Citrine who were trying to convince the party of the pressing need to support rearmament. At this point the majority of the parliamentary party was not persuaded by their arguments.[94] Even Attlee and Morrison, who in other respects now worked so closely with Dalton, Bevin and Citrine, could not be won over. The PLP had opposed National government rearmament since it was first introduced in July 1934. Now in March 1936, when the National government published its White Paper containing plans for substantially increased rearmament, the NCL, PLP and NEC rejected the arguments of Dalton and his allies and decided to oppose the new measures. Dalton dismissed the prevalent views as 'mere anti-armament sentiment'.[95] However, the Labour party had always consciously seen itself as a party of peace. The coalition of interests in the Labour movement was held together by its common commitment to domestic social reform, and this was generally thought to require a peaceful international environment. At its simplest it inspired the belief that expenditure on arms was inimical to the achievement of any substantial social improvement at home. Moreover, since the Great War a deep suspicion of the morality of private arms manufacture had permeated the whole party. An article written for the *Daily Herald* by Attlee in 1936 epitomised these views. He condemned the 'instruments of destruction' and contrasted the National government's willingness to sanction arms expenditure with its failure to spend on depressed areas.[96] This meant that when Bevan spoke strongly against rearmament (and against Dalton) at a meeting of the PLP in February 1936, he was expressing sentiments shared by many in the party.[97] The same was true of Cripps when in March he criticised the way that the National government considered itself 'too hard up to provide decent standards for the unemployed or for the workers', but that when 'it comes to armaments . . . no one was going to discuss the question of cost'.[98] The Socialist League campaign against rearmament thus added an important voice to that section of the Labour party opposing National government rearmament and echoed the deeply-held Labour sentiments.

Cripps had first linked his opposition to League of Nations sanctions with opposition to National government rearmament in September 1935, and Bevan had done likewise.[99] Moreover, ahead of the general election in November 1935 Cripps had forthrightly demanded 'resistance to any increase of British armaments by a capitalist Government'.[100] However, until March 1936 opposition to rearmament had been only a tangential part of the Socialist League programme. Then the publication of the National government's White Paper on Defence on 3 March prompted the Socialist League into action. The Socialist League objected to the plans laid out in the White Paper and immediately wrote to the NCL expressing the hope that it would 'definitely oppose the government's rearmament plans'.[101] Shortly afterwards, its concerns further heightened by Hitler's remilitarisation of the Rhineland, the Socialist League began a comprehensive campaign against National government rearmament.

The Socialist League shared the view held by many British politicians that while Germany's remilitarisation of the Rhineland indicated a severe deterioration in the international situation it was not necessary to take action against Germany.[102] This view was often based on a belief that the clauses of the Versailles Treaty, which had been broken, were in any case unjust. Trevelyan considered that sanctions 'would be entirely out of place' because the 'basic complaint of Germany is justifiable, namely the inequality of her position', though he recognised that Hitler's actions increased the international tension.[103] Brailsford thought likewise. He held that Hitler had been 'violent and unscrupulous', but that he really had little alternative to a unilateral revocation of the Rhineland clauses.[104]

Yet the Rhineland crisis did give impetus to the campaign against rearmament. Later in March 1936 the Socialist League National Council issued a 'Seven Point Resistance Plan to Rearmament and the National Government'. It welcomed the decision of the NCL to oppose the White Paper. However, it not only wanted the PLP to vote against the arms estimates, but also called on the TUC to refuse to 'collaborate in the munitions production'. It saw this 'on the industrial side' as the 'logical consequence of the political opposition expressed to the White paper by the National Council of Labour' and emphasised that without this Labour opposition would be ineffective. This was an important way in which Socialist League opposition to rearmament went beyond that of the NCL. The National Council opposed any attempts to 'dilute' labour by bringing in unskilled or semi-skilled workers alongside skilled ones to work in industries that were vital to armament production. It also made an opposition to military and industrial conscription central to its campaign. It wanted to see 'mass demonstrations organised by the NCL' and urged that the May Day demonstrations should be used to build opposition to National government rearmament. The Socialist League National Council also hoped that local areas would set up special committees to maintain the momentum of opposition to war preparations.[105]

The Socialist League's anti-rearmament campaign soon gathered momentum. Its Seven Point Plan was placed on the front page of *The Socialist* in April 1936, together with an article by Cripps explaining the reasoning behind this strong stance. He argued that the preparations for war were 'to maintain the existing class domination over European and Colonial peoples alike'. The National Council was 'resolute in its opposition to Fascism', but held that 'the desire to stabilise British and French imperialism is as much responsible for the present war danger as are the expansionist aims of Hitler or Mussolini'. The National Council's main aim remained the overthrow of the National government.[106]

From this point on 'all the campaign conferences and meetings organised by the League' were devoted 'to arousing active opposition' to National government rearmament and the policy laid out in the White Paper.[107] In many ways these nationwide conferences followed the precedent of those arranged by the Socialist League against sanctions in September 1935. They involved the Socialist League operating as a semi-independent mass organisation, propagandising its ideas within the wider movement and aiming in particular to win over local Labour parties and trades councils to its stance. Yet on this occasion the NEC and the TUC General Council could not object because opposition to rearmament was official party policy, and so they did not respond in any way to the Socialist League's initiative. Moreover, given the extent of anti-armament feeling within the Socialist League and the wider Labour movement, these conferences appear to have been united in contrast to the divisions that appeared the previous autumn over sanctions.

The Stockport conference, addressed by Cripps and Mellor was 'well attended' and public meetings on the same day in Stockport and Walkden were 'a huge success'. To be sure, the Bolton meeting was 'not at all well attended'. But at Reading 'both the conference and the meeting were very well attended and enthusiastic'. On the weekend of 4 and 5 April there was a series of 'good' conferences in South Wales – in Cardiff, Pontyrhyl, Maesteg, Caerau and Blackwood. The one in Bevan's constituency of Ebbw Vale was 'in spirit excellent'. There were also meetings in the North East – in Sunderland, Birtley, Shildon and Durham. There were mass meetings in London – the ones at Balham and Tooting, and Fulham, being perhaps 'the most successful'. Cripps, Bevan and Mellor spoke at Fulham where 'an audience of over 600 received them enthusiastically'. It seems a number of local Labour parties and trades councils responded, after Socialist League initiatives, to the anti-rearmament campaign – Balham and Tooting, Worcester Park, Stepney, Fulham, Chelsea, Kensington, St. Marylebone, St. Pancras, Islington, Bethnal Green and Hendon being examples. In Stepney, the Limehouse and Whitechapel and the St. George's Labour parties passed resolutions on the lines of the Socialist League's 'Seven Point Resistance Plan'. Furthermore, the Stepney Trades Council formed a 'Council for Peace and Democracy' advocating 'class resistance to War and War Preparations' and arranged a conference of all local Labour, Trade Union and Co-operative organisations to protest against rearmament and particularly against industrial conscription, linking the protest with demands for improved conditions for the working-class. The Islington branch of the Socialist League got part of the National Council's Declaration published in one of the local newspapers, and the Hendon branch similarly persuaded a local newspaper to publish anti-war propaganda.[108]

Significantly, opposition to rearmament had widespread support within the Socialist League. In a way that vividly illustrates the contradictory response of the Left to the rise of fascism, it was even endorsed by those who had favoured the use of sanctions against Italy. Trevelyan was clear that 'collective security leaves no justification for rearmament'.[109] Brailsford argued that it was ill advised to 'pretend that Tory England is arming to defend democracy against Fascism'. The purpose of the escalating arms budgets, he contended, was 'to maintain the gains of the last war' and 'preserve investment and trading monopolies overseas'.[110] And Kingsley Martin surely spoke for many when he wrote in February 1936 that the collapse of the League of Nations coupled with rearmament meant 'a fatal compromise; no definition of policy, but armaments for no policy, or for any policy which a more reactionary successor to Mr Baldwin may think fit to use them'.[111] Furthermore, Murphy was willing to introduce the National Council's resolution on opposition to rearmament at the Socialist League annual conference in June 1936 making a very stark contrast with the previous year's conference when he had opposed so publicly Cripps and Mellor over collective security. Murphy's speech now showed that he was in complete accord with the official Socialist League stance on rearmament. He spoke of the 'gravest danger of the Labour movement being committed to the policy of collaboration with the National government on the basis of national defence' and urged 'mass agitation' within the Labour movement to highlight these dangers.[112]

The Socialist League also gained ILP support for its campaign against rearmament. Like the Socialist League, the ILP was critical of the way it appeared that the TUC was collaborating in the 'actual operation of rearmament'.[113] As soon as the National government published its White Paper, the ILP NAC had issued a memorandum calling on ILP branches 'to approach other sections of the working class with a view to . . . common action' and to try 'to overcome all organisational barriers'.[114] Now the ILP also lavished praise on the Socialist League's Seven-Point Plan opposing rearmament[115] and collaborated closely with it in the preparations for May Day demonstrations in London.[116] Indeed, on May Day evening itself the ILP was represented at a meeting at the Memorial Hall at which Mellor spoke and which resolved to undertake a 'great resistance campaign throughout the country to the . . . new rearmament proposals'.[117]

V

At the same time as undertaking its campaign against rearmament, the Socialist League increasingly refined the nature of its support for the united front. In an article on the front page of *The Socialist* in March 1936 Cripps made it clear that the Socialist League was completely opposed to a popular front which would include Liberals as well as working-class parties. Consistent with the Socialist League's class interpretation of politics, Cripps argued that – like the popular front governments which had recently been formed in Spain and then France with Liberals as the largest single partner – these 'coalitions or groupings may be considered effective for the immediate purposes of opposition to reaction' but that 'they carry within them the seeds of their own disintegration unless the working-class parties are prepared to abandon the class struggle as the basis of their political action'. If a popular front coalition achieved power, Cripps concluded pessimistically 'the working-class movement is either condemned to the futility of reformism or the coalition naturally splits down the line of class interests'. Adamantly, Cripps insisted that if 'we accept the view taken by the Socialist League that it is impossible to save democracy for its own sake, since it can only effectively be preserved by turning it into an effective instrument for achieving socialism, then obviously there can be no question of any association or grouping with capitalist parties or individuals, however radical or progressive they may appear'.[118]

At this stage the thrust of these arguments was not contested within the Socialist League, but there was no doubt that the scope for potential future difficulties certainly existed. The Comintern meeting in summer 1935 had actually declared itself in favour of the idea of popular front – the domestic corollary of its support internationally for the League of Nations – while suggesting that for the time being a united front would be more achievable in British circumstances where there was no existing tradition of co-operation between the Labour and Liberal parties. Whereas the Socialist League clung to the dictates of its class-based philosophy, for the CPGB the difference between a united and popular front was therefore simply one of tactics. Indeed, as Pollitt put it: 'there can be no real and effective people's front unless there has been already united action within the Labour movement itself'.[119] For now though, the more pro-Soviet figures in the Socialist League could, of course, happily endorse its central call for CPGB affiliation.[120]

Like the Socialist League, the ILP's class-based opposition to the notion of a popular front intensified in response to events in France and especially to those in Spain. At one level Brockway thought the success of the popular front in Spain was 'inspiring'. However, he argued it was 'when the Government fails – as on a Liberal programme it inevitably must fail – to realise their hopes of economic improvement', that 'the real decisive struggle will arise'. Brockway saw the popular front Republican government in Spain fulfilling the role of the Kerensky government 'which preceded the real revolution in Russia'. His overriding concern was that the workers would 'tie themselves to support the Liberal Government in such a way that they are led to damp down the necessary working-class revolt which must occur if the political revolution is to be succeeded by the social revolution'.[121]

As the year progressed, Lee made clear her views about the inevitable class-based tensions within the French People's Front.[122] Meanwhile, Brockway continued to focus on events in Spain, speculating that divisions would soon develop between the Liberals and working class elements in the coalition, and emphasising the government's unwillingness to deal with issues of national autonomy for Basques and Catalonians.[123] By this stage Brockway had developed his ideological opposition to the popular front, relating it to differing interpretations of fascism:

> If your view is that fascism can be resisted separately from capitalism, you will see in the coalition of capitalist and socialist forces in the People's Front an instrument to defeat fascism . . . if your view is that fascism is a stage in the development of capitalism which will inevitably become a danger as the decisive struggle comes near, you will regard any tactic which moderates the struggle against capitalism itself as a mistake.[124]

Significantly, the ILP's perspective on Spain was cemented by its identification with the Workers' Party of Marxist Unity (POUM), which was affiliated to the International Bureau and whose leader, Joaquin Maurin, had contributed an article to the *New Leader* in February.[125] Brockway now argued that the POUM alone – which remained outside the Republican government – saw 'clearly the limitations of the present victory and the need to prepare the workers for the coming revolutionary struggle'.[126] At the meeting of the International Bureau in Paris on 9 and 10 May, Brockway,

McGovern and Stephen met Maurin, whose 'story of the Spanish situation was of thrilling interest and revolutionary importance'.[127] Brockway later remarked that his 'description of the situation in Spain was one of the most masterly analyses I have ever heard' and claimed that 'he made a deep impression on me'.[128] Needless to say, he was delighted that Maurin agreed to speak at the ILP Summer School in August 1936.[129]

Unlike the Socialist League, the ILP's emphatic rejection of the popular front did not contain latent tensions. With the secession of the RPC, its most pro-Soviet members had left the party. However, the ways in which the ILP could advocate a united front – given its continued reluctance to re-affiliate to the Labour party[130] – did remain more problematic. For this reason, the ILP NAC continued to develop its call for 'a federal association of workers' political organisations which permitted freedom of propaganda and action', securing endorsement of the idea at the annual conference[131] and subsequently advocating it through the *New Leader*.[132] On 3 and 4 July the NAC asked the Executive Committee 'to prepare detailed proposals for the application of the principle of working-class federation to both national and local conditions'.[133] Yet the ILP still had great difficulty formulating its view of the CPGB demand for Labour party affiliation. While it continued to insist that it did 'not believe that affiliation to the Labour party is the way to working-class unity',[134] it hesitantly argued that the NEC should allow the CPGB to join because it was willing to accept the restrictions this would involve.[135]

VI

Meanwhile, as the Abyssinian forces looked increasingly likely to capitulate to Italy in early summer 1936, the Socialist League adopted a more openly critical stance towards the NEC-TUC grouping than at any point in the past. In April Cripps argued that by only applying half-hearted sanctions against Italy, the National government's overriding concern 'not to endanger Italian capitalism' had become clear.[136] To Cripps this represented 'the last straw' confirming his suspicions and meaning that the Labour party 'definitely cannot have anything more to do with this Government and its foreign policy'.[137] The fact that the NCL then reiterated that 'Labour's foreign policy is based upon support of the League [of Nations]'[138] prompted Cripps to argue that when 'today Labour politicians speak of National Unity under a National Government they unwittingly imply the complete surrender of the Labour Party and all it stands for to the capitalists'.[139] Likewise, Mellor now admonished the TUC which, he claimed, was 'busy appealing to the Government to let it help in the production of munitions' instead of representing genuinely working-class interests.[140]

The Socialist League annual conference at Hanley confirmed this more critical line. Crucially just before the conference met – on 1 June – the Socialist League National Council made a highly significant decision: Mellor was elected to replace Cripps as chairman of the Socialist League. From this point on Mellor adopted a higher profile role and intrinsically carried more weight in the Socialist League. However, given the convergence of Cripps and Mellor's views, and the fact that Cripps continued to fund the League, very little difference in overall direction was expected. The decision was taken because the previous year's conference had decided, in an uncontroversial resolution, that no individual could hold the post of chairman for more than two successive years.[141] Cripps himself moved the motion proposing Mellor and the Council as a whole was keen that 'there be no misunderstanding as to why Stafford Cripps was resigning chairmanship of the National Council' when the change was announced to the Socialist League conference.[142]

In any case, at the Socialist League annual conference itself the National Council won overwhelming rank and file approval of the two main planks of its policy: a united front and opposition to rearmament. Mellor moved the resolution declaring support for a united front and CPGB affiliation to the Labour party. The motion asserted that it was 'most urgent to secure unity of policy and action by the working class of this country' as well as between the working class internationally. Mellor stressed the 'significant change' in the immediate policy of the CPGB, and the way in which different capitalist forces were themselves joining together throughout the world. He emphasised that the resolution also involved opposition to all forms of collaboration between the industrial and political Labour movement and capitalist parties and organisations. Setting the Socialist League sharply at odds with the NEC and the TUC General Council, Mellor also argued that the CPGB's 'drive and energy – and with all its faults – was wanted now as something that would break down the complacency and the bureaucracy in the Labour movement'. This was undoubtedly a popular policy in the Socialist League – it was adopted almost unanimously with the only dissenting voice of the 91 delegates present being that of Davidson, an obscure North London member.

The National Council's resolution opposing rearmament prompted a passionate debate lasting for two hours, during which the danger of military and industrial conscription from the 'reactionary militarist' elements in the National government was discussed. Moreover, Reg Groves, the secretary of the London Area Committee who had just been elected on to the National Council, stressed that the National government's rearmament proposals 'carried with them a threat against trade union conditions'. He further argued that the Socialist League should highlight this in order that the trade union rank and file might be won over to the Socialist League viewpoint. Once again the conference was significantly in favour of the National Council's stance: the resolution was eventually passed by 74 votes to 17.[143]

The NEC and the TUC General Council were undoubtedly concerned by the Socialist League conference's endorsement of a united front. When the Socialist League Executive Committee met on 11 June 1936 it had appointed Mellor, Cripps, Groves and Murphy to a sub-committee charged with drafting a resolution for the Labour party conference 'supporting the Communist Party affiliation to the Labour party' which was quickly sent to the Labour party.[144] This now served to harden the NEC's own stance against Communist affiliation. In late June Morrison's London Labour party issued a forthright warning to its members that they must not associate with Communists. Morrison also took pains to stress that the democratic Labour party was fundamentally different to the CPGB, which was in favour of revolutionary violence in order to achieve a dictatorship.[145] A little later Attlee argued that the Labour party could not consider CPGB affiliation because the latter owed 'allegiance to the Third [Communist] International, which is, in fact, the creation of another government' and meant that it 'obeys an external authority'.[146] On 16 July the NCL issued a statement which summarised and developed these arguments. It dismissed the united front as the 'latest manoeuvre in the ceaseless effort of the revolutionary Communist party to capture the democratic Labour movement'. And it made the dramatic speculation that if CPGB affiliation was accepted then 'further finance will be made available from abroad to consolidate the success and to reinforce further inroads into the ranks of the Labour party and the trade unions'.[147]

However now that the recent Amalgamated Engineering Union (AEU) and MFGB conferences had voted narrowly in favour of accepting CPGB affiliation to the Labour party, the Socialist League accused the NEC and the NCL of ignoring rank and file support for Communist affiliation.[148] Murphy – writing as 'Trade Unionist' in *The Socialist* – was highly critical of the TUC General Council, claiming that it was 'more anxious to avoid a struggle than to wage one'. He pointed to their reluctance to embrace the growing rank and file mood for CPGB affiliation. Provocatively he warned that if they 'meet this new wave of mass interest and action with the formal answers of bureaucrats instead of confidently placing themselves at the head of the movement and daring to lead the workers unitedly into action to secure their demands, they will assuredly produce the biggest internal crisis the British Labour movement has yet experienced'.[149]

The Socialist League did, moreover, try to muster support behind its advocacy of a united front by linking it with key contemporary issues in the

Labour movement. In the first place, of course, the united front was linked
to opposition to rearmament. Immediately after the Socialist League
conference, the Executive Committee agreed to make opposition to
rearmament central to its autumn campaign.[150] Significantly, opposition to
rearmament provided a basis for united action with the CPGB, which –
though supporting collective security – also opposed rearmament.[151] It also
found wide support within the Labour movement as a whole. In late July
1936 the PLP rejected the arguments in favour of supporting National
government rearmament made by Dalton and voted by 57 votes to 39 to
continue its policy of opposition.[152] The PLP argued that this was 'not a vote
for the abolition of the service concerned', but rather 'a vote in opposition to
the policy of which the Estimate is the expression' because 'the government
has shown plainly that it cannot be trusted to pursue an honest League [of
Nations] policy' and 'has never explained how its armaments policy is related
to League [of Nations] requirements'.[153]

The Socialist League also linked its advocacy of a united working-class
front with opposition to the National government's Unemployment
Assistance Board (UAB) regulations. These were issued on 9 July 1936 and
maintained both the concept of a means test and a distinction between the
long and short term unemployed for unemployment benefit. The NEC and
the TUC General Council were themselves opposed to the new UAB
regulations – the NCL criticised them and the PLP attacked them in the
House of Commons. However, the connection that the Socialist League
forged could not have sat easily with the NEC given its firm opposition to
Communist affiliation. In *The Socialist* Mellor argued that 'the real
significance of the unemployment regulations' was that they provided 'an
issue on which the whole political and industrial strength of the working-
class movement can be mobilised in a struggle not merely against the
regulations but against the whole policy and purpose of the National
Government'.[154] The clear inference was that opposition to the UAB
regulations could provide an issue around which to form a united front.

When the Socialist League Executive Committee met on 30 July 1936,
it planned a campaign against the UAB regulations, calling for nation-wide
demonstrations in the week before they were to come into operation in
November. Significantly, on the suggestion of the London Area Committee,
the committee decided to ask Groves to draft a 'pamphlet on the new UAB
regulations and their relations to the armaments plan'.[155] The Socialist
League seized on this point. Murphy stressed the connection between the
Means Test and opposition to National government rearmament to the
Socialist League rank and file in early August. Writing to all branch
secretaries and Area Committees, he explained how the leadership wanted

its members 'to take a leading part in developing the campaign of the
Labour movement' against the new regulations of the UAB and the Means
Test. He was clear that 'the whole campaign should be conducted as a fight
against the Government's war preparation programme and special emphasis
should be made of the new conditions imposed upon single men' who would
now find it more difficult to claim unemployment benefit. Murphy added
that it was 'exceedingly significant that at the moment these conditions are
imposed the Government simultaneously intensifies its campaign of
recruiting for the Armed Forces'.[156]

Murphy simultaneously conveyed these points to the NEC.[157] Middleton's
reply, however, made it very clear that the Socialist League's approach
differed from that of the NEC. He said that demonstrations against the UAB
regulations were being organised but contended that 'the proposal that the
Government's attitude to the Unemployment Regulations should determine
the Party's attitude to the Government's War Preparations also seems to link
up two subjects which are entitled to separate and independent
judgments'.[158]

VII

Since the sanctions crisis in the previous autumn the Socialist League had
remained united but now, in summer 1936, a number of Socialist League
members broke ranks and began to favour a broader popular front. In June
1936 two members of the Socialist League in London – Jim Delahaye and
Davies – began to speak publicly in favour of a popular front. In early July
Delahaye even wrote to the *New Statesman* giving his address and asking
anyone interested in advocating a popular front 'of persons from as far left as
the Communist party to as far right as the democratic Tory' to contact him.[159]

At the same time other, more prominent, Socialist League figures
tentatively began to advocate the same course. Bevan seems to have carefully
considered the advantages of a broader-based popular front at this stage. He
was very much in favour of aligning with the CPGB and the ILP, arguing
that this would give the Labour party 'a transfusion of blood'. He further
contended that to make 'an arrangement with the Liberals without making
any similar arrangement with the Communist party and the ILP' would be
'disastrous' as it 'would merely convert the Labour party into a left centre
party . . . bound to repeat the tragic history of the German social democratic
party'. However, he held that 'a combination that stretched from the Liberals
through the Labour party to the Communist Party and the ILP would still
leave the Liberals as hostages of the Left'. Bevan did 'not regard the
association of the Left Liberals as absolutely essential to the alignment', but

tentatively supported the idea on the pragmatic basis that he could 'appreciate the fact that there would be some leaders in the Labour party who would be prepared to take in the Communist party on the Left if they could balance themselves by taking in the Liberals on the Right'.[160]

At this stage Brailsford did not openly disagree with the Socialist League's united front policy either, but there is some indication that he was beginning to favour a popular front. Having wavered over supporting sanctions in September 1935, the League of Nations' subsequent failure to deal with the Italian-Abyssinian dispute led him to conclude that the 'institution was insincere'. He saw a possible solution in 'turning the League into a true federal government' provided this was initially done 'on a small scale' of 'some common social philosophy'. Crucially, Brailsford argued that if this could not 'yet be frankly socialist or communist', then it might 'be on what we nowadays call the People's Front basis': he envisaged socialist states like the Soviet Union joining Liberal democracies like France.[161] Brailsford did maintain the important proviso that a Labour government would have to be in power in Britain before such an international alliance could be formed to check the threat from the 'German giant'.[162] However, since he could advocate the popular front internationally, it appeared that it might be only a matter of time before he came round to supporting a broader alliance within Britain.

Cripps and Mellor were concerned to prevent any ruptures within the Socialist League and reaffirmed the Socialist League's definite commitment to a united front and its converse rejection of any kind of popular front. Significantly, in July 1936 Cripps defined the type of programme which he saw as underpinning a united front. There was nothing original in the programme; in fact it contained the core elements of Socialist League policy since 1932. However, the statement was important in distancing the Socialist League from demands for a more broadly based popular front, which would have necessitated a more moderate programme capable of appealing to progressive Liberals, and would have had to be framed in such a way as to downplay the Socialist League's class-based anti-capitalist rhetoric. Instead Cripps started directly from the premise that they were 'working for the co-operation of all working-class parties and sections on the basis of a socialist policy at home and an anti-imperialist policy abroad'. While he held that 'the maximum of unity is desirable if reaction and fascism are to be defeated or even held in check in this country', he was clear that there 'must, however, be some limit to the catholicity of opinion within any front that is going to adopt a positive policy for government and not merely a negative policy for opposition'. He therefore laid out 'a minimum programme of action for the first term of office of a socialist government as the basis upon which we should be prepared to accept and welcome co-operation'. In line with Socialist League policy, he was clear that the 'central point . . . in our policy must be the challenge to and overthrow of capitalism' but that this must be done 'within democracy and without the violence of revolution'. In effect, this meant nationalisation of the joint-stock banks as well as the Bank of England, and control of international trade 'in order to achieve economic co-operation with other Socialist states as a foundation for the nucleus of a peaceful world confederation'. Abolition of the Means Test, improvement of working conditions, especially in mining, and the repeal of the Trades Disputes Act were also mentioned, as was a 'great works programme financed by the nationalised credit of the country' to reduce 'unemployment during the transition period.'[163]

At the same time the Socialist League Executive Committee under Mellor's guidance set about removing from the League's ranks those who were definitely in favour of a popular front. In the first week of July 1936 Mellor personally interviewed both Delahaye and Davies and asked them to account for their support of a popular front. When Mellor reported back to the Executive Committee on 9 July, he described how he had apparently 'explained that their actions in relation to the promotion of a People's Front movement was outwith the policy of the League and the Executive could not agree with it' because the 'League was in favour of a Workers' Front'. Forthrightly, Mellor 'advised the two comrades that if they pursued their present line of action, they would have either to resign their membership of the League or the National Council would have to take disciplinary action'. Mellor was taking a strong stance but the committee was in full agreement.[164] Faced with such overt pressure from Mellor, Davies immediately drafted a letter of resignation. Delahaye also wrote to the Executive Committee expounding 'his views on the proposals to organise a People's Front Movement' and indicating 'that if these were considered incompatible with views of the SL he must resign'. Needless to say, his offer was duly accepted. Significantly, with a desire to quell further dissent, the Executive Committee also instructed the General Secretary 'to state in [the] next letter to the branches that the National Council is taking steps to secure the loyalty of members to National Conference decisions as per instructions of the Hanley Conference [and] has accepted several resignations of members'.[165] For now, it was possible for Cripps and Mellor to keep these incipient divisions submerged but they were set to develop later in the summer when the attention of the Socialist League, and that of the Labour movement as a whole, turned to the fast moving events in Spain.

4

THE OUTBREAK OF THE
SPANISH CIVIL WAR

July 1936 to October 1936

In summer 1936 British politics, and particularly those of the Left, focused on the question of how to respond to the outbreak of the Spanish Civil War. The details of the conflict – beyond the fact that the Republican government, supported by the socialists, was fighting against a fascist-nationalist coalition under Franco – were not readily known in Britain. However, as more information emerged, the Socialist League began to interpret the war in Spain as part of an international class war. Emphasising the German and Italian assistance being given to Franco, the Socialist League campaigned against the NCL's support for the policy of non-intervention taken by the National government, and moved closer to actual collaboration with the ILP and the CPGB. Under the impetus of the war, the Socialist League, questioning the most effective way to resist fascism in practice, also experienced sharpened divisions between those who supported a popular front and the majority who remained committed to its official line of support for a united front. In the meantime, the ILP criticised the Soviet Union's reluctance to intervene in Spain at this stage, building on its earlier criticism of Soviet foreign policy. Moreover, responses to the first Show Trials in Moscow in late August 1936 then prompted the ILP to begin to develop a distinctly anti-Stalinist assessment of the Soviet Union – a perspective that was also shared by some in the Socialist League.

I

The Spanish Civil War was precipitated by a right-wing revolt from parts of the army and the fascist party on 17 July 1936. Spanish politics had been turbulent for some time. In 1931 the second Spanish Republic had been created, but in 1933 a coalition of the centre right (CEDA) had won power. The Socialists (PSOE) had joined a *Frente Popular* in late 1935, together with the Communists (PCE) and Republicans, and had triumphed in the general election of February 1936. During the popular front government's first few months in power disillusionment developed with the effectiveness of the centre-right opposition. The fascist Falange party and the army now received growing support and by July felt sufficiently confident to stage the revolt, which began in parts of Spanish-controlled North Africa. The Republican forces tried to put this down but in doing so had to rely on the Socialists as well as the POUM.[1]

Initially, the Socialist League and the NCL made broadly similar responses to the outbreak of war in Spain. The NCL immediately appealed for funds to provide humanitarian relief for the Spanish workers. When the Socialist League Executive Committee met on 30 July 1936 it warmly endorsed this decision. It asked its branches 'to call special meetings, organise collections etc' and called for 'a voluntary levy of one day's pay per adult member for the Spanish workers' but stressed that 'all monies [were] to be sent to League headquarters and forwarded to the Labour Party Fund by Head Office'.[2]

However, during August the NCL showed increasing signs of supporting non-intervention. This was the policy which had been agreed between the British and French governments and it forbade the sale of arms to either of the belligerent sides in Spain. At first the French government under Leon Blum had agreed to supply arms to the legitimate Republican government, but in late July it had reconsidered its position and adopted a policy of neutrality. Britain and France formalised this agreement in stages on 8 and 15 August. They sought to create a Non-intervention Committee in the hope of preventing the Spanish Civil War from developing into a general European conflict. Portugal accepted non-intervention on 21 August, and Germany and the Soviet Union soon followed. Significantly, at the same time an official Labour delegation met Eden twice – on 19 and 26 August – to discuss the policy. The NCL itself then met on 25 and 27 August and decided to support non-intervention – a far-reaching decision which was endorsed at the private Labour movement conference on 28 August.[3] Tom Buchanan has cast invaluable light on the institutional dynamics underlying this course of action. He has shown that Bevin and Citrine were concerned that more extensive involvement in Spain would have divided the Labour movement in an extremely factious dispute. In particular, he has emphasised their concern not to alienate Catholic members of the Labour movement by openly supporting the anti-Catholic Republican side.[4]

Whatever the NCL's reasoning, the Socialist League now began to adopt a very different policy towards Spain. At a time when only a limited amount was known about the war and Spanish politics more generally in Britain[5] (and undoubtedly within the Socialist League), Brailsford as a leading commentator on international affairs did much to shape Socialist League thinking. He outlined his views in a weekly article for *Reynolds News* as well as occasionally in the *New Statesman*, and it seems likely that he also took the opportunity to discuss them with other prominent Socialist Leaguers.

At the beginning of August 1936 Brailsford was one of the first people in Britain to make clear the extent of the Italian and German involvement in the Spanish Civil War. As a well-connected foreign affairs correspondent, he was well placed to acquire knowledge of the situation. Brailsford claimed to have heard 'from informants who should know the facts that General Franco received money to finance his rebellion both from Rome and Berlin'.[6] In subsequent weeks Brailsford provided further information that Mussolini was sending a large number of aeroplanes with trained pilots to Franco along with other vital military supplies.[7]

Brailsford was sure that the Spanish workers were 'waging a class war against the exploitation of the aristocratic landlords, the monastic orders, and their few big capitalists'.[8] The most controversial point here was the criticism of the Catholic Church but Brailsford was undeterred. He argued forthrightly that the Catholic Church was 'a belligerent in the class war'. The Spanish Left was hostile to the Church but Brailsford argued that according to eyewitnesses 'when churches were burned, it was because they were used by the rebels as forts or arsenals'. Brailsford argued that the 'main cause of the hostility is economic' because the 'Church owns nearly one-third of the land in Spain, and its reputation as a landlord does not stand high'.[9]

However, it was perhaps more important that Brailsford perceived the Spanish conflict as part of the 'international class war' given the extent of foreign involvement in the conflict. He argued that if Franco triumphed 'the military prospects of the fascist coalition in Europe would be vastly improved' but that if 'the republic can consolidate itself, its friendliness is of the greatest value to the international People's Front'.[10] Brailsford held that Hitler sought to be 'the leader of Property in its struggle against the working-class, not in Germany only, but in Europe as a whole'.[11] One of his main points was that Germany and Italy could now work together because the 'ambitions of Italy have shifted from central Europe to the Mediterranean, North Africa and the East'. Brailsford held the National government responsible for devising the neutrality policy and for forcing France to support it.[12] He argued that it was 'class prejudice' which explained British neutrality – emanating from the fear that the Republic was controlled by the workers, and, perhaps, even by the Communists.[13] He sensationally speculated that 'the Foreign office is in private life almost as eager as Mussolini himself to acclaim the victory of fascism in Madrid'.[14] Importantly, Brailsford also differentiated the Spanish Civil War from the

Italian-Abyssinian dispute, arguing that in contrast to the Abyssinian people who lived in a feudal society the 'Spanish people are fighting our battle . . . against the two dictatorships that are planning to enslave Europe'.[15]

As the NCL looked increasingly likely to support non-intervention, the Socialist League called a special meeting of its Executive Committee on 18 August 1936 to agree on a statement about the Spanish situation. Brailsford had set the parameters of the debate through his articles, but it was Reg Groves who submitted a draft of this crucially important document. Along with Barbara Betts, Groves had been elected on to the National Council for the first time in June 1936 and since then they had both become active members of the Executive Committee. Groves's statement was accepted 'after full discussion and amendment' and 'circulated to branches and individual members of the League'.[16]

The Socialist League statement, which was published in full in *The Socialist* in September, was underpinned by concern for 'the international consequences of the Spanish struggle'. It argued that a fascist victory in Spain would 'intensify the danger of war, for it . . . [would] encourage the reactionary forces in Britain, France and other European countries and strengthen the military position of the Fascist Powers'. The idea of the Spanish conflict as part of the international class war in which there could be 'no neutrality' was also brought out. With the fascist states aiding Franco, the Spanish workers were said to be fighting 'a major engagement in the world workers' fight against Fascist aggression and for Peace, Freedom and Socialism'. The Socialist League statement acknowledged that a powerful argument in favour of supporting the Republican side was that Franco's fascists were rebels 'in arms against a constitutionally elected government'. However, it maintained that the real issue was whether the war would end in 'a fascist or a workers' Spain'. The Socialist League, therefore, called upon its members 'to agitate against any restrictions on the provision of arms and supplies to the anti-fascist forces in Spain and to demand that the British government shall accede to any request of those forces for help in the fight against fascism'. The Socialist League considered the matter to be so important that it also demanded the recall of Parliament.[17]

Nearly 50 years later Groves wrote an account describing the Socialist League Executive Committee's discussion of the resolution on the Spanish Civil War. He recalled that at the Executive Committee meeting, 'Cripps, returning from a meeting with Government ministers, surprised everyone by supporting non-intervention. It would, he thought, stop supplies reaching Franco's forces. "I have Eden's word on it", he added'.[18] The Socialist League Executive Committee minutes show that Cripps was not present at its special meetings on 18 and 24 August when the Spanish Civil War was discussed. Nevertheless, it is possible that Cripps expressed support for non-intervention to his Socialist League colleagues on other occasions around this time, which may have confused Groves as he reflected on events so long after they had happened. A Labour delegation had, in fact, recently seen the Foreign Secretary. And Cripps does seem to have been temporarily in favour of non-intervention. At the private Labour movement conference on 28 August he argued that the agreement had at least 'immobilised intervention against the workers' side' and that they should not apply pressure to end it 'because it would be against the interests of the Spanish workers to do so'.[19] In 1939 Morrison, who had opposed non-intervention at the Labour movement conference, also pointed out to the *Daily Herald* journalist Hannen Swaffer that Cripps had refused to support his opposition to non-intervention in August 1936.[20] If this was the case, then perhaps the weight of opinion against non-intervention within the Socialist League persuaded Cripps to change his position. Mellor certainly objected strongly to Cripps's faith in Eden. Writing in *The Socialist*, Mellor emphatically made the point that the National government's adoption of non-intervention was nothing 'but a calculated diplomatic manoeuvre for the Edens are never, in the ultimate, friends of the workers, however much they may seek to disguise their purpose'.[21] In any case, from late August 1936 Cripps himself became a firm opponent of non-intervention. When he addressed his East Bristol constituents on 29 August his change of position was clear: he opposed non-intervention and made the standard Socialist League arguments that the war in Spain was part of an international class war in which the National government was sympathetic to Franco.[22] Above all, this incident shows that Cripps was not always the principal arbiter of Socialist League policy and was even prepared to change his position in line with the majority opinion of the League.

The Socialist League's stance against non-intervention aroused substantial enthusiasm and surely caused the NCL great concern. The Socialist League's hastily convened meeting at the Essex Hall on 21 August in London, which endorsed the official Socialist League statement on the Spanish Civil War, was 'most successful' and raised £150.[23] Martin's *New Statesman* had initially endorsed the idea that foreign governments should not intervene in Spain – on the basis that this would actually help the Spanish government, and possibly enable France and Britain to convince Hitler and Mussolini to remain neutral.[24] However, when it became clear that neither Italy nor Germany intended to honour the Non-intervention Agreement, Martin changed his stance and aligned with the Socialist League. By late August Martin was even arguing that until non-intervention became effective, Britain and France should aid the Republican government to the same extent that the fascist powers were arming Franco.[25] Laski became a particularly vehement opponent of non-intervention. He wrote an impassioned letter to the *Daily Herald* expressing his disbelief at the Labour party's failure to demand that the government 'allow the Spanish government to exercise . . . [their] right to purchase arms here'. Referring to the actions of the NCL, he stressed that he did not think that 'a small fund and some telegrams' was sufficient to 'exhaust our duty to the Spanish workers'.[26]

Significantly, even those who had left the Socialist League during the past year were now firmly in agreement with its stance. Pritt, who had recently resigned from the Socialist League, became a staunch supporter of the Republican side in the Spanish Civil War and an equally strong opponent of non-intervention, which he memorably described as being 'rather like a Christian declaring himself neutral in the struggle between God and the Devil'.[27] Similarly Trevelyan, who had gradually ceased to be an active member of the Socialist League because he disagreed with its policy towards League of Nations sanctions against Italy, was now was in complete accord with the Socialist League's stance over Spain. He viewed the Labour Movement's conference's endorsement of non-intervention on 28 August with 'alarm' and 'disappointment'.[28]

II

Nevertheless, enthusiasm over Spain merely masked the fact that a number of prominent figures within the Socialist League now came out more decisively in favour of a popular front. The fact that the Socialist League was so actively supporting a popular front coalition in Spain made it more difficult for it to justify its adherence to a united front in principle, another reminder of the Left's constant conflict between theoretical and practical considerations. At its special meeting on 18 August 1936, the Socialist League Executive Committee grappled directly with the question of how to frame its statement of support for the Republican side in Spain, while conveying its own preference for a united front. Eventually the committee agreed to stress that while the 'workers are fighting alongside the Liberal government' for the time being, it hoped that 'defeat of the militarists . . . [would be] a necessary preliminary to the winning of full economic and political power for the Spanish workers and peasants'.[29] Yet, according to Groves's recollection, the committee still remained uncomfortable with the phrasing and with the dilemmas that the Spanish Civil War provoked.[30]

In this context Murphy began to advocate a popular front within Socialist League circles and tried in particular to win support for the idea from others on the National Council. In his autobiography Murphy recalled how he had come to 'the conclusion that no other course lay before those who wanted to see a government which would seriously stand for collective security against the aggressor powers than that they must form a People's Front strong enough to bring about the defeat of the National Government'. He was in favour of CPGB and ILP affiliation to the Labour party. However, in keeping with broader Comintern policy, he 'was not prepared to make this into the principal question of the campaign in which all three organisations would appear on the same platforms and openly flout the decisions of the Labour party, thus leading to the League's expulsion'. When Murphy came up against the staunch resistance of 'William Mellor's powerful influence', he decided that there was now 'little left in the policy of the Socialist League' which he 'could wholeheartedly support' and so decided to resign in early September 1936. Murphy had been at odds with the official Socialist League line since June 1935 but it was the impact of the Spanish Civil War that now prompted his resignation. Indeed, Murphy later wrote that the 'civil war in Spain gave the urgency to every effort for which we [those advocating a popular front] strived'.[31]

Murphy formally tendered his resignation on 7 September 1936 and the Socialist League Executive Committee considered the matter on 10 September. Murphy had given three months' notice of his resignation, but the committee decided that his resignation should take effect immediately. Murphy was to be paid weekly for the next three months but to forgo any further payment if and when he gained new employment. The decision had to be ratified at the next National Council meeting on 20 September, but Murphy was told that in the meantime he did not need to work at head office. Significantly, the committee decided to 'ask him not to take part during that same period in any outside activities and propaganda which would be incompatible with his position as Secretary of the League'. The Executive Committee 'also decided that, pending the decision of the National Council, no reference should be made to the letter of resignation to the branches of the League, or publicly, and that Comrade Murphy be requested to observe this'. Mellor was assigned to see Murphy and to inform him of the decisions.[32] The Executive Committee clearly feared that Murphy's resignation could polarise opinion within the Socialist League over the merits of a popular or united front at a time when Socialist League support for the Republican side in Spain had already complicated matters. Accordingly, the Executive Committee attempted to minimise the publicity which would be given to Murphy's resignation and to limit the contact that Murphy now had with other members of the Socialist League.

The National Council meeting on 20 September 1936 accepted the recommendations of the Executive Committee about Murphy as a matter of course and appointed the assistant secretary, Margaret McCarthy, as full-time secretary. The National Council agreed on a press statement explaining Murphy's replacement by McCarthy. It blandly noted that 'Murphy has for some time been at variance with the National Council of the Socialist League on certain questions of policy', which had 'now led to his resignation and its acceptance by the Council'.[33]

The same National Council meeting was also faced with two separate proposals about the popular front written by Brailsford and L. Anderson Fenn, with whom Murphy had recently discussed the popular front.[34] Fenn was a member of the National Council and treasurer but, because he lived outside the Greater London area, he did not sit on the Executive Committee. Brailsford had, of course, been on the National Council since the League's formation and regularly attended the Executive Committee. Brailsford had endorsed an international popular front in early July and under the impetus of the Spanish Civil War his support for the concept had grown further.[35]

Almost as soon as the war broke out, Brailsford was impressed by how united the Republican forces seemingly were. He argued that the 'tactics of the Popular Front, as well established in Spain as in France, may be proof against internal dissensions on the Left'.[36] On 31 July 1936 he wrote to Cripps explaining how his 'mind had been moving, at first reluctantly, but in the end decisively in favour of a Front Populaire in this country' and stressing that it was the deteriorating 'international situation' – and principally the events in Spain – that had led him to this conclusion. Brailsford did not want to advocate such a course publicly because he knew it would affect his 'relations with the Socialist League'. Nevertheless, by setting out his views so fully, and by making it clear that he recognised that he 'may have to resign from the SL', he possibly also sought to convince Cripps to support a popular front. With the complexities thrown up by the Spanish Civil War, Brailsford held out some hope of persuading the Socialist League since he considered that it would not necessarily 'be bound to oppose it'.[37] Cripps did not reply to Brailsford for nearly three weeks. In the meantime Brailsford continued to voice his support for an international peoples' front.[38] He also gave a tentative public endorsement of a popular front in Britain. While stressing once again that if 'we had in England a Government that would take its stand with France and Russia in an international People's Front, the fascist coalition would be checked', he added suggestively that to 'get such a government, and to get it soon, it is our duty to forget party'.[39] It is unclear how Cripps responded to Brailsford: they spoke on the telephone about the matter on 18 August.[40] Whatever was said, Brailsford now started to draft a memorandum on the popular front for consideration at the National Council.

At the National Council meeting on 20 September Brailsford's and Fenn's memoranda on the popular front were considered in detail and there was a 'general discussion' of the issues involved. Mellor was undoubtedly aware that the Spanish Civil War had sharpened divisions not only within the Socialist League but also the wider Left on these points. Tawney, for instance, was in favour of 'establishing an ad hoc Council, composed of such representatives of all parties as would join, in order to put pressure on the government in connection with the Spanish situation'.[41] For this reason at the Socialist League meeting 'no vote was taken but it was agreed that . . . members of the National Council should proceed in their work on the lines of the League's Conference decisions' supporting the united front. Significantly, however, it 'was also agreed that the Executive Committee and the National Council consider the whole situation after the Labour Party Conference'.[42] In contrast to early July when Mellor had easily secured the Executive Committee's agreement to discipline Delahaye and Davies for their support of a popular front, he now clearly preferred to gloss over the issues.

III

The ILP's stance on the Spanish Civil War was formulated during August. It initially welcomed the NCL's decision to open a fund for the assistance of the victims of fascist violence but, at the same time, announced its intention to 'send money to Spain to be used by our comrades in the way they think best in their situation'. In some ways this was a formal response to the appeal issued by the International Bureau for funds to be sent directly to its own affiliated organisation in Spain – the POUM.[43] Time and again the ILP championed the role of the POUM. Initially noting the apparent unity of the Spanish working-class movement, the *New Leader* contended that 'the Workers' Party more than any other has been preparing for this unity of action'.[44] Later in the month, and fearing the fragmentation of the working class, Brockway argued that it was 'not too much to say that the one hope of maintaining working-class unity in Spain rests with the Workers' Party'.[45] The ILP's support of the POUM was cemented further by actual links established in Spain by John McNair. Following a decision taken by Brockway and Maxton at the ILP Summer School, McNair, who was the Assistant Secretary of the International Bureau, was sent to Barcelona as its representative in mid-August.[46] On his return to Britain in September McNair testified from first-hand experience of the value of the ILP contribution of £100 and medical supplies to the POUM.[47] Unsurprisingly too, the *New Leader* also gave extensive coverage to the plight of Maurin, who had been unable to speak at the ILP Summer school because of the escalation of events in Spain, and who was first reported to be in danger[48] and then presumed dead.[49]

At the same time as glorifying the role of the POUM, the ILP made further demands for united action in Britain, which increased in intensity as it became clear that the Republican government was not receiving international assistance in the same way as the fascists. As early as 31 July Brockway had commented on Italian and German aid being given to Franco.[50] The following week he demanded that the 'ban on the purchase of arms by the Spanish Government from other countries shall be ended'.[51] In a context where the debate over League of Nations sanctions was very familiar, Brockway argued that, in effect, 'sanctions are being applied against the Spanish Government' because '[g]overnments of other countries are refusing to allow armaments to be exported to it'.[52] When the ILP NAC met on 1 and 2 August it agreed to send a letter to the Labour party, the Co-operative Society and the CPGB noting, with respect to Spain, the 'overwhelming demand for united action among the rank and file of all sections of the working class' and suggesting the need 'to avoid working-class conflicts in the face of our common capitalist enemies'. It did, however, stress that underlying differences would mean there was a need for 'liberty of advocacy and action outside the agreed programme'.[53] Under the impetus of the Spanish Civil War, the ILP was therefore returning to its call for working-class unity on a 'federal basis'.[54]

One particular reason at this juncture for the advocacy of such 'liberty' was that the ILP had become the most forceful critic of the Soviet Union's stance towards Spain, building markedly on its earlier criticisms of Soviet foreign policy. Even by the end of July, Brockway had singled out the Soviet Union for attack. Noting that there was 'no indication that its Government has taken advantage of the rule permitting the supply to *de facto* Governments in order to help Spain', he argued pointedly that 'Socialist Governments should ally themselves, not with capitalist governments, but with other socialist governments and with the working-class movement in capitalist countries'.[55] He further argued that while the Comintern had always asked workers of all countries to prioritise the defence of Soviet Russia, the Soviet Union now 'applies an arms sanction to the Spanish workers in their desperate struggle with the fascists'.[56] Brockway's *New Leader* editorials also attacked the CPGB, and particularly Pollitt, for claiming that the Spanish Civil War was about the defence of democracy and 'constitutional government' instead of the class struggle. This, he contended, was 'an expression of the spiritual rot which has set into the whole Communist Movement'.[57] Brockway even remarked that it was frankly hypocritical for Pollitt to ask the National government to help the Spanish government in light of the Soviet Union's desire to uphold neutrality.[58]

Brockway's criticism clearly had wider resonance. In late August the Welsh Divisional Council of the ILP passed a resolution calling specifically on the Soviet Union 'to render every possible assistance and materials necessary for the struggle in Spain'.[59]

Crucially, the ILP's commitment to the workers' cause in Spain meant that it began to argue that the workers must prepare 'for direct action against the National government if the situation so develops that the Government threatens intervention in its imperialist and capitalist interest and against the Spanish workers' revolution'.[60] It read the events in Spain positively for the workers, drawing particular attention to Catalonia which it saw as unlikely 'to return to Liberal capitalist democracy' in a way that would greatly concern capitalist governments.[61]

With the parameters of its policy established, throughout September the ILP attempted to mobilise its rank and file.[62] There was a wave of activity in North London, with Maxton, Brockway and McNair speaking at a meeting in Shoreditch Town Hall on 4 September which raised £40.[63] Jennie Lee and McGovern also spoke alongside Brockway and McNair on 18 September in Battersea Town Hall.[64] In other areas concerted efforts were made to establish 'united working-class action' on behalf of the Spanish workers. In the North East, Gateshead ILP – with its firm tradition of working closely with the local Socialist League branch – was one such example. The Southampton ILP also offered to form a 'municipal united front' with the local Labour party over Spain.[65]

IV

Responses to events in the Soviet Union also complicated the debate over the united front with the Communists. As the first wave of Show Trials took place between 19 and 23 August 1936, views of the Soviet Union's internal regime became central to factional struggle between the Left and the Labour party for the first time. Altogether sixteen prominent Communist Party members were tried in Moscow for counter-revolutionary activities. Grigori Zinoviev and Lev Kamenev, who had been very prominent in the Communist Party in the early and mid 1920s, were the best known of the accused. They had been sentenced to ten and five years' imprisonment respectively in 1935 for the murder of Sergei Kirov, the Soviet leader in Leningrad, in 1934. The charges were now extended to cover their involvement with the Nazi secret police and an unsuccessful conspiracy to assassinate Stalin and several other prominent leaders. It was suggested that Trotsky had been the prime influence behind the conspiracy and, since he was now in exile, he was tried in his absence. The charges were clearly very elaborate, but perhaps the most notable feature of the trial was the seemingly implausible confessions made by the accused in court. The impact of the Show Trials was more significant still, coming so soon after the high hopes stimulated by the announcement of the new Soviet constitution in June 1936 which, promising a major extension of the franchise and a modest improvement in civil liberties, had been greeted with great excitement on the Left. For instance, even though the Soviet Union was to remain a one-party state, Brailsford heralded it as firm evidence that the dictatorship was transforming itself into a genuine parliamentary regime.[66] And the *New Leader* argued emphatically that the new constitution marked 'the passing from the stage of proletarian dictatorship to proletarian democracy'.[67]

However, after learning the outcome of the trial in late August 1936, the ILP began to develop its existing criticism of the Soviet Union – which had been fuelled by its involvement in the League of Nations and its failure to act in Spain – into a specifically anti-Stalinist critique. The ILP was quick to stress that it was unable 'to accept as authentic much of the evidence'.[68] Instead the *New Leader* considered that the 'most likely' explanation of the confessions was 'that physical and mental exhaustion, plus the hope of a possible reprieve . . . influenced the minds of the defendants'.[69] Yet, crucially, the ILP position did not rest on the authenticity of the evidence but on a broader interpretation of the Soviet Union's domestic political system. Brockway speculated that there must have been 'considerable cause for the extensive opposition which has clearly arisen', arguing that it would be 'impossible to isolate a revolt among leaders of such quality from a wider opinion among large masses'.[70] From this perspective, it was unsurprising that the ILP endorsed the statement issued in early September by the International Bureau calling for an inquiry by a commission representative of the international working-class movement as a whole.[71]

In contrast to the ILP, the Socialist League's initial public reaction to the trials was relatively restrained and hesitant. Internally, however, the trials threw the Socialist League into a state of disarray. On 10 September 1936 the Socialist League Executive Committee considered them for the first time and agreed that the matter was so important that it should be discussed at the forthcoming National Council meeting for which Groves was asked to draft a resolution.[72] Groves's resolution, which was passed at the National Council on 20 September by six votes to one, took a similar line to the ILP in supporting the request made by the International Bureau for an independent inquiry. The resolution further urged the government of Norway, where Trotsky was in exile, to facilitate the inquiry and, more critically, asked the Soviet Government 'to co-operate by allowing access to such documents and persons as may be found necessary'.[73]

Groves can fairly be called a Trotskyist. He had been a member of the CPGB in the 1920s but had become increasingly frustrated with its leadership – Harry Pollitt and Rajani Palme Dutt – which he considered was more committed to following instructions from the Comintern than to promoting revolution in Britain. Along with Harry Wicks and Stuart Purkis, Groves formed the Balham Group in 1930 in an attempt – not least through the publication of Trotsky's writings – to promote a line which was more independent of Moscow within the CPGB. This strategy, however, was not successful, and the CPGB leadership expelled the Balham Group in August 1932, dismissing it – with some justification – as Trotskyist.[74] After this point Groves became increasingly involved with the Balham Labour party which apparently 'elected him as delegate to the Labour Party Conference in 1935 where he was refused admittance'.[75] Against this background, therefore, Groves's stance towards the trials is not that surprising. What is more important is that his arguments found favour within the wider Socialist League National Council, which was most certainly not Trotskyist. Indeed, it seems that the Socialist League's demand for an investigation into the Show Trials only hinted at the real views of some its members. In early October 1936 Pollitt noted with disgust how the Socialist League 'at their last Executive meeting' devoted so much of their time to scurrilous attacks on the Soviet Union'.[76]

Brailsford was the most openly critical. He powerfully argued that the purge 'recalls Hitler's slaughter of his rivals' and that 'there was no scrap of evidence against them [those executed] save confessions so abject that only terror could have extorted them'. 'Civilised justice does not rely on confessions', Brailsford stressed, arguing that the 'whole procedure is a relic of the Middle Ages, worthy rather of the Inquisition than of a Socialist Tribunal'. He felt qualified to offer an opinion because he actually 'knew several of the victims and the suspects'. Above all he was disappointed that 'we must read the news from Moscow with shame'.[77] Significantly, Brailsford was so outspoken in his criticism that he soon found himself embroiled in a public row with the former Socialist Leaguer Pritt who – after attending the trial in Moscow – now became one of its most significant apologists, writing a book entitled *The Zinoviev trial* in late 1936.[78] Brailsford openly criticised Pritt for failing in the midst of his praise of the Soviet criminal justice system to recognise that 'from the earliest days of the Revolution the Bolsheviks always drew a sharp distinction between ordinary criminal cases and political affairs' in which 'they frankly avowed that they were waging the class war'.[79]

It seems likely that many of the Socialist Leaguers actually took a very similar line to that of Martin. The *New Statesman* had been optimistic in June 1936 that democracy was 'coming on apace in the USSR' in light of the new constitution.[80] By late August it was puzzled as to why the Soviet secret police had been allowed to hold the trial at this point and speculated that it was in order 'to show their importance and activity before the introduction of the new constitution which may curb their power'.[81] The journal was less sure about the confessions – initially describing them as 'wholly unconvincing' and 'worthless in the circumstances'[82] but then suggesting that they 'may have contained the substantial truth'. The *New Statesman* developed the possibility of this insight in more depth than the ILP and importantly in a way that did not inhibit its developing anti-Stalinism. It stressed that 'intrigues and rivalries . . . are inseparable from dictatorship' and was 'compelled to wonder whether there may not be more serious discontent in the Soviet Union than was generally believed'.[83]

Perhaps most significantly of all though, Laski became privately critical of the Stalinist regime. Along with the committed fellow travellers Strachey and Gollancz who continued unquestioningly to support Stalin, Laski had been one of the selectors for the pro-Communist, and pro-Soviet, Left Book Club since its formation in May 1936.[84] He had welcomed news of the new Soviet constitution in June 1936, saying that it allowed for 'gains in individual freedom' that were 'politically inconceivable in Germany or Italy'.[85] Laski was recognised by the CPGB as a very important sympathiser and so they were naturally worried about his response to the Show Trials in August 1936. Even before the sentences were passed, Laski wrote to Pollitt that the 'trial is a travesty of justice from any angle, if it is accompanied by the kind of mucous ballyhoo the Soviet press and the wireless has organised against these men'.[86] For Laski the proceedings of the trial must have been particularly disappointing. In 1935 he had written a book praising the Soviet justice system.[87] With his deep sympathy for the Soviet Union and significantly, considering its cause as his own, he now wrote: 'We ought not to imitate German methods just at the time when we want the average man to understand that Soviet Communism is the strength of all that means hope for civilisation'.[88]

At this stage, however, the most hostile public responses to the Show Trials came from the moderate section of the Labour party.[89] Citrine was one of the first British Labour figures publicly to criticise the purges. Speaking on 27 August, he was adamant that 'the confessions were extracted by means that have not yet been properly disclosed, from men who were kept in prison for months'. Citrine dismissed the idea that the Soviet Union was a dictatorship of the proletariat, arguing instead that 'Russia, as other dictatorships, was governed by a handful of men and that the great mass of the people had but little or no voice in the governing of the country'.[90] As soon as the trials were over, the *Daily Herald* argued frankly that they 'offend every decent impulse of democratic labour movements'. It remained uncertain 'whether the evidence is bogus or genuine', but was pessimistic either way. If the evidence had been faked and the confessions extorted, it considered that 'the Soviet Government has committed an act of terrorism worthy of ranking with the supreme achievements of fascism'. On the other hand, if the evidence was genuine then 'this was the price and cost of dictatorship, whether Communist or fascist. It drives opponents of government policy to terrorism, because it allows them no opportunity of securing any but a violent change of government'.[91]

Significantly, while the Labour party did not make any official pronouncement on the trials, the *Daily Herald* readily linked developing views about the repressive internal regime in the Soviet Union to the on-going debate about Communist affiliation. Despite the considerable overlap between its interpretation of the trials and that of much of the Left, it nonetheless asked if this was 'the sort of outlook that British Labour could ever want brought into its own ranks by the acceptance of Communist affiliation'.[92] Provocatively, the paper argued that if the CPGB was accepted into the Labour party, its members might one day turn on their new colleagues on the orders of Stalin as readily as they now condemned the old Bolsheviks who had been put on trial in Moscow.[93]

V

Meanwhile, ahead of the Labour party conference, intra-party tension mounted between the Socialist League and the NCL. Trade union support for non-intervention had been secured at the TUC meeting on 10 September 1936. Citrine had argued that non-intervention would be in the best interests of the Spanish government and that it would prevent the war from developing into an international conflict.[94] Bevin had been a little more cautious – moving a resolution endorsing non-intervention but stressing that it must not be disadvantageous to the Spanish government. The Congress then voted by 3,029,000 votes to 51,000 to endorse non-intervention.[95] In this context, Cripps outlined the major points at stake between the Socialist League and the NCL. Reiterating established views about the international class struggle and the imperative of opposing the National government, Cripps argued that it was just as important to attack the NCL, which was entering into 'partnership with the National government' by endorsing non-intervention and by conditionally supporting rearmament. Indeed, Cripps contended that the NCL's stance made it all the more important to form a united front of 'every force that can represent any body of workers . . . in a resolute opposition to the National government'.[96]

Groves now developed the Socialist League's arguments about how co-operation with National government rearmament would lead to an attack on trade union and workers' conditions. He argued that the TUC meeting had 'kept a significant silence about the Government's increased armament plans' because 'the General Council is preparing to support the government's Arms Plans . . . without rousing too great a protest from the rank and file'. Groves then outlined what he saw as the dangers if the TUC was 'getting ready to co-operate openly in the creation of a British war-machine equal to or greater than that of Hitler-Germany'. He argued that the 'pre-requisite for the bringing into being of the German war-machine was the destruction of the workers' organisations'. He recognised there were crucial differences between Germany where the capitalists had 'absolute power' and Britain where 'the workers' movement still exists' and 'the capitalists govern through a democratic state'. This meant that in Britain, faced 'with the need to create, in a short time, a powerful war machine and a pre-war mobilisation of industry and man power, the ruling class seeks to secure a "National Unity" equivalent to the totalitarian regime of Hitler by winning over the leaders of Labour . . . by various means; by "honours"; by giving them government posts; by flattery; by bluff and thinly-veiled threats'. In a context where Citrine had just been knighted, these arguments had particular bite. Groves, however, took his argument further, by contending that inevitably 'the very carrying through of the armaments programme brings in its wake such an attack upon working class conditions that it becomes imperative for the Government to hamper, restrict, intimidate and finally to seek to crush the workers' organisations'.[97]

The TUC meeting's endorsement of non-intervention moved Bevan to assume an important role in the Socialist League's attack on the NCL. In his biography of Bevan, Foot pointed out that he 'saw the new event in its full setting' and that the 'note struck in his speeches was deeper and stronger than he had sounded before in dealing with the foreign situation'.[98] In September 1936, as the Republican hold on the Spanish capital, Madrid, came under increasing threat from Franco's advancing forces, Bevan argued that its fall would be a serious setback for the Labour movement worldwide. Not only would it 'give plausibility to the rebels' claim to be the *de facto* government of Spain', but the 'spiritual consequences for the workers everywhere would be hardly less serious'. Bevan argued that the 'forces of socialism would be devitalised' because at a time when 'we are beginning to throw off the feeling of defeatism caused by the collapse of the German working-class movement this new set-back might plunge us into despair'. In this critical situation, and with the fascist states arming Franco, Bevan savagely dismissed the TUC's attitude as 'a piece of black treachery of the Spanish workers'. Instead Bevan urged the Labour movement 'to use every endeavour to force the British government to allow the Spanish government to purchase arms in this country'. Bevan argued that such action was absolutely crucial because what 'British Labour does might well turn the balance in favour of those French forces which are working for the Spanish government'.[99]

During September the Socialist League also organised a number of meetings to build support for overturning non-intervention at the party conference. Mellor, Groves and Horrabin drafted a resolution for discussion at these meetings, which contained the same principal points as the Socialist League's earlier official statement in August: the need for the Labour party to press for the rejection of non-intervention and for the recall of Parliament to discuss this latest development in the international class war.[100] In an attempt to boost further its campaign the Socialist League Executive Committee decided to ask Morrison to speak at its Essex Hall conference, which was planned for 25 September and was to form the centrepiece of the Socialist League campaign. This would have had the effect of showing that a very prominent figure on the NEC, and the leader of the London County Council (LCC), was very publicly at odds with the NCL line.[101] Morrison was contacted and given a copy of the resolution.[102] However, he replied that he might possibly 'be out of London on this date, but in any case, having regard to the fact that I am a member of the National Council of Labour I think it would be rather difficult for me to be a speaker at your meeting'.[103] Despite Morrison's unwillingness to attend, the conference at the Essex Hall was a success. It was chaired by Mellor and addressed by Bevan as well as Isobel Browne of the Spanish Medical unit and R. C. C. Stewart, a representative of the Catalonian Defence Department, and it raised £35. Within the capital, smaller meetings were also held in Islington, Stepney, Bethnal Green, Balham, Battersea, Hackney, Hendon and St. Pancras. And in the provinces the Socialist League held demonstrations in Pontymister in South Wales, Newcastle and Brighton.[104]

The Socialist League increasingly took its own initiative in distributing the money it raised for the Spanish workers rather than relying on the NCL. By the middle of August 1936 the Socialist League was becoming concerned about the way in which the money it forwarded through the NCL for the Spanish workers was being distributed.[105] On 24 August the Executive Committee considered the possibility of sending the money it had raised 'direct to the Socialist Party in Spain'.[106] On 10 September the Executive Committee, on the recommendation of the former suffragette Sylvia Pankhurst, agreed to send £5 through an intermediary – Francesco Nitto – for the purpose of sending technical personal aid to Spanish workers.[107] By 1 October the Socialist League was distributing its money in more complicated ways. It sent £50 to the Medical unit for supplies and £10 to the Catalonian Defence Department 'for repayment in two months, the

League to take responsibility for the amount should it not be forthcoming within that time'. Significantly, the Executive Committee also agreed 'to take into consideration when allocating further sums the possibility of sending them direct through the POUM'. [108] Betts exemplified the Socialist League's growing allegiance with the POUM, which was to be of great significance over the next year. In an analysis of Spanish politics in *The Socialist*, she had stressed that of all the factions on the Republican side it was the POUM which appeared to be 'going forward to great things'.[109]

Nevertheless, the Socialist League remained uncertain whether it should engage in joint activities with the CPGB and the ILP.[110] After its conference in June, the Socialist League had maintained a cautious distance from the CPGB. The Executive Committee had stated that it did 'not approve of making requests of the Communist Party for information concerning its campaigns'.[111] However, the Spanish Civil War prompted the Socialist League to rethink its position. The Socialist League now came very close to arranging a meeting at which its representatives would speak on the same platform as those from the CPGB and the ILP. At a special meeting on 24 August the Executive Committee agreed to write to the NCL asking it 'to organise a nation-wide demonstration and Albert Hall Meeting in support of the Spanish workers and against the neutrality policy of the National Government during the weekend following the TUC conference'. Significantly, the Executive Committee decided that should 'the National Council of Labour refuse to organise such a meeting . . . the League in co-operation with the recognised working-class bodies, i.e. Labour party, Communist Party, ILP, Co-operatives, etc. should call the meeting'. It was agreed that Mellor would take the chair and that Cripps and Bevan for the Socialist League, Pollitt for the CPGB, Maxton or Brockway for the ILP, and Lansbury for the Labour party would be invited 'on the understanding that they speak in support of the resolution'. The Socialist League considered the matter so pressing that it told the NCL it wanted an answer 'within three days'.[112] Nevertheless, despite the NCL's subsequent endorsement of non-intervention, the Socialist League did not go through with its threat. Perhaps the Socialist League leaders realised how this action might jeopardise its own position within the Labour party. The Socialist League exhibited the same cautious attitude towards the ILP when it invited the Socialist League to send delegates to an international anti-war conference in Brussels on 19 September 1936. The Executive Committee now decided that 'no action be taken' and to inform Brockway accordingly.[113] Brockway persisted in his attempt to draw the Socialist League into joint activity and made a personal appeal to Cripps, drawing attention to their shared opposition to rearmament and desire to bring about 'common action

between all socialists . . . against fascism'.[114] Cripps replied that the Socialist
League's view, affirmed by the National Council on 20 September, was that
'as regards the whole question of unity . . . it is important until after the Conference at Edinburgh that we should not commit ourselves in any way'.[115]

VI

When the Labour party conference met on 5 October 1936 at the Usher Hall
in Edinburgh, the issues at stake between the NEC and the TUC General
Council and the Socialist League came to a head in unpredictable and
dramatic ways. The Spanish Civil War was discussed on the first day of the
party conference with Greenwood introducing the resolution supporting
non-intervention but describing it as 'a very, very bad second best' in a
situation that could easily develop into a wider, European war.[116] Trevelyan
spoke against the resolution arguing that the consequences of non-
intervention would be the creation of another fascist state in Europe, which
would increase the danger of war.[117] However, he was strongly rebuked by
Bevin.[118] Bevan spoke against the resolution stressing that the non-intervention agreement had already been broken because Franco was receiving
arms from Italy and Germany.[119] He, in turn, was also refuted by Attlee who
played down Bevan's assertions and emphasised the need to investigate the
alleged breaches of the agreement.[120] The resolution was then passed
overwhelmingly by 1,836,000 to 519,000.

The conference then debated a deliberately ambiguous resolution on
foreign policy which attempted to reconcile the views of those in the
movement, such as Dalton, Bevin and Citrine, who were willing to sanction
National government rearmament with the views of those who were not.
Accordingly, the resolution affirmed the Labour party's commitment to
armed collective security through the League of Nations but criticised a
'purely competitive armament policy' and stressed that it reserved 'full
liberty to criticise the rearmament programme of the present government'.[121] The resolution was passed by 1,738,000 to 657,000 but inevitably
Labour's intra-party debate over rearmament, in which the Socialist League
played a full part, continued.

The conference also debated the question of a united front. Jack Little,
the delegate from the AEU, moved the resolution calling for united
working-class action in view of the danger of fascism.[122] Mellor spoke very
strongly in favour of the resolution, making it clear that this involved ILP
and CPGB affiliation. He argued this would improve the Labour party's
electoral prospects because although the membership of both bodies was
small, they represented 'big trends of thought . . . big movements of opinion

and action'.[123] However, after Dalton argued against the motion on behalf of the Executive, it was rejected by 1,805,000 to 435,000.[124]

Now the events at the party conference became somewhat more dramatic as the fraternal delegates from Spain arrived at the Usher Hall. It seems that Cripps may have been party to carefully worked out plans to use these delegates to help overturn the NCL's support for non-intervention. On 18 September 1936 Zilliacus had contacted Cripps with whom he fairly regularly corresponded. Zilliacus revealed that, at his suggestion, the foreign minister in the Spanish Republican government, Alvarez del Vayo, had arranged to send a workers' delegation to Britain. Zilliacus now asked Pablo de Azcarate, the new Spanish Ambassador in London, to contact Cripps and to arrange a meeting between Cripps and the workers' delegation from Spain so that Cripps could also put them in touch with the Miners' Federation which was known to be very strongly against non-intervention. Zilliacus also made the suggestion that 'they should not only see as many people as possible in London, but should be in Edinburgh at the time of the Labour conference and ask for seats in the audience'. He hoped that then either Cripps or the miners would 'demand in the conference that the leader of the delegation be invited to address the conference as a fraternal delegate' so that the conference 'might go on to reversing the "non-intervention" policy'.[125] It is not clear how far these plans developed but it is clear that Cripps knew the Spanish delegates might try to win sympathy from the conference.

In the event, the fraternal delegates Jimenev de Asua and Isabel de Palencia – who had once lived in Scotland and spoke English with a Scottish accent – were allowed to address the conference, and made emotional speeches pleading for aid for the Spanish socialists and claiming that Germany and Italy were continuing to ignore the Non-intervention Agreement.[126] Significantly, the majority of the delegates now appeared to turn against non-intervention.[127] Attlee and Greenwood were sent to London to consult Neville Chamberlain, who was standing in for Baldwin. On their return the following day Attlee introduced a new resolution which called upon the Labour leaders to conduct an 'investigation of the alleged breaches of the Spanish Non-intervention Agreement . . . with the utmost speed'.[128] Cripps now moved an extremely important amendment. He asked if an additional sentence could be added to the resolution stressing that the conference 'declares its conviction that the fascist powers have broken their pledges of non-intervention'. Such was the mood of the conference that Attlee said he could not 'see any objections at all to accepting that statement'.[129] Cripps had modified the resolution showing that, for once, the Socialist League had found an effective policy with which to attack the NCL.

5

THE FORGING OF A UNITED FRONT

October 1936 to January 1937

In the immediate aftermath of the Labour party conference in October 1936, the Socialist League took the momentous decision to associate more closely with the Communist party and the ILP. In the first place the Socialist League began to co-operate with the two parties in support both of the hunger marchers and the anti-fascist campaign in the East End of London. At the same time leading members of the Socialist League also entered into negotiations with the ILP and the CPGB for the initiation of a Unity Campaign. These discussions, however, were greatly complicated by the CPGB's longer-term commitment to a popular front as well as by the hostility of the ILP to Soviet foreign policy. In the event, the creation of the Unity Campaign was largely facilitated by the Soviet Union's decision to intervene in Spain, which temporarily convinced the ILP to put its reservations to one side. Nevertheless, serious differences of opinion remained only partially submerged beneath the surface. To the CPGB's alarm, the ILP tentatively linked its anti-Stalinist critique to the Soviet Union's actions in Spain. Furthermore, within the Socialist League itself Groves became a powerful opponent of the Unity Campaign.

I

The hunger marches are one of the most evocative images of Britain in the 1930s. The Communist-dominated NUWM had led hunger marches – in which groups of unemployed men from the provinces walked to London – in the 1920s. However, it was only as unemployment rose in the 1930s that a large number of marches were organised. The most famous of these was the Jarrow Hunger March in 1936. By this point unemployment, as a whole, was falling but it remained extremely high in certain areas – particularly those, like the North East, in which the old 'heavy' industries were concentrated. The Jarrow March, which was publicised by the town's Labour MP Ellen Wilkinson, sought above all to draw attention to this lingering regional high unemployment. Two hundred men then left Jarrow on 4 October 1936, planning to arrive in London on 7 November where, in order to provide a welcome and publicity, a Provisional London Reception Committee had been established.[1] The ILP and the CPGB were actively involved with this committee but the NEC kept a deliberate distance.[2]

Many in the Socialist League had previously been uncertain whether to defy the NEC and become actively involved in united demonstrations with the Communists against unemployment, the majority of which were organised by Wal Hannington's NUWM. For Bevan, in particular, with his roots and constituency in South Wales where unemployment was high and the Communist presence strong, this seems to have been an acute dilemma. Foot's biography explains that, on occasions in 1933 and 1934, Bevan had shared platforms with Communists in South Wales and had found himself personally at odds with the NEC.[3] Nevertheless – unlike the ILP which had been involved with the NUWM since 1932 and had co-operated with the Communists in supporting the earlier hunger marches of 1932 and 1934[4] – the Socialist League as a whole refrained from joint activities with the CPGB over unemployment until autumn 1936. Then on 1 October its Executive Committee seriously considered sending representatives to the Provisional London Reception Committee for the Jarrow hunger marchers.[5] Betts attended an initial meeting of the reception committee just as an observer but when the Executive Committee met again on 15 October it made a firm commitment to support the hunger marchers, and to associate with the CPGB and the ILP. It now appointed Mellor and Groves as well as Betts as its permanent representatives.[6] The Socialist League's unanimous decision 'actively [to] associate itself with the Hunger Marchers' Reception Committee' was a new departure as the Security Service noted, adding that 'Cripps is quite prepared to have his name added to the Committee's letter headings'.[7] The Socialist League had considered joint action with the Communists and the ILP over Spain in August 1936, but had eventually decided against the idea.

The Socialist League Executive Committee now became deeply involved with the organisation of the reception for the marchers in London.[8] It worked closely with the London Trades Council to see that local trades councils organised representative reception and solidarity committees in various parts of London. The Socialist League also encouraged its branches elsewhere in the country to do their utmost to ensure that their local trades council 'responds to the Committee's appeal to bring *all* working-class organisations into action without delay . . . to help to secure accommodation for the marchers . . . and to nominate Socialist League speakers for the demonstrations'.[9] On 5 November the Socialist League Executive Committee agreed that Borrett should represent the Socialist League at an ILP meeting in support of the hunger marchers in Hackney on 8 November.[10] When the National Council met on 7 November it 'approved the League's association with the Hunger Marchers' Reception Committee' and stressed emphatically that it 'did not propose to prevent members from speaking on platforms with members of the Communist party or the ILP'.[11] This was, however, merely formal approval for a policy which had already been accepted by the Socialist League rank and file: when the marchers arrived in London later on 7 November, Socialist League branches were involved with local reception committees in Wood Green, Fulham, Islington, Poplar, Willesden and Hammersmith.[12] The Executive Committee then took a particular interest in helping to organise the large Hyde Park demonstration on 8 November.[13] Bevan spoke at the demonstration itself. He argued that the hunger marchers had 'for the first time in the history of the Labour movement achieved a united platform'. He stated defiantly that 'Communists, ILPers, socialists, members of the Labour party and the co-operators . . . have joined hands together and we are not going to unclasp them'.[14] His article in November's *Socialist* criticised the NEC's initial refusal to support the Hunger march and argued that its subsequent success had shown 'that given the right lead there is a real desire for struggle amongst the rank and file of all working-class parties'. Emphasising the Socialist League's close association with the CPGB and the ILP, he contended that on 'this occasion it is significant that the lead was given by a combination of forces to which we may have to look more and more in the future'.[15] The Socialist League initiatives continued over the next couple of weeks. On 13 November Mitchison hosted a reception at his home for 60 of the Hunger Marchers, which was attended by many of the National Council as well as representatives from Socialist League branches in South Wales, Scotland, Northumberland, Durham and the Midlands.[16] Furthermore, Mellor and Groves spoke in support of the Hunger Marchers at a large mass meeting in Trafalgar Square on 15 November.[17]

II

The Socialist League also took an active role in anti-fascist activities against Oswald Mosley's British Union of Fascists (BUF) in the East End of London. Just as in the case of the Jarrow Hunger March this meant working closely alongside the ILP and the CPGB and in defiance of the NEC. Throughout 1936 the BUF had been attempting to build up working-class support in areas of high unemployment such as South Wales and Lancashire. It had mobilised most support, however, in London's East End after a series of meetings at which a very crude message of anti-Semitism had been expounded. In response, many local people – led by Communists and Socialists – confronted the BUF in ways that often led to violence. These clashes included the famous 'Battle of Cable Street' on 4 October 1936 when nearly 100,000 people gathered in Stepney in order to prevent a Blackshirt (i.e. fascist) procession from passing along its intended route.[18] Groves reported to the Socialist League Executive Committee on the fascist disturbances in the East End for the first time on 24 September 1936. At once the Executive Committee agreed that the London Area Committee should organise meetings in the East End as well as an aggregate meeting of all East End London members.[19] This was in clear defiance of the official Labour party line which was to discourage such rank and file protests while criticising the BUF itself. The aggregate meeting took place on 14 October and made plans for a series of mass meetings in different parts of East London over the next three weeks. The following day the Socialist League Executive Committee 'unanimously approved' the London Area Committee's plans, which were outlined by Groves, for the East-End campaign against fascism. The Executive Committee also gave the London Area Committee authority to raise funds for the campaign; branches or area committees were only usually allowed to collect funds for Head Office.[20]

The Socialist League's London Area Secretary, Andrew Campbell, took a major role in the anti-fascist campaign. He had helped to formulate the London Area Committee's policy which attributed the appeal of fascism in the East End to the absence of effective socialist propaganda and, crucially, held that 'the only way to combat the fascist menace in the East End is for the entire movement to unite in an endeavour to make up lost ground'.[21] The London Area Committee's campaign involved a public meeting at Bromley Public Hall on 25 October 1936, at which Mellor, Horrabin, Frank Winocaur and Campbell spoke, as well as one in the Devonshire Hall in Hackney on 3 November. Both these meetings seem to have been successful. The centrepiece of the London Area Committee's campaign was a conference at Whitechapel Art Gallery on 31 October. There were 125 delegates present – including representatives from the CPGB, the ILP, the League of Youth and various Jewish organisations. Groves chaired the meeting and Mellor gave the opening speech introducing the resolution which was seconded by Lewey of the local Trades Council. After fully discussing the issue, the delegates then 'unanimously approved' the conference resolution, which declared that the riots and disorders were 'due to the deliberate attempts of fascist organisations to divide the working people of this district by the systematic spreading of racial and religious antagonisms'. The resolution also called on the government to ban 'all fascist propaganda and demonstrations as essentially provocative in character and purpose' and argued that 'the hesitations and equivocations of the government on this matter can only be ascribed to a sympathy with the political aims of the Blackshirts, or a desire to utilise the disorders to ban socialist, communist and trade union assemblies'. In contrast to the approach of the NEC, the resolution recognised the 'decisive power of the organised workers of East London' and called for a 'socialist propaganda campaign throughout the East End' and a mass trade union recruiting drive. A committee of 25 was then elected to carry on this work.[22]

The Socialist League also published a pamphlet called *East End Crisis*, which was written by Groves and widely distributed in East London.[23] This adapted the Socialist League's anti-capitalist philosophy to attack anti-Semitism by stressing that the workers should not attribute their problems to Jews – even Jewish employers – but to the capitalist system itself.[24] This mirrored the position adopted by the *New Leader* that: 'We are not pro-Jew or anti-Jew. We are pro-worker and anti-capitalist . . . We boldly claim for Jewish workers the same rights as for all workers.'[25] Moreover, Mellor gave the London Area Committee's anti-fascist stance high-level backing and embraced the co-operation with the ILP and the CPGB. He agreed that 'Mosley's aggression in the East End can only be effectively withstood by the people of the East End themselves'. He was supportive of the London Area Committee's conference, which was 'so widely representative of *all* working class organisations in the East End'. Firmly pitting the stance of the Socialist League with that of the ILP and the CPGB and against the NEC, he argued that 'Mosley's attempt to import Nazi racial principles into London cannot be defeated by the "stay away" policy of the *Daily Herald*' but 'can only be countered by an appeal to class loyalty'.[26]

The Socialist League took other steps to associate itself with anti-fascism and against anti-Semitism. On 22 October the Executive Committee accepted the Jewish Socialist Organisation as a branch of the Socialist League which was to be known as 'The London Jewish Branch of the Socialist League'. The branch had to accept the rules of the Socialist League but significantly it was also 'agreed that the Executive Committee and National Council would consult the new Jewish branch on specific Jewish issues'.[27] Moreover, the Executive Committee later agreed to send one of the League's most high-profile members – Brailsford – as a representative to the first meeting of the newly-constituted London Jewish Branch of the League.[28]

III

The Socialist League's co-operation with the ILP and the CPGB in supporting both the Jarrow Hunger March and the anti-fascist campaign in the East End of London provided the backdrop for a more significant joint undertaking. In the weeks immediately following the Labour party conference in October 1936 Cripps, Mellor and Bevan took the initiative and met Brockway and Maxton as well as Pollitt and Dutt on a number of occasions at Cripps's chambers in the Middle Temple to discuss the possibility of a Unity Campaign.[29] The discussions were kept secret from the rest of the Socialist League – even from the Executive Committee and the National Council. This was later to prove a contentious strategy but it was consistent with the way in which the Socialist League leadership had previously conducted informal negotiations with the ILP and the CPGB.

The basic proposal was for a united front through the Labour party against fascism and against the National government. The Socialist League, the ILP and the CPGB shared an opposition to National government rearmament. Indeed, Pollitt had a particular desire 'to strengthen this division that is existing within the Labour party on the rearmament policy', and considered that 'if we utilise Cripps for this purpose, then it is of the utmost importance that we should give every consideration to him and see what we can do in that direction'.[30] Moreover, the three parties shared a desire to support the Republican side in Spain by providing arms. Of course, the CPGB stance was problematic here because the Soviet Union was not yet assisting the Republicans. Nevertheless, important informal links existed between the CPGB and members of the Socialist League. At the Central Committee on 10 October Pollitt reported that Brailsford had recently been to see him to discuss the possibility of sending volunteers and supplies to Spain. Pollitt noted: 'The importance of this is that six months ago they [the Socialist League] would never have dreamt of coming anywhere near the communist party office.'[31] Finally, the three parties agreed that the core elements of a domestic programme would include abolition of the Means Test and the Unemployment Assistance Board Scales, a National Plan of work for the distressed areas, the 40-hour week, non-contributory pensions at 60 and nationalisation of certain industries including mining, banking and armaments.

The Socialist League's ability to contemplate the Unity Campaign at this juncture was strengthened by the fact that none of its prominent members were any longer pushing for a popular front. Brailsford, who had submitted a memorandum advocating a popular front to the Socialist League National Council in September 1936, was now suddenly and firmly behind a united front, striking a very different note to the summer. He argued that to 'rebuild' the Labour party its members needed to 'realise their unity as a class' and this meant that 'the Socialist League, still inside the Party, should form a close working alliance with the two organisations [the ILP and the CPGB] outside it' which 'have this sense for class highly developed'. Significantly, Brailsford dismissed the idea of a popular front with the Liberals whose leaders were 'no more alive than our own'.[32] Despite his recent criticism of the Show Trials, an on-going commitment to the defence of the Soviet Union – stimulated by the war in Spain but clearly harking back to an earlier pro-Soviet affinity – underpinned his attitude. He argued that both Liberal and Labour leaders have 'played the parasite over Spain; both would repeat this treason when Russia's hour of danger comes'.[33]

At the same time other prominent figures in the Socialist League who had supported a popular front now resigned. The Socialist League's treasurer, Fenn, who had submitted a proposal for a popular front at the same time as Brailsford in September, wrote to Mellor in mid October 1936 expressing his desire to resign as treasurer and from the League altogether. This was reported to the Executive Committee on 29 October, which also heard that George, another National Council member, had telephoned Mellor to explain that he was sending his resignation. The Socialist League's most prominent advocate of a popular front – Murphy – had become secretary of the People's Front Propaganda Committee, which he helped to form along with Delahaye and Davies who had left the Socialist League in July.[34]

Even so, it was clear from the outset that the Socialist League's task of forging an agreement between itself, the ILP and the CPGB would be a difficult one. Altogether the negotiations really were 'one long political struggle'.[35] During the previous year relations between the CPGB and the ILP had seriously deteriorated. Indeed, it did not bode well that at the very first meeting between the three parties, Pollitt asserted that 'under no circumstances would we be identified with Brockway and the ILP unless it changed the whole of its line'.[36] Furthermore, the CPGB was concerned about how its involvement with the ILP and the Socialist League would affect its relations with the Labour party. When the CPGB Central Committee gave approval for discussions to proceed on 10 October 1936, it also expressed concerns that this might antagonise the official leadership of the Labour party to which it remained their central aim to affiliate.[37] The ILP also had serious reservations about the whole Unity Campaign proposal. Most importantly, unlike the CPGB it did not want immediately to affiliate to the Labour party. As a result of these obstacles some of the negotiations took on a very informal nature from an early stage. For instance, in her autobiography Barbara Castle (nee Betts) recalls that she and Mellor entertained Pollitt at her flat in central London.[38]

Other serious differences of opinion between the CPGB, the ILP and the Socialist League came to the fore during the negotiations. The CPGB was willing to subordinate its longer-term preference for a popular front in favour of an immediate united front but there was still considerable opposition to the overall CPGB line. Crucially, this came not just from the ILP but also from the Socialist League. Pollitt noted that while Cripps avoided the issue, it soon 'became clear that Mellor was wholly opposed to the conception of the People's Front'.[39] After further meetings Pollitt was commenting, with exasperation, on 'this complete opposition to any conception of the Peoples Front'.[40] These abstract disagreements over the merits of a popular and united front also related to more tangible differences: the CPGB wanted the freedom to advocate an immediate alliance between the National government, France and the Soviet Union – the kind of international popular front advocated by the Soviet Union – whereas both the ILP and the Socialist League considered it imperative first to establish a socialist government in Britain which would then seek an alliance with any other states controlled by the working class. For the CPGB this difference over foreign policy formed the 'greatest obstacle towards reaching agreement'.[41] Time and again during the negotiations it was a point of dispute.[42] Crucially, of course, it related to the question of whether the Socialist League and the ILP were willing to agree to curb their criticism of the Soviet Union. The ILP had been critical of the Soviet Union's foreign policy since it joined the League of Nations in 1934. Since September 1935 – with the Soviet Union's support of sanctions against Italy – the Socialist League had also accused the Soviet Union of differentiating between the foreign policy that was best for itself and that which was best for the international working class. More recently still, the ILP had been outspoken not just in expounding its anti-Stalinist assessment of the Show Trials but also in its condemnation of the Soviet Union's failure to support the Republican side in Spain. It was not unsurprising therefore when Pollitt told the Politburo in early November that so far as the Socialist League and the ILP were concerned, he was 'perfectly clear that there is not an atom of support for the whole of the foreign policy and peace policy of the Soviet Union and the Communist International'. Indeed, he contended that: 'I never listened to so many studied insults of the Communist Party as I listened to. At the right time, and the right place, I shall let myself go, but I had to hold the chair etc in order to relieve my tension a little.'[43]

IV

Despite the extended negotiations throughout October, it was only at the
end of the month that the Socialist League branches were cryptically
informed that at the National Council meeting planned for 7 and 8
November 'consideration will be given to the future of the working-class
movement and the Socialist League in the light of present events and of the
discussions and decisions which took place at Edinburgh'.[44] Furthermore, it
was only on 5 November that the Executive Committee as a whole first
discussed the negotiations with the CPGB and the ILP and decided, after
receiving a draft by Mellor on the 'principle of united activity', that the
National Council should consider the matter. Interestingly, it was also
agreed that the document should not be circulated before the meeting. The
London Area Committee clearly suspected, however, that negotiations had
been taking place. It now wrote to the Executive Committee asking for a
statement on its position regarding the united front.[45]

At the National Council meeting on 7 and 8 November, Mellor 'reported
that conversations had been taking place between Stafford Cripps, Aneurin
Bevan and himself acting as individuals with leading members of the
Communist party and of the Independent Labour Party, to see whether it was
possible to arrive at agreement as a basis of joint action by the three
organisations for working-class unity'. Mellor then presented the draft
document. There was a strong sense of affront – a number of Council
members 'expressed the view strongly that the members taking part as
individuals should have reported to the Executive Committee their intention
so to do'.[46] There was a long discussion in which 'questions were asked of
the chairman and Stafford Cripps as to the meaning and position *vis-à-vis* the
League and other parties to the document and its clauses'. Even so, the
document was unanimously approved in principle. Groves seems to have
been the most cautious in his approval – asking the Council to add an
addendum (which was narrowly approved) stressing the League's
commitment 'in so far as it is not inconsistent with the policy of the
League'.[47] Retrospectively, Groves expressed the view that the 'discussion
was inevitably steered to the documents and no serious consideration was
given to the merits, wisdom, or consequences to the SL of the proposed
campaign'.[48] Cripps had spoken very strongly in favour of the Unity
Campaign and had been supported most notably by Mellor, Brailsford,
Mitchison, and Horrabin. However, Groves felt that the 'provincial members
were almost all uneasy about the proposed campaign, but were manoeuvred
into a detailed discussion of the unity agreement, and so into an implied
approval of the campaign itself'.[49] Even so, Borrett advanced the only major

reservation: that in light of recent events the Socialist League should not
pledge 'support in all circumstances of methods used by the Soviet Union'.
Significantly, this was seconded by Betts and carried without dissent.
Furthermore, the National Council now agreed that Mellor and Cripps
should act as the negotiators and delegated authority to the Executive
Committee not only to approve the step-by-step negotiations but also 'to
make final decisions' provided that it communicated these to members of
the National Council for approval. The National Council also approved the
policy of keeping the document 'strictly private' and, by implication, of not
informing the Socialist League rank and file.[50]

Cripps and Mellor reported to the Executive Committee on 12 November
1936. There had been further unity negotiations but the differences over
criticism of the Soviet Union and the international popular front remained.[51]
Having thought more about the Unity Campaign in the time since the last
Executive Committee meeting and the National Council, Groves now
expressed his unhappiness with the negotiations. He asked for copies of the
unity document, as amended by the National Council, to be sent to all
Socialist League members. However, the rest of the Executive Committee –
fully aware that the National Council had sanctioned the policy of keeping
the document confidential, and conscious too of the delicate nature of the
negotiations – voted against him.[52]

There was a further round of negotiations on 19 November[53], at which
both the CPGB and the Socialist League agreed on a compromise that would
allow the campaign to proceed.[54] Pollitt now left for Moscow to secure the
Comintern's approval for participation in it.[55] An emergency Socialist League
Executive Committee meeting was called for the next day to sanction the
decision – but this proved so short notice that neither Cripps nor Groves was
able to attend. In any case, Mellor now asked the Executive Committee to
agree that the CPGB could independently demand that the National
government adopt a pact between itself, the Soviet Union and France while
the Socialist League and the ILP retained the right to stress the need for a
socialist government in Britain that should then seek an alliance with 'all
other states in which the working class has political freedom'. Mellor also
persuaded the committee to accept that all three parties should 'agree to
abstain from any general criticism of the policy of the Soviet Union or its
government, and in the event of any party considering it necessary in a
particular case to criticise them, before any such criticism is made, the three
parties will meet to discuss the matter with a view to preventing any break
in unity'. Significantly, even this carefully worded compromise had proved
insufficient for the ILP. Nevertheless, the Socialist League Executive
Committee approved the Unity Campaign and actually agreed 'that in the

event of the ILP's inability to accept the document the campaign should go forward with the CP and the SL, but that every possible effort should be made to obtain the co-operation of the ILP'. It authorised the negotiators to work out details of how the campaign might be co-ordinated nationally and locally and how it would be launched. The willingness to pursue the Unity Campaign without the ILP testifies, of course, to the commitment to the idea of those present – obviously Mellor but also Betts, Borrett, Brailsford, Elvin and Mitchison. They recognised that this was different from the type of united front endorsed by the National Council and so they also agreed that National Council members should be consulted as to whether they were willing to proceed without the ILP.[56]

Groves was very clearly opposed to the idea of continuing the Unity Campaign without the ILP. It seems that as soon as he heard the Executive Committee's decision he personally wrote to all the National Council members indicating his own objections.[57] At the Executive Committee meeting on 26 November 1936 Groves expressed 'regret that a definite vote had not been taken' on the resolution concerning the Socialist League's willingness to pursue the Unity Campaign if the ILP withdrew.[58] He certainly knew he had one influential supporter – Deborah Barker who was the National Council representative for the South West. She was 'against continuing with the campaign unless the ILP will agree to join us' because she thought it left the League liable to be asked why it did not 'merge with the Communists if it is in agreement with them, especially considering the fact that we are the smaller body'. She was, however, reluctant for a National Council meeting because of the expense.[59] In any case, the Socialist League was still desperately trying to secure the ILP's agreement, with Mellor maintaining the pressure on the ILP.[60] In fact, he actually arrived late at the Executive Committee meeting on 26 November having been in negotiation with the ILP.[61]

V

Pollitt had considered it unlikely that the ILP would 'give up its anti-Soviet campaign'[62] but the Socialist League's persistence might well have proved crucial. On 24 November the ILP Executive Committee had appeared immovable.[63] Yet on 3 December Brockway announced its acceptance of a slightly rephrased Unity Agreement. The ILP was still not prepared to apply for re-affiliation to the Labour party, insisting that the Labour party would have to be democratised before it would consider doing so. Importantly, however, the ILP was now 'prepared to subordinate criticism of the policy of the Soviet Union in view of the necessity to mobilise support for Soviet

Russia arising out of its action in relation to Spain and in view of the necessity to maintain the spirit of unity in the Unity Campaign'. The ILP also said it was willing to consult the CPGB and the Socialist League before criticising the Soviet Union.[64]

A desire to support the Republican government in Spain had been a common, and uniting, force for the Socialist League, the CPGB and the ILP in October and November, which the Socialist League no doubt exploited to help the negotiations along.[65] The commitment made at the Labour party conference in early October 1936 to investigate the fascist breaches of non-intervention was only half-heartedly fulfilled and this maintained aid for Spain as a common left-wing cause. On 28 October a Labour movement conference, guided by Citrine and Bevin, supported a resolution calling on the British government to act jointly with the French to take the initiative in an international agreement that would restore the Spanish government's right to the arms it needed for its defence. Significantly, however, the resolution did not demand that the National government should actually supply arms to the Republicans.[66] As Buchanan put it, this 'did not constitute an unequivocal rejection of Non-intervention, but rather evoked the distant prospect of joint intervention by the British and French governments'.[67] Similarly, Attlee and Greenwood made the case for the restoration of the rights of the Spanish government in the House of Commons on 29 October but this was not followed by any consistent campaign in Parliament or by other co-ordinated attacks on the National government's policy.[68] This greatly stirred passions on the Left and prompted local collaboration between the ILP and the Socialist League. In Gateshead, for instance, the ILP and Socialist League formed a joint committee after the Labour town council refused the ILP application for a street collection on behalf of the Spanish workers.[69] Furthermore, this shared perspective on Spain meant that even before the ILP had agreed to enter the Unity Campaign, it joined the Socialist League and the CPGB in signing an open letter, published on 21 November, which criticised the Labour movement for lacking any sense of urgency over Spain and demanded that it 'launch a great campaign for allowing arms to be exported to the Spanish government'.[70] Most importantly of all though, it was the Soviet Union's decision in early October to abandon non-intervention and begin supplying arms to the Republican side that underpinned the ILP's willingness to forgo its ability to criticise the Soviet Union.

When the Unity Campaign negotiations began, the ILP had still been highly critical of the Soviet Union's inaction in Spain. Indeed, Brockway publicly drew comparisons between this and 'tendencies within the Soviet Union itself' – such as the Moscow trial – and argued that these were having

'a disturbing effect on Communist Party members everywhere'.[71] Meanwhile
Lee attributed the scale of the vote against Communist affiliation at the
Labour party conference explicitly to disillusionment over Soviet policy in
Spain.[72] Moreover, on initially hearing the news that the Soviet Union
planned to help the Republican side in Spain, the *New Leader* was decidedly
ambiguous. It welcomed the development but stressed that it was 'three
months late' and that the Soviet Union had already 'betrayed the international working class movement and the international fight against
fascism'.[73] As time passed, however, the *New Leader* became more positive,
contending that in the light of the Soviet Union's changed policy, 'the
movement of the world mobilised behind her'.[74] Brockway even expressed
the hope that the Soviet Union might 'have reverted to the sound socialist
principle of acting with and for the workers and not in alliance with
capitalist governments'.[75] Ominously, Brockway noted his concern that if
'Russian arms do come the Spanish workers will be deeply grateful; but they
do not expect the Russian comrades to make the supply of arms dependent
in any way on an endorsement of Communist policy'.[76] Within a couple of
months, of course, incipient differences in Spain between the Communist
party and the POUM would cause serious difficulties between the CPGB
and the ILP but for now at least the Soviet Union's action in Spain
temporarily united the Left.

VI

Just as the Socialist League courted the ILP, it also tried to mobilise the fast-
growing constituency parties movement behind the Unity Campaign.
Pimlott has provided a superlative account of the development of this
movement, which pushed for the resolution of long-standing grievances.[77]
Since Henderson's reforms of the party structure in 1918 the constituency
parties had wanted greater representation on the National Executive. Of the
23 places on the NEC, 11 were nominated by the affiliated trade unions, five
by local Labour parties, four by women and there was also a treasurer. Yet
all the places were voted for by the whole party conference which was, of
course, dominated by the trade unions and so local parties could only
actually nominate candidates to five of the 23 places. During the early 1920s
there had been unsuccessful demands to give the local parties direct
representation on the NEC. As the 1920s progressed, however, these
demands receded as the rapidly expanding local Labour parties at least began
to feel that they had some influence because the proportion of MPs sponsored
by local Labour parties steadily increased – including, for example, Attlee
from 1926. Nevertheless, one effect of the 1931 electoral debacle was to

destroy the link between the PLP and the constituencies. This meant that, as Pimlott puts it: 'In the 1930s the expanding individual membership felt a new sense of isolation and impotence'.[78] It was against this background, therefore, that from 1932 Ben Greene had started to organise the disparate local parties all demanding common reforms – initially through a number of unsuccessful ventures. However, in 1935 he formed the Home Counties Labour Association (HCLA), which was committed to work for greater and/ or more direct constituency party representation on the NEC, and the momentum of the campaign quickly developed. In March 1936 R. St. John Reade set up the Bristol and District Labour Association to work in a similar way to the HCLA. Then in June 1936 the Socialist League annual conference agreed to sponsor the constituency parties' campaign.[79] At the Labour party conference, in October 1936, the constituency parties' demands were rejected on the recommendation of the NEC. However, this precipitated the formation of the Provisional Committee of Constituency Parties immediately after the party conference of which Cripps became chairman and Greene secretary and included Charles Gainsworthy, St. John Reade and Bevan as prominent members.[80]

A latent antagonism now developed between the Socialist League and the constituency parties, which prevented the Socialist League from mobilising the Constituency Parties Movement behind the Unity Campaign. Greene explicitly argued that with the strengthening of the constituency parties the Socialist League should recognise that 'the day of affiliated socialist societies is past', which meant that the Socialist League 'must adjust itself to the fact that the only place for socialists in this country is inside the local Labour party as active members'.[81] At the same time the Socialist League remained determined to see that the constituency parties endorsed its policies. Cripps and Mellor reported the formation of the new Constituency Parties Committee to the Executive Committee on 15 October 1936. There was some discussion on the relationship between the two bodies and Cripps was asked to draft a resolution for the National Council.[82] The National Council meeting on 7 November approved Cripps's report, which argued that it was 'the duty of the Socialist League to encourage in every way this demand for democracy within the party and to foster the growing revolt of the Constituency Parties against bureaucratic domination in the movement'. It also stressed that support for the constituency parties' campaign should be secondary to 'its settled and approved policy' which had to be kept 'in the forefront of propaganda'. Above all, Cripps was convinced that this 'new movement amongst the constituency parties should be utilised by the Socialist Leaguers to bring the Constituency parties behind the Socialist League policy'.[83] Mellor reiterated this sentiment once the Unity Agreement

had been reached. He argued it was important that the aims of the constituency parties' movement were 'not confined solely to matters of
machinery' but were instead actively concerned with policy differences.[84]
However, Greene was not willing simply to acquiesce in support for the
Unity Campaign as the frank exchange of views when he attended the
Socialist League Executive Committee meeting on 10 December made
clear.[85]

VII

Preparations for the launch of the Unity Campaign now got underway.
When the Socialist League Executive Committee met on 3 December it duly
agreed to the rephrased Unity Agreement, which now stressed that the
parties did 'not abrogate their right of constructive and friendly criticism'.
The Executive Committee also appointed Cripps, Mellor and Mitchison as
its representatives on the Unity Committee, and endorsed Betts's suggestion
to call a special national conference of the League in order to mobilise rank
and file support.[86] The newly formed Unity Campaign Committee then met
for the first time at Cripps's chambers at 3 Elm Court on 9 December 1936.
Brockway and Aplin attended on behalf of the ILP, while Dutt and J. R.
Campbell were the CPGB delegates. Cripps was appointed as chairman and
Mellor as secretary. Most of the committee's business then concerned the
drawing up of a list of those individuals they might approach to sign the
manifesto and a discussion of plans for a nationwide campaign.[87]

Meanwhile, Groves's opposition to the Unity Campaign was growing. It
seems likely that he had been the sole dissentient when the Executive
Committee had accepted the Unity Agreement on 3 December.[88] Now at its
meeting on 10 December 1936 he stressed that while he supported the idea
of a special national Socialist League conference, he was keen that 'the
branches should have the full information concerning the Unity Campaign
before them and be given time to reflect on the document'. It also seems
highly probable that he was one of the two members who opposed the
motion, which was carried by four votes to two, that the conference should
be restricted to branch delegates.[89]

The Socialist League branches were also becoming increasingly curious
about the nature of the special conference. In *The Socialist* Mellor had
attempted to begin mobilising support for the Unity Campaign without
actually revealing the agreements that had been made. He had claimed that
since the Labour party conference the National Council had 'given anxious
and intense consideration to the future of the League and of the working-
class movement in this country'. He argued that joint activities over Spain

and the hunger marches were 'demonstrations of the essential oneness of the Left within the broad movement of the working class'. Working through the Labour party he urged that 'theoretical differences' be put 'into proper perspective' so that 'allies in the working-class fight must be comrades in the working-class army'.[90] These guarded indications of the direction in which the League was moving inevitably did not satisfy many of the branches. The Cleator Moor and Briton Ferry branches wrote to the Executive Committee 'asking for information as to the subject matter of the conference'. The Battersea branch asked 'for fuller information' and protested that visitors were not to be allowed to attend the conference. Most provocatively, the Balham and Tooting branch – of which significantly Groves was a prominent member – informed the Executive Committee that the question of conference procedure had been placed on the agenda of the London aggregate meeting due to be held on 19 December 1936. The Executive Committee was very concerned. It replied frankly that 'it could not agree to the inclusion of the item on the agenda'. The committee also agreed that the secretary 'attend the Aggregate meeting for the purpose of stating that the Executive Committee was not in favour of having the matter discussed'.[91] The Executive Committee's protests were to no avail. Despite even Mellor's presence at the aggregate meeting on 19 December, the discussion still focused on the Unity Campaign and the forthcoming national conference. A resolution was passed which asked 'the National Council Executive Committee to furnish all branches with full details of the Unity negotiations which are said to have been conducted with the Communist party and the ILP and of the suggested procedure at the National Conference to be convened in the New Year'. The resolution stressed 'emphatically . . . that no agreements or decisions should be made with these organisations without first getting the support and consent of the membership as expressed at a fully mandated and informed National Conference'.[92]

On the same day as the London aggregate meeting was held, reports of the Unity Agreement and speculation about the forthcoming Unity Campaign appeared in the *Daily Herald* and the *News Chronicle*.[93] The Socialist League leadership was clearly surprised and unsettled by these reports but was not prompted to give its rank and file members more information. Instead Mellor wrote to the branches merely reiterating the bland press statement that the 'National Council of the Socialist League has had under consideration the question of unity of the working-class movement within the framework of the Labour party and the trade unions' and 'has reached certain decisions which are to be reported to a Special conference of the League'. He explained that 'the National Council of the League has no comment to make on statements in certain newspapers purporting to know more about the policy of the National Council and the activities of the Socialist League than the National Council itself'. Nevertheless, Mellor attempted to quell dissent by saying there was 'not the slightest need for any disturbance within the ranks of the Socialist League'. Moreover, he made the issue one of confidence in the leadership by stressing that 'all loyal members of the League will at this time place confidence in the National Council of the League' and that 'speculative discussion on the reports in the press can serve no useful purpose and will be seriously damaging'.[94]

The press revelations did, however, prompt the Executive Committee to call an emergency meeting on 21 December. The committee now decided to set a firm date for the proposed Socialist League special conference; it was to be held in London on 16 and 17 January. The Executive Committee agreed that members of the National Council and branch delegates would be able to vote and that other members of the League would simply be able to attend as visitors. So far as the procedure of the special conference was concerned, the Executive Committee made some important decisions. It was decided that the Socialist League Head Office would post the unity document to the branches on Wednesday 13 January 1937 and the branches would be asked to call branch meetings on 14 or preferably 15 January. It was also agreed that 'copies of the document shall be numbered and shall not pass out of the hands of branch secretaries save to branch delegates'. On each occasion there was one dissenting member – it again seems very likely that this was Groves. It was agreed unanimously, however, that the purpose of the conference was to reject or ratify the Unity Document.[95]

<h2 style="text-align:center">VIII</h2>

As the Socialist League special national conference drew closer, tension mounted between the Socialist League and the NEC. At the Labour party conference in October 1936 Dalton had been elected as chairman of the NEC for the forthcoming year. He was resolved to working very closely with Bevin who was chairman of the TUC General Council. Even before the Unity Campaign their tolerance of Cripps and others in the Socialist League, who they believed were damaging the party's electoral chances, was already stretched. Dalton made a note after a private meeting with Bevin which captures this sentiment. Bevin had a particular desire to 'face up Cripps to the question "Do you want us to win or not. What are you playing at?"'[96]

Once the plans for the Unity Campaign became public, the NEC and the TUC General Council decided to attack the Socialist League in an unprecedentedly vicious manner in the *Daily Herald*. This was in marked contrast to the policy of ignoring the Socialist League and giving little coverage to its activities which they had adopted for the previous year. On 19 December 1936 when the *Daily Herald* reported the agreement between the three bodies, the editorial attempted to mobilise opinion against the Socialist League by arguing that 'the doctrine and policy of its leaders have for some time been indistinguishable from that of the Communist party'. It contended that 'the SL, like the ILP and CP, believes in the prosecution of the class war, in the certain breakdown of democracy, the workers' revolution and the dictatorship of the proletariat' whereas the 'Labour party believes in appealing to all democrats for informed support, in the practicability of democratic advance towards socialism, in constitutional government'. Finally, the editorial argued that it was 'an act of open defiance and of provocative disloyalty surely without precedent in the Labour party's history'.[97] The *Daily Herald* editorial on 29 December 1936 intensified the attack on the Socialist League. It dismissed the Unity Campaign as 'a rebellion against the elected leaders and the endorsed policy of the Labour party' which they had failed to change 'democratically and constitutionally in the Labour party annual conference'. It forthrightly argued that the 'leaders of the alliance are, therefore, rebels and dissenters, and in the case of the Socialist League they are men who are deliberately breaking the pledge to observe party policy'. The publicity surrounding the launch of *Tribune* (originally known as *The Tribune*) on 1 January 1937 to spearhead the Unity Campaign then simply added further fuel to the intra-party debate. In early January, the *Daily Herald* made much of the Socialist League leadership's disdain for, and high-handed attitude towards, its membership. Publicly revealing the Socialist League's plans for the procedure to be adopted at its Special Conference, it stressed that the branches would have insufficient time to discuss the National Council's proposals before their delegates left for the conference – particularly those from the North. The Socialist League leadership was accused of attempting to 'stampede the conference' because the branch delegates would at the very least have no time to discuss the resolution among themselves.[98]

The CPGB was clearly disturbed by these news reports, and urged Mellor to issue a public statement. Mellor, however, refused to do this, arguing 'let the *Daily Herald* fire its guns; it is Xmas and New Year and no one will take any notice'.[99] Even so, the NEC and the TUC General Council's sharp response did force the Socialist League to consider the possibility of its own expulsion from the Labour party. The Executive Committee commissioned a memorandum by Mitchison to consider the options and on 5 January 1937 discussed the matter at length. The general view on the committee was that 'if the SL was disaffiliated no useful purpose could be served by its separate existence' and it was agreed that the National Council should be informed accordingly.[100] Ominously, just three days later, the NEC decided to issue a statement – obviously aimed at the Socialist League – which appealed for loyalty to the party conference decisions against Communist party affiliation and a united front.[101] The statement, which was issued on 13 January, stressed emphatically that party members should not associate with bodies pursuing united front activities or those 'which are being promoted to weaken the party's organisation and electoral power by association with other political bodies which do not share the party's determination to achieve our democratic socialist objectives'.[102]

IX

At the same time divisions were also developing within the Unity Campaign Committee. When it met on 16 December 1936 it agreed a manifesto along the lines of the Unity Agreement, and decided that Mellor should allocate to each committee member a list of potential supporters to approach personally. However, the divergences of opinion over a united or popular front almost came to a head. The Communist representatives raised the possibility of Strachey 'and (or) Communist party representatives speaking on specific Popular Front platforms'.[103] According to Brockway it was the Socialist League representatives who were most critical, arguing that this would undermine the Unity Campaign. Nevertheless, a full-blown dispute was avoided and the CPGB permitted to address popular front meetings because the ILP also wanted 'liberty to take an independent line outside the agreed scope of the campaign'.[104]

Soon, however, more serious differences between the CPGB and the ILP began to come to the fore. In the very early stages of the campaign their relations had been superficially amicable. On 4 December 1936 Brockway produced a piece for the *New Leader* dissociating himself from the Trotskyists, which genuinely represented his views but, given the timing, was also surely an attempt to placate the CPGB. He wrote that while he shared their opposition to Stalin's doctrine of 'Socialism in one Country', he considered that 'Trotskyists are everywhere a source of mischief in the working-class movement'.[105] Significantly, moreover, at the end of November the bulk of the Trotskyist Marxist Group had finally left the ILP.[106] The ILP conference in April 1936 had decided that groups within the party should be banned, putting the Marxist Group under pressure. Thereafter some of its members had continued to work inside the party but a group led by James had moved steadily towards resignation.[107] The CPGB noted their departure with satisfaction.[108] Nonetheless, friction developed between the ILP and the CPGB as tensions escalated in Spain between the Soviet-funded Communist party and the POUM. After a Unity Campaign Committee meeting in late December Brockway wrote to Mellor complaining that Pollitt had criticised a POUM regiment for deserting a critical position.[109] Furthermore, by early January 1937 Brockway was again tentatively linking his anti-Stalinist analysis of the Soviet Union's domestic regime with events in Spain. He noted with alarm in the *New Leader* that the Comintern had started to accuse the POUM in Spain of providing 'new confirmation of what was disclosed at the Moscow Trial': the POUM leaders were accused of acting as fascist agents and attempting to assassinate prominent Republican leaders.[110] The POUM had been accused of plotting to assassinate Caballero, the social democratic Prime Minister, Arzana, the President of the Republic, and la Pasionaria, the popular female Communist leader and acclaimed orator.[111] Brockway was equally critical at news that the Comintern was demanding the exclusion of the POUM from the Spanish government.[112]

So far as the position of the Unity Campaign was concerned, the ILP was clearly treading a fine line. At one of the Unity Campaign Committee meetings, the CPGB 'had a quarrel' with Brockway 'because of the character of the material in the *New Leader* on the Soviet Union and Spain and because of an article he had written giving away what was going on in this committee'.[113] On 25 December the *New Leader* had published the ILP's two reservations concerning its insistence that the Labour party was democratised before the ILP would apply for affiliation, and its stated disagreement with the Soviet Government's foreign policy.[114] According to Brockway, 'Pollitt and Dutt were furious when they arrived at the next Committee; they regarded the publication of the ILP reservations as a betrayal of the secrecy of the negotiations between the three bodies. I was flabbergasted; the negotiations had been secret, but no suggestion had been made that the conclusions should be secret.'[115] For the time being, however, these differences could be glossed over – particularly because the ILP still felt a seemingly sincere commitment to 'close our ranks' behind the Soviet Union, which was 'faced with grave danger from the capitalist governments' in Spain.[116]

Parts of the Socialist League were also concerned by the CPGB attitude to the POUM. Since October 1936 the Socialist League had been increasingly co-operating with the ILP to support the POUM. The Executive Committee had discussed the possibility of support for POUM at length on 15 and 29 October, and finally decided to send £15 to the ILP to be used for medical supplies for the POUM.[117] Moreover, in late October Cripps and Mellor had spoken on the same platform as Brockway at a

meeting organised by the Catalan Defence Committee of the ILP.[118] Now at
the Socialist League Executive Committee on 5 January 1937, Groves drew
attention to the CPGB attacks on the POUM and asked that the Socialist
League make a public protest. At this stage the rest of the committee was
probably concerned not to disturb the Unity Campaign and so voted against
his proposal.[119] Nevertheless, his points undoubtedly struck a chord; when
Groves brought up the issue again just over a week later, the committee
agreed that Mellor should raise the matter with the Unity Campaign
Committee.[120]

X

By this point Groves had stepped up his efforts against the Unity Campaign
in other ways within the Socialist League. He had taken the unprecedented
step of writing directly to the branches of the Socialist League, timing his
letter so that it would arrive at the same time as the official letter from Head
Office containing the Unity Document. He emphasised the extent to which
the leaders of the League – Cripps and Mellor – had not properly consulted
the National Council or even the Executive Committee about the
negotiations. He claimed the circular that was to be issued to the branches
on 13 January wrongly gave 'the impression to branches that the National
Council is unanimously in support of the document coming before the
conference'. He argued that the National Council had not met since 7
November when it had 'only considered a preliminary draft to which
members of the Council had several objections'. He claimed that even 'the
Executive Committee has not met to discuss the resolution which has been
issued to branches for the conference' and that the 'consequences of the
agreement for united action on the lines of the document were not, and never
have been, discussed by the Council'. Groves went on to argue that the
'Council has never considered the possibility of the dissolution of the League
in the event of Transport House action, although it has now been made
apparent that certain members of the Executive Committee visualise such a
situation'. In an attempt to arouse rank and file feelings of grievance, Groves
argued that the 'conference is to be confronted with an accomplished fact'.
He revealed not only that the Unity Agreement had already 'been signed by
representatives of the League and the other organisations' but that 'public
meetings have been arranged to further the campaign which is now being
planned by a committee on which are League representatives'. Provocatively,
Groves argued that this showed 'contempt for the membership', and 'that
the National Council as a whole would never have agreed to such a
procedure'. Despite having given his consent at the Executive Committee

meeting on 21 December, Groves now argued that the 'straight choice of an "accept" or "reject" document makes it impossible for the conference to come to a decision which will allow forms of united action without completely destroying the League'. He did not want the conference 'to be hustled into decisions without insisting on full opportunity to formulate the kind of policy which will preserve and strengthen the League'.[121]

To an extent Groves's arguments were disingenuous. They were deliberately intended to exploit a feeling of discontent on the part of some of the provincial branches about the way the Socialist League worked.[122] Groves himself knew that the National Council had actually authorised the Executive Committee to approve the unity negotiations. Groves also knew that the Executive Committee effectively ran the Socialist League and that it was largely under the influence of Cripps and Mellor. He had been secretary of the London Area Committee in 1935 and on the National Council and Executive Committee since June 1936. It seems that his most important objection had more to do with his unwillingness to cease criticism of the Soviet Union but perhaps he considered that arousing rank and file objections to the autocratic Executive Committee would be more effective. In his own retrospective account Groves argued that during the Unity Campaign negotiations there were not only differences between the ILP and the CPGB but 'fundamental differences too, between the SL and CP' and that 'as arbitrator, Cripps jettisoned the policy and purposes of the SL'. He argued that 'the ambiguities, privately-circulated codicils and "addenda of explication" attached to the Unity agreement, mirrored in miniature the false-seeming and double dealing infecting the Socialist Left everywhere'. His most important objection was that:

> The SL became involved in the erection of an unreal façade of unity, behind which the brutal realities of Russian government policy operated unseen and unchecked; and the SL found itself recruited into a conspiracy of silence about the misdoings of the Russian government in which had already been enlisted an impressive array of British intellectuals – writers, publishers, academics and politicians.[123]

At the Socialist League national special conference on 16 and 17 January 1937 Cripps, Mellor and Brailsford spoke very strongly in support of the Unity Campaign but predictably they were publicly opposed by Groves and a lengthy debate ensued.[124] In the end the resolution was passed by 56 votes to 38, with 23 absentions. This narrow result, however, then precipitated rumours that Cripps had persuaded a number of provincial delegates, who were actually mandated to vote against, that disaffiliation of the Socialist League was very unlikely.[125] Cripps had certainly stressed this point at length during the conference debate but whether he had made personal appeals to delegates in less clear.[126] Nevertheless, in response there were counter rumours that Stonham, a Head Office employee and a close associate of Groves, had 'used his position as an official of the League to influence' Shildon, Whitley Bay and Chester-le-Street branches in the North East to oppose the National Council's resolution.[127] Later on 17 January special conferences organised by both the CPGB and the ILP also approved the Unity Campaign. The plans to launch the Unity Campaign the following week could now proceed. Nevertheless, the close outcome of the Socialist League conference had actually served to exacerbate further the divisions within the Socialist League.

Groves immediately organised a meeting for the conference delegates who represented branches that were opposed to the Unity Campaign. Other members of the London Area Committee, such as Andrew Campbell, attended the meeting as did delegates from South Wales, Lancashire and Cumberland so that 20 branches were represented in total. They agreed to set up a special ad hoc committee to represent the interests of those members of the Socialist League who wanted to remain loyal to the aims and constitution of the Labour party. Groves did not sit on the committee but it included those he knew well from his Balham Group days as well as from his time as Secretary of the London Area Committee: Garry Allighan who was the *Evening Standard* radio critic, Harry Wicks, Arthur Wimbush, Arnold Bennett and, of course, Campbell. It was authorised 'in the event of a critical situation arising from the Unity Agreement . . . to take all necessary steps . . . to enable us to consult together as to the most desirable future action'.[128] The Socialist League Executive Committee was very concerned. In the same circular as it instructed its branches 'immediately to get into contact with the local branches of the Communist Party and the ILP and establish Unity Campaign Committees', it also added that 'any branch which receives a communication from or on behalf of London or any other members of the League purporting to act as a Committee appointed by a meeting of visitors and delegates to the conference held after the conference closed, with reference to the decisions of the Conference, should immediately communicate with the Head Office'.[129] The Socialist League had often contained opposing factions – particularly when Murphy had been general secretary and had supported a popular front – but this level of organised dissent to the Cripps-Mellor line was unparalleled. It did not bode well for the prospects of a wider Left unity in the coming months.

6

THE UNRAVELLING OF THE UNITY CAMPAIGN

January 1937 to May 1937

The Unity Campaign was launched in a blaze of publicity at a meeting in the Free Trade Hall in Manchester on 24 January 1937. Despite capturing the headlines and initially appearing to make progress, the campaign soon ran into difficulties. A further round of Show Trials in Moscow and growing bitterness in Spain between the Communists and the POUM effectively undermined any real prospects of Unity. Despite the political constraints of the campaign, a public strand of anti-Stalinism nonetheless persisted within the ILP and led to considerable tensions with the CPGB on the Unity Campaign Committee. As the NEC disaffiliated the Socialist League, and then declared that membership of it was incompatible with membership of the Labour party, international developments also served to intensify the opposition of the Groves group within the Socialist League. Amid rapid organisational decline and increasingly bitter internal debate the Socialist League National Council then decided – with far-reaching consequences – to dissolve the League.

I

Ahead of the Unity Campaign's inauguration in Manchester a double-page spread on unity in *Tribune* on 22 January 1937, to which Cripps, Pollitt and Maxton contributed, had set the scene. Lansbury, who remained a well-respected figure in the Labour movement, had publicly given the campaign his support.[1] Laski had also announced his willingness to sign the Unity manifesto and gave his influential backing to the campaign.[2] The *New Statesman* had adopted a line that was broadly sympathetic to the Unity Campaign arguing that, in contrast to the NEC, it was at least 'trying to do something about the really vital questions of the hour – the fascist aggression in Spain, rearmament . . . and the struggle . . . to displace the National government and set up a government of the Left in its place'.[3]

Mellor chaired the meeting at the Free Trade Hall in Manchester where, for the first time, Cripps spoke alongside Pollitt and Maxton. The three speakers adumbrated the broad anti-fascist theme and launched the Unity Manifesto outlining the demands of the campaign.[4] Cripps dramatically accused the Labour party leadership of increasingly favouring 'class collaboration' with the National government – particularly over rearmament. The need for more active support of the Republicans in Spain was also emphasised. There were calls for the NCL to demand that not only the embargo on the supply of arms but also the ban on British volunteers for the Spanish Republican government, which had just recently been introduced by the National Government, be lifted.[5] The ILP had been particularly vocal in this respect.[6] The *New Leader* had publicised the activities of the ILP contingent under Bob Edwards which had left for Spain just before the law banning volunteers came into operation.[7] And at exactly the point when the Unity Campaign was launched, it called for a national conference 'representing the combined strength of the political, industrial and co-operative sides of the working-class movement' to discuss the matter.[8] Altogether, this meant that the Unity Campaign stance on Spain was different from that of the NCL, which was still only providing hesitant opposition to non-intervention and was completely unwilling to sanction the use of British volunteers.[9] There was widespread acknowledgement that the first Unity Campaign meeting was a success. The official figures claimed that 3,763 people had attended and signed the Unity 'pledge cards', while another thousand people were reported to have attended an overflow meeting at the Theatre Royal. Altogether more than £250 was raised.[10]

Beneath this outward success, however, the divisions within the Socialist League remained. The special ad hoc committee, set up by Groves and his associates, wrote to all Socialist League members and then specifically to the secretaries of all the London branches. Ostensibly the letters simply noted that it was 'in no way a committee elected to agitate against the National Council or the Conference decisions' and that it regretted the leakage of information about its formation to the press.[11] Nevertheless, the letters also obviously served to draw attention to the committee's continued existence and to the names of its leaders. Inevitably, the Socialist League leadership was unsettled and demanded that the list of members be returned.[12]

Further problems were created by the CPGB's renewed criticism of Groves. On 18 January 1937 the *Daily Worker* made a savage attack on him.

It accused him of leaking the confidential material about the Socialist League before the Special National Conference to the *Daily Herald* in an attempt to build opposition within the Socialist League to the Unity Campaign. It said he had been expelled from the CPGB because of his 'Trotskyist . . . disruptive activity'. The *Daily Worker* portrayed Groves's position as part of a wider battle with Trotskyism. It said Groves's actions were 'true to type' and compared them to Trotskyism in the Soviet Union which 'organises the murder of the leaders of the CP, and acts as the agent of the secret police of Hitler', and to Spain where it had 'organised the fight against the Spanish government and the Popular Front in the most critical hours of the struggle'.[13] The CPGB was vehement in its opposition to Groves under pressure from the Comintern.[14] On 20 January it issued a circular to all its organisations repeating the accusations and emphasising 'the necessity of an increased struggle against Trotskyism in Britain'.[15]

The CPGB stance created a difficult dilemma for the Socialist League leadership. It now came under pressure both to defend Groves publicly despite its own opposition to his actions, and at the same time to attempt to undermine the opposition of his group. The first Socialist League Executive Committee meeting after the special conference on 21 January received a letter from Bennett – who was on the special ad hoc committee – concerning the *Daily Worker* attack on Groves and demanding 'that the EC demand a public withdrawal'. The London Area Committee also called for an 'unqualified withdrawal'. At the committee meeting itself Groves made similar demands. However, after a prolonged discussion, it was finally agreed to send a letter to the *Daily Worker* containing the Special Conference resolution and simply 'stating that at the National Council meeting R. Groves had said that he was not responsible for the information contained in the press and that the NC had accepted his assurance'.[16] The Executive Committee was perhaps further swayed to take this stance by information that identified Allighan as the likely source of the press leakage. At the same meeting the Executive Committee also discussed the position of the special ad hoc committee. Mellor was particularly concerned that Campbell had written to all the branches of the League. By seven to one – probably Groves – the Executive Committee decided that the membership of the committee was frankly 'inconsistent' with holding any other official position within the Socialist League and agreed to communicate the decision to Bennett, Allighan and Campbell.[17]

Groves remained unhappy that the Executive Committee had not made a stronger protest to the CPGB and tried to muster more rank and file support. Studer, the secretary of his own Balham and Tooting branch and a member of the publications department at Head Office, now wrote to Cripps arguing that the *Daily Worker* attack went well beyond the 'friendly and constructive criticism' permitted under the Unity Agreement. Studer argued that under the Unity Agreement the three groups had agreed 'not to attack any other group or its personnel supporting the unity campaign' and that in his view this undertaking had 'already been violated by the Communist Party'. Studer accused the CPGB of 'mudslinging and slander' by making 'a quite unauthorised assumption that he had given information to the *Daily Herald*.[18] Nevertheless, the attempt to influence Cripps was to no avail. Cripps was very unsympathetic to the idea of making a stronger protest to the CPGB on behalf of Groves. He argued that Groves's action had been 'very undesirable and unauthorised' and that frankly 'Groves only has his own actions to blame for what has occurred'.[19]

II

Meanwhile tension continued to mount amid widespread speculation that the NEC would discipline the Socialist League. After the Socialist League special national conference the NEC immediately demanded a copy of both the resolutions passed and the Unity Manifesto.[20] The *Daily Herald* predicted that disaffiliation of the Socialist League was nothing less than the 'bounden duty' of the NEC.[21] This prompted a number of calls not to expel the League. Nineteen prominent Labour figures from Lancashire petitioned the Labour party to this effect.[22] On 25 January 1937 Cole, Lansbury, Addison, Pritt and John Parker wrote to the NEC appealing that they should not begin a 'heresy hunt' against those in the Socialist League as this would have 'only a tendency to disrupt the party, to weaken the Labour movement, and to drive active party workers . . . into disgruntlement and apathy, if not altogether out of the party'.[23]

However, such demands did not affect the determination of the NEC to take immediate disciplinary action. Cole had sent a copy of the letter to Bevin reiterating the appeal.[24] Bevin was not, of course, a member of the NEC but he was working very closely with Dalton in an attempt to check the Labour left and, as such, his opinion counted for a great deal. Bevin was completely opposed to the idea of co-operation with the Communists. He stressed that 'we will not be tools of Stalin' and 'dominated by the Communist international' because 'the communists . . . are out to destroy the trade unions like every other dictatorship'. He retained a dislike of the middle-class, intellectual nature of the Socialist League with its repeated disregard for conference decisions, and argued that 'Cripps is driving himself out'. Above all, he considered that the Socialist League's latest campaign – inevitably involving much publicity – was a serious distraction for the party from the work that the NEC Policy Committee had been doing on the party's new programme:

> As to the working of the party itself I have given nearly all my spare time for the past six years preparing for the next Labour government so that we won't be caught as we were before without a policy and our schemes ready. We have dealt with cotton, coal, transport, electricity, water, pensions, hours of Labour, and so on and when the appropriate moment arrives it will be put over to the electorate. If they vote for us I am certain that the policy decided upon can be translated into action but we cannot turn off our course at the instigation of all these various sections whose main contribution is purely intrigue. No-one is a greater adept at that than . . . Mellor.[25]

Influenced by these considerations the NEC, under Dalton's chairmanship, decided to disaffiliate the Socialist League both nationally and locally at its meeting on 27 January. It had dismissed the possibilities of either suspending the League or of giving it a week's grace. With one dissenting member, it decreed that the Socialist League's National Council 'must have known' that supporting the Unity Campaign 'in direct defiance of the Labour party . . . would render the League ineligible for continued affiliation to the Labour party especially having regard to the statement on Party Loyalty issued by the Executive dated January 12th, 1937'.[26] Curiously, the *Daily Herald* on 28 January also gave further information, which had not been sent to the Socialist League. It revealed that Mellor's candidature for Labour at Coventry had also come up for discussion, and that the NEC had 'refused to endorse his nomination'. Provocatively, the *Daily Herald* warned that this 'may be taken as an indication of what will happen in the future. Candidates put forward or recommended by the Socialist League will automatically be rejected'.[27] Indeed, a few days later Campbell, who was a prospective Labour party candidate at Hendon, received a letter from Middleton 'asking him to state what his position was in view of the disaffiliation of the Socialist League'.[28] Perhaps Campbell's well-publicised opposition to the Unity Campaign inclined the NEC to give him, unlike Mellor, a chance to affirm his loyalty to the Labour party.

The Socialist League Executive Committee considered the disaffiliation of the Socialist League on 28 January. Neither of the two principal critics of the Unity Campaign – Groves and Borrett – was actually present at the meeting but they both wrote asking for a National Council, and possibly even another National Conference, to be called to consider the matter. Perhaps in an attempt to pre-empt later discussion when Groves and Borrett would be present, the Executive Committee considered this as a resolution advanced by Groves and seconded by Borrett. The overwhelming view on the Executive Committee, however, was that 'it was not practicable at the present time to call a National Conference and that in view of the fact members of the Council were engaged at meetings in connection with the Unity Campaign during weekends it would not be desirable to have a meeting of the Council prior to the normal date at the beginning of March'. A particular concern was that calling another conference so soon after the last one would frankly be 'politically unwise'. The Executive Committee solicited the opinion of members of the National Council about this matter but found that many of them – including Dodds, Waters, Wigglesworth, Barker and Palmer – were similarly reluctant to call an early National Council.[29]

The rest of the meeting involved 'a long discussion and consideration of a draft' statement on the Socialist League's disaffiliation that had been prepared by Mellor. Eventually it was agreed to issue a statement to the press and the NEC. The statement objected to the NEC's comment that 'the National Council must have known such action would be contrary to the cause of unity in the ranks of Labour' as being 'totally without foundation'. It also drew attention 'to the point that in spite of the fact that membership of the Socialist League had not been declared incompatible with membership of the Labour Party action had been taken against the chairman of the National Council in connection with his prospective candidature at Coventry'. It stressed that 'the Executive Committee of the Socialist League protests against such unconstitutional and discriminatory action' especially since the 'nomination was not made by the Socialist League, which has no branch in Coventry'. The statement also pointed to the 'undeniable fact that members of the Labour Party, prominent as well as rank and file, have repeatedly appeared on platforms in joint activity with the CP and the ILP' and that 'prominent members of the party have appeared on platforms with Tories and Liberals', in both cases 'without any action being taken by the Party Executive Committee'.[30] At one level the Socialist League was drawing attention to the thousands of ordinary Labour party members engaged in joint activity with Communists and the ILP on a range of issues – perhaps most notably the hunger marches. Dodds noted from her own experience as an active Gateshead Borough Councillor that the technical ban on co-operation was 'completely inoperative' and that she 'could give heaps of cases of Labour party co-operation with Communists, in the past; and going on now'.[31] The Gateshead branch of the Socialist League, for which she kept the minutes, had always shared premises with the local ILP in an apparently very amicable arrangement.[32] At another level the Socialist League case was a direct reference to two high-profile cases. The first of these was the University Labour Federation (ULF), whose President was Greenwood, which had been operating a united front since January 1936 when it had incorporated the Communist-led Federation of Socialist Societies and then seen its membership rise from 1500 to 3017.[33] The second reference was to Citrine who had appeared with Churchill at the Albert Hall in December 1936 in support of the pro-rearmament 'Arms and the Covenant' campaign.

At the same time the Socialist League's own newspaper – the *Socialist Broadsheet* which had replaced *The Socialist* in January 1937 and was edited by Horrabin – carried a more forceful reply by the Socialist League to its disaffiliation by the NEC. Mellor asserted it was frankly 'a lie' to suggest that the Socialist League was disloyal to the Labour party when all it had done was to 'challenge the bureaucracy which seeks to drive the party into the paths of class collaboration and national unity'.[34]

Although Groves and Borrett were not present at the Executive Committee meeting on 28 January 1937 to press their own views in response to the disaffiliation of the Socialist League, they were most certainly opposed to the decision to continue defying the NEC. Borrett wrote to the Executive Committee ahead of its next meeting on 4 February 'asking that her dissent to the contents and publication of the press statement on the Labour party's attitude to the Unity Campaign be recorded'. Groves immediately stated that he also wanted to be associated with this protest.[35]

At this stage no one on the Executive Committee favoured the immediate dissolution of the League. When Barker, the National Council representative for the South West, wrote to suggest such a course, the Executive Committee quickly dismissed it. They were emphatic that 'there was every reason for the continuance of the League at present'.[36] This was in sharp contrast to the view taken by the Executive Committee on 5 January 1937 when it had considered the same question in a hypothetical sense and decided that 'if the SL was disaffiliated no useful purpose could be served by its separate existence'.[37] Nevertheless, there was now a real fear that many Socialist League branches might start slowly to disintegrate under pressure from the NEC. Consequently, the Executive Committee wrote to them stressing that since membership of the Socialist League had not been declared incompatible with membership of the Labour party this allowed 'continued activity on the part of branches of the Socialist League'. Furthermore, the federal structure of the Labour party meant that it would be left to local Labour parties actually to disaffiliate Socialist League branches in their area. Where possible, therefore, the branches were urged to remain affiliated and to try to get resolutions passed opposing the dissolution of the League.[38]

III

By this point a further round of Show Trials, which opened in Moscow on 24 January, had caused yet more splinters within the Unity Campaign. This time seventeen Communist party members, including Karl Radek, a prominent journalist, and Grigory Sokolnikov, the former Soviet Ambassador to London, were accused of plotting to kill Stalin and to destroy socialism under the influence of Trotsky. Once again, those accused confessed spectacularly. While these trials were very similar in format to those in August 1936, the political reaction to them on the Left was different in a number of ways – all of which related to the Unity Campaign.

Given that the Unity Campaign was launched on the same day as the trials began in Moscow, the Left was inevitably less vocal about them than it had been the previous August. Nevertheless, their criticism did not disappear altogether. Indeed, when news of the second Moscow trial was received, the ILP was initially unrestrained in its criticism. Through the *New Leader*, it expressed its 'distress' and 'bewilderment'. It stated forthrightly that it was 'impossible to believe' the charges, and that this made an international investigation even more imperative.[39] The Scottish ILP was at this point holding a conference and, even though the Moscow trials had not been put on the agenda, the delegates voted in favour of an addendum calling for an international working-class commission to investigate the situation.[40]

This inevitably caused ruptures within the Unity Campaign Committee, and meant that Cripps, Mellor, and Mitchison had to work hard to ensure that the campaign did not fall apart within a week of its launch. The attack on the trials by Brockway in the *New Leader* prompted the Politburo of the CPGB to commission a report by its representatives on the Unity Campaign Committee. This concluded that the *New Leader* article was 'a definite breach of the agreement that was signed by representatives of the three parties'. Nevertheless, the CPGB representatives were persuaded by Cripps, Mellor, and Mitchison to recommend continuing with the Unity Campaign. The Politburo accepted this course, but stressed that 'if it were not for the situation the Socialist League has placed itself in . . . and particularly the position of Comrades Cripps, Mellor, and Mitchison, we would find it impossible to give permission for our speakers to take any further part in any demonstrations along with Fenner Brockway'.[41] It seems that at the Unity Campaign Committee meeting the CPGB representatives had been impressed to see 'Cripps emphatically dissenting from the attitude of Brockway and the *New Leader*'. Even so, it was only after 'arrangements were made for a further meeting at which the whole question of Trotskyism could be put both to the ILP and the Socialist League' that the CPGB allowed the issue to drop.[42]

After this point – in the constrained atmosphere of the Unity Campaign – the ILP criticism of the trials abated. Indeed, when the NAC met on 6 and 7 February 1937 it endorsed the demand for an impartial investigation into the Moscow trials but stressed that it 'expresses no judgement on the matter at issue, and instructs the party to refrain from doing so'.[43] Similarly, ahead of the ILP conference in early April 1937 the NAC prepared a resolution which attested to the enduring pro-Soviet sentiment that still existed alongside the ILP's developing anti-Stalinism. The resolution praised the Soviet Union's 'social and economic developments', pledged to defend it from capitalist attack, and only hinted at certain 'causes of disquiet'.[44] At the conference itself, the Trotskyist Ernie Patterson, a one-time member of the Marxist Group who had chosen to remain in the ILP, sharply criticised the methods of the trials and the wider 'bureaucracy of Stalinism'. Nevertheless, Carmichael, who introduced the NAC resolution, emphatically stated that 'the party is not prepared to declare out of hand, that the trials are frame ups, or that the prisoners are duped or drugged'. He stressed that 'the evidence at present available is inadequate to reach a final judgement' and that, as such, there was a need for an impartial international inquiry. He was strongly supported in taking this approach by Maxton. With this endorsement from the leadership, the resolution won an 'overwhelming majority' and the proposed amendments were 'decisively defeated'.[45]

The CPGB had hoped that *Tribune* might criticise the *New Leader*'s initial hostility to the second wave of Show Trials.[46] It did not, but it did remain conspicuously silent – no doubt in part because Cripps, who had staked so much on the Unity Campaign, largely funded *Tribune* which was edited by his close colleague Mellor. Nevertheless, the absence of comment in *Tribune* does stand out – even in the context of the Unity Campaign. Michael Foot, who was a journalist on the paper at the time and a member of the Socialist League sitting on its London Area Committee, was clearly very disappointed. Reflecting after twenty years, he wrote that:

> all papers have their Achilles heels, their blind spots, or what, less
> charitably, may be called their streaks of cowardice. Ours was the
> Russian trials. We said nothing or next to nothing on the subject
> . . . Our excuse was that we . . . were engaged in a unity campaign
> on the supreme issue of . . . the international crisis . . . Let us hope
> that we have learnt the moral which might be put in a maxim to
> be inscribed above every editorial chair: 'Never funk the truly

awkward issues; they are the very ones your readers most want to hear about. And if by any chance they don't, to hell with them!'[47]

Cripps's own view was that the trials were an 'internal matter for Russia'.[48] However, even amid the on-going Unity Campaign, others in the Socialist League found it more difficult quietly to acquiesce. In December 1936 Brailsford and Horrabin, along with Groves, Purkis, and Wicks, had formed the British Provisional Committee for the Defence of Leon Trotsky, which sought to safeguard Trotsky's right to asylum and to help organise an independent inquiry into the Moscow trials.[49] In *Reynolds News* Brailsford voiced the concerns of those who wished to remain critical of Stalin.[50] Indeed, Foot felt a particular debt to Brailsford on this score. He later described with admiration how Brailsford 'stripped aside the curtain of lies and saved the honour of socialist journalism in face of the inconvenient horror'.[51] Similarly, in the *New Statesman* Martin reiterated the line he had taken in August 1936 – criticising the nature of Stalin's dictatorial regime irrespective of whether the confessions had been somehow painfully extorted or were actually true and exposed 'a regime in which the only way to express discontent is in conspiracy and the only way to suppress conspiracy mass execution'.[52]

The *Daily Herald* also responded in the same way as it had in August 1936. It argued that the charges were 'fantastic', and directly compared the trials and executions to Hitler's purge of the paramilitary arm of the Nazi party – the Sturmabteilung (SA) – on 30 June 1934, which had been a pivotal event in revealing the brutality of the Nazi regime.[53] Significantly, in a context where Left criticism (and particularly that of the Socialist League) was muted, the moderate wing of the Labour party also used the trials for overtly political objectives. With the aim of directing disapproval of the Moscow trials into opposition to the Socialist League, the editorial in the *Daily Herald* said its decision to disaffiliate the League marked a desire 'to keep itself clear of . . . theories of violence and dictatorship which are working themselves out so tragically . . . in a court in Moscow'.[54]

IV

In the first months of the Unity Campaign tension continued to simmer between the ILP and the CPGB over Spain. The ILP was kept informed of events there through a number of channels. Brockway interviewed the POUM leader Julian Gorkin in Paris,[55] and a visit to Britain by Johan Matteo – a member of POUM who was technically a French citizen – was also arranged.[56] Most importantly, however, the ILP was fed information by

McNair, the International Bureau's representative in Spain. McNair's presence had been welcomed by the POUM Executive which even allowed him to meet Communist representatives on five separate occasions in order to call for unity.[57] With such a personal commitment to the POUM, it was neither unsurprising that he championed its cause as often as possible[58] nor that his information was favourable to it.

In early February Brockway wrote 'with reluctance and regret' about the continued 'campaign of the most vicious kind . . . now being worked up against the POUM'. Stressing the need for united action against fascism across Europe, in Britain and especially in Spain, he contended that this should not mean 'that we hide political differences or stop agitation for political lines which we regard as essential. But it does mean that the difference is maintained on a political level, without bringing about charges of treachery and going over to the enemy.' He did not want 'our unity to be destroyed by the disunity elsewhere' and – rather incredibly – suggested that Maxton, Cripps and Pollitt might address unity meetings in Barcelona, Valencia and Madrid.[59] As the Communist criticisms of the POUM intensified further, Brockway argued boldly that there was not 'a shred of evidence' against the POUM.[60]

Nevertheless, as a result of the on-going Unity Campaign the ILP did make a certain effort to overcome its differences with the CPGB. While the NAC's conference resolution on Spain stressed that 'Social Revolution, and not capitalist democracy, is the issue in the struggle against fascism', it also demanded an 'all-in conference of British working-class organisations to mobilise support for the Spanish workers and for the lifting of the embargo on arms and volunteers for the anti-fascist forces'.[61] At the ILP conference itself, McGovern, who moved the resolution, stated frankly that 'Soviet Russia should never have attached conditions to its practical support'. His most vehement criticism was, however, reserved for the Labour party whose attitude he condemned as the 'greatest tragedy of all'.[62] Lee – who had been in Barcelona at the beginning of the year[63] – took a similar stance, arguing that the 'greatest offender within the whole working-class movement of the world was the British Labour party'. Moreover, while she was clear that the attacks on the POUM had to be explained, she contended that 'however delayed and hedged with conditions Communist aid is now being splendidly given to the Spanish Government' and she even went on to praise the 'great work . . . being done by the Communists in Spain'.[64] Lee's attitude clearly went beyond a simple attempt to conciliate the CPGB, pointing instead to the larger practical dilemmas of reconciling the Soviet Union's role in combating fascism in a context where the British Left was not itself in a position to influence international events in any significant way.

A similarly ambiguous stance – constrained both by events in Spain and Britain – influenced the course of the debate at the ILP conference on the workers front. After Brockway had moved a resolution reiterating the ILP's support for the proposal, Lee argued that 'there might come a time when we would be glad even for the existence of a Popular Front Government'. This was met by loud 'cries of No!' which prompted her to attack 'those whose only care was the saving of their own souls, and who preferred to keep themselves without sin whatever the cost'. She argued, above all, that 'a situation might arise in which a Popular Front government would be the last bulwark against fascism'. Crucially, Brockway then added that the POUM had decided to enter a popular front government as a 'temporary expedient' instead of remaining outside the mass working-class movement altogether. Significantly, he argued that if 'similar circumstances ever arose here . . . the ILP might have to adopt the same policy'.[65] In the event only four delegates voted against the workers' front.[66] Nonetheless, the debate had shown how the actual practice of supporting a faction in Spain had influenced the ILP's ideas about how to fight fascism in Britain. There are indeed clear parallels here with the way in which the Socialist League's support for the Republican side in summer 1936 had led some of its members to advocate a popular front in Britain.

The ILP's occasionally less dogmatic attitudes towards the struggle in Spain and the popular front did not however markedly reduce friction between itself and the CPGB. On 27 March an article appeared in the *Daily Worker* arguing that the ILP's whole stance was a 'stab in the back' and ultimately serving the interests of fascism. Brockway responded strongly, saying that this was the 'beginning of the kind of language which has been used to denounce the political line of the POUM in Spain. The next stage will be to denounce the ILP as "Trotskyist-fascist".'[67] This was, of course, a particular concern for the ILP leadership which remained determined to distance themselves from Trotskyism. Reviewing C. L. R. James's *World Revolution*, Brockway wrote dismissively about its 'biased . . . Trotskyist . . . view' and contended that the 'fault of Trotsky and his disciples is that they can see nothing else than the mistakes of Soviet Russia and the Communist International' and that 'in every country they have become a negative and destroying force' for whom 'Communists become as hateful as fascists'.[68]

V

Against this background the Unity Campaign enjoyed mixed success. Initially it had appeared quickly to gather momentum as 11 large meetings were held. In late January Bevan and Mellor addressed those at Cardiff,

Swansea, Llanelly, Newport, and Merthyr in South Wales.[69] In February there were further large meetings in Hull, Birmingham and Hamilton. Cripps spoke to a crowd of 3,000 in Bristol on 13 February when he stated frankly that 'James Maxton and Harry Pollitt ought to be leaders in the Labour movement today'.[70] Cripps also addressed a large meeting in Glasgow on 21 February.[71] By the end of February the Socialist League's own figures claimed that 19,000 people had attended these demonstrations. Moreover, the League contended that 11,769 people had filled in the pledge cards of the Unity Campaign, £700 had been raised and that 39 unity committees had been formed.[72] It seems that the Unity Campaign attracted considerable support from energetic younger Labour party supporters and members, many of whom were in the Labour League of Youth. For the past two years the Socialist League had courted the League of Youth in the hope of securing its support for the Socialist League's policies. In particular, the Socialist League annual conference in June 1936 had supported the League of Youth in its opposition to the NEC's plans to reduce its maximum age of membership from 25 to 21, which the League of Youth considered as an attempt to reduce its numbers and influence.[73] Now the Socialist League explicitly sought to capture the 'enthusiasm of the young' behind the Unity Campaign.[74] To a large extent, the Socialist League was successful and members of the League of Youth, such as Ted Willis, became very active supporters.[75]

At the same time there was an equivocal response to the Socialist League Executive Committee's decision that membership of the special ad hoc committee was incompatible with membership of the London Area Committee. Campbell clearly wanted to remain secretary of the London Area Committee. He told one of its meetings on 3 February 1937 that he had resigned from the special ad hoc committee and informed the Executive Committee of his decision. Allighan, however, was determined to remain a public opponent of the Unity Campaign. There had been a frank exchange at the Executive Committee meeting on 28 January when Allighan had been interviewed about the press leakage. He 'emphatically denied' that he had given information to Ernest Hunter, the political correspondent of the *Daily Herald*. He admitted that he had seen Hunter both before and after the special conference but said that in 'neither case had the conversation been on the question of the League's policy and the Unity Campaign'. Curiously, however, he said that Hunter had asked him directly if 'Groves had sent him any document'. Nevertheless, without any firm evidence otherwise, the Executive Committee reluctantly accepted Allighan's statements.[76] Allighan now continued to stand firm. He had not replied to the Executive Committee indicating whether he would resign from the London Area

Committee or from the ad hoc committee. He was being deliberately adversarial as he told the London Area Committee on 3 February that 'he could not accept the resolution of the Executive Committee'. It was no surprise, therefore, that on 4 February, after hearing a report on the matter from Horrabin, the Executive Committee made plans to deal harshly with Allighan. It was agreed that if Allighan did not reply within a week to a further letter, and did not deny the report, then the 'National Council may be compelled to exercise their discretionary powers under the last paragraph of rule 1'.[77] This stated that members 'who do not conform to the principles and policy of the League may be expelled . . . by the National Committee'.[78]

Once again the Socialist League leadership soon found itself in the difficult position of having to defend its dissentient members. The CPGB representatives on the Unity Campaign Committee requested that the London Area Committee should pledge to support 'loyally' the Unity Campaign before it was allowed to appoint three of its members to serve on a proposed London Unity Campaign Committee charged with the responsibility of promoting the campaign in the London area. The Socialist League Executive Committee readily endorsed the idea of the London Unity Campaign Committee and informed the London Area Committee accordingly. However, it also agreed that Mitchison 'should inform the secretary of the Unity Committee that the EC unanimously thought the request for an assurance' of loyalty was inadvisable. The view was 'that if the London Area Committee duly accepted the instructions they would carry them out loyally'.[79]

Meanwhile, the opposition of Groves on the Executive Committee continued. His attempt to force the issue of the *Daily Worker* attack now failed. Mellor raised the matter with Pollitt after further pressure from the Balham and Tooting branch.[80] However, the CPGB reply suggested the matter was not one on which they were prepared to move. The CPGB confirmed that they refused to publish the Socialist League's letter about Groves in the *Daily Worker*. The Secretariat was adamant that 'no publicity will be given to Groves and his Trotskyist associates who aim to disrupt and destroy the Labour movement'. Mellor said the Unity Campaign Committee would consider the POUM and the Soviet Show Trials the following week.[81] Even so, he does not seem to have pushed the point too strongly and a few weeks later readily accepted that the matters 'had been postponed for discussion at a later date'.[82] Groves now had to be satisfied that the *Socialist Broadsheet* would publish his letter denying that he had leaked any information about the Socialist League special conference in January to the *Daily Herald* and criticising the CPGB for claiming that he had done so.[83] At this point, however, Groves did develop a more effective line of criticism.

On 18 February 1937 he argued that, irrespective of the merits of the campaign, the Unity Campaign Committee was not sufficiently accountable to the Socialist League. This argument found wide support on the Executive Committee. When Groves proposed that the Executive Committee should be supplied with 'the documents issued by the Unity Committee, together with the minutes of its meetings', this was unanimously agreed.[84]

VI

Following its disaffiliation by the NEC, the Socialist League now entered a period of considerable organisational decline. Of course, some branches – such as Shildon and Miles Platting – had opposed the Unity Campaign from the outset and these had dissolved soon after the special conference.[85] Many more branches – such as Birtley in the North East – did not want to defy the NEC and so disbanded once the Socialist League had been disaffiliated.[86] Similarly, others such as Aylesbury and Mitcham now decided that their finances could not cope with a split from the local Labour party. Many more branches simply disintegrated at a rate that the Executive Committee could not calculate. Moreover, while there had been 27 new head office members enrolled by the end of February, many more had simply allowed their membership to lapse.[87]

Throughout February further speculation then suggested that the NEC would expel prominent members of the Socialist League from the Labour party at its next meeting.[88] Attlee was reluctant for the NEC to pursue such a course.[89] On the other hand, Greenwood was determined to see the leading Socialist Leaguers expelled.[90] Cripps himself added to the speculation by dramatising the danger of his own personal expulsion from the Labour party.[91] However, on 24 February the NEC decided not to take any action immediately. It stressed that while the 'recent position cannot continue indefinitely', there was a need to give the Socialist League 'time to consider where they stand'. Significantly, the NEC did not mention Mellor's parliamentary candidature or that of Wigglesworth, the National Council member. Mellor had written personally to the NEC about the matter on 2 February but had received a curt reply.[92] The general view at the NEC meeting 'was opposed to any kind of heresy hunt directed against a few individuals who, as a result, might become political martyrs'.[93] There was also an awareness – as the NEC's memorandum made clear – that any action could be politically damaging in the weeks before the LCC elections on 4 March and so it was agreed that no decision would be taken until the NEC's next meeting in late March.[94]

G. R. Strauss, who was a prominent member of the LCC holding positions as chairman of the Highways Committee and vice-chairman of the Finance Committee, had made the Unity Campaign a live issue in the forthcoming elections. Strauss was a wealthy supporter of Cripps who had given £6,000 to help set up *Tribune*.[95] He had signed the Unity Campaign and now insisted in *Tribune* on 12 February that co-operation between the Labour party, the ILP and the CPGB would be an invaluable aid to success in the elections.[96] In mid-February the Unity Campaign Committee discussed the possibility of issuing a statement in support of the Labour party for the LCC elections. However, in deference to Morrison's wishes – he pleaded with Cripps as LCC leader that such a move would detrimentally affect the London Labour party's electoral prospects – the committee decided not to issue a statement but did offer 'the services of any of our speakers at any of your meetings'.[97] This policy was strongly endorsed by the Socialist League Executive Committee on 18 February,[98] and so Morrison probably pushed for inaction over the leading Socialist Leaguers in order to preserve what he saw as a valuable truce.

VII

With the Socialist League suffering falling membership and under pressure from the NEC, the Groves group now stepped up its attack on the Unity Campaign. On 25 February the Socialist League Executive Committee discovered that Donald Barber – a member of the National Council and Executive Committee between 1933 and 1934 and now a prominent member of the London Area Committee – had sent another circular to a large number of Socialist League members on behalf of the special ad hoc committee. Criticising the fact that Allighan had now been forced to resign from the London Area Committee, the circular informed members that the ad hoc committee 'has remained in being, because it believes it to be essential to continue the work of unifying the left inside the Labour party, and to counteract the harm which may well be done to this cause by the ill-timed and ill-based "Unity" campaign'. The circular also argued that 'a number of branches have resigned or broken up in the face of the unnecessary difficulties created by the "Unity" campaign'. Significantly, for the first time the ad hoc committee now argued that the CPGB was dominating the Unity Campaign.[99]

This latest circular from the ad hoc committee put the Executive Committee on the defensive. Mellor wrote to all branch secretaries and head office members in an attempt to justify the League's stance. He argued that after full consideration the Executive Committee had decided that membership of the ad hoc committee was incompatible 'for a member of the League holding an official position, such for instance as membership of the Area Committee whose function it was to encourage and co-ordinate branch activities in conjunction with the National Council and in consonance with the general policy of the League, to be a member of an unofficial committee not provided for in the constitution of the League, the purpose of which was, in certain events, to take action independent of the National Council'. Mellor argued that the Executive Committee simply 'acquainted the three comrades involved who were members of the L[ondon] A[rea] C[ommittee] with that decision, and it was then up to them either to resign from the London Area Committee or resign from the ad hoc body'. Finally, Mellor dismissed as 'without foundation' the argument that the Communists dominated the Unity Campaign but he found it more difficult to put a favourable gloss on the League's declining membership.[100]

Although Campbell had resigned from the special ad hoc committee there was some speculation that he may have given Barber the list of provincial branch secretaries, which the Executive Committee knew he had not returned. In any case, Campbell was still only reluctantly supporting the Unity Campaign. The Executive Committee noted that, as London Area Secretary, he had not done enough to form new branches in the area. The Executive Committee agreed to write 'informing him that in view of the urgency of the matter the Executive Committee recommended that the Assistant Area Secretary should be given authority to act in this situation'.[101]

Groves had maintained that the Socialist League should associate itself more closely with the POUM in face of criticism of it by the CPGB. Now, as relations between the POUM and the Communist party in Spain worsened, his group pressed these points more forcefully. In mid February the London Area Committee had passed a resolution 'expressing solidarity with the POUM as the only party in Spain which has raised the slogan of working-class power and declaring disgust at the slandering and lying attacks made upon the POUM by the Communist press'.[102] Following Groves's earlier request the Socialist League had convinced the Unity Campaign Committee to circulate copies of its leaflets, pamphlets, manifestos and, more reluctantly, its minutes to the Executive Committees of its three constituent organisations.[103] Now that the Socialist League Executive Committee knew more about the Unity Campaign Groves turned this to his advantage. At the Executive Committee meeting on 11 March 1937 Mitchison read the minutes of the Unity Campaign Committee from 2 March. Groves – supported by Borrett – moved that 'members of the Executive Committee on the Unity Committee support any request by the ILP for the cessation of the slanders in the Communist party press against the POUM'. Cripps and Mellor were not present at the meeting but only two of Horrabin, Mitchison and Elvin opposed the motion. The motion fell, but the closeness of the vote meant that the matter was placed on the agenda of the National Council meeting.[104]

Those opposing Groves's motion – as Cripps and Mellor no doubt would have done – were prepared to put their own affinity with the POUM aside for the sake of the continuance of the Unity Campaign. Nevertheless, there was sufficient sympathy in the League for the POUM that, together with the animosity on the subject between the ILP and the CPGB, it was not possible to offer anything approaching an agreed Unity Campaign platform on Spain. Significantly, the Unity Campaign Committee's divisions over Spain meant that it missed a considerable opportunity to express rank and file Labour dissatisfaction with the NCL, which had continued to provide only hesitant and faltering opposition to the National government's support for non-intervention.[105] Now, on an issue on which the Labour party leadership was out of step with the mass of its members, the initiative fell to the HCLA. At one of its meetings on 13 March 1937 the Labour Spain Committee was formed, which set out to be more than just a fund-raising body and to mobilise the wider discontent with official policy over Spain.[106]

Nevertheless, the Unity Campaign Committee was able to advance an agreed platform on National government rearmament. In February the National government had announced its intention to raise a £400 million loan for rearmament and to spend £1,500 million in five years on war preparations. Brockway was quick to condemn this development, arguing that the 'Labour movement should undertake a nationwide campaign to oppose rearmament, to make clear that a National Government which has betrayed the Spanish workers cannot be trusted with armaments, and to refuse all Trade Union collaboration or concessions for the sake of the rearmament programme'.[107] Significantly, moreover, the Socialist League Executive Committee was perfectly happy even to ask Groves to draft a document on the Socialist League's stance,[108] which it then endorsed – with only very minor changes – at its meeting on 11 March 1937.[109] Similarly, the Unity Campaign Committee was quickly able to agree on a statement, which was issued on 6 March. This argued that the National government was 'sacrificing the future in the interests of imperialism and embarking upon a course that means the lowering of the standards of the workers, a piling up of debt and the causing of a crisis that will be resolved by armed force'. Revealing the basic level of pro-Soviet feeling that the Socialist League, the ILP and the CPGB undoubtedly still shared, it emphasised that the National government's policy was 'based upon a determination to leave the Soviet Union and the smaller democracies at the mercy of fascist aggression so that British imperialism in the Mediterranean, Africa and the Far East may be preserved'.[110] The Unity Campaign Committee's stance on rearmament struck a chord with many in the Labour movement who still opposed rearmament. Had the committee been able to produce a similar joint statement on Spain its ability to influence Labour policy might have been greater.

VIII

The Socialist League now entered a deep crisis. Before the National Council meeting on 12 and 13 March, Cripps had decided that he was no longer willing to continue supporting the League financially. He was now funding *Tribune* – to which he had recently given £18,000[111] – as well as the constituency parties movement.[112] Perhaps he considered that these might prove to be more effective instruments for influencing the Labour left in the longer term than the Socialist League. It is also possible that the increasingly factious nature of the Socialist League made Cripps willing to jeopardise its existence. The National Council recognised that Cripps's decision meant there was an urgent need 'to submit proposals regarding the future of the League in view of the fact that it had been made clear that the League would not in future be able to depend upon financial assistance from members of the NC'. Groves moved that the Council should issue an appeal to raise £1000 before the next National Council meeting. A sub-committee of Groves, Borrett, Horrabin and McCarthy was now formed charged with ensuring that as many members as possible were contacted and that, in particular, branch secretaries and officers were encouraged to make a special effort to raise the sum required. Even so the prospects did not look promising. McCarthy tendered her resignation as secretary 'on the ground that it was necessary to reduce the expenditure of the League to a minimum'. She was persuaded, however, to remain in her post until 8 April, by which time the response to the appeal would be known. Altogether these pressures on the Socialist League made it necessary for the National Council to decide that the first item on the agenda for the Socialist League conference was the 'present situation of the League, political, organisational and financial and its future'.[113]

Now that the LCC elections were over and the Labour party had retained control with an increased majority, the NEC began to take a tougher stance towards the Socialist League. The first indication of this was Morrison's action against Strauss, who – echoing comments in the *New Leader*[114] – was now loudly praising the efforts of Communists during the LCC election campaign. Their formal offer of help had been rejected but they had worked with local Labour parties in some places and elsewhere had adopted a stance critical of the Conservatives and supportive of Labour. Strauss argued that, despite the Conservatives' best efforts, the 'scare value of Communists' was 'practically negligible' and that co-operation had helped 'to raise the spirit and efficiency of the Labour party electoral machine and secure striking results at the poll'.[115] Morrison had remained silent during the campaign but now decided to act.[116] On 16 March he recommended to the new LCC Executive Committee that Strauss not be re-elected to his committee posts. Ominously, the committee passed the motion 'without discussion' during a meeting that lasted only four minutes.[117]

The NEC then decided to act to crush the Socialist League. On 24 March it resolved that 'membership of the Socialist League is incompatible with membership of the Labour party and continued membership of the League renders members ineligible for membership of the Labour party' from 1 June.[118] The same information was communicated directly to Mellor – in response to his letter of 2 February concerning his parliamentary candidature.[119] The NEC wanted to sideline the Socialist League quickly so that it could concentrate on publicising its new programme through a nationwide campaign.[120] On 8 March the NEC had published *Labour's Immediate Programme*, which had been drafted by Dalton and Durbin. Dalton later described how it was intended 'to arouse interest, to maintain self-confidence, and to blanket and discredit the disloyalists'.[121] He had become particularly concerned that the Unity Campaign – which he regarded as 'a piece of clotted nonsense' – was 'a most exasperating diversion of the party's mind and energies'.[122] The *Immediate Programme* gave details of the measures that a majority Labour government would implement in a single five-year term. It promised planning through the national investment board, and nationalisation of the Bank of England – but significantly not the joint-stock banks – and of coal, power and transport. It also laid out plans for a 40-hour week, and the abolition of the Means Test. The significance of the programme was in its concrete plans for the implementation of most of its policies.[123]

The situation had now changed drastically as the Socialist League Executive Committee recognised when it considered the matter on 30 March 1937.[124] The NEC's action initially provoked some sympathy for the Socialist League from the wider Labour movement. The National Union of Distributive and Allied Workers (NUDAW) passed a resolution, supporting a united front and protesting against the Socialist League's disaffiliation, by 69,266 to 34,101. The Shop Assistants' Union passed a similar motion but by a smaller majority.[125] Lansbury again intervened. He now dismissed the NEC's new stance as 'sheer madness' and pleaded 'for freedom for individual members to form a subsidiary or other bodies in an endeavour to further the cause of socialism'.[126]

An Emergency National Council meeting was called to discuss the League's position on 4 April. It considered three options: Cripps and Barker favoured 'dissolving at once and . . . making the fight on the Unity attack which would be certain to follow from Transport House'; Groves and Borrett wanted the Socialist League to remain in existence but to abandon the Unity Campaign; Mellor and Betts wanted to continue with both the Socialist League and the Unity Campaign. There was a long discussion in which the two most powerful figures in the Socialist League – Cripps and Mellor – disagreed over a fundamental question of policy for the first time. Mellor made the argument that immediately disbanding the League would be 'letting down the other two signatories to the campaign'.[127] Eventually, however, the National Council decided on a compromise between the different views: the League should remain in existence until after the Labour party conference in October and then disband if the conference vote went against the Unity Campaign.[128] The National Council now agreed to write to the NEC protesting about its 'unprecedented action', stating that such 'action has never previously been taken against a purely propagandist body such as the SL which does not enter into electoral competition with the Labour party and which is not an organisation declared to be ancillary or subsidiary to the Communist party'. The National Council expressed its hope that the Labour party conference would overturn the decision and said that the 'policy and action' of the Socialist League would be determined at its conference at Whitsuntide.[129] Significantly, at this point the compromise resolution seemed to have wide support among the Socialist League leadership. Mellor was optimistic that the Socialist League would gain support for the Unity Campaign at the Labour party conference.[130] Cripps considered that the compromise resolution made by the Council was 'quite a good one' even though his personal preference was for 'the closing down of the League'. Cripps was apparently conscious that 'when one is working with a number of people one cannot be too autocratic!'[131]

Now the NEC responded sharply. It told the National Council that they 'should realise their action in initiating the "Unity Campaign" in defiance of repeated conference decisions was equally unprecedented'.[132] On 9 April 1937 the NEC issued a document entitled 'The Labour Party and the So-Called "Unity Campaign"' which was the most powerful criticism yet of the Unity Campaign and the Socialist League's involvement with it. It questioned the sources of funding for the campaign – remarking that these were 'not disclosed'. It further attacked the CPGB for taking 'not only its money but also its orders from Moscow'. It dismissed the Unity Campaign as 'sham unity', and it called for efforts to concentrate on publicising the *Immediate Programme*.[133] These points were reiterated in the *Daily Herald's* editorial which articulated the NEC and the TUC General Council's concern that the Unity Campaign was 'disruptive and distracting' and 'doing far more to reduce the effectiveness of Labour than to harm the government'.[134] Dalton took the attack even further. He said publicly that the Unity Campaign 'was being financed by one or two rich men who are using their private wealth in constant attack on the policy and leadership of the party'.[135]

The NEC's attack forced the Socialist League to adopt a defensive posture. Cripps publicly asked Dalton to name the rich men.[136] The front page of *Tribune* on 16 April gave coverage to the whole debate and claimed that the Unity Campaign was largely self supporting.[137] Brockway's *New Leader* editorial made the same points and was particularly keen to refute the idea that the campaign was a 'Communist manoeuvre'.[138] In response, Dalton replied that the CPGB was certainly funded from Moscow, and that the Socialist League was 'little more than a rich man's toy' funded massively by Cripps who also funded *Tribune*.[139] Altogether these debates damaged the momentum of the Unity Campaign as Pollitt recognised in a memorandum submitted to the Unity Campaign Committee later in April.[140]

IX

At this juncture Cripps became determined to see that the Socialist League reconsidered its position and disbanded immediately. Pimlott has argued that Pollitt 'perhaps persuaded' Cripps to favour this course.[141] There was certainly some pressure from Pollitt on Cripps to dissolve the League – as the memoirs of Brockway make clear.[142] However, this is by no means the whole story. Cripps had been disillusioned with the Socialist League even before the NEC declared that membership of it was incompatible with that of the Labour party. Cripps had favoured immediate dissolution at the National Council on 4 April 1937 but had agreed to a compromise. Now Pollitt's was not the only or even the most influential voice pushing Cripps in this direction. Laski, whose advice Cripps valued highly, warned that 'once there is expulsion . . . there will be a slow erosion of any effective influence the campaign can have'.[143] Moreover, perhaps on top of Cripps's existing reservations, the intense NEC attack on the Socialist League, which Dalton had made decidedly personal, was important to his change of position. Beatrice Webb, whose husband Sidney had discussed the position of the Socialist League with Cripps on 6 April, speculated that 'Stafford says and does things without considering the consequences – and when the consequence occurs, in an unpleasant fashion, he does not always stick to his guns.'[144]

However, it seems likely that the most important factor in turning Cripps's mind definitely in favour of immediate dissolution was the strength of feeling in his own constituency of East Bristol, which was conveyed to him by Rogers, his agent, and Barker, the Socialist League National Council representative for the South West. A meeting of the Socialist League branch in Bristol on 4 April had voted by 19 to 8 in favour of immediate dissolution. However, when Barker, the National Council representative for the South West, arrived at the meeting immediately after returning from the meeting of the National Council she attempted to pass a resolution along the lines of the National Council compromise. This had proposed that only the loss of the debate on the Unity Campaign at the Labour party conference in October would trigger dissolution. Many members had already left the meeting by the time Barker arrived but she managed to persuade those remaining to endorse the compromise.[145] Significantly, Rogers was completely opposed to such a course. He now wrote to Cripps arguing that, from his local knowledge, many members of the League would resign before the Labour party conference. Rogers was particularly concerned about the 'further complication of Labour councillors who are members of the SL and who will seek re-election next November'. He argued that these councillors would come under considerable pressure either to resign from the Socialist League or to refrain from contesting the seats. Rather than facing expulsion from the Labour party, Rogers's own view was that it 'would be far more spectacular to have cheated the LP by the dissolution of the League than to wait and find that the annual conference will, without doubt, support the National Executive decision'.[146]

Barker had been surprised at the strength of rank and file feeling in favour of immediate dissolution. She herself had been one of the only leaders of the Socialist League to favour dissolving the League as soon as the NEC disaffiliated it in late January and had not wavered since.[147] Nevertheless, 'in the face of views expressed in Council, in order to preserve unity' she had advocated the compromise to her own branch thinking that they would accept it. Now Barker accepted Rogers's analysis of the likely local effects of the decision and also strongly urged Cripps to reconsider the situation. She made clear her view that if the League remained in existence after 1 June the Bristol Labour party '*will* operate this ban' partly because of ill-feeling between the Borough Labour party and Rogers and the East Bristol District.[148] Erroneously, Cripps had assumed that the Bristol Labour party would not actually ban the Socialist League.[149]

After another meeting in Bristol on 12 April both Rogers and Barker again wrote to Cripps stressing that the Socialist League rank and file in Bristol were overwhelmingly in favour of immediate dissolution.[150] Rogers told Cripps forthrightly that the 'suggestion to dissolve after the Labour Party Conference was not favourably received'. Furthermore, Rogers warned 'that if they resign from the League it will do considerable damage to you by the capital that the press and Labour Party officials will make out of it . . . not only will they say that your supporters were not remaining true to you but that many were prepared to remain with the LP while you were willing to split it'.[151] The weight of both Cripps's agent in East Bristol and the Socialist League National Council representative advising immediate dissolution, and making clear the potential implications for Cripps's own position as MP for East Bristol, must have forced Cripps to rethink and decide to pursue the course he had himself originally favoured more strongly.

As a result another National Council meeting – the second in 14 days – was planned for 18 April in order to reconsider the issue.[152] At the meeting Mellor outlined the possible resolutions on the future of the League that the National Council could put before the annual conference and there was a 'full discussion'. It is likely that Cripps, Barker and Mitchison spoke strongly in favour of immediate dissolution. Significantly, the option favoured by Groves – 'that the League should continue but, in the light of the Party Executive decisions, withdraw from the Unity Campaign' – was discounted. The National Council then agreed to reach a decision by a system of alternative votes on three resolutions. The first of these was that the League could dissolve on 1 June, but encourage its former members to continue their active involvement with the Unity Campaign. The second was that the League could remain in existence and pursue the Unity Campaign. The third option was the compromise position reached on 4 April: the League could continue with the Unity Campaign until the Labour party conference but dissolve if the vote there went against it. The result of the alternative voting was 27 for dissolution, 16 for continuation and 11 for compromise. This showed how far views had changed in just two weeks. In a straight vote on dissolution eight (including Cripps) voted for, four (including Mellor) voted against, and there were two abstentions.[153] It was agreed to send the National Council's recommendation to the branches 'for them to amend, substitute, mandate upon' together with a statement of the reasons behind the National Council's decision. At this point only Groves continued to oppose the decision and insisted that he was completely disassociated from the majority on the National Council.[154]

The National Council was concerned to prevent any dissent within the League from the Groves group from becoming public. Accordingly, the National Council decided that it would not issue a press statement. The statement to the branches prepared by Mellor, Cripps and Horrabin urged them to ignore any press reports. Most of all, the National Council was concerned that the debate, which it anticipated at the annual conference, should not receive press coverage. It was decided that 'the conference open in private session and that the report and the discussion on the future of the League be taken in private session'. It was agreed 'that in the private session National Council members be permitted to express their own individual views, but that a statement on the major decision be given in public session by the chairman speaking on behalf of the conference'. Furthermore, it 'was agreed that the procedure of presenting this statement for vote but not for discussion might have to be employed'.[155]

X

Now that the National Council had decided to recommend immediate dissolution of the Socialist League, its membership fell still further. There are no accurate figures for Socialist League membership at this point. By the time of the Socialist League annual conference in May 1937, Groves and his supporters argued that since the launch of the Unity Campaign, it had fallen from 3,000 – the number of members for which it paid affiliation fees in 1935 and 1936[156] – to 1,600.[157] The National Council report tried to give a more positive picture – it claimed that eight branches had dissolved but that five new ones had been formed. It also claimed that 12 individual members had resigned.[158] The National Council's figures related to the information the Executive Committee had received but, since many branches had simply silently disappeared and many members become quietly inactive, the estimates of the Groves group may have been more accurate. At the National Council meeting on 13 and 14 March 1937 McCarthy had reported 'that the general organisation of the Area Committees was in a weak state'.[159] Cripps's outright refusal to fund substantially the League's activities had meant that in March when the branches were informed about the arrangements for the annual conference, they were told that in contrast to previous years it would 'not be possible this year to give financial assistance to enable delegates to attend the conference'.[160] The dire financial situation had not been helped by the financial appeal launched in March, which only raised £24.[161] Moreover, at the National Council meeting on 18 April, Horrabin had raised the question of whether to produce another issue of the *Socialist Broadsheet*. He said 'that he felt little finance would be forthcoming from the sale of a third issue in the light of experience with the previous two'. The National Council agreed that no further issues would be produced.[162] For the first time since 1934, when *The Socialist Leaguer* had been launched, the Socialist League did not have a journal of its own.

There were now also concerns that, for the first time, the Unity Campaign was losing momentum. Indeed, the Unity Campaign Committee discussed at length how it might be reinvigorated.[163] So far the campaign had enjoyed moderate success. By 19 April 34,399 pledge cards had been signed and 93 local unity committees formed.[164] This meant that in the two months from the end of February 22,550 more cards had been signed and 54 more local committees established.[165] To be sure, the figures were not as high as those for membership of Gollancz's Left Book Club, which had 45,000 members a year after its formation in May 1936.[166] However, membership of the Left Book Club was a less political commitment than support for the Unity Campaign. It is perhaps more significant to recognise that support for the Unity Campaign far outstripped the combined membership of the Socialist League, the ILP and the CPGB.

Against this backdrop of organisational decline, the Groves group further criticised the Socialist League leadership. On 25 April Allighan, Arthur Bennett – the organising Secretary of the Youth Committee – and Barber wrote to the branches on behalf of the special ad hoc committee protesting strongly about the National Council's decision. They argued that this meant the 'one organisation of the Socialist left within the Labour movement is to be destroyed'. They accused the League leaders of 'disastrously deceiving' the special conference by saying that they would not be expelled from the party over the Unity Campaign. And they called for the League to be reconstituted 'with its original policy and purpose'.[167] Provocatively, Campbell had already produced an article for the *New Leader*, which not only called on Socialist Leaguers to stand firm until the Labour party conference in October but also – in the event of the rejection of the Unity Campaign at the conference – advocated the creation of a 'new Revolutionary party', possibly including the CPGB, but centred around a 'closer affiliation between the ILP and the Socialist League'.[168] At the same time the *New Leader* revealed that Campbell had written for the paper under a pseudonym in October 1936 when he had similarly broached the idea of a 'new socialist party' comprising the Socialist League, the ILP, and the constituency parties but crucially not the CPGB.[169]

The supporters of Groves also began to argue that Cripps had been put under pressure from the CPGB to favour dissolution of the League. At a meeting of the Hendon branch of the Socialist League Campbell apparently made a ferocious attack on Cripps to this end. Cripps was enraged. He wrote to Campbell saying that he would 'no doubt appreciate that this statement is slanderous and as such would entitle me to bring an action against you'. Cripps did not intend to press the matter at the present time but he frankly told Campbell: 'I must warn you that you must carry on your arguments without making false statements and that you must not repeat gossip given you by members of the National Council'.[170] Cripps clearly had Groves in mind. Groves later recorded his belief 'that the proposal for the dissolution of the SL had originated with the CP, and [had been] pressed by that organisation as being in the best interests of the unity campaign'. Groves himself did not actually know what had been said at the Unity Campaign Committee. However, his dislike of the CPGB inclined him to think that it 'wanted to be rid of the SL, with its dangerous potential as a centre for revolutionary socialist ideas'.[171] In any case, Campbell was prepared to show the letter to his London Socialist League colleagues – perhaps in an attempt to build further opposition to Cripps.[172]

Despite these tensions the Socialist League, the ILP and the CPGB made significant efforts to present a façade of unity for May Day. During the high-profile demonstrations in Hyde Park, Maxton spoke alongside Pollitt and Strauss. Meanwhile Brockway addressed the same audience as J. R. Campbell, one of the CPGB representatives on the Unity Campaign Committee, and Groves appeared on the platform with the Communist Dave Springhall.[173] However, behind the scenes there was a struggle over whether the platform should call for a popular or united front. The ILP and the CPGB were clearly at odds, with the *New Leader* describing the original resolution – which the ILP succeeded in amending slightly – as 'worded carefully to avoid a class character' and as 'so moderate and respectable that any Liberal could speak to it and vote for it'.[174] Furthermore, on May Day itself tensions were also apparent in the way that the ILP contingent carried POUM placards.[175]

XI

At the Socialist League annual conference on 15 May 1937, Cripps introduced the National Council's resolution recommending dissolution. The resolution protested about the NEC's decision to disaffiliate the Socialist League and to make membership of the League incompatible with that of the Labour party. It argued that many other members of the Labour party had worked with the CPGB on a range of issues 'without any such disciplinary measures'. The resolution expressed the hope that the Labour party annual conference would reverse the NEC's decision. However, in the meantime it stated that the Socialist League conference was 'determined to do its utmost to prevent any splits or breakaways from the Labour move-ment' and 'prepared to sacrifice its own organisation rather than allow its continued separate existence to be made an excuse for further disunity in the ranks of the workers'. The resolution committed the Socialist League 'to dissolve and to terminate all membership in the Socialist League as from

May 31st 1937, so as to obviate the friction and difficulties within local
Labour parties and Trade Unions which would otherwise be created . . .
during the period intervening before the next annual party conference'. The
resolution asked 'the National Council to take all necessary steps . . . to wind
up the Socialist League' and empowered its members 'to reconstitute the
Socialist League if in their opinion such a course becomes possible as a result
of any decision arrived at by the annual party conference'.[176]

In the private setting of the conference, a passionate debate now ensued.
In all, the debates over the future of the Socialist League lasted 12 hours.[177]
Mellor had only reluctantly accepted the dissolution of the League and so it
was Cripps who spoke most strongly on behalf of the National Council's
resolution. Cripps was most critical of the Groves line of continuing the
Socialist League but abandoning the Unity Campaign. He argued that 'in
the light of existing circumstances national and international' such a League
would be 'meaningless and would merely introduce another dissentient
element into the already too disunited working-class movement'. Cripps's
most damning criticism of Groves and his followers was that their persistent
opposition to the Unity Campaign had enabled the NEC to take such strong
disciplinary action. He claimed that 'the lack of uniformity and the activities
of some of the individual members of the League in continuing to oppose
the Unity Campaign has played a part in encouraging the Labour party
Executive to act as it has done' and move beyond merely disaffiliating the
Socialist League.[178]

Having sharply dismissed the Groves line, Cripps argued that the two
remaining options before the conference were to continue with the Socialist
League 'as an integral part of the Unity Campaign' or to dissolve the Socialist
League and for individual members then to play a full part in the Unity
Campaign. Cripps, however, was clear that continuing the League would
'allow the *Daily Herald* and the rest of the capitalist press to give the
impression that we are splitters, or are encouraging a breakaway from the
movement'. Just as a similar course had left the ILP isolated, Cripps argued
that the Socialist League would 'forfeit all the sympathy and support for our
cause in the Labour movement'. He asserted that it would 'give the
appearance of walking out of the party to preserve our own little
organisation'. Cripps suggested that, to an extent, continuing the League
was futile. He said that the League would soon 'disintegrate' because there
were 'many members of the League who, faced with the choice between the
League and continued Labour party membership (even with the danger of
exclusion because of their unity campaign activities) . . . would undoubtedly
chose the latter'. Cripps now powerfully stressed that he himself could 'not
in the present circumstances or any like them be a member of any political

body outside the Labour party'. If he was personally expelled from the
Labour party, he planned to 'remain an independent' and not be 'a member
of any other political party . . . and this would preclude . . . continued
membership of a Socialist League that was outside the Labour Party'.[179]

Cripps also took the opportunity to dismiss the possibility of the Socialist
League remaining in existence until after the Labour party conference – the
compromise initially endorsed by the National Council. He argued that
before October in 'many Labour parties disciplinary action may have been
taken; the mind of the movement will be turned away from the true issue of
a militant united working-class party to an issue of an organisational
character in which we shall be widely figured as a second ILP'.[180]

Cripps then made the case strongly for the immediate dissolution of the
Socialist League so that the challenge could 'be made by countless
individuals upon the basis of their right to appear with CPers and ILPers and
urge unity within the Labour movement'.[181] Cripps had information from
Barker that on the Unity Campaign the 'Bristol East LP as a whole might
make a stand and that other divisions might follow suit'.[182] He also believed
that in Manchester the local Labour party was '100% for unity'.[183] With
these considerations in mind, Cripps argued that this would 'be a much
broader basis of challenge than that which could be made by the SL alone'
since the Left as a whole was 'very much greater in numbers than the
membership of the League'. In this context, he insisted that dissolving the
Socialist League would thwart the NEC and that the Unity Campaign would
not suffer 'in the slightest' as a result. On the contrary, he argued that if the
Socialist League members allowed themselves to be expelled from the party
it would 'create great difficulties . . . for the thousands of Labour party and
TU members connected with that campaign who are not Socialist Leaguers'.
Above all, Cripps contended that it would be 'far better for us all to fight to
stay in the party on the same basis and not to embarrass our case by
introducing the question of rival organisations'.[184]

Groves now spoke strongly against the National Council resolution. His
own views had been dismissed by the National Council at its meeting on 18
April. Nevertheless, Groves's branch – Balham and Tooting – put forward
an amendment embodying his objections. Its central demand was to
'reconstitute the Socialist League as a revolutionary socialist organisation
within the Labour party by withdrawing from the existing Unity Agreement
of the ILP or CP'; it supported a united front in principle but not in this
particular manifestation. The resolution went on to repeat the claim that
'leading members of the National Council of the League secured a bare
majority at the special conference for the Unity Agreement only by denying
that this would necessarily lead to disaffiliation and individual expulsions'.

It attacked the way that 'many of those who led the League into the Unity Agreement and its present situation are now in favour of dissolving the League in order to themselves remain within the Labour party'. The crux of the position put forward by the Groves group, however, was that the Communist party were 'using the Unity Movement to secure a Popular Front Movement and a Popular Front foreign policy'.[185]

Despite the heated debate, the Groves group were outnumbered by five to one: its amendment was rejected by 51 to 10 and the National Council's resolution endorsed by the same majority.[186] Many of those present seemingly agreed with Betts who spoke for dissolution arguing that it was 'not a funeral' but 'a conscious political tactic'.[187] Brailsford had been in Spain for the past six months and now returned to Britain in time to attend the Socialist League conference. He was opposed to the dissolution of the League, arguing that it would be 'a political blunder of the first magnitude'.[188] However, Brailsford was clearly out of touch with recent developments as the delegates recognised.

Immediately after the conference the Socialist League began to wind up its affairs. A final Emergency National Council met before the League's decision was announced to the press. An Executive Committee meeting was then planned for 24 May to oversee the final payment of the League staff and to relinquish control of its offices at 3 Victoria Street,[189] while Mitchison – as liquidator – contacted the branches and asked them to settle their accounts.[190] Despite the positive gloss that Cripps and others, such as Betts, had tried to put on the situation, with hindsight the Socialist League's forced dissolution was undoubtedly a major blow. For the remainder of the 1930s the Labour left would take a different – and markedly less cohesive – form.

7

THE FINAL SHATTERING OF UNITY

May 1937 to March 1938

After the Socialist League disbanded on 1 June 1937, Cripps and Mellor tried to maintain the organised Labour left in some form. Initially, they sought to use the Unity Campaign Committee, but when the NEC prohibited their involvement with that organisation, they shifted their attention to the Constituency Parties Movement. However, once they came up against the determined opposition of Greene, their plans to use the constituency parties as a vehicle of the left were also thwarted. By the end of the Labour party conference in October 1937 the forces of the Labour left were even more loosely grouped than in the summer. Meanwhile, the ILP's relationship with the CPGB completely broke down as the ILP increasingly linked its criticism of events in Spain with those in the Soviet Union and developed further its biting analysis of the Stalin dictatorship. Left-wing unity fractured in other ways too. Brailsford – one of the Labour left's most consistent critics of the Stalinist purges in the Soviet Union – refused to denounce the Communist tactics in Spain and so came under attack from the ILP. Furthermore, in early 1938 the influential Laski broke ranks with others on the Labour left, and particularly those in the Left Book Club, by publicly criticising the Soviet Union for the first time.

I

The NEC responded quickly to the Socialist League conference's decision to dissolve. On 26 May 1937 it called on all Labour party members to 'refrain from any further joint activities with the Communist party and the ILP'.[1] This meant that if former members of the Socialist League continued as individuals to be involved with the Unity Campaign and to speak on the same platforms as Communists and ILPers they would be liable for expulsion. A few days later the NEC actually threatened to discipline Strauss who was scheduled to appear with Pollitt and Maxton at Hull on 6 June.[2] The NEC's action had been anticipated and it seems that the initial response of Cripps, Mellor and Strauss himself was to continue with the Unity Campaign as they had planned.[3] Elvin also favoured this course though he was not consulted.[4] However, when the matter was discussed at two meetings of the Unity Campaign Committee on 1 and 5 June, it was decided that the campaign would 'take a new form' in the face of the NEC's attempt 'to isolate the supporters of Unity, before the October conference, from the great body of the party and the trade unions'. It was agreed that the Unity Campaign Committee itself would disband and that instead its Labour supporters would form a Labour Unity Committee, while the CPGB and the ILP worked 'wholeheartedly for unity in their own spheres'.[5]

This decision obviously constituted a complete *volte-face* on the part of the former leaders of the Socialist League, overturning the decision made at their conference less than three weeks previously. Indeed, as recently as 21 May, Cripps had continued to insist that the central justification for the difficult decision to dissolve the League was the continuation of the more important Unity Campaign. In *Tribune* he had stated that:

> Organisations like the Socialist League are implements to be used by bodies of persons who are out to attain specific objectives, and immediately their use becomes inappropriate in the circumstances of the time they should be laid aside and some fresh implement taken up which can be used more effectively. The effective implement of the moment is without doubt the Unity Campaign . . . I regard the Unity Campaign and all it means and stands for as the one real hope for the working-class movement of this country today . . . It was because I wanted the challenge to come on this basis that I was in favour of winding up the Socialist League.[6]

There were a number of reasons why the former Socialist League leaders were willing to cede to NEC pressure and not challenge its decision by continuing the Unity Campaign in its original form. Firstly, the CPGB was keen for the existing Unity Campaign Committee to disband.[7] In his concluding speech at the CPGB annual congress on 31 May 1937, Pollitt openly suggested that it was desirable for the Unity Campaign to continue in such a way that no disciplinary action could be taken by the Labour party.[8] Furthermore, at the meeting of the Unity Campaign Committee on 1 June, it was the CPGB representatives who proposed that the committee should be reconstituted to comprise only the Labour party advocates of unity.[9] The CPGB representatives were 'very insistent' on this course and managed to win the support of Mitchison and Laski.[10] The nominal reason for the CPGB's stance was that continuing the campaign in its current form would further divide the Labour party and 'prejudice any chances of a successful victory for unity' at the Labour party conference.[11] However, it appears likely that, above all, the CPGB was reluctant to antagonise the NEC because one of its longer-term objectives was to affiliate to the Labour party.

Secondly, 'the increasing friction over Spain between the ILP and CP did not hold out very good prospects'.[12] Throughout May the ILP and the CPGB had attacked each other with growing ferocity as the intensity of the struggle within the Republican side in Spain increased with violent clashes between Communists, anarchists and POUM supporters which resulted in hundreds of casualties. This bitter in-fighting culminated in the POUM being declared illegal in June and its leaders being imprisoned. In the meantime the British Communist press had argued repeatedly that the POUM was responsible for the rising which had begun on 3 May.[13] The ILP, however, had vehemently taken the line officially adopted by the POUM: that it associated itself with the workers only once they had already taken to the streets.[14] McNair, who was actually in Barcelona with Orwell at this point, gave strong endorsement to this view.[15] The ILP also took its analysis further, connecting it to its earlier criticisms of Soviet foreign policy. It now argued that Communist influence was being 'exerted everywhere against revolution' because it was so desperate to have Britain and France as allies against Nazi Germany.[16] For this reason Brockway argued that the 'ferocious attacks of the Communists upon POUM and the ILP are an attempt to direct away attention from the anti-working class and counter-revolutionary policy of the Communist party in Spain'.[17] Altogether this meant that Maxton was unwilling to see Strauss expelled for what he regarded as a lost cause and was ready to see the Unity Campaign move on to a new footing.[18]

Thirdly, the momentum of the Unity Campaign had already begun to falter. For instance, a document produced by Aplin on 24 May for the Unity Campaign Committee revealed that the campaign had a cash deficit of nearly £250 and proposed a range of economies including a total cessation of grants to local committees and more rigid control over publicity expenditure.[19] Similarly, Unity meetings were increasingly less well attended. Rogers told Cripps about a meeting held in Bristol in early June for which '1,000 circulars were sent out but there were only 50 people in attendance', suggesting that 'many people signed the cards without accepting any responsibility'.[20]

Finally, it seems that a particularly important factor in persuading Cripps to support a change in the form of the Unity Campaign was information that rank and file opinion favoured this course in the light of the NEC's decision. Significantly, Cripps had received this information before attending the Unity Campaign Committee meeting on 1 June. Just as in April when they had told him that local feeling was inclined towards the dissolution of the Socialist League, Barker and Rogers now informed Cripps that the final branch meeting of the Bristol Socialist League on 30 May had voted by 16 votes to 7 to withdraw from the Bristol Unity Committee and to establish a Labour Unity Committee without the Communists and the ILP. Barker had been appointed secretary of the new Bristol Labour Unity Committee and the chairman of the soon to be disbanded Bristol Socialist League, Councillor Watson-Allan, had given his firm approval. Cripps was told that even before the NEC had made its latest announcement, there had been a strong local feeling that continuing with the Unity Campaign was 'causing a big cleavage in the party with consequent disruption . . . within the wards and divisions or on the city council'. He was also made aware of the view held by some of the rank and file that 'the brunt of the work had fallen upon the SL and Labour party members already active in the Movement [and] that the other two organisations had not pulled their weight'. Undoubtedly aware that her information about Bristol had influenced Cripps in the past, Barker now explicitly suggested the formation of 'Labour Unity Groups' on a nationwide scale.[21]

II

The Unity Campaign Committee's decision to disband, even though its former constituent parties continued to work separately for a united front, made it appear that the Unity Campaign had been abandoned.[22] In doing so, it gave impetus to the efforts of Groves and his followers who had been contemplating their next move since the Socialist League annual conference. Arguing that the Socialist League had been dissolved for the sake of the Unity Campaign which had now itself been 'officially terminated by its sponsors', they formed the Socialist Left Federation in early June 1937. The two most prominent members were Groves and Barber, with McCarthy employed as secretary. In certain respects, the federation aimed to emulate the Socialist League. It described itself as an 'organisation of militant socialists within the Labour party' strongly opposed to 'class collaboration', the popular front and capitalist rearmament and advocating an alliance with the Soviet Union. It was, however, distinctly Groves's organisation and accordingly critical of the CPGB.[23] At this point the ILP publicly announced how it had come 'frankly [to] regret the changed form of the campaign' and that it was now clear that – so far as the Socialist League was concerned –

'there was no need for its dissolution'.[24] From this perspective the ILP gave strong support to the Socialist Left Federation.[25]

Meanwhile the Unity Campaign continued in its new form with its old aim of winning support at the Labour party conference. Cripps and Strauss launched the new Labour Unity Committee at the Hull meeting on 6 June, at which Strauss had been due to share a platform with Pollitt and Maxton.[26] The new committee met for the first time on 10 June at the House of Commons, and elected Cripps as chairman, Strauss as treasurer, Mellor as honorary secretary and Robert Entwhistle as secretary.[27] In its first two months the Labour Unity Committee organised a number of conferences and rallies across the country. In late June a special conference for Labour women delegates was held at which Betts 'stated the case for unity and for the decision to conduct the campaign by means of Labour councillors'.[28] Cripps echoed similar sentiments when he spoke at a demonstration of 500 people in Cardiff on 19 June.[29] At Newcastle on 4 July a meeting addressed by Cripps, Mellor and Laski was attended by 2,000 people and raised £36.[30] And on Unity Sunday – 18 July – there were further meetings in Brighton, Leeds, Stockton-on-Tees and Hackney.[31]

Nevertheless, developments in the Soviet Union further hindered the prospects for a successful unity campaign of any sort. Throughout 1937 the purges in the Soviet Union had continued. There were no further Show Trials but many thousands of people were arbitrarily arrested and sentenced either to substantial periods of imprisonment or to death. Furthermore, a whole new dimension was added to the problem in June 1937 when it emerged that the purges had been extended to the highest ranks of the Red Army: eight generals, who were accused of passing information to the Nazis, were executed after being tried in secret. A lack of information about the charges meant that these trials did not gain as much attention as the more sensational Show Trials. Nevertheless, they prompted the ILP to repeat the argument it had made the previous year. It contended that the situation in the Soviet Union was dire, irrespective of whether 'the governing ranks of the Soviet Union are honeycombed with treason and moral depravity; or . . . Stalin is a despot who has destroyed every man of distinction and independence around him by an incredible "frame-up" in order to rule the rest of his party by terror'. The *New Leader* was clear that it was impossible to know 'because in Russia there is neither honest justice nor free discussion'.[32] Once again, the ILP was careful that its anti-Stalinist position should not be considered Trotskyist, a term which it rightly argued that the Communists 'applied indiscriminately'.[33] For example, Brockway was keen to disassociate himself from the report of the American Commission for the Defence of Trotsky in May 1937, arguing that it was biased in favour of

Trotsky – not least because even the organisation's title did not give the impression of impartiality.[34]

Importantly, the ILP also made the connection between the events in the Soviet Union and those in Spain more explicit than ever before. In early July the *New Leader* stressed that so far as the 300 arrested members of the POUM were concerned, it was 'no accident that the Spanish Communist Party press – like the Russian press in relation to the purge in the Soviet Union – has already prejudged the issue, has found the arrested men and women guilty of being agents of fascism and has demanded the death penalty'.[35] The ILP called on every section of the working class to protest at the Spanish Embassy in London about the persecution of the POUM.[36] Brockway himself visited Spain at this point and was in close contact with McNair and Orwell, who had both established contact with the new underground POUM executive.[37] Significantly, on his return Brockway took pains to introduce a distinction between the Communists and the rest of the Spanish government, arguing that the suppression of the POUM was the 'work of the Communist-controlled police force' and that he was 'able to say definitely that the arrests of the POUM leaders in Barcelona took place against the wishes of all the non-Communist members of the Catalan Government in office'.[38] Brockway also argued that – based on his own experiences – members of the International Brigade were 'becoming disillusioned by the changing character of the struggle in Spain'.[39] Significantly, Brockway recalled in his autobiography that his visit to Spain at this crucial time enabled him 'to understand as never before the Moscow technique of dealing with political prisoners'.[40]

At its meeting on 17 July the ILP Executive Committee accepted the basis of a detailed report by Brockway and formalised the party's stance on the POUM. Its official policy was now to ask that 'those who have been imprisoned shall be freed and that the POUM shall be restored to legality'. It also endorsed the proposal made by the International Bureau that an 'International Commission of representative socialists should go to Spain to encourage the widest agreement between all sections of the working class anti-fascist forces and to inquire into the charges made against the POUM and to secure a fair trial for the prisoners'.[41] By the end of July the ILP MPs (Maxton, Stephen, McGovern and Buchanan) had even decided to cable directly to Juan Negrin, the prime minister of the Spanish government in Valencia, to ask for the POUM prisoners to be released.[42] Furthermore, the International Bureau – meeting at the ILP summer school in the second week of August – also responded to reports of the death of Andres Nin, the POUM General Secretary and former Minister for Justice in the Catalan government, by deciding to send an immediate delegation, which included

Maxton, to Spain.[43] Significantly, Maxton's report of his activities there repeated the distinction made earlier by Brockway between the Communist party and the Spanish government, arguing that the latter wanted to see a 'fair trial' of the prisoners.[44] This inevitably worsened the ILP's relations with the CPGB. In early August the Politburo decided that the *Daily Worker* should cease to advertise any ILP activities.[45] At the same time Pollitt was privately describing the ILP as nothing less than 'an enemy of the Party'.[46]

Interestingly, other left-wing individuals were far more reluctant than the ILP to forge a link between Soviet actions in Spain and those in Moscow, further undermining the appearance of unity at this juncture. Famously, Kingsley Martin, who was at times as critical of the Russian purges as the ILP, refused to publish articles sent to him from Spain by Orwell which were sharply critical of the Communists.[47] In his autobiography Martin explained that he simply saw a distinction between events in Spain and the Soviet Union. He considered that 'Stalin did not imagine Spain as anything but Spanish and his idea was to keep the war going as long as possible'. Martin also apparently thought 'that whatever else was true the war would certainly be lost if its direction fell into the hands of the Anarchists'. While retrospectively conceding that he underestimated the scale of Communist atrocities in Spain, at the time he considered it was inevitable that the Spanish government gave the Communists 'too much power because no country except the Soviet Union was aiding the Republican cause'.[48] Amid the rise of fascism, the realities of international power politics had convinced Martin that it might be necessary to trust the National government to use League of Nations sanctions against Italy in 1935. Now the same underlying considerations inclined him to take a benevolent view of Soviet tactics in Spain.

Brailsford took a similar stance to Martin, just as he did over sanctions. Having visited Spain between January and May 1937, Brailsford was broadly supportive of the Communist position there. Perhaps as an expert on foreign affairs, he was even more aware than Martin of the *realpolitik* which gave the Communists a great influence over the Republican side.[49] In any case, it was completely accurate that, as Pollitt told the CPGB Central Committee meeting on 16 January 1937, Brailsford was 'working exceedingly well with the party on the Spanish campaign'.[50] Indeed, Brockway was sharply critical of Brailsford's position on Spain.[51] Furthermore, by the end of the year Brailsford was engaged in a detailed correspondence with Orwell over his assertion that during the May uprising the POUM had attacked the Spanish government with ammunition stolen from government arsenals.[52] At the same time, however, Brailsford continued to be outspoken in his criticism of the Soviet purges.[53] By now his relationship with the Soviet Ambassador,

Maisky, had completely broken down. According to Beatrice Webb's diary the Maiskys were 'much hurt by Brailsford's defection', having 'been very intimate with him'.[54] Moreover, in July 1937 Brailsford became embroiled in a heated dispute with Dutt. Ostensibly the debate was over Brailsford's acceptance of the authenticity of a memorandum printed in the *News Chronicle*, which was reputedly written by Stalin to explain the charges levelled at the Red Army generals but which had been disowned by the Soviet Union. However, what was really at stake in the debate, which was played out in the pages of the *New Statesman* with Martin supporting Brailsford, was Brailsford's views of the Soviet regime. It provided an opportunity, once again, for him to voice his doubts about the 'reliability of Soviet justice in political affairs', and to condemn the Stalinist regime as a 'terror based on lies'.[55]

Against this inauspicious background it was little surprise that the Labour Unity Committee was soon in financial difficulties. Cripps donated £50 on 21 July but the funds remained slightly overdrawn. As early as July the committee had considered the possibility of winding itself up after the party conference given the precarious state of its finances.[56] And on 23 August Entwhistle had to ask Cripps for an advance of £150.[57] Moreover, wider feeling within the Labour movement was now turning more noticeably against the united front. By the end of July conferences of the National Union of Railwaymen (NUR), the TGWU and the MFGB, which collectively held enough votes to carry both the TUC meeting and the Labour party conference, had rejected resolutions calling for a united front with the Communists and the ILP.[58] The impact of the purges also inhibited the Left's ability to push for a firmer stance on Spain – one of the core demands of the united front. Pollitt brought out this point in a private letter to Robin Page Arnot, the CPGB representative in Moscow, in October 1937:

> one of the obstacles in getting leading labour people interested in Spain, is the argument, which I understand has been very extensively used in all circles, of the trials and executions in the Soviet Union. This question has played a very big part here and comes up every day. In spite of all the arguments which we are able to bring against them we have not been able to do much, and the position is exceptionally difficult.[59]

III

The Socialist League leaders had, since October 1936, sought to use the constituency parties' movement as an important ally in their struggle against

the NEC and the TUC General Council. However, with the demise of the
Socialist League and the Unity Campaign Committee forced to change its
tactics, Cripps and Mellor's attempts from June 1937 to make the
constituency movement part of the Labour left represented a new departure.
On the face of it, this was an attractive strategy for Cripps and Mellor as the
constituency movement had been rapidly expanding throughout the first six
months of 1937. In February and March regional committees had been set
up in Yorkshire, East Anglia, the Midlands, the North West and the West
Country. The Provisional Committee became the committee of a new
National Constituency Parties' Association with a head office run by Greene
in London.[60] Moreover, it looked increasingly likely that the constituency
parties' demands made at the Labour party conference in 1936 for changes
to the constitution of the Labour party, which Dalton had undertaken to
investigate, would be met. Following local investigations, a meeting of the
NEC's Organisation Sub-committee in early June had agreed to sponsor the
constituency parties demands to elect their own representatives on to the
NEC (instead of having the constituency party places elected by the whole
Labour party conference consisting mainly of affiliated trade-union votes), to
allow proxy voting by constituency parties not represented at conference,
and to increase the local parties' representation on the NEC from five to
seven.[61] The NEC itself endorsed these demands later in June.[62]

However, there had always been uneasiness between the leaders of the
Socialist League and Greene, and this made it very difficult for Cripps and
Mellor. Greene had resigned from the board of *Tribune* on 8 March 1937.
Now that Cripps and Mellor began to take more interest in the constituency
parties' movement this ill feeling increased. Greene wrote frankly to Cripps
saying:

> It appears that since the Socialist League has been dissolved some
> of its members believe that the associations can be made to serve
> the same purpose. If this idea is acted upon immense damage will
> be done to our constituency organisations. Under no circum-
> stances must the constituency and local party organisations or
> the Associations be allowed to become dominated by any group
> tied to a specific policy other than that of the Labour party
> nationally.[63]

Greene was very concerned that 'in certain constituencies a concerted effort
is being made to remove from positions of influence those who are opposed
to the United Front proposals'.[64] His particular grievance was that in
Manchester, Taylor – a long-standing figure in the local Labour party who

did not support the Unity Campaign – had not been chosen as the constituency parties' representative for the Labour party conference and instead a candidate favoured by the members of the Manchester Labour Unity Committee had been selected. However, Greene considered that this was only part of a broader trend because there was 'evidence of very similar activities in other widely separated parts of the country'.[65]

A conference of the constituency parties was planned for 3 October 1937 – just before the Labour party conference. A few days beforehand Greene had told Cripps he was going to raise the question of Cripps's chairmanship of the Committee of Constituency Labour Parties because there were 'many important considerations involved as to the connection of the committee with the Unity Campaign'.[66] In an attempt to prevent an attack on his leadership, therefore, Cripps told the conference frankly at the outset that 'the committee had no concern with the Unity Campaign'.[67] By the time of the Labour party conference, Greene's persistent opposition had clearly thwarted Cripps and Mellor in their plans to convert the constituency parties' movement into the organ of the Labour left.

IV

By this point the tension between the former leaders of the Socialist League and the NEC had also increased further. In late August the NEC, in conjunction with the Conference Arrangements Committee, decided to apply the three-year rule to the 43 resolutions submitted calling for a united front so that they could only be discussed by references back to the NEC annual report. This was obviously a tactic to limit the amount of discussion on the issues as Laski recognised in an article in *Tribune* that was sharply critical of the NEC.[68] Furthermore, on 4 September 1937 Cripps spoke strongly against the NEC's persecution of the supporters of Unity to a crowd of 2,000 at Manchester.[69] Two days later he spoke at a Labour Unity Committee meeting in Norwich – where the TUC itself was currently meeting.[70] At the same time the NEC decided to reject the parliamentary candidature of Mellor – this time for Stockport – on account of his support for the Unity Campaign. As soon as he heard the news Cripps publicly labelled this as an act of 'victimisation', asking why such action was not also being taken against himself, Laski and Strauss. Cripps threatened to withdraw from the on-going speaking campaign to boost Labour party membership but the NEC still refused to alter its decision.[71] Cripps now withdrew his services and Laski, Strauss and Horrabin followed suit.[72]

At the Labour party conference itself Cripps moved references back to the sections of the NEC report explaining its rejection of the united front and justifying its treatment of the Socialist League. He argued that, with the deteriorating world situation, 'the fundamental test of antagonism . . . is class, and that association with working-class parties and persons is right and necessary, whereas association with capitalist parties or persons is fundamentally wrong, and is fraught with dangers to the party'. He also drew attention to what he called the 'selective victimisation' of Mellor. However, it was clear that Cripps no longer thought it possible to win support from the Labour movement for the united front. His request was the more limited one to 'ask conference to preserve to the members of the party the full right to proclaim publicly their views on all particular issues'.[73]

Laski seconded Cripps's references back. He stressed that 'if the Labour movement of this country is to preserve its integrity and to maintain its freedom, unity of the working-class is the fundamental condition of its achievement'. He stated frankly that if he had 'to chose between appearing on a platform in the pursuance of our common aim with Mr Harry Pollitt or with Mr Winston Churchill, I have no doubt at all that my proper place is with Mr Harry Pollitt'. However, like Cripps, Laski did not seek to change the conference's opinion on the united front. He said that he accepted that the 'party has decided, through its Executive, that association in this campaign with members of the Communist party is outside the terms of its constitution'. He simply argued: 'I ask from this conference the right on the public platform and in the press, where I disagree with the views of the Executive, to take all the steps that are open to me as a member of the party to persuade my fellow members that majorities are not always in the right'.[74] Finally, Strauss – with his own demotion on the LCC by Morrison in mind – advocated unity. He argued that the NEC had not acted 'fairly' since it had failed to take any action against co-operation with Communists on the hunger marches or over Spain and had not said anything to those who shared platforms with Churchill. In keeping with the more limited lines of attack followed by Cripps and Laski, Strauss concentrated on the treatment of those who supported the united front rather than on the issues themselves.[75]

Morrison replied for the NEC. He argued that the united front with the CPGB would not improve Labour's electoral prospects: it would simply associate the Labour party with 'every one of the absurd announcements that they cannot help making from time to time'. He argued that for the CPGB to talk of unity was absurd since they were opposed to Trotsky and to the POUM. Morrison's central argument was that the purpose of the united front was 'to capture the party for the Communist party'. Referring to Cripps and the other former Socialist Leaguers, he said that 'they ought not to act as the agents and instruments of people who are not interested in the welfare and prosperity of this party and its unity, but want to make mischief'. He argued that this was why association with Communists was a very different issue to association with other political parties.[76] The debate on the united front was not a dramatic one. As Cripps himself had recognised in September, the outcome was 'a foregone conclusion'.[77] The conference overwhelmingly rejected both references back – the one concerning the Socialist League by 1,730,000 to 373,000, and the one about the united front by 2,116,000 to 331,000.[78] Although Cripps, Laski and Strauss had only asked for their views to be tolerated, this was a smaller number than had voted for the united front in the previous year. Even *Tribune* conceded that this was a 'heavy defeat' for unity.[79]

On the other hand, most of the constituency parties' reforms were endorsed. Admittedly, the NEC abandoned the proposal for proxy voting and this was, in turn, rejected. At the same time, however, the proposal to increase the size of the NEC from 23 to 25 was narrowly endorsed. More important still, substantial majorities accepted the proposals for both direct and separate election to the NEC and to increase the number of constituency party seats from five to seven. Bevin had wanted the reforms only to come into operation after the next Labour party conference, which was scheduled for May 1939.[80] Yet the conference voted that the reforms should come into place immediately, and Cripps, Laski and Pritt were promptly elected as three of the constituency party delegates to the NEC.[81]

Despite appearances, however, the events at the party conference actually dispelled the notion of any explicit association between the Unity Campaign and the Constituency Parties' Movement. In his speech at the conference Greene took pains to deny that the constituency parties had any connection with left-wing policies. He stressed frankly that if 'there is any idea that the constituency party organisation that has sprung up is in any way connected with policy proposals, that idea is completely and absolutely wrong'.[82] On closer examination, it was also apparent that the relationship between Cripps, Laski and Pritt and the constituency parties was ambiguous. A significant number of the constituency delegates who voted them on to the NEC also voted against the Unity Campaign and the Socialist League – suggesting that while they were personally popular, their policies not always were. The minority vote for the reference back of the NEC's report on the Socialist League was 373,000, which included union votes, and the potential constituency party vote was 502,000. The minority of 331,000 in the united front vote included one large union, the NUDAW with 137,000 votes, three smaller ones – the Shop Assistants with 40,000 votes, the Dyers, Bleachers and Textile Workers with 39,000 votes and the Furnishing Trades Association with 2000 votes – as well as part of the Woodworkers' vote of about 21,000. This made a total union vote of 234,000 and so the total constituency party vote for the Unity Campaign must only have been about 92,000 out of a possible 502,000.[83] It was altogether appropriate, therefore, that when the Constituency Parties conference re-adjourned on 5 October Cripps resigned as chairman.[84] By later the same month, Cripps was content to offer the services of *Tribune* simply as 'a forum for . . . discussion and exchange of views' by the constituency parties.[85]

V

In the aftermath of the Labour party conference, it became apparent that the organised Labour left in the form of the Socialist League had completely disintegrated. The NEC and the TUC General Council had clearly defeated the Socialist League over the attitude that should be taken towards National government rearmament. The party conference had endorsed *International Policy and Defence* which embodied the views of Dalton, Bevin and Citrine that collective security must be underpinned by rearmament – even under the National government. This meant that the conference had approved the PLP's decision in July to abstain on, instead of voting against, the arms estimates. According to Dalton the Labour left's support for arming the Republicans in Spain had made it more difficult to deny the need for rearmament in Britain.[86] To be sure, the former members of the Socialist League remained opposed to National government rearmament with Bevan, for instance, speaking passionately against its acceptance at the party conference.[87] However, the issue was now closed.

Similarly, the NEC had ensured the conclusive rejection of the united front. On 16 October 1937 the Labour Unity Committee wrote to its local committees asking them to wind up their affairs. The explanation given was that the change in the party constitution 'which has opened up a direct avenue of approach between the constituency parties and the National Executive, affords also an opportunity for the left and the supporters of the Unity Campaign to press upon the party, both at the centre and in the localities, the increasing need for a definite socialist policy in home and international affairs'.[88] The reality was that the Unity Campaign was at an end.

Tribune now operated as the mouthpiece of the Labour left and on the NEC Cripps, Laski, Pritt and Wilkinson (who had been elected in the women's section) worked closely together as a left-wing faction.[89] Moreover, Cripps began to minimise the extent of the differences between himself and the NEC. His donation of £1,000 to the Labour party's campaign fund just after the party conference symbolised this rapprochement.[90] At the same time, *Tribune* strongly endorsed the NEC's formation of a Spain Campaign

Committee which involved Cripps and Wilkinson.[91] It similarly welcomed the Labour party's commitment to reinvigorate the League of Youth, stating that this merited 'a burying of past disputes'.[92] Cripps had, however, already begun to move towards this more conciliatory position in June when he had given the *Immediate Programme* guarded approval, saying that it had 'similarities' to the policies advanced by the Socialist League so that there was 'plenty of room for common agreement even upon that programme'.[93] Significantly, the *Immediate Programme* had been 'carried unanimously' without any left-wing opposition at the party conference.[94] Meanwhile, Groves's Socialist Left Federation, without any high-profile Labour figures to ensure publicity, had become increasingly inactive.

By this point the ILP's attitude towards to the Labour party was also undergoing a substantial change with longer-term implications for the shape of the Left. As tension had increased between the ILP and the CPGB during the summer, the ILP had made increasingly favourable noises about re-affiliation to the Labour party, marking a complete contrast of course with its reluctance over the issue during the Unity Campaign negotiations. Fearing 'isolation from the mass movement of the working class', by the end of July Brockway declared that he was 'prepared to consider any opportunity which arises for closer association with the Labour party so long as the minimum of required freedom is guaranteed'.[95] In his speech at the ILP Summer School in early August, he was even more forthright in expressing his personal view that 'membership of the Labour party would be justified' because the Labour party's federal structure would allow the ILP sufficient freedom to advocate its revolutionary socialist policy. Moreover, clearly viewing re-affiliation as a serious possibility, he laid down a number of conditions: that the ILP remained a distinct unit, that it was able to continue to publish its own literature, to undertake its own propaganda and to voice policy in parliament, and that it retained the right 'to criticise in comradely spirit the official policy or the policy of other sections'. Significantly, Brockway argued that so far as the Communist party was concerned 'the importance of unity is not so urgent because it does not represent the mass movement of the working class'.[96]

One potential difficulty for the ILP was that, with the PLP now abstaining during votes on rearmament, it was effectively at odds with official Labour party policy on the issue. The ILP MPs continued to vote against all rearmament in Parliament, having received the unanimous support of the NAC to do so on 2 August.[97] Summing up the ILP stance, Maxton considered it 'unthinkable at this juncture that we should fail to oppose the creation of a great war machine in this land, which we can never visualise as being used to further the ends of the working class at home or abroad, but which may well be used as an instrument of their continued subjection'.[98] Significantly though, and demonstrating its desire to move closer to the Labour party, the ILP argued that the 'very fact of the Labour leadership's disastrous policy at the present time underlines the necessity for activity by revolutionary socialists within the Trade Union Movement, and ... the Labour Party'.[99]

VI

Throughout the rest of 1937 and into early 1938 a combination of domestic political and international developments brought about a further significant fracturing of the Left. Following the decisive rejection of the united front at the Labour party conference even the façade of association between the CPGB and the ILP was abandoned in early November.[100] This, in turn, unleashed some of the most damning criticisms of the Soviet Union from the ILP. Discussing the Soviet Union's actions in Spain, McGovern argued that he could 'now understand the Trotsky purge in Russia'. His views could not have been clearer when he declared that: 'No honest person who is a member of the Communist party can defend this murderous campaign in Spain. I accuse the Comintern of brutality on a par with Hitler, Mussolini and Franco'.[101] At this stage McNair also dramatically claimed to have 'positive knowledge that Andres Nin ... was murdered by the orders of the head of the Communist police'.[102] Focusing directly on the Soviet Union's domestic regime, both the ILP heavyweights – Brockway and Maxton – now expressed their own disdain for the elections in the Soviet Union which took place under its new constitution in December. Brockway noted that superficially the elections showed 'overwhelming support for the Stalin regime', but added that this had to be balanced against an awareness that 'belonging to the opposition ... involves the danger of imprisonment or death' as the trials and purges had made vividly clear.[103] The same issue of the *New Leader* carried an article by Maxton. In contrast to his intervention at the ILP conference in April in favour of suspending judgement on the purges, he now urged 'those in power in the Soviet Union' to abandon 'their present tactics of ruthless suppression'.[104]

From this point on, the ILP's criticism of the Stalinist regime gained further momentum. In January 1938 the ILP forged a particularly powerful connection in attributing the 'growing evidence of political tyranny' in the Soviet Union directly to the nature of dictatorship itself, asking: 'Is it dictatorship rather than the Communist Party which is responsible'? The ILP recognised the necessity of having 'some form of temporary dictatorship' because of 'the futility of hoping that the change from capitalism to socialism will take place by democratic parliamentary methods'. However, it now argued that it had been naïve to hope that the Soviet Union would develop into 'a socialist community in which equality and liberty were allowed expression', given the clear 'absence of proletarian democracy'.[105] Crucially, the ILP's stance was in line with that of the International Bureau as a whole. Meeting in conference in late February 1938, it 'denounced with indignation the calumnies which have been published against the POUM' as well as criticising 'in the strongest possible language the trials of revolutionary leaders of proved worth and . . . the long series of arrests, imprisonments and executions which have taken place'.[106]

In contrast, most of the Labour left continued to refrain from criticising the Soviet Union, thus maintaining an important distance between itself and the ILP. Betts spent some time in the Soviet Union in autumn 1937 and produced a series of articles about her experiences there, looking specifically at the role of women but also more widely discussing Soviet culture and society.[107] Not only were these articles overwhelmingly positive, but Betts had been explicitly told by Mellor before she left that she was 'not being sent in order to engage in the Trotsky vs Stalin controversy, or to become yet another authority on the inner meanings of Soviet internal and foreign policy'.[108] In November 1937 Mellor then openly stated that he found his 'attitude towards the Russian trials and towards Trotsky more nearly expressed in the Webbs' postscript to their new edition of *Soviet Communism*'.[109] The second edition of their book, first published in 1935 and then famously reprinted without the question mark in the title, had attempted to put a favourable gloss on recent developments.[110] Mellor's public standpoint was, therefore, clear when he added that 'it might not be a bad thing if the wisdom of the Webbs percolated into other quarters'.[111] Meanwhile, *Tribune* juxtaposed its more sympathetic views of the Soviet Union with the more ambivalent attitude of the *Daily Herald*. Complaining about the *Daily Herald*'s coverage of the celebrations for the 20th anniversary of the Russian Revolution, it argued critically that it did not contain 'a single word of appreciation for the immense Socialist reconstruction, not a sign of feeling for the course of the Russian workers, no expression of solidarity with them in their work – just an "objective" description of what had been going on in Red Square, conveyed in a most unfriendly tone'.[112] *Tribune* took the same stance when the *Daily Herald* criticised the lack of democracy in the Soviet Union following the elections there in December. It argued that:

> this Revolution is certainly not completed. It still has to face
> immense difficulties, internal and external. The transformation of
> what was a backward, semi-medieval country into a complete

socialist commonwealth needs the work of decades. It is still growing and expanding in the fields of production and of liberties. The new constitution is another stage in the journey – a journey, the *Daily Herald* would do well to remember, the workers of Great Britain have not even begun.[113]

In fact, *Tribune* was only critical of the Soviet purges on one occasion. In late December it published an open letter to Stalin asking him if he was 'aware that the continued necessity for purges and executions in the Soviet Union is causing friends of Russia in other countries serious concern'. It called for an 'authoritative and calm statement' about the reasons for them and – accepting the verdicts passed in court but mirroring the kinds of questions asked by the *New Statesman* and the *New Leader* – asked whether 'the malaise which has led to the action against former leaders of the Revolution is confined to a small stratum of prominent persons, corrupted in various ways, or whether it goes deeper'.[114]

At the same time the Labour left did not express any criticism about the Soviet Union's role in Spain.[115] Indeed, when Strauss reviewed Brockway's *Worker's Front*, which had been published in January 1938 and was deeply critical of the Communist attack on the POUM, he argued that despite the defeat of the POUM the 'morale of the Spanish workers [was] as excellent as anyone would wish'.[116] The Labour left's stance was underpinned – as it had been since October 1936 – by close co-operation with the CPGB on issues ranging from organising food for the Republican side through to more general attempts to campaign against non-intervention.[117]

Against this background of Labour left quiescence, however, Laski's actions soon caused ripples. Ironically, it was in response to Stalin's claim in January 1938 that the purges were over, that Laski voiced his unhappiness with the Soviet Union publicly for the first time. Writing in the high circulation *Daily Herald*, he welcomed the halt to the purges but argued that the whole incident showed the 'need for far fuller light than we have upon the internal position in the Soviet Union' and the overriding imperative 'not to assume that whatever is done there by its Government is, necessarily, what should have been done'. Laski's view was that 'wholesale errors have been committed', which showed more than ever 'that the duty of criticism is one that no Socialist can abdicate'.[118] Crucially, this was the accusation with which he then powerfully charged the Webbs. Reviewing the second edition of their *Soviet Communism*, Laski asked: 'are not Mr and Mrs Webb disturbed at . . . the wholesale character of the purges that have taken place'?[119]

Now Laski's comments were far from the most stinging criticism of the trials given by the British Left but they were enormously significant. Laski was a figure who was closely linked with the Communists – not least through the Left Book Club – and had long been particularly notable in his support of the Soviet Union.[120] As such the importance of his public criticism was noted at the time.[121] He had, of course, expressed private doubts about the first Show Trials to Pollitt in August 1936. Laski had then continued to feel uneasy about trials and purges throughout 1937, even though he had spoken repeatedly in favour of the Unity Campaign, and indeed as recently as early January had written in *Tribune* that the Soviet Union embraced 'new and richer values which are certain to transform for the better all the basic values of civilisation'.[122] However, he had voiced so many concerns privately to the CPGB that by the end of October 1937 they considered him a 'weak and vacillating force'.[123] By this point he had even reneged on a promise to Dutt to write an article for *Labour Monthly* commemorating the twentieth anniversary of the Russian Revolution. He said he was unwilling to do this while the purges continued, his personal acquaintances were still imprisoned, and his letters to both Stalin and Litvinov about these matters remained unanswered. To the CPGB's consternation, Laski was also becoming increasingly uncomfortable about appearing at Left Book Club rallies.[124]

VII

The final round of Show Trials, which took place in March 1938 in spite of Stalin's earlier statement, exposed the full extent of the Left's fragmentation. This time Nikolai Bukharin – a former leader of the Comintern and editor of *Pravda* – and Genrikh Yagoda – the former head of the GPU, the Soviet secret police – were the most prominent of the accused. The trials themselves were broadly similar to the previous ones but on this occasion the ILP was predictably even more outspoken in its criticism.[125] The ILP MPs Maxton, Buchanan, McGovern and Stephen, along with Brockway as ILP General Secretary, issued a public letter, asking Stalin to end the purges, on 11 March 1938. The letter dismissed the trial as an 'outrageous travesty on the most elementary human rights and a bestial crime against the most fundamental advances towards social decency registered by mankind'. It explicitly blamed the 'system of bureaucracy' for stifling 'democratic expression' and forcing opposition 'to take secret forms', even though it still held that the confessions were simply 'inconceivable'. Above all, the leading ILPers accused the Soviet Union of 'resorting to methods and practices that savour of the Fascist Terror'.[126] Elsewhere Brockway reiterated the same note of uncertainty about the evidence that he – and many others – had expressed in the past, but this did not undermine the intensity of his criticism.[127]

The ILP conference in April 1938 also vented its opposition to the trials and purges much more fully than the previous year. Indeed, the mood of the conference was so against the recent events in the Soviet Union that a resolution defending the Moscow trials only received 2 votes to 111. Brockway moved a NAC resolution which, while once again pledging to defend the Soviet Union against aggression and contending that the 'basis of the workers state remains', condemned 'developments of a reactionary nature' – most notably, of course, the trials and purges – which meant that the 'inner democracy of the C.P. has been destroyed' and 'state bureaucracy was now in control'. Interestingly, the ILP also stressed how 'trades unions have lost their independence' – an argument implicitly inviting comparisons between the Soviet Union and Nazi Germany. Emphasising that thousands of people had been killed, the ILP resolution asserted that it was frankly impossible to 'remain silent on the internal political happenings'. Lee argued that 'where they could not praise they should be silent', but in contrast to the previous year when this had basically been the stance of the conference, her argument was rejected.[128]

Meanwhile Cripps and Mellor, with their close affinities to the CPGB, remained silent, with the limited *Tribune* coverage of the trials making it clear that it was determined 'not to attempt assessment of the evidence or take sides'.[129] Others on the Labour left responded to the trials in the same way they had done to the previous ones.[130] Martin's anti-Stalinist stance was clear when he wrote that 'since open criticism is forbidden, secret opposition must, of course, have developed to serious lengths in Russia, where, as under other dictatorships, it becomes impossible to distinguish between a plot and a difference of opinion'.[131] Brailsford likewise continued to attack the trials.[132] There is also evidence that Laski's concerns were further heightened. Patrick Gordon Walker, who was at the early stages of a long career as a Labour politician, met him as news of the trials was breaking on 1 March 1938 and recorded the incident in his diary:

> Laski was ringing up Brailsford about the new Bukharin trial. Laski very disturbed. Said he could not believe allegations. Getting very worried about Soviet Union. Even said he regretted learning Russian.[133]

In the following weeks Laski added to his analysis of the situation in the Soviet Union. He made clear in *Tribune* that he had no doubt that it was 'definitely a dictatorship' which with sheer 'ruthlessness' had 'suppressed those hostile to its authority'. He was equally adamant that in 'the classic sense of absolute liberalism, freedom does not exist in the Soviet Union' given the inability to express divergent opinions. Nevertheless, unlike others such as Brailsford, Martin and the ILP, Laski could not bring himself to accept the parallels between the Soviet Union and Nazi Germany which had become central to their anti-Stalinist position. Indeed, reiterating a position very similar to that of Brailsford before 1936, Laski still insisted that the Soviet dictatorship 'with all its faults . . . is wholly different in character from that of Mussolini or Hitler'. He argued that the 'atmosphere of contingent war' since 1933 had prevented the Soviet Union from relaxing its standards.[134] He contended that:

> the logic of the Russian system involves, in all normal circum-
> stances, an ability to move forward to the revivification of
> principles of freedom. That is not the case with the fascist
> dictatorships. By their nature they involve the domination of the
> many in the interest of the few; by their nature, also, they involve
> military adventure which means the perpetual strains and stresses
> of nations organised for war.[135]

With the Left more openly divided than ever, the Labour party's response to the trials was incredibly revealing. While the *Daily Herald* gave ample coverage to the events, it only gave the trials editorial space on one occasion when it expressed its dismay, saying that belief 'in the charges, the evidence, the confessions is impossible to the sane mind'.[136] Of course, perhaps little new could be said about the trials by this point. However, a more speculative political explanation is also possible. In the past it had clearly served the aims of the TUC-controlled *Daily Herald* constantly to reiterate its indignation at the events in Russia in order to discredit the left wing and its demands for a closer alliance with the Communists. Now, with the Socialist League disbanded and the ILP looking to rejoin the Labour party, the lack of comment can be taken as signifying a Labour party belief that the most serious threat to its hegemony had been defused. With hindsight, therefore, it seemed that Dalton had indeed been right when he had predicted that the party conference in October 1937 would be seen 'as marking the end, for some time to come, of a number of major controversies, and a clearing of the decks for our campaign for power'.[137] In the remaining 18 months before the outbreak of war, the Left increasingly capitulated to the NEC-TUC grouping.

8

THE APPROACH OF WAR

March 1938 to August 1939

In May 1937 Neville Chamberlain replaced Baldwin as prime minister and, amid further deterioration in the international environment, took appeasement of the fascist dictators to new lengths. Against this background the Labour left increasingly took a pragmatic view of the situation, initiating various popular front proposals, giving conditional support to National government rearmament, and – after September 1938 – advocating an immediate strategic alliance with the Soviet Union in a way that diminished its own public pro-Soviet identity. Meanwhile the ILP remained firmly committed to a working-class war resistance strategy, disdaining the various popular front initiatives but beginning to co-operate closely with the pacifist movement as it campaigned against the National government's plans for conscription. The ILP also experienced an extended internal crisis, which was nominally over Maxton's response to Chamberlain's actions during the Munich crisis, but actually brought up larger questions about the party's relationship with the Parliamentary Group. Crucially, in these years the ILP shed the final vestiges of its pro-Soviet identity. It now developed its anti-Stalinist position to argue that the Soviet Union's actions in Spain had weakened the international anti-fascist cause, and in 1939 even abandoned its long-held commitment to defend the Soviet Union. By summer 1939 it had also become clear that both the Labour left and the ILP had failed to construct serious alternatives to the policies of the NEC-TUC grouping. The Labour left considered it had no choice but to accept the crushing defeat of its latest popular front proposal, and the ILP was attempting to re-affiliate to the Labour party.

I

In late 1937 and early 1938 the Labour left and the ILP shared a similar response to the threat of war between Nazi Germany and the 'capitalist'

and 'imperialist' National government: working-class mass resistance. The
ILP was emphatic in asserting that it was not willing to fight in a war on
behalf of the 'imperialist "Commonwealth" of exploited coloured peoples',[1]
stressing that in the British Empire 'liberties of speech and press and
association are denied as they are in the fascist countries' and drawing
specific reference to the 'brutalities of our ruling class in India'.[2] Similarly,
Tribune spoke of the British 'colonial Empire where the methods of fascism
flourish'.[3] Moreover, the Labour left and the ILP both emphasised that
opposition to rearmament and a central commitment to defending the
Soviet Union were the core components of a broader war resistance
strategy.[4] Indeed, despite his growing concerns about the Soviet regime,
Laski invoked memories of the 'direct action' which the Labour movement
had threatened when the British government looked likely to intervene in
the civil war in Russia against the Bolsheviks and suggested that '[w]hat
the councils of action did in 1920 we may have to again in the near
future'.[5] These demands from the Left for working-class mass resistance
intensified in response to Japanese aggression towards China in early 1938.
When dockworkers in Middlesbrough and London refused to load goods
for Japan, the *New Leader* pointedly asked: 'Why not all of us', lamenting
the inaction of the TUC.[6] By endorsing independent working-class action
of this kind, the ILP was effectively returning to the policy of 'working-
class sanctions' that had caused such bitter dispute in 1935 and 1936.
Now, however, it was seemingly uncontroversial. *Tribune* also made similar
demands.[7] It criticised the decision of the LSI and the International
Federation of Trade Unions (IFTU) on 16 January merely to encourage
working-class parties to urge economic sanctions through moral pressure,
and was strongly supportive of the statement by John Marchbank, of the
NUR, calling for Labour movements to refuse to handle Japanese imports
and exports.[8]

The class-based policy of the ILP could not have been clearer. As McNair
stated: 'We are not for our country right or wrong because we have no
country, but we are for our class right or wrong'.[9] Significantly, this policy
was in tune with the stance taken by the international conference of
Revolutionary Socialist parties and Groups which met in Paris on 19
February 1938. McGovern, Brockway, Aplin, Edwards, McNair and Audrey
Brockway represented the ILP at this meeting which rejected 'social
patriotism' in wartime and stressed the imperative of defending the Soviet
Union.[10] Eden's resignation as foreign secretary – on 20 February – marked
out differences between him and Chamberlain.[11] Even so, Brockway was
clear that for 'socialists who recognise the real character of the rival
imperialisms . . . there can be no thought in this situation of identifying

themselves with one capitalist class against another . . . Our duty is to oppose both at home and abroad by class action'.[12]

Not long after this point, however, many on the Labour left converted to the idea of a popular front. This was a pragmatic attempt to maximise their potential influence, but which also necessarily distanced the Labour left from the ILP.[13] In the immediate aftermath of Eden's resignation, Cripps was still publicly arguing that a 'united working class is the one hope for peace in this country and the world' and asserting 'the inability of the good or bad intentioned imperialist to solve the problem of war and peace'.[14] Similarly, after the Austrian Anschluss with Germany on 13 March 1938, which sparked fears for the safety of Czechoslovakia, Cripps stated that this was 'the moment not to talk of combining with reaction to defend our country' and urged that it was necessary to 'redouble an effort for victory for the British working class'.[15] However, by late March Cripps was increasingly thinking that 'an anti-Chamberlain front would be the best way of accomplishing something at the moment'[16], and was keen 'to get everybody to join in behind the Labour party . . . before it is too late'.[17] Moreover, at the beginning of April the first public appeal for a broader coalition appeared in *Tribune*. Significantly, the central motivating factor was not Austria but Spain where Franco's forces were advancing into Catalonia. Calling for 'the maximum support for smashing non-intervention in Spain and supplying the Spanish government with arms', it appealed 'to all genuine opponents of the Chamberlain government, both inside and outside the ranks of the Labour party, to force a General Election which would sweep Chamberlain and his government from office'.[18]

Soon afterwards Cripps set about organising a tremendously important conference at the Queen's Hall in London on 23 April that was to consider ways of assisting the Republican side in Spain and sought to attract 'all those to the Left of Neville Chamberlain'.[19] The speakers, on the Labour side, were to be the Co-operative MP A. V. Alexander, Wilkinson, Pritt, Trevelyan, Philip Noel-Baker, David Grenfell and Cripps. They were to be joined by the National Labour MP Harold Nicolson, the Liberal leader Sir Archibald Sinclair, the Liberals Wilfred Roberts and Megan Lloyd George as well as by A. J. Cummings of the *News Chronicle*, the Duchess of Atholl, Gollancz and the Bishop of Chelmsford.[20] Given that 'the position of Spain' was 'the keystone', this meant that Churchill and Eden – with their well-known lack of support for the Republican side – were excluded.[21]

Ahead of the conference, Cripps gave the public reasons behind his change of stance in favour of a popular front. He argued that 'events move rapidly today and it is necessary to reconsider one's opinions and decisions in the light of changing events'. He interpreted Eden's departure as 'a stiffening of the pro-fascist elements in the Cabinet' and argued that on an electoral basis there was simply 'no immediate prospect of a purely Labour government' while the 'psychological effect of the unity of progressive forces could be very considerable throughout the country'. He contended that there would be no difficulty in agreeing on foreign policy: in fact, individuals would join because they were 'more inclined to support democracy, peace and collective security'. So far as domestic policy was concerned, Cripps accepted that 'any idea of real socialism would have to be put aside for the present' so that through 'temporary co-operation' it might be possible 'to save democracy . . . then resume our attempt to bring about social democracy to Great Britain'.[22] Cripps then reiterated these themes at the conference itself, making it clear that he hoped such a movement would precipitate a general election.[23]

There were, of course, other reasons underpinning Cripps's *volte-face*. Given that 'quite a lot of our people have been seriously upset by the Russian trials, with a consequent reaction against communism', it seemed unwise 'to force unity work just at the moment' and this meant that a broader front, in which the Communist presence would be less conspicuous, was more pragmatic.[24] The movement for a popular front in Britain had been developing since 1936, but for a long time it had been overshadowed by the Unity Campaign and its aftermath. Since the middle of 1937, however, momentum had been gathering – particularly among those with whom Cripps was closely aligned – and this reached a crescendo around the time of the Austrian Anschluss. Martin now argued very strongly in favour of a popular front in the *New Statesman and Nation*. Explaining his reasoning to Cripps, he asserted that if there was 'half a chance of preventing war by the Winston sort of policy, I feel I ought to say so'. He went on:

> I have always tried to make a distinction between a war we ought
> to risk which would genuinely be in the interests of socialism in
> Spain, and a war for the British Empire. It is now, I am afraid
> obvious that they would be the same thing, and it seemed to me
> no good merely to say that one would be opposed to war because
> it was capitalist, nor that one would be opposed to the necessary
> home consequences of such a decision. I found this an almost
> intolerable position to take up, but I saw no alternative.[25]

Brailsford, who had first tentatively endorsed the popular front in summer 1936, now also came out strongly in its favour. Furthermore, Laski began to argue that, in the face of the fascist threat, the French popular front had much to teach the British Left. He considered that a similar arrangement in

Britain might 'have the same beneficial results for democracy' and mean that instead of 'a policy of piecemeal surrender to the fascist powers, as in . . . Abyssinia and Spain, it would present them with a challenge to aggressive action fairly certain to change for the good the balance of our civilisation'.[26] However, perhaps the longest-standing, and most consistent, advocate of a popular front was G. D. H. Cole, who, in June 1937, had published *The People's Front* – a book which had made a significant impact given, as Pollitt aptly noted, 'the influence of Cole in the Labour Movement, especially on some of the younger men'.[27] Through his book Cole sought to encourage the formation of 'a People's Front wide enough to include everyone who can be persuaded to accept a democratic and progressive immediate programme in national and international politics, even if they cannot yet be got to accept the full socialist creed'.[28] The Spanish Civil War had convinced him of the need to act quickly in order to save 'democracy from total eclipse',[29] and led him to pin his hopes on an international pact of pooled security – with a popular front Britain, the Soviet Union and France as its core.[30] Crucially Cole had dedicated the book to Cripps, arguing that they were 'fundamentally on the same side'.[31] Significantly, moreover, in his book Cole stressed that there was 'no conflict of view between advocacy of the People's Front and advocacy of working-class unity';[32] he envisaged the former operating with a 'united working-class movement as its rallying point and as the principal contributor to its strength and solidity in action'.[33]

II

In the next few months the Labour left developed its advocacy of a popular front. In the first place, a direct attempt was made to persuade the NEC to consider the idea. Cripps informed Middleton in late April that, along with Pritt, Laski and Wilkinson, he planned to table a proposal in favour of a popular front at the NEC's next meeting on 5 May 1938.[34] Their memorandum argued that the current 'drift . . . in face of European perils' made it essential to defeat 'the Chamberlain government at the earliest possible moment'. Repeating the argument recently made by Cripps, it contended that 'an effective victory by the Labour party alone is highly improbable at the next election'. It therefore explicitly advocated a popular front – a 'combined fight' involving Labour party co-operation 'with other anti-government parties' including the Liberals as well as the ILP and the CPGB – asserting that it was 'better to join forces with anti-socialist democrats than to see both socialism and democracy perish'.[35]

Reflecting the priorities of the Labour left, the memorandum put the question of Spain above that of Austria but curiously contained no reference whatsoever to the Soviet Union.[36] Previously many of the Labour left advocates of the popular front had stressed that it, like the united front, was underpinned by a desire to protect the Soviet Union.[37] Trevelyan, one of its most prominent supporters, was greatly concerned by the tendency, even within the Labour party, to 'ignore Russia'.[38] He considered that the Chamberlain government's 'vital preference for the fascist dictators over Russian democracy' was 'the central world fact today'. He was equally clear that 'the only hope for the world lies in collective action between the Western democracies and Russia'. Nevertheless, Trevelyan recognised that 'a lot of people in the Labour party' considered it 'unpopular and unwise to proclaim to the world that we should get in line with Soviet Russia'.[39] Cripps fully appreciated this and was well aware of the need to tread carefully. He lamented to Trevelyan that he had 'no idea what an excuse the recent trials have given those who are anti-Russian in the party!'[40] Perhaps, therefore, it was on the pragmatic grounds of avoiding a contentious issue that any mention of the Soviet Union was omitted. Despite this concession, Cripps's advocacy of a popular front still pitted him firmly against the moderate majorities on the NEC, who had produced their own statement on the matter in advance, thus ensuring that Cripps's memorandum was rejected. They argued that it was not clear whether Liberal support would improve the Labour party's chance of defeating the National government and that association with the CPGB would be actively detrimental to its prospects.[41]

After the setback of rejection by the NEC, the Labour left turned its attention to more indirect ways of influencing the Labour party. Cripps's freedom of action was now restricted because, as he put it, 'the decision of the Labour party . . . prevents me as a member of the National Executive from doing anything unless I am prepared to withdraw from the Executive of the party, and I am not prepared to do this at the present time, as I believe that the nucleus of any such [popular front] movement . . . must be of the Labour and Trade Union movement'.[42] Cripps and *Tribune* had previously demanded that a special Labour party conference should be called to discuss the fast deteriorating international situation.[43] *Tribune* now reiterated this plea[44] as well as giving space to those advocating it – printing, for instance, letters from Brailsford and Joseph Pole of the Labour Spain Committee.[45]

At this point the Labour left's stance on rearmament also underwent a significant change. Instead of opposing it so long as a capitalist government remained in power, it began to attach conditions to its support for National government rearmament. This adjustment was related to its growing support for a popular front, as well as a deepening awareness of the seriousness of the international situation. Crucially, one of Cole's objections to the Unity Campaign had been its complete opposition to rearmament. He was prepared to criticise the National government rearmament programme 'on the grounds both that it is excessive and that the Government has provided no satisfactory assurance of the purpose for which the armaments are to be used'. However, he did not 'oppose British rearmament altogether' and contended that he could not 'be a party to creating a situation in which an incoming Government of the Left might find itself unable to resist fascism, or to become an active partner in an international democratic front, for lack of adequate military resources'.[46] Importantly, by early April 1938 Cole had developed his position into one of conditional support for rearmament: he now asserted that he 'would not advise anyone to lift a finger in order to speed up the output of munitions except in return for a clear and satisfactory declaration of the policy which the munitions are destined to serve'.[47] In a similar spirit, the 'Emergency Conference on Spain' on 11 April, which had been organised by the Labour Spain Committee and the HCLA, had passed a resolution involving a 'flat refusal to negotiate over any fresh facilities for rearmament until Non-Intervention is cancelled'.[48] Now in mid May *Tribune* argued that the Labour movement 'in conference should declare that it refuses, industrially and politically, to co-operate with the government in rearmament . . . *so long as* the government refuses to come decisively to the aid of the Spanish government by ending non-intervention [and] refuses to follow the path of collective security by building a peace front with the Soviet Union [and] with France'.[49]

Mellor was clear that this double-pronged policy – involving advocacy of a special Labour party conference and conditional support for rearmament – was the line *Tribune* should take.[50] Foot summarised Mellor's argument:

> William claimed that the vital question was one of policy and not of organisation. He argued that instead of calling for a Popular front which would make the fight with the Executive an organisational fight and which would involve a split and possible expulsions we should lay all the emphasis on the issue of policy and call for a Special Conference. By a question of policy he meant, of course such questions as refusing to support the Arms programme . . . as the government persisted in their refusal to defend democracy.[51]

Mellor's reason for adopting this stance was that he still favoured a united front and, supported by Betts, was strongly opposed to *Tribune*'s shifting allegiance to a popular front.[52] Over recent months he and Cripps had indeed become 'increasingly incompatible'.[53] Their relationship then completely

broke down in July once Cripps secured funding for *Tribune* from Gollancz
which was premised on support for a popular front. Technically, the agreement – which sought 'to draw together as closely as possible the elements of
the political left in the Labour party' – simply gave the Left Book Club two
pages in *Tribune*, promised to expand its circulation (though Cripps continued
to underwrite its running costs), allowed the Left Book Club to nominate one
of its directors, and stressed that it did 'not in the least affect the political
control of *Tribune*'.[54] In reality, however, as Foot recognised, with 'Gollancz's
. . . presence on the Board . . . above all the fact that the sales will be largely
dependent on him – his control will be bound to become predominant'.[55]

Mellor now resigned 'on the Board's request',[56] and plans were made to
replace him with Foot. This placed Foot in a very difficult dilemma: he had
worked under Mellor and respected him greatly but he had also visited the
Cripps family home, having befriended John Cripps while he was an
undergraduate at Oxford University. So far as Mellor's line was concerned,
Foot 'did not entirely agree with him at the time and afterwards . . . argued
it out with him'. Foot had initially considered that 'it was impossible for us
to do other than give tentative support to the Popular Front supporters as
we wanted their aid against the Executive'. However, following the NEC's
rejection of the popular front memorandum, he had reconsidered the benefits
of Mellor's suggested line. After much thought Foot decided not to accept
the post of editor and to resign with Mellor for a combination of political
and personal reasons. Foot recognised that Gollancz's objection to working
with Mellor was 'partly a political objection' based on his lack of enthusiasm
for the popular front. Whatever differences there may have been between
them, Foot had no doubt he preferred 'William's politics to Gollancz's
politics'. He also disliked the 'highhanded manner' that he considered
Gollancz had so far exhibited towards *Tribune*.[57] Reflecting on his decision
the morning after he had written to Cripps, he felt it was 'the only possible
decision' given that it had been such 'an appalling humiliation for
William'.[58] The *Tribune* Board then appointed the pro-Communist H. J.
Hartshorn as editor,[59] and the agreement with the Left Book Club then
formally came into operation on 16 September.[60] Overall, these events in
summer 1938 undoubtedly marked a pivotal juncture for the Labour left,
involving a break in the Cripps-Mellor axis that had underpinned it since
1934.

III

Meanwhile the ILP remained firmly committed to working-class mass
resistance to overthrow the National government. It advocated this course

strongly as the international situation deteriorated in March 1938,[61] at the same time as the Executive Committee called for assistance for the German and Austrian workers.[62] Like the Labour left, the ILP continued to regard Spain as a more pressing issue than Austria.[63] At the ILP conference in Manchester in April 1938 the resolution urging both mass resistance in support of the right of the Spanish workers to buy arms and an organised refusal to make, handle or transport materials to Franco (as well as to Germany, Italy and Japan) was passed without dispute.[64] Resolutions opposing National government rearmament and pledging the ILP to defend the Soviet Union were also smoothly endorsed. Indeed, when the Keighley and Bristol branches moved an amendment questioning the commitment to the Soviet Union, they found 'no support in the conference'.[65]

At the same time the ILP strongly opposed the growing calls for a popular front on the Labour left, sharply criticising the ideas put forward by Brailsford and Martin.[66] At the ILP conference, Aplin introduced the NAC resolution which advocated a workers front and rejected the popular front, but accepted a 'position that sometimes common action with non working-class organisations is justified, so long as that action is limited to specific objects'. However, even this aroused hostility from some of the delegates. Ernie Patterson – the Trotskyist delegate from Clapham – led the opposition, proposing an amendment stating that the ILP would never participate in any kind of popular front. He used the example of the POUM and 'begged the delegates to learn from that experience'. His view found strong support from Jack Huntz of the London ILP but was opposed by Lee who argued that 'those who opposed the Popular Front in the Labour party were not the militant elements, but were the "Tammany Hall bosses of Transport House" to whom socialism is an alibi'. C. A. Smith countered this by arguing that he saw it as a simple dichotomy: 'we either maintain capitalism by a Labour government or a Popular Front government, or we make a frontal attack on capitalism'. At the end of the debate the resolution was carried and the amendment rejected. It was a close result, however, and on reflection the NAC interpreted it as clear evidence that the membership did 'not wish to be compromised into support of class collaboration policies'.[67]

The ILP developed its opposition to the popular front in the months after its conference. In May it responded to the growing calls for a 'Peace Alliance' from various circles by asserting its view that 'there must be no general political . . . alliance' but that if 'Liberals and Tory Democrats are prepared to join with the working class in demanding "arms for Spain" their co-operation should be welcomed'.[68] The *New Leader*'s 'Peace Alliance Supplement' further stressed that it sought a specifically working-class alliance.[69] Above all, the ILP made clear that its opposition to the popular front was linked – in several ways – to its ever-increasing dislike of the CPGB. Brockway argued that one of the 'worst features of the Popular Front policy advocated by the Communist Party is the betrayal of the colonial workers which it involves', citing as an example that since the Soviet Union had entered into a military alliance with France, Communist stimulation of revolt in the French colonies had stopped.[70] The ILP, as it defined itself less and less in terms of the Soviet Union, was increasingly interested in the plight of 'subject peoples' in the European empires and how they would be affected by a 'capitalist' and 'imperialist' war.[71] On a more specific level the ILP objected to the CPGB decision to support the 'Peace Alliance' candidate instead of Groves, who had resurfaced as the official Labour candidate, at the Aylesbury by-election in late May.[72] Pollitt's refusal to appear on the same platform as Brockway during the 'Spain Week' organised by the Hampstead Spanish Relief Committee was also eagerly reported with the intention of exposing 'the sectarianism of the Communist Party'.[73] It was, however, once again over events in Spain that the ILP was most critical of the CPGB.

In the worsening international crisis, the ILP further developed its anti-Stalinist viewpoint to argue explicitly for the first time how the Soviet Union stood to undermine the anti-fascist cause. In early June McNair called for the POUM prisoners to be tried or freed, contending powerfully that the 'processes and practices of Stalinism have been imported into Spain, with the well-known system of terrorism which seeks the physical suppression of all critical or oppositional tendencies. And this is while Franco is hammering at the gate.'[74] Once a planned trial was announced in July, charging the POUM leaders (as the Comintern had previously outlined) with provoking the uprising in May 1937 and of being agents of Franco, the *New Leader* reacted angrily. It openly expressed concern that 'both judges and lawyers in Spain with a reputation for impartial and independent judgment and advocacy have been steadily removed and that the legal machine is now dominated by members of the Communist Party'. Speculating that the prisoners would be found guilty and sentenced to death, it powerfully argued that 'it would be a crime to be silent, not only as a matter of justice to the POUM prisoners, but to the cause of anti-fascism itself'.[75] The International Bureau reiterated these sentiments at its meeting in Paris on 16–17 July, expressing its hope that 'the Republican Government will be kept clean from a blot which would seriously lessen its moral authority to resist the tyranny which is fascism'.[76] Furthermore, in late July Maxton, Brockway and McNair issued a public appeal stating that 'it is the duty of the international working class to prevent the recurrence in Barcelona of such gravely disturbing events as the Moscow trials'. Beyond refuting the evidence and stressing the record of the prisoners, it drew attention to the fact that they were to be tried by a Special Tribunal of Espionage and High Treason which had been set up at the end of June the previous year – just after the arrest of the prisoners – but had retrospective powers. The statement went on:

> This Tribunal is the same type as those in Italy and Germany against which the whole working-class movement has protested. The trial of prisoners by a Tribunal set up after their arrest recalls the worst features of militarism and fascist dictatorships, and is absolutely indefensible from a democratic, to say nothing of a genuine socialist, standpoint.[77]

Overall, this meant that by the time the outcome of the trial was known in early November, with the POUM leaders imprisoned for leading the Barcelona uprising but having the other charges withdrawn, this came as no surprise at all for the ILP.[78] In any case, even by the time of its summer school in August 1938 ILP relations with the CPGB had already reached a new low. Here Brockway stated frankly that 'a workers front with the Communist party is impossible whilst it has no recognition of working-class morality and democracy'.[79]

The ILP's deteriorating relationship with the CPGB inversely reflected its moves to establish a closer relationship with the Labour party. Early in 1938 Cripps had approached Maxton, informing him that he had the authority of Attlee and George Dallas, the chairman of the NEC, 'for the encouragement of discussions' between the two parties.[80] The ILP's conditions for affiliation were effectively the same as the previous year: organisationally the desire to remain a unit, and, so far as policy was concerned, a freedom to oppose rearmament.[81] Now at the ILP conference, the resolution on the ILP's relationship with the Labour party – which stated 'the necessity of working-class unity . . . and the need for a permanent structure for common action on a federal basis' – found 'general support'.[82] This was very much the spirit in which the Executive Committee had authorised the London ILP to give support – 'without compromising the policy of the ILP' – to the Labour party candidate in the West Fulham by-election earlier in April.[83] The composite amendment, which was moved by Carmichael on behalf of the NAC in light of Cripps's recent approach, did however arouse more dispute. This instructed the NAC 'to approach the Labour party for the purpose of securing the maximum common action against the National government'. It sought an electoral understanding but made clear that 'any proposals involving change in the organisational relationship of the party were to be submitted to a special conference'. Significantly, Carmichael argued that it would appeal greatly to the workers and 'make a Popular Front impossible'. Nevertheless, Patterson again led the opposition. While he had firmly opposed any kind of popular front, he was happy for the ILP to work with other working-class parties for 'specific objects' but 'deplored any approach for re-affiliation to the Labour party'. Smith took a similar stance – welcoming co-operation on certain issues but arguing that re-affiliation would mean an end to the ILP's independence and would 'muck up' the ILP's international relationships. There was also opposition to the composite amendment from Emrys Thomas, the South Wales representative on the NAC. Altogether this meant that even after Carmichael gave his assurance that the NAC was 'not being mandated to approach the Labour party to seek affiliation', the composite amendment was only carried by 55 votes to 49.[84]

Even so, after the ILP conference there was a greater impulse for action. In mid May there were preliminary discussions between the secretaries of the ILP and the Labour Party.[85] On 14 June Maxton, Brockway, Aplin, Stephen and McGovern met the NEC, enjoying a 'friendly discussion'[86] during which Maxton made a significant concession in stating that the question of Standing Orders was 'of quite small importance today'.[87] Following another joint meeting the NEC reported to the ILP its position that 'the affiliation of the ILP to the Labour Party would be the satisfactory way of bringing about co-operation between the two parties'. This view was then submitted for the consideration of the whole NAC within which, of course, there were marked differences of opinion as the ILP conference debate had made vividly clear.[88] On 21 July – ahead of the NAC meeting at the end of the month – the ILP Head Office issued a statement asserting that no commitments had yet been made and that if it were decided to consider affiliation further, a full conference would be held.[89] In the event, however, the NAC did not come to a clear decision. In its subsequent press statement, the NAC simply said that the 'authority of the ILP representatives would be limited to clarifying any doubts about the conditions of affiliation'. It did not, however, call a special conference or make a proposal for re-affiliation. Instead it planned to meet again to consider the matter.[90] In short, although the possibility of re-affiliation was stronger than at any other point since 1932, the issue remained unresolved.

IV

As the Czech crisis deepened in late August and September, with Hitler vociferously demanding control of the German-dominated Sudetenland and seemingly ready to invade Czechoslovakia, events in central Europe now assumed a greater importance than those in Spain for the Labour left.[91] In this context, the Labour left called on the National government to form a pact with the Soviet Union, which itself had a treaty commitment to Czechoslovakia.

Crucially, for the first time, an alliance with the Soviet Union was advocated as an immediate policy, rather than one that a future Labour government would pursue. This was yet another indication of the Labour left's more realistic appraisal of the international situation. Moreover, in portraying the Soviet Union primarily as a strategic – rather than an ideological – ally, the Labour left was also, in effect, aligning with the Labour party which had increasingly begun to present the Soviet Union in this way.[92] The Labour left had quietly dropped any talk of war resistance. In early August Laski had adumbrated the new line when he argued it was necessary to 'make it clear how firmly opposed the workers of this country are to a policy of consistent surrender to the fascist dictators'. While he maintained that he had 'no sympathy for an imperialist war', he stressed that 'we cannot, as a movement stand helplessly by and see Mr Chamberlain connive at the slaughter of what remains of European democracy to add prestige to the moral vandal of Berlin and Rome'.[93] In September Strachey put forward similar arguments in *Tribune*.[94] For once, the advice given by Martin in the *New Statesman* – on this occasion that Britain 'should not guarantee the status quo' in central Europe[95] – did not have much wider resonance on the Labour left.

By now, *Tribune* – under Hartshorn's occasionally unrestrained editorship – had introduced aspects of a more unapologetically pro-Soviet tone,[96] which served to obscure the important change that had occurred in the immediate policy advanced by the Labour left. For instance, *Tribune* criticised the National government for apparently contending that Hitler had found 'Soviet traitors who were willing to join him', significantly arguing that this ignored 'the rather important consideration that such Soviet traitors have all been caught and shot!'[97] Plainly this view of the Show Trials went far beyond the silence on the matter previously maintained in *Tribune*.

On closer examination, however, the Labour left's changed stance was clear. Responding to news of the Munich Agreement on 29 September, through which Chamberlain and the French agreed to cede the Sudetenland to Germany, *Tribune* stressed that 'Chamberlain's method of postponing war by concession after concession after concession to fascism is the one thing that will make war inevitable'.[98] The Left Book Club selectors reiterated what was quickly becoming the core position on the Labour left: the immediate call for 'a firm, unqualified and public declaration by Britain, France and the Soviet Union to Germany, telling Hitler in so many words that an attack on the Czechs would be considered an act of war against them',[99] which was then to be followed by the formation of a Peace Alliance of Labour, Liberal and Communist figures into 'a government which is organised solely to defeat fascism abroad'.[100] By this point even Martin had repudiated his earlier position, and was denouncing Chamberlain strongly.[101]

Cripps's own trajectory also makes clear the re-evaluation that had taken place on the Labour left. As news of the crisis broke, Cripps was returning – by sea – from a holiday in Jamaica and, as the diary he kept makes apparent, underwent a transition in his thinking. On 28 September – when he felt war was 'inevitable' – he faced up to the difficulty 'of those like myself who have uniformly the attitude that the present Government cannot be trusted to wage a war because fundamentally they are out after the wrong things'. Significantly, he asked himself 'whether it is better now to allow the present government to try and call that halt by waging war or whether it is necessary to continue to point out to the workers the acute danger and indeed the uselessness of allowing such a government as the present to wage any war'.[102] Cripps was clearly in a dilemma, as Peter Clarke has recognised.[103] But the important point was that he went so far as to consider the pros and cons of joining a wartime government – a considerable move from the policy of class-based war resistance, even if he could not envisage reconciling himself to 'the imperial policy of the war government'.[104]

On receiving news of the Munich agreement Cripps welcomed the peace but considered just as strongly that it was 'tragic that Hitler should have got his way on yet another occasion with all Europe apparently at his mercy and dictation'.[105] Now on his return to Britain, Cripps approached his arch rival Dalton, as well as Morrison, as he sought to gather support within the Labour party for a wide parliamentary alliance against Chamberlain, which was crucially to include Conservative opponents such as Churchill, Eden, Amery and Harold Macmillan.[106] Cripps's basic argument that 'had a strong bloc of closely-knit peace-loving states, including France, Russia, Czech, ourselves and our Dominions, spoken with firmness and determination, there would have been no war and no danger of war',[107] was widely accepted on the Labour left. But his willingness to approach even Churchill – who was perceived as being on the right of the Conservative party and remembered for his role in crushing the General Strike – showed how far his concept of the popular front was broadening under the pressure of international events. In any case, however, the plans soon fell apart because of Eden's reluctance to get involved.[108]

Throughout the rest of 1938 the Labour left continued to champion the popular front cause. Together with the Left Book Club, it was strongly supportive of the two progressive candidates in by-elections at this point:

A. D. Lindsay, the master of Balliol College, who was defeated in the Oxford by-election, and the journalist Vernon Bartlett who triumphed at Bridgwater.[109] Meanwhile, as the Labour left remained clear that 'it might be necessary to employ or to threaten the protective use of force . . . as a means of safeguarding the common people from . . . those who are attempting to rule the world by violence through the methods of fascist dictatorships',[110] it was increasingly concerned to distance itself from pacifism. Cripps publicly stated that while he had 'a very great admiration for the followers of pacifism', he did 'not regard it as a practical policy for the present time'.[111] This was in marked contrast to the way that pacifism had been welcomed within the Socialist League ranks and, as such, it precipitated some difficulties with Ruth Dodds – the former Socialist Leaguer and a Quaker.[112]

V

The ILP's response to the growing Czech crisis in late summer 1938 was to maintain its commitment to both strands of its war resistance policy: emphasising its readiness to take independent working-class action against Germany, Italy and Japan, and its desire to overthrow the National government. It had reiterated this throughout August.[113] Now, as fears of war mounted in September, it forthrightly asserted that it would not 'support a war for British imperialism even against German fascism' given that in the British Empire there was 'a repression and a misery every whit as great as the tyranny and exploitation in Germany'.[114] As the month progressed, and the likelihood of war increased still further, the ILP argued that the brewing conflict was only nominally over the Sudetenland and was actually 'the pretext for a settlement of accounts between German imperialism on the one hand, and British and French imperialism on the other', a situation in which working-class interests were 'neither on the one side nor the other'.[115] Similar appeals for mass resistance were made time and again,[116] and echoed by the manifesto issued in mid September by the International Bureau.[117] Furthermore, distancing its stance from that of the Labour left, on 25 September the ILP NAC unanimously adopted a statement outlining its 'unconditional opposition to any form of support to the Government for war'.[118] This was the type of view expressed on 25 September at a meeting in Hyde Park addressed by Brockway as well as by Edwards, Huntz and Kate Spurrell, the NAC representative for the South West.[119]

Significantly, at this critical juncture the ILP began to collaborate closely with the pacifist movement. On 17 September at a conference held at the

Trade Union Club, the ILP, the Parliamentary Pacifist Group, the Peace Pledge Union (PPU), the No More War Movement and the Society of Friends agreed to set up an ad hoc committee.[120] The following week left-leaning pacifists – such as Alfred Salter and C. E. M. Joad – joined Horrabin, Orwell and the ILP in calling for war resistance and the overthrow of the National government.[121] And on 2 October George Johnson, the East Anglian representative on the NAC, emphasised publicly that while the ILP differed from the PPU, it was certainly 'prepared to co-operate in opposing war'.[122]

During the debate on the Munich agreement in the House of Commons on 4 October, however, the relationship between the ILP MPs and the wider party again came into question, just as it had over 'working-class sanctions' in 1935 and 1936. Before the debate Brockway, Aplin and McNair had urged Maxton not to endorse the settlement – even amid the general sense of relief at the avoidance of war. However, when Maxton made it clear that he 'would not commit himself', Brockway became 'apprehensive'.[123] Maxton's speech itself was – as Brockway recognised – an 'indictment of war-making imperialism, German and British'.[124] Indeed, despite his well-known opposition to the Great War and consequent imprisonment, there can be little doubt that Maxton opposed war on anti-capitalist, rather than on truly pacifist, grounds.[125] More controversially though, Maxton also stated that: 'I congratulate the prime minister', arguing that he had secured a widely desired 'breathing space'.[126] Brockway was deeply disturbed, objecting to Maxton's speech 'from a revolutionary socialist point of view for two reasons: first, for the praise of Chamberlain and, second, for its omission of any denunciation of the terms of the Munich Pact'.[127] At Brockway's request an emergency meeting of the Executive Committee, which comprised Brockway, McNair, Aplin, Maxton, Stephen and McGovern, was called for 13 October.[128] Ahead of this meeting the Parliamentary Group of the ILP met and unanimously agreed to the line taken in the debate. With the Parliamentary Group standing firm, at the meeting of the Executive Committee Brockway and Aplin nevertheless argued that they wanted publicly to dissociate themselves from what they described as 'the unreserved praise given to Mr Chamberlain's action' by the Parliamentary Group. On Stephen's suggestion the Executive Committee agreed that it would not prevent them from doing this, and so Brockway promptly issued a personal statement with which Aplin later expressed his agreement. The statement stressed that the Munich Agreement had been 'an imperialist truce which, so far from removing the danger of war, has been the signal in all the countries concerned for intensified rearmament'. It then reiterated the established ILP view about the imperative of 'overthrowing all imperialism', beginning with the National government.[129]

After this internal dispute the ILP tried to concentrate on those aspects of party policy which united it. An editorial in the *New Leader* stated that while 'there have been differences in the ILP on the British Prime Minister's role in the recent war crisis' this did 'not mean that there are differences in the Party regarding our resistance to war or the imperialist peace' or 'about the policy now to be pursued'. The ILP turned its attention to opposing strongly the rearmament programme of the National government 'bringing all sincere anti-war sections behind it',[130] and explicitly continuing to embrace its links with the pacifist movement. Indeed, in December Brockway gave a lecture to the PPU in which he stressed that while the ILP was 'not pacifist' and supported a social revolution, there was nonetheless a desirable 'broad basis of co-operation between pacifists and revolutionary socialists on immediate issues'.[131] Meanwhile the ILP emphasised its continued support for a workers front. It contended that the events of September had shown the 'futility of the Popular Front tactic', in particular by revealing how the capitalist powers had not involved the Soviet Union in the all-important conference at Munich.[132] The popular front triumph at Bridgwater then merely provided another occasion for the *New Leader* to stress its desire to 'put up the most uncompromising opposition to all our war preparations and war, either by the National government or that more representative National government which Mr Bartlett and the Popular Frontists would like to see'.[133]

The ILP also undertook a new initiative in launching a campaign against conscription in late October in response to the National government's announcement of a proposed National Register. In doing so, it gained the signatures of 47 Labour MPs and parliamentary candidates – including Groves, Horrabin and Salter – to a manifesto offering 'strenuous opposition to the proposed Register'.[134] Although it was nominally voluntary, the ILP considered that it would be an 'advance towards the totalitarian state'.[135] On this issue, like many others, the ILP was very much in tune with the International Bureau which discussed the matter at its conference on 30 October.[136]

Despite pulling together over such issues, the debate over the action of the Parliamentary Group during the Munich Crisis continued to reverberate within the ILP. It was a major issue on 4 and 5 February 1939 when many of the ILP divisional conferences were held. At the London conference, the delegates for Croydon and Clapham moved resolutions demanding the expulsion of the Parliamentary Group. These was defeated but, nonetheless, a resolution was adopted which repudiated the congratulation given to Chamberlain and demanded that 'immediate steps be taken to bring the [Parliamentary] Group within the discipline of the Party'. In contrast – and unsurprisingly given Maxton's support in the area – the Scottish Conference was markedly more supportive of the position adopted by the ILP MPs, accepting Maxton's report on the issue by 64 votes to 12. The position adopted by the Welsh Divisional Conference was between these two extremes. There was a lengthy debate after which it was resolved that 'utterances were made which could be used against the party but urging that the damage done would be intensified by further controversy'.[137] Two weeks later at the North East Divisional Conference, Tom Stephenson – the NAC representative for the area – dealt with the controversy in some depth. The conference itself was divided on the wisdom of the speech, but 'unanimously disapproved of the publicity given to the opinion of the Clapham branch that Maxton should be expelled'.[138] The whole episode now had one direct impact: before the ILP national conference Maxton declined nomination as chairman of the NAC, though he remained a national member of the NAC,[139] and was replaced by Smith – his long-standing opponent.[140]

At the ILP conference – which met at Scarborough between 8 and 10 April – Smith led the opposition against Maxton and the ILP MPs. On behalf of the City branch he moved the reference back that their speeches 'did not adequately represent the policy of revolutionary socialism' and had projected a contradictory message. He held that it was necessary to clarify that the ILP was a socialist rather than a pacifist organisation so that similar sentiments would not be expressed in the future.[141] This was clearly a contentious point because the ILP had been readily co-operating with the pacifist movement since the previous September. Furthermore, in January it had established the No Conscription League, which included representatives from the Parliamentary Pacifist Group.[142] Even so, Patterson, on behalf of the critical Clapham branch, readily reiterated its demand either to expel the Parliamentary Group or to 'define the position of the Group in relation to the Party and lay down the basis of their parliamentary activities'.[143]

McGovern was the first to defend the position of the Parliamentary Group. He sarcastically 'asked if the party didn't want a capitalist war or a capitalist peace, what the hell did it want'. He 'genuinely believed . . . Chamberlain had secured peace and he hoped the workers would profit in the breathing space'. He took an unapologetic stance and accused Brockway and Aplin of acting in a 'scurrilous manner'. He added that Brockway was a 'double-crosser' and accused the London section of the party of being 'fireside theoreticians and middle-class dilettantes with no contact with the working class'.[144] The debate intensified further as Brockway spoke. He said that if he had behaved in the way described by McGovern, he was 'unfit' to be party secretary and promptly resigned, remaining a national member of the NAC and becoming political secretary, with his former post being taken by

McNair. Brockway spoke at length, explaining why he had felt it necessary to disassociate himself from the MPs' speeches in October. He argued that he frankly objected to their praise for 'a criminal peace'.[145] Brockway, however, did not press his points further. Not only did he have a fundamental respect for Maxton's convictions,[146] but also he subsequently recalled that:

> I could not [speak] . . . with the same confidence as when I had intervened in the not dissimilar debate on the Abyssinian issue. My mind was obsessed by the larger international crisis which was approaching and I did not want to emphasise any differences in the Party; I knew that the members, divided though they were about imperialist peace, would be united absolutely in opposition to imperialist war.[147]

The debate then continued as Aplin argued that the attitude of the Parliamentary Group had not been in the interests of the international working class. Linking it with another live issue in the ILP and responding to McGovern, he contended that the settlement had simply given the National government a 'breathing space' to impose conscription.[148] Finally, Maxton asserted that he had advanced the party's policy in the terms that he understood it. He claimed to have been 'hurt' by the actions of Aplin and Brockway, and by the London Division. He also said that 'if he had realised that five words out of his speech would have caused six months of controversy in the party, he would never have used them'. Johnson then wound up the debate on behalf of the NAC, declaring that Maxton's speech was 'a magnificent socialist utterance'. The reference back was defeated by 65 votes to 43, and the motion to expel the Parliamentary Group rejected by 'a large majority'.[149] As Maxton put it, this meant that 'the party did not like what we did, but is not prepared to chastise us for it'.[150]

VI

In January 1939 Cripps embarked on a further popular front initiative.[151] He produced a memorandum which he sent to Middleton on the 9th, calling for a special Labour party conference to consider the matter. He made his argument on electoral grounds, contending that at such a time of crisis, and with the Labour party not able to defeat the National government by itself at the next election, a need arose for 'the use temporarily of some tactic which will enable the essential extra electoral strength to be mobilised'. This Labour-led 'progressive democratic block' was to consist of Liberals,

Communists and ILPers; it was to be held together by a shared commitment to the 'protection of the democratic rights, liberties and freedom of the British people from internal and external attack' and a 'positive policy of peace by collective action with France, Russia [and] the United States'.[152] More forcefully than ever before, the Labour left was publicly asserting the ideological imperative of defending Britain and merely using an alliance with the Soviet Union as a means to this end.

There were a number of factors behind Cripps's decision to issue his memorandum. He was frustrated that the NEC had decided, at the end of November, not to co-operate with other groups in opposition to Chamberlain on the basis that this would mean a departure from socialism.[153] Cripps was also involved in an on-going dispute with George Shepherd – the National Agent – over the legal advice which he had given to the local Labour party in Bridgwater justifying their decision to back Bartlett: 'that if it had decided not to run a Labour party candidate, it was within the competence of the local Labour Party to recommend their members in the constituency to support any other candidate who was in fact running'.[154] At the same time Cripps knew his popular front line was gaining popularity on the former Socialist League left. Naomi Mitchison, for instance, wrote to him explaining that she could consider supporting a Liberal candidate because even if it was not 'really socialism . . . it may be the best thing to do at the moment . . . until the immediate danger is over'.[155] Once again, the interpretation of events relayed to Cripps from his Bristol constituency seems to have played an important part in his actions. In November Rogers warned him that recent events in Bridgwater would encourage 'other Labour parties throughout the country, similarly placed, to now go in on the same basis as this contest was fought', i.e. to support progressive or non-Labour party candidates, with a consequent danger that 'the initiative would pass from our hands to the Liberal Party'. This led Rogers to suggest that it would be 'most harmful for local constituencies to be left on their own to make their own arrangements' and that there 'must be a proper understanding and a leadership from the top'.[156] Cripps was also moved to act by what he – and Bevan among others – saw as the tendency of the Labour party 'to give the appearances of being drawn into some association with the National government on such matters as the National Register'.[157] He was further concerned about the 'danger of the formation of some middle party or group' led by the dissident Tories.[158] Unlike in the aftermath of Munich, Cripps clearly did not now envisage Churchill being part of his popular front. The memorandum itself spelt out a progressive domestic programme that would have been unacceptable to most Conservatives.[159] Moreover, when he had sent it to Middleton,

Cripps had specifically stated that Churchill stood for 'reactionary imperialism'.[160] Finally, Cripps's action was motivated by a concern that at any point the 'anti-Government feeling' could 'be swung over to the support of the Government by some international event, by a change in Chamberlain's foreign policy or by an appeal to National Unity if the crisis deepens'.[161]

The memorandum was put on the agenda of the NEC meeting on 13 January where it was proposed by Cripps and seconded by Pritt.[162] Although the proposal also received support from Wilkinson, it was rejected by 17 votes to 3, with Laski not voting because he was in America at this point.[163] Having anticipated the result, Cripps now put in place the next stage of his plan. In his correspondence with Middleton he had stated that if the NEC did not accept the memorandum or 'take any definite action in the direction indicated', he would 'claim the right to circulate it'.[164] Later the same day Cripps did just that, sending a circular to all Labour MPs, candidates and local parties.[165] The NEC quickly struck back. It issued a statement, broadcast by the BBC on the evening of the 14th, which argued that Cripps's appeal would serve only to 'bring confusion and division within the party'.[166] Cripps responded that this was 'an attack upon myself'.[167] He also complained to the BBC that it was 'taking sides in the discussion' by broadcasting the statement.[168] The intensity of the debate was similar to that after the launch of the Unity Campaign when rumours had abounded that Cripps would be expelled. A further NEC meeting was scheduled for 18 January but Cripps was unable to attend because of a business meeting.[169] Despite a discussion with Dalton, Cripps refused to change course.[170] The NEC meeting referred the matter to the Organisation Sub-committee which was to produce a report for the next NEC meeting the following week.[171] The highly critical report accused Cripps of 'deception' – principally because he had already printed copies of the memorandum for posting before the NEC met on the 13th. It argued that Cripps had made an improper attempt 'to change party direction and leadership', and recommended that unless he reaffirmed his allegiance to the party and withdrew the memorandum, he should be expelled.[172] This report was considered at the NEC meeting on 25 January, at which Cripps provocatively argued that his service over the past eight years made a reaffirmation of loyalty 'unnecessary', and that he would not withdraw the memorandum. The recommendations were then endorsed by 18 votes to 1 with only Wilkinson voting against. Laski was still in the United States and Pritt was absent through illness.[173] Cripps had been expelled and his party commitments cancelled.[174] He did, however, swiftly make it clear that he wanted to appeal against the ruling at the Labour Party Conference.[175]

VII

Cripps now set to work organising what became known as the Petition Campaign. The petition itself reiterated the same points as his memorandum and called on the Labour, Liberal and Co-operative parties to form a government that would 'defend democracy, protect our democratic rights and liberties against attack at home and abroad, organise a Peace Alliance with France and Russia [and] rally the support of the United States'.[176] In the planning stages Cripps was optimistic of securing support from the *News Chronicle*, the *Manchester Guardian*, *Reynolds News*, *Time and Tide* and the *Daily Worker*. He was also hoping to secure endorsement from the *New Statesman* and planned to work through the Left Book Club. Meanwhile Cripps had decided that he was 'not prepared to guarantee the finance especially in view of the cost of *Tribune* at the moment' but was certainly happy to be 'personally liable for the costs incurred' provided he had the 'unwavering backing of all the rest of the group'.[177] By the end of January, the Petition Campaign had moved into offices at Cliffords Inn on Fleet Street and was employing E. P. Young as a full-time Organising Secretary. Cripps then formally launched the campaign in a speech at Newcastle on 5 February. He outlined the electoral reasoning behind his argument and emphasised the dire international situation. He stressed the importance of the Soviet Union, which, he argued, could 'be of inestimable assistance in the struggle against fascism and war' but would not align with 'a government such as the present one' which was 'pro-fascist', having overseen the 'betrayal of Spanish democracy' and refused to take any action in support of China.[178]

Beyond those in his immediate *Tribune* circle, Cripps had already had promises of support from a raft of Labour left figures such as Naomi Mitchison and G. D. H. Cole.[179] In addition, Cripps had the full support of Trevelyan who, after a period of relative political inactivity, asserted his willingness to throw himself into the campaign, not least by attending the Newcastle meeting.[180] Trevelyan's great motivation, of course, related to the imperative of forming an international alliance with the Soviet Union. He privately told Cripps that, with the launch of the campaign, he hoped the National government might be 'frightened into approaching Russia'.[181] Furthermore, Cripps knew that he could count on the support of his East Bristol constituency, which had so often proved important in the past.[182]

Significantly, Cripps also received backing from prominent Liberals such as Richard Acland and Wilfred Roberts.[183] Just as it had in April 1938, Spain proved to be the unifying issue for the Liberals and the Labour left at this juncture. With Barcelona looking increasingly likely to fall to Franco,

Roberts had told Cripps that 'what is happening in Spain makes me and other Liberals desperate to be allowed to help the Labour party to defeat the National government'.[184] Indeed, it was not coincidental that on the evening of his expulsion from the Labour party – 25 January – Cripps, together with Wilkinson and Bevan, had spoken alongside Roberts and Lady Violet Bonham Carter at a meeting convened at the Queen's Hall in London in the (now rather vain) cause of 'Arms For Spain'.[185] The precise form that Liberal co-operation with the Petition Campaign should take was, however, problematic. The issue exercised the participants at the *News Chronicle*'s Policy Conferences, who were wary of associating themselves too closely with the 'erratic' Cripps.[186] By the same measure, Cripps was unsure about the extent to which he should work with the Liberals – as he made clear to both Acland and Roberts.[187] Here Cole offered Cripps some advice:

> I feel that it is essential, if we are to have a chance of carrying the conference at Whitsun, to be careful how we (or rather you) handle the Liberals between now and Whitsun. If there were to be any known pact between you and the Liberal party before Whitsun, I feel sure it would be used at the conference to discredit the ideas for which we stand by representing it as positive 'treason' (something more than 'disloyalty') and that the argument would go down with a great many Trade unionists and local Labour Party leaders in the industrial districts, especially in the North. As long as there is a hope of carrying the Conference, it is essential to appeal as Labour party people, and not so as to be represented as persons engaged in favouring a 'Centre party', or fostering a Liberal revival.[188]

This presumably struck a chord with Cripps who had always been keen to prevent the appearance of forming a new or 'rival party'.[189] The result was that the Liberals worked in a 'parallel campaign'.[190] Within this framework, Cripps quickly gained the support of J. M. Keynes, who – being in 'full sympathy' – agreed to sign the petition and even donated £50 to the campaign funds.[191] Meanwhile, Bonham Carter became a particularly energetic supporter,[192] and the campaign also acquired the backing of J. B. Priestley.[193]

Despite Cripps's cautious attitude to Liberal support, tension continued to mount with the NEC, which encouraged Labour speakers to criticise Cripps for his actions over the past few years, ranging from his attitude towards League of Nations sanctions in 1935 through to his pursuit of the Unity Campaign in 1937. This led to heated correspondence as Cripps accused the Executive of obscuring the issue now at stake.[194] The NEC was equally unwilling to allow Cripps to appeal to the Labour party conference, initially arguing that this was without precedent before eventually conceding that the Conference Arrangements Committee would consider the matter in April.[195] Furthermore, amid claims that the Petition Campaign was recruiting new members into the Labour party, the NEC issued a circular asserting that 'agreement with Sir Stafford Cripps's present speeches cannot be accepted as a qualification of membership for the Labour Party'.[196]

Cripps certainly had his supporters. Cole readily signed a letter circulated by Strauss in support of Cripps's memorandum.[197] Will Lawther of the Miners' Federation and Alfred Barnes, the chairman of the Co-operative Society, did likewise.[198] Bevan was particularly forthright in his support. He publicly argued that it was simply 'absurd' that the NEC wanted to prevent a leading figure from making 'known to his fellow party members what he thinks should be done in times of crisis'.[199] Others now withdrew their support. Despite his early backing of Cripps, Pritt chose not to sign the Petition, instead deciding to 'obey party discipline'.[200] Similarly, Wilkinson decided to remain loyal to the Labour party and promptly resigned from the *Tribune* editorial board.[201] Nevertheless, throughout February the Petition Campaign appeared to make progress. By the end of the month the Labour party had received 94 resolutions from local Labour parties protesting against Cripps's expulsion, in contrast to 59 explicitly supporting the NEC's action.[202] Moreover, the campaign had organised a 'complete canvas . . . in one of the wards of Dalton's constituency at Bishop Auckland, and got 81% of the electors to sign'.[203] Indeed, it was in the context of seemingly growing rank and file support that the participants at the *News Chronicle* policy conferences repeatedly discussed the possibility that the campaign might well 'split the Labour Party'.[204]

In early March the NEC broadened out its attack by deciding to threaten Cripps's most prominent supporters. It wrote to Bruce, Young, Bevan, Strauss, Trevelyan and Lawther, informing them that involvement in the Petition Campaign was inconsistent with membership of the Labour party.[205] At the same time the NEC produced a statement which argued that the Petition Campaign sought to create 'a definite and independent political party' and stated that 'having now dealt with the leader of the "Popular Front" campaign, it cannot avoid taking similar action against others who associate with that campaign, and who thereby violate the conditions of their party membership'.[206] At this juncture Tawney tried to mediate the situation. While he had supported a popular front since 1936, he disagreed with the course Cripps had recently taken 'on some of the questions of tactics'. However, after discussing the matter with Cripps in detail he got in touch with Morrison to try and facilitate a compromise. Tawney proposed that in return for Cripps calling off the campaign, the NEC would agree to postpone any further disciplinary action until after the Labour party conference and also accept that 'in a list of constituencies to be agreed upon local Labour parties should be free, if they so desire, to select and support candidates not officially endorsed by the Executive'.[207] Tawney, however, was unable to make further progress with his proposal, and intra-party relations quickly deteriorated. On 15 March Bevan, Strauss, Young and Bruce wrote to the NEC provocatively claiming the right to put their own views in front of the party and refusing to give any assurances whatsoever about their future behaviour.[208] Trevelyan chose not to sign the letter: he was not 'quite confident' that it was 'the right line of action' and considered an open letter to Attlee instead.[209] Perhaps Trevelyan's judgment was correct as the letter only served to heighten the tension. Backed by equal amounts of support from local Labour parties for its line as against it,[210] on 22 March the NEC decided to send an ultimatum to the signatories giving them a week to withdraw from the campaign and assert their loyalty to the party.[211] When they refused to do so, they were expelled on 30 March. Ominously, however, they subsequently claimed that they could not accept this verdict.[212]

VIII

The entry of Nazi forces into Prague on 15 March 1939 – in direct defiance of the Munich agreement – prompted Cripps's next move. As Chamberlain increasingly looked set to abandon appeasement and to take a firmer stance against Hitler,[213] Cripps wrote to the NEC declaring that he was 'ready at any time to meet the Executive . . . for the purpose of seeing whether any or what accommodation can be arrived at which will succeed in maximising the opposition to the National government'. Cripps was concerned that 'people should be asked now to rally behind the National government which has so manifestly misled and deceived them in the past'.[214] Nevertheless, amid the fraught atmosphere of intra-party struggle, the NEC decided not to take any action.[215] It also continued to expel prominent local supporters of the Petition Campaign.[216]

Inevitably, tension increased. Gwen Hill, Cripps's secretary in East Bristol and now the parliamentary candidate for Bristol West, as well as the chair of the South Paddington Petition Committee, was convinced that 'the only thing now for the Left wing to do is to stand firm and refuse to compromise with the NEC and let them do their worst'.[217] She and Lyall Wilkes, the parliamentary candidate for Newcastle Central, wrote to other parliamentary candidates, asking them to sign a letter to the NEC in order to demonstrate support for Cripps and the Petition Campaign as well as to protest about the other expulsions and the wider attempt to 'stifle discussion'.[218] At the same time *Tribune* linked its advocacy of a popular front with opposition to conscription and the demand for an alliance with the Soviet Union. It contended that 'with a Labour-led progressive Government in power allied with the Soviet Union conscription will be unnecessary'.[219] Apparently – with 'a true People's Government' – 'volunteers would come forward in ample numbers'.[220] At a point when the Labour party was opposing conscription and advocating an alliance with the Soviet Union but not, of course, supporting a popular front, this argument was surely intended to resonate widely.[221]

Despite these efforts, the Petition Campaign – like the Unity Campaign – began to lose momentum after a couple of months. During the second half of March, the final Republican strongholds had fallen to Franco. As Michael Foot aptly put it, this 'more than any edicts from Transport House, had broken the spirit of the Left';[222] it had clearly had more impact than the Prague coup. Indeed, before the event Cripps had predicted that the 'fall of Spain is going to react seriously on our people especially those who have done so much work in that cause'.[223] By this stage the Co-operative Party had also rejected the popular front. The only union support the Labour left could now rely on came from the NUDAW, the National Union of Clerks and the South Wales Miners.[224] A conference of the Petition Committees was planned for 11 June, and Cripps's statement for submission, which he prepared before the Labour party conference, was decidedly pessimistic. It contended that 'the situation for us has deteriorated very much since the campaign was first started' not least because of 'the rather unexpected violence of the opposition by the Labour party'.[225]

The debates about whether Cripps – no longer a Labour party member – was to be allowed to address the party conference had remained unresolved.[226] Now on the first day of the conference at Southport on 29 May, the issue was debated. Mellor spoke in support of Cripps's right to speak,[227] and the NEC agreed to let the conference as a whole take the decision. When it decided (by a small majority) that Cripps should speak,[228] he then outlined his case, emphasising the technical arguments about the right to issue the memorandum irrespective of the broader merits of the popular front.[229] Needless to say, he failed to capture the attention of the conference. Dalton then replied for the NEC that it had been necessary to act against Cripps in order to prevent 'disintegration and demoralisation' from permeating the Labour movement.[230] It was no surprise when the delegates approved Cripps's expulsion by 2,100,000 votes to 402,000 and then chose to reject the popular front by an even larger majority.[231]

The Labour left had been squarely defeated. Cripps, Bevan, Strauss and Young immediately applied for re-admission to the party, promising to 'abide by the decision of the conference on the Popular Front' because 'its immediate political practicability' had been 'destroyed'.[232] For the time being though, they remained outside the party as the NEC replied that it would consider the matter in due course, effectively shelving it.[233] The Petition Campaign was clearly at an end. Brailsford told Cripps that frankly 'it would be a mistake to keep the petition organisation in being'. Brailsford was deeply despondent, stating: 'My own feeling is that I now see nothing the Left can usefully do', and deciding 'to drop out of active politics for some considerable time'.[234] Cripps shared Brailsford's perspective, recognising the need to 'sit back for a bit now and watch what happens',[235] and telling Laski 'there are times when it is wise to withdraw in order to advance the better later'.[236] For these reasons, Cripps wrote in *Tribune* that the result at the Labour party conference 'must mean the end of the Popular Front campaign', and urged those who had been involved 'to throw themselves into the work of the Labour Movement'.[237] At the conference of the Petition Committees on 11 June, Cripps developed the same themes,[238] and gained acceptance of a resolution that 'the Petition Campaign be forthwith wound up and the local and central committees be disbanded'.[239]

The Labour left was in disarray. Laski planned to raise the question of the re-admittance of Cripps, Bevan and the others into the party at the NEC meeting on 28 June. Significantly, Laski had avoided even seeing Cripps for the past few months. He considered it important to show that he had been 'cut off from this dispute, directly and indirectly . . . if I am to exercise any influence on the Executive'.[240] Laski had, of course, been in the United States during the early part of the year but this was not the only factor which had prevented his involvement. While supporting Cripps's overall line, his firm view was that 'if we are beaten on the NEC we must accept defeat or resign'. He had opposed the Petition Campaign but at the same time had considered that the expulsions were 'utterly unjustifiable'.[241] His efforts to mediate on Cripps's behalf were, however, to no avail. The NEC meeting, after discussing the matter, simply referred it to the Organisation Sub-committee, which was mandated to produce a report ahead of the NEC's next meeting in September.[242] The left-wing bloc on the NEC, which had enjoyed some success since October 1937, had clearly been shattered.

The rejection of the popular front and the expulsion of its leading advocates not only adversely affected sales of *Tribune*,[243] but also brought its relationship with the Left Book Club into doubt. Before the party conference, Cripps had speculated that if the popular front was defeated, it might be possible to continue the campaign through the Left Book Club.

He was, however, aware that this might be problematic since the club sought to have a 'purely educational basis'.[244] In a context where the Labour left was seriously discredited, these concerns led the Left Book Club Selection Committee to become aware of 'certain disadvantages inherent in the existing arrangement':

> While it has always been made clear that the Left Book Club pages were completely autonomous and had no organic connection with the rest of the paper, nevertheless there was a tendency to identify the Club with the paper as a whole: not only had this never been the intention, but it was obvious that, if an idea got abroad, one of the basic principles of the Club would be destroyed – its all-inclusive character, and its refusal to identify itself with any party or group.[245]

As a result the Selection Committee decided to sever its connection with *Tribune*, with the final Left Book Club pages appearing in July. At the same time Gollancz resigned from the *Tribune* board. Now that the Left Book Club no longer contributed its own section, he was concerned that if he had not done so, he and the Left Book Club would still 'necessarily be definitely identified' with the *Tribune*'.[246] The agreed statement produced by the Left Book Club about the decision also noted *Tribune*'s desire to 'lighten' its tone, and stressed that in this context it was considered desirable to drop the Left Book Club pages and place the whole paper under the editor's control.[247] However, it seems that the prime motivation for the dissolution of the arrangement came from the Left Book Club side.[248]

In the final months before the outbreak of war, Cripps – outside the Labour party[249] – devoted much of his effort to attempting to build alliances with other critics of Chamberlain, including Churchill.[250] He also began to see Baldwin as a potential prime minister.[251] Meanwhile, *Tribune*'s main line was to continue to call for an alliance with the Soviet Union, and to lament Chamberlain's lack of enthusiasm for the idea.[252] Significantly though, once again, it suggested that a strategic alliance with the Soviet Union was necessary to save Britain (and British democratic values) from fascist aggression.[253] In the context of impending war, this surely testifies to the reduced importance of the Soviet Union in the Labour left's identity.

IX

In early 1939 the ILP continued to press its case for a united front. As Cripps issued his memorandum, the *New Leader* asserted that 'his proposed solution

... would only make the situation worse'.[254] Similarly, in March the ILP argued that the root cause of the fall of Republican Spain was divisions between 'bourgeois Republicans and the revolutionary workers', with the former being 'out for the maintenance of their class under any conditions' in such a way that necessarily 'destroys the case for Popular Frontism'. The ILP was absolutely clear that any 'collaboration with capitalism leads to disaster and betrayal.'[255] During the Prague Coup, the ILP again argued in favour of 'independent working-class action against fascism, imperialism and war' and suggested an international working-class conference to consider the matter. Its reasoning here was the same as it had been during the Munich crisis: this was another potential conflict between rival imperialisms, adding that 'the very same tyrannies which Hitler commits in Germany are committed in the British Empire'.[256] The *New Leader* reiterated the same arguments after Britain offered a guarantee to Poland, further asserting that Poland was 'admittedly semi-fascist'.[257] It was no surprise at all, therefore, that at the ILP conference in April, a resolution urging 'international working-class action by organised refusal of supplies to fascist countries' was smoothly endorsed.[258]

Crucially, however, the Soviet Union was no longer central to the ILP's war resistance policy, marking an important break with the past. Brockway gave the first public indication of this change of position in late March. Calling for an international working-class congress to organise mass resistance, he significantly made no mention at all of the Soviet Union.[259] Events at the ILP conference the following month then made the ILP's new stance clear. An amendment which demanded an explicit commitment to defend the Soviet Union, contending that it was 'still the object of attack by the capitalist powers', was lost, showing that the ILP was steadily abandoning the remnants of its pro-Soviet identity.[260] This was, of course, part of a longer-term process of which the responses to the purges and to the persecution of the POUM in Spain had been important parts.[261] Moreover, this change on the part of the ILP also mirrored developments in the international organisations to which it affiliated. At the beginning of May, McNair and Edwards took part – as the ILP delegates – in the formation of two new international organisations. These were the New Revolutionary Marxist Centre which replaced the International Bureau and crucially included the International Communist Opposition,[262] and the International Workers Front Against War which was also notably critical of Stalin.[263]

Despite clear differences with the Labour party over its policy of mass resistance, the ILP nonetheless continued to have a serious internal debate over the merits of re-affiliation. In late October 1938, the ILP Executive Committee had 'unanimously decided that the policy of supporting Labour party candidates against the candidates of the National government should be maintained'.[264] A month later the ILP NAC had formalised this position in writing to the Labour party proposing a 'united campaign . . . on agreed issues' and an 'electoral agreement for by-elections and the General Election'.[265] In keeping with past ILP policy, extended discussion over a contentious issue was not permitted in the *New Leader*.[266] Consequently, some of the most intense arguments took place in the ILP's lower-circulation discussion organ *Controversy*.[267] Re-affiliation was, however, one of the main topics of discussion at the divisional conferences on 4 and 5 February 1939. At the London conference the proposal for Labour party affiliation was 'heavily defeated', while at the Scottish conference, 60 delegates voted against affiliation, 11 in favour of conditional affiliation and 18 in favour of re-affiliation. In the Midlands a resolution favouring conditional affiliation was carried, while in Wales a more ambiguous resolution was passed which endorsed the 'principle of working-class unity' but expressed 'concern' about the attitude of the Labour party and the TUC towards rearmament and the National Register.[268]

At the ILP national conference on 8–10 April, the debate was equally intense. Opening the discussion, Maxton made it clear that the NAC itself was divided over the question of re-affiliation. Lee was strongly opposed, arguing that it was particularly inopportune to consider affiliation at the point when the Labour party was 'lining the workers up behind the Government for war'. She was also clear that if the ILP did affiliate it would not, in any case, be able to exert much influence as the trade union block vote would 'ensure defeat for whatever we say'. Bob Edwards then highlighted 'the present isolation of the party' as he introduced a report produced by a specially convened committee. Importantly, this suggested a compromise which would allow individual ILP members to work inside the Labour party without the need for ILP affiliation. Aplin then entered the debate, explaining that he had been a signatory to the report, but had since withdrawn his support and now opposed re-affiliation. He linked his attitude on the issue to his views on the action of the Parliamentary Group over the Munich crisis, contending that he now ceased to believe that 'as a disciplined revolutionary body, it [the ILP] could work with advantage within the ranks of the Labour party'. Patterson also argued that he had changed his stance as a result of the controversy over Munich, but claimed for rhetorical effect to draw the opposite affiliationist conclusion. From his Trotskyist viewpoint, he was clearly deeply disaffected with the ILP and, seeking to increase discord, argued that it might as well join the Labour party because, in any case, it 'would not develop into a revolutionary party'. Carmichael, by contrast, was genuinely in favour of affiliation, arguing that

the ILP 'could give a lead to the rank and file of the Labour party' against
fascism. He was clearly moved by concerns about the ILP's isolation from the
Labour movement, contending that it was 'not enough to have a correct
policy. That policy must have a chance of application'. The veteran Fred
Jowett, on the other hand, was adamant that the ILP should not 'be
associated with the reactionary policies of Transport House'. Brockway then
wound up the debate. He repeated his view that affiliation should be
regarded 'as a matter of tactics', determined by how best the ILP could 'work
for the revolutionary socialist view . . . in the wider mass movement'. If the
ILP could not accept a situation in which, despite remaining a unit, it could
not vote against the Labour party in parliament, i.e., that it could not adhere
to Labour's Standing Orders, then he argued that the committee's
compromise was the best course to follow. The result of the debate was
mixed. Straightforward affiliation was defeated by 63 votes to 45; the
committee's report was also rejected by 68 votes to 42; while conditional
affiliation was endorsed by 69 votes to 40. This was clearly inconclusive, and
accordingly Maxton simply said that he interpreted 'this decision as a desire
by the conference that negotiations with the Labour party should
continue'.[269] The confusion was then only increased when the new NAC
chairman Smith wrote a piece in the *New Leader* immediately after the
conference strongly opposing Labour party affiliation. His central argument
was that 'far from agreeing with its [the Labour party's] policy of supporting
the British government in a war, I regard this "social patriotism" as a
mixture of poltroonery and treachery'.[270]

In the months after the conference, the ILP continued to chart a
contradictory path so far as its relations with the Labour party were
concerned. In the first place, the ILP was sympathetic to the plight of the
leaders of the Petition Campaign, arguing that 'we cannot help asking
ourselves whether their expulsion does not mean that the organised public
expression of minority views are no longer permissible within the Labour
party'.[271] Secondly, the ILP continued to go beyond the Labour party in its
campaign against conscription, which it saw as an integral part of its overall
war resistance strategy. The ILP conference had been unanimous in its
opposition to the National Register.[272] At the conference too, William
Ballantine, a member of the NUR Executive who was chairman of the No
Conscription League, was elected on to the NAC as a national member.[273]
Now the ILP also made opposition to conscription central to its May Day
demonstrations in London, Bradford and Manchester.[274] As Smith readily
emphasised the ILP continued to be willing to unite with 'pacifists, both
socialist and non-socialist' in order to encourage resistance to conscription.[275]
Indeed, at a North London conference of the No Conscription League on

24 June, Smith spoke alongside speakers from the PPU.[276] With the Labour party constantly reiterating its support for an immediate policy of collective security, a statement issued by the ILP in July made its divergence in policy clear:

> The ILP will not support any war under any Government whilst Britain remains a capitalist state. We will not support a war under the National government, under a Peace Front government, or under a Labour government.[277]

Even so, the question of Labour party affiliation continued to be a live one. In late April Buchanan, who favoured affiliation, resigned from the ILP and re-joined the Labour party.[278] There was also press speculation that McGovern and Stephen might follow suit.[279] Significantly neither of them was any longer on the NAC, having previously been Scottish representative and a national representative respectively. By early July it appeared that the Labour-ILP negotiations had reached deadlock, with the Labour party claiming that 'very little useful comment could be added' to the negotiations that had taken place before the ILP conference and asserting the importance of the observance of Parliamentary Standing Orders.[280] However, in this context, and with Brockway now in regular contact with Middleton,[281] the NAC began to consider its stance very closely once again. Significantly, as it did so it faced stiff opposition from Patterson who repeatedly accused the ILP of abandoning its revolutionary socialist beliefs and in particular attacked the two most forceful advocates of re-affiliation – Stephen and McGovern.[282] As a result, the Executive Committee took the decision to expel Patterson for 'anti-party political conduct', thus precipitating a row with the London Divisional Council, which – by a majority of one – decided that it would not operate the ban. This, in turn, led the Inner Executive to suspend the London Divisional Council and to summon a conference of branches from the London and Southern Counties, which then duly passed a resolution asserting – in contrast to Patterson's comments – that the ILP was indeed a revolutionary socialist party.[283]

Despite Patterson's opposition, by this point momentum was building in favour of re-affiliation. At a meeting on 5 August a majority on the NAC now came out in favour, and agreed to recommend it to the membership at a special conference on 17 September. The NAC asserted that the ILP remained 'opposed to rearmament and national service for the defence of a capitalist-imperialist state, to conscription, and to the sham "Peace Front" proposal' but argued that there were 'thousands within the Labour Party who share the ILP view on these matters' and that there would therefore 'be the opportunity to maintain them'. The NAC also stressed that affiliation would 'not mean an end of the organisational independence of the ILP' as it would 'continue as a political unity, with our own branches, our own conferences, our own *New Leader*, our own literature, our own meetings'. At the same time, however, the NAC wanted the ILP to 'recognise the L[abour] P[arty] as the political expression of the working-class movement of Great Britain and . . . logically co-operate within it'.[284] Although the outbreak of the Second World War prevented the ILP special conference from taking place, it was nonetheless clear that a chapter in the history of the Left was closing; by deciding to apply for re-affiliation, the ILP NAC was conceding defeat in its battle with the Labour party.[285] Just as significantly, the announcement of the Nazi-Soviet Pact on 23 August was about to test the Left's views of the Soviet Union which had been so painfully developed during its internal debates in the 1930s.

CONCLUSION

During the course of the 1930s the Left had become increasingly sceptical about the value of the Soviet Union – the world's first socialist state – as an ideological ally against the rise of international fascism. In the early part of the decade the Left held a distinctly pro-Soviet identity, but the entry of the Soviet Union into the League of Nations, the Comintern's role in the Spanish Civil War and, of course, the Show Trials and wider purges in the Soviet Union subsequently threw its assumptions into question. By the end of the decade the Left was defining itself in more complex ways – partly in terms of a greater ambiguity towards the Soviet Union, and partly in terms of a marked hostility towards it.

The Left did not, by any means, respond uniformly to the international developments of the 1930s. In fact, it was the Left's deep-seated divisions over the Soviet Union which, at critical moments, enabled Labour's moderate majorities seriously to discredit it. This was what happened to the Socialist League during the sanctions crisis in September and October 1935. Similarly, divisions over the Soviet Union ruptured the Unity Campaign in 1937, not just setting the ILP at odds with the CPGB but also permeating the Socialist League and creating divisions within its ranks that the NEC-TUC grouping could then exploit. As the Second World War approached, the increasingly critical stance towards the Soviet Union taken by the ILP separated it from the Labour left grouped around *Tribune* which publicly insisted that, above all, the Soviet Union was an essential strategic ally. With the CPGB focusing its attention on securing entry to the Labour party, both the ILP and the Labour left became increasingly marginalised from wider support. As a result, by summer 1939 they both became willing to operate within the framework of the Labour party.

Other characteristics of the Left have been illuminated by a close analysis of the 1930s. On many different occasions a significant gulf has been noticeable between the Left's heady rhetoric of 'revolutionary socialism' and its actual stance in practice where both the Labour left and the ILP worked within a parliamentary democracy.[1] In particular, it was unclear whether the

Left ever really envisaged 'mass resistance' taking place. Nevertheless, it remained a central part of the ILP's programme for the entire decade and it was only in 1938 that the Labour left moved away from such a position.

The fast moving events of the 1930s also brought into sharp focus a related dilemma facing the British Left: how to reconcile its preferred theoretical stance with the reality of a situation in which it was not able to influence international developments, or even domestic politics, in any meaningful way. This quandary explains Brailsford and Martin's willingness to consider endorsing the National government's use of sanctions against Italy in 1935. It also accounts for the Labour left's increasing advocacy of a popular front and its conditional backing of National government rearmament, as well as the ILP's decision to re-affiliate to the Labour party.

Both the Socialist League and the ILP experienced a fraught relationship with their relatively limited number of rank and file members. Maxton used his influence effectively to overturn the ILP annual conference's support for 'working-class sanctions' against Italy in 1936. Cripps and Mellor were constantly seeking to exclude the Socialist membership from any influence over decision-making – a process that became particularly evident as a result of the twists and turns of policy during, and immediately after, the Unity Campaign. There was, indeed, a distinctly hypocritical note to Cripps's frequent accusation that the NEC was acting in a high-handed manner. Crucially, however, in a number of instances the Socialist League branch in Bristol – Cripps's parliamentary constituency – did have a discernible impact on the overall direction of policy.

The precise contribution to the Left made by women, such as Betts, Wilkinson and Lee, has also been elucidated in more detail. Pamela Graves has argued that in the 1920s women pushed for distinctly 'feminist' or certainly gender specific reforms, but that by the 1930s gender conflict disappeared within the Labour party as women adopted positions alongside men on the central issue of the response to international fascism.[2] While such issues are not, of course, a major theme of this book, it confirms this picture so far as the Left is concerned.

Above all, a detailed examination of the Left's ideological trajectory in the 1930s has shown that – even before the Nazi-Soviet Pact – an anti-Stalinist outlook had firmly emerged in the ILP and on certain parts of the Labour left.[3] In a number of ways this involved a condemnation of the characteristics of Stalin's dictatorship and an explicit comparison with that of Hitler. As a concept anti-Stalinism was distinct from the type of domestic anti-communism which had developed in the Labour party during the 1920s as the CPGB had repeatedly attempted to infiltrate it. This continued to pervade the Labour party, and particularly the trade union movement, in the

1930s and was epitomised by an extreme wariness of Communist attempts to 'make mischief'.[4] While some of those adopting an anti-Stalinist position – such as Groves in the Socialist League and Patterson in the ILP – could be defined as Trotskyist, many others could not. Indeed, at one level anti-Stalinism was critical of Stalin as the symbol of the whole political culture – based on suspicion – that had developed in the Soviet Union and produced the Stalin-Trotsky split in the first place.

Anti-Stalinism had not developed consistently across the Left. Throughout the 1930s Cripps and Mellor, of course, remained silent about internal developments within the Soviet Union, while pro-Stalinist figures such as Pritt continued passionately to defend them. Nevertheless, as information about the Soviet purges appeared in Britain, Brockway and Maxton, together with Brailsford and even Laski, criticised these events as a betrayal not only of socialism but of an even more basic sense of social justice. Unlike the others, however, Laski refused to accept that the Stalinist dictatorship was the same as that in Nazi Germany. Moreover, some of those who were vehement in their criticism of the purges – such as Brailsford – were still supportive of the Communist position in Spain and thus publicly at odds with the ILP which championed the POUM and explicitly incorporated Soviet actions in Spain into its anti-Stalinist outlook. Importantly, Orwell's anti-Stalinism had been formed in the opposite way to that of much of the ILP: his views were very much shaped as a result of his experiences in Spain and it was only later that he integrated the purges into his analysis.[5]

The Left's views of the Soviet Union soon came under scrutiny as a result of the Nazi-Soviet Pact and then the Soviet invasion of Finland at the end of November 1939. Famously, Pritt published *Light on Moscow*, which was extremely sympathetic to the Soviet need to reach an agreement with Nazi Germany, and then *Must the War Spread?*, a controversial apologia for Soviet actions in Finland that led to his expulsion from the Labour party.[6] By this point, however, such attitudes were clearly unusual. Indeed, *Tribune*'s initial response to the Nazi-Soviet Pact was consistent with its portrayal of the Soviet Union as an essential strategic ally since September 1938. It contended that the pact had resulted from Chamberlain's failure to build bridges with the Soviet Union,[7] and Bevan even called for renewed efforts to reach agreement.[8] Yet after the Soviet invasion of Finland, *Tribune* began to take a more critical line, albeit one that contained elements of the pro-Soviet identity it had never fully abandoned even after it ceased publicly to present the Soviet Union as an ideological ally. *Tribune* now declared that: 'We deplore her for her aggression, but we support her for her socialism.'[9] Despite the relatively restrained tone, this stance led to a breach with the CPGB and, in early 1940, to the dismissal of the ardently pro-Soviet Hartshorn as *Tribune* editor.[10]

Elsewhere on the Left, the underlying anti-Stalinist perspective shaped the ways in which early wartime international events were interpreted. The ILP, for instance, juxtaposed its criticism of Stalin with its opposition to war in Britain. Speaking in the House of Commons on 24 August 1939, McGovern memorably condemned the 'bloodstained handshake of Stalin and Ribbentrop'.[11] Some of the ambiguities of the ILP's anti-Stalinist outlook of the late 1930s also persisted. Even after the Soviet invasion of Finland, the official ILP stance remained emphatically opposed to British involvement in a war against the Soviet Union. In March 1940 the *New Leader* declared that it would 'resist war with Russia to the last ounce of our strength. Many of the achievements of the October Revolution remain in Russia despite Stalinism and we shall certainly not line up with British capitalism to destroy them.'[12] Clearly, opposition to Stalinism was not yet synonymous with opposition to the Soviet Union. Nonetheless, C. A. Smith contended that he was prepared to fight against 'Stalin's latest crime' provided he was not aiding 'British imperialism',[13] showing just how far anti-Stalinist attitudes had progressed in some parts of the ILP.

On the Labour left Brailsford described the Nazi-Soviet Pact as 'a violation of public morality for which nothing in the record of the Soviet Union had prepared us'.[14] The invasion of Finland then led him publicly to argue that:

His [Stalin's] Russia is a totalitarian state like another, as brutal towards the rights of others, as careless of its plighted word. If this man ever understood the international creed of socialism, he long ago forgot it. In this land the absolute power has wrought its customary effects of corruption.[15]

At the same point, Martin powerfully contended in the *New Statesman* that the Soviet Union – together with Germany and Japan – represented a 'new totalitarian idea', opposed both to democracy and socialism.[16]

Anti-Stalinism also facilitated a patriotic response to the Second World War by parts of the Left. This was the outlook made famous by Orwell in *The Lion and the Unicorn* in 1941 which celebrated the distinctive characteristics of English life that were under attack from fascism.[17] Crucially, it was also evident in some of Laski's writings.[18] Partly, of course, this was a straightforward reaction to the external threat facing Britain at this point as well as to the broader features of the 'People's War'. It was, however, made possible because – unlike the early 1930s – the Left no longer saw the Soviet Union as any kind of exemplar. At a time of crisis, they accordingly looked not to the Soviet Union but, despite its faults, to Britain.

The Left's interpretations of the Soviet Union's actions in the early stages of the Second World War were similar to those of the Labour party and the TUC, building on a common perspective established at the time of the purges.[19] At the TUC meeting in early September 1939 Citrine spoke of 'a dictatorship in Russia as severe and cruel as anything that has happened in Germany'.[20] Similarly, on receiving news of the Soviet invasion of Finland, the *Daily Herald* called it an 'inexcusable a crime as Hitler's invasion of Czechoslovakia'.[21]

Undoubtedly though, it was on the Left that an anti-Stalinist critique had been most forcefully developed. Never having been overtly pro-Soviet to anywhere near the same degree as the Left, the Labour party had not found the events of the 1930s as deeply unsettling. A further layer of explanation is also possible: the Left has traditionally attracted individuals who tend to take world events to heart. This means that while they sometimes prevaricate in ways that undermine their political positions, they also often develop more insightful analyses.

After 1940 anti-Stalinism did not develop in a linear manner.[22] Once the Soviet Union entered the Second World War on the side of the allies in 1941 the Labour party and the Left quickly expressed renewed respect for the Soviet Union, seeing it – once again – as a key partner in the fight against Hitler. Indeed, Stalin himself was rehabilitated as 'Uncle Joe'. By the time Labour came to power under Attlee in 1945 this pro-Soviet enthusiasm had already begun to recede and soon, as the Cold War intensified, initial concerns about Soviet aims for expansion in Eastern Europe developed into fully-fledged criticisms of Stalin and his regime. As a Soviet attack on Western Europe was mooted as a serious possibility and Britain drew closer to the United States, the Labour party explicitly likened Stalin's actions and methods to those of Hitler. This view had quickly taken hold on the centre right of the party. By 1947 it was being expounded by Bevin as foreign secretary and by Dalton as chancellor of the exchequer. Initially the left wing of the Labour party hesitated and still tried to portray the Soviet Union in a favourable light, thus temporarily obscuring its earlier anti-Stalinist traditions. It was a full year later that the Labour left, including *Tribune*, became forthright in its indictment of Stalin.

The irony is that the foreign policy of Attlee, Bevin and Dalton – all of them opponents of the Left in the tactical struggles of the 1930s – rested in important respects upon an analysis of Stalinism that the Left had itself done much to formulate. An abiding image of the Left's discomfiture in the 1930s is of Bevin's brutal demolition of its case against sanctions. But, as so often in politics, there was a two-way traffic in ideas. From a longer-term perspective, the Left's anti-Stalinist critique was not so easily scorned and marginalised. Indeed, many of its insights undoubtedly became central to Labour's international outlook in the 1940s – and arguably for the rest of the twentieth century.

NOTES

Introduction

1 D. Blaazer, *The Popular Front and the Progressive Tradition: Socialists, Liberals, and the Quest for Unity, 1884–1939* (Cambridge, 1992).

2 See, in particular, ibid., chs 5 and 6.

3 Ibid., p. 157, is explicit on this point, citing H. N. Brailsford, *Property or Peace?* (1934), p. 54.

4 H. Pelling, *A Short History of the Labour Party* (1961), ch. 5. Pelling entitled this chapter, covering 1931 to 1939, 'The General Council's Party'. This emphasis is repeated in all subsequent editions including the most recent with Alistair Reid.

5 B. Pimlott, *Labour and the Left in the 1930s* (Cambridge, 1977), pp. 18–19; B. Pimlott, *Hugh Dalton* (1985), p. 212.

6 Elizabeth Durbin and particularly Richard Toye show how the NEC assumed responsibility and that the trade unions were largely uninvolved: E. Durbin, *New Jerusalems: The Labour Party and the Politics of Democratic Socialism* (1985), chs 4, 10, 12; R. Toye, *The Labour Party and the Planned Economy 1931–51*, (Woodbridge, 2003), chs 2 and 3.

7 T. Buchanan, *The Spanish Civil War and the British Labour Movement* (Cambridge, 1991), esp. chs 1–4.

8 Pimlott, *Labour and the Left*, p. 5.

9 Ibid., pp. 42, 6.

10 Ibid., esp. pp. 1–5 and *passim*.

11 P. Seyd, 'Factionalism within the Labour Party: The Socialist League, 1932–37' in A. Briggs and J. Saville (eds), *Essays in Labour History 1918–39* (1977), pp. 204–31. R. G. Dare, 'The Socialist League, 1932–37' (unpublished Oxford D. Phil., 1973), is the only full length study of the Socialist League but is stronger on its formation and initial development than on its responses to international developments after 1935. M. Cowling, *The Impact of Hitler: British Politics and Policy 1933–40* (Cambridge, 1975), pp. 27–31, is also insightful. In addition, Durbin and Toye have added to the picture by closely examining the Socialist League's role in Labour party debates over economic policy: Durbin, *New Jerusalems*, esp. pp. 85–6, 204, 207–8, 212–15 and 223; Toye, *Labour Party and Planned Economy*, pp. 61–3. See also Pimlott's earlier article: B. Pimlott, 'The Socialist League: Intellectuals and the Labour Party in the 1930s', *Journal of Contemporary History*, 6, 3 (1971), pp. 12–38.

12   J. Jupp, *The Radical Left in Britain 1931–41* (1982). This builds markedly on
     the outlines offered in R. E. Dowse, *Left ingfbe Centre: The Independent Labour
     Party 1893–1940* (1966). However, G. A. Cohen, 'The Independent Labour
     Party, 1932–39' (unpublished University of York D. Phil., 2000) [hereafter
     Cohen thesis], is now the fullest account. T. Buchanan, 'The Death of Bob
     Smillie, the Spanish Civil War and the Eclipse of the Independent Labour
     Party', *Historical Journal*, 40, 2 (1997), pp. 435–61, is also extremely useful.
13   Pimlott, *Labour and the Left*, pp. 54–6; Seyd, 'Factionalism', pp. 218–19; Dare,
     'Socialist League', pp. 312–18.
14   D. Howell, *MacDonald's Party: Labour Identities and Crisis 1922–31* (Oxford,
     2002), p. 7.
15   A. J. Williams, *The Labour Party and Russia, 1924–34* (Manchester, 1989), esp.
     chs 11 and 14, and pp. 161, 232. See also A. J. Williams, 'The Labour Party's
     Attitude to the Soviet Union 1927–35: An Overview with Specific Reference
     to Unemployment Policy and Peace', *Journal of Contemporary History*, 22,
     1 (1987), pp. 71–90.
16   There is very limited consideration in Pimlott, *Labour and the Left* and Jupp, *Radical
     Left*. The ways in which different individuals on the Left responded to these events
     is, of course, better known. F. Leventhal, *The Last Dissenter: H. N. Brailsford and his
     World* (Oxford, 1985), is among the best biographies in this respect.
17   B. Jones, *The Russia Complex* (Manchester, 1977), ch. 2, which purports to
     consider Labour's views of the Soviet Union actually focuses narrowly in its
     coverage of the 1930s on extremely pro-Soviet (if not Stalinist) figures such as
     Sidney and Beatrice Webb as well as D. N. Pritt. Repeating contemporary
     Communist claims, the 'official' history of the CPGB, N. Branson, *History of the
     Communist Party of Great Britain 1927–41* (1985), p. 142, argues that in the
     1930s 'the ILP was to an increasing extent influenced by Trotskyists . . . like
     Brockway'. In contrast, those with a Trotskyist outlook themselves have
     criticised the ILP for being insufficiently Trotskyist: S. Bornstein and A.
     Richardson, *Against the Stream: A History of the Trotskyist Movement in Britain
     1924–38* (1986), esp. ch. 8.
18   The Left frequently discussed Stalinism and also occasionally referred to its own
     stance as anti-Stalinist. See, for instance, *New Leader*, 13 January 1939.

Chapter 1

1   The authoritative account of the critical years between 1922 and 1931 is
     Howell, *MacDonald's Party*. A useful overview can be found in A. Thorpe, *A
     History of the British Labour Party* (1997), ch. 3.
2   For this paragraph see specifically Howell, *MacDonald's Party*, chs 4, 15–17;
     Dowse, *Left in the Centre*, chs 3, 9–11; R. K. Middlemas, *The Clydesiders: A
     Left Wing Struggle for Parliamentary Power* (1965), chs 8–9; G. Cohen, 'The
     Independent Labour Party, Disaffiliation, Revolution and Standing Orders',
     History 86, 2 (2001), pp. 200–21, at pp. 204–7; and more generally N.
     Riddell, *Labour in Crisis: The Second Labour Government 1929–31* (Manchester,
     1999).
3   Generally for this paragraph see Howell, *MacDonald's Party*, pp. 288–303; Jupp,
     Radical Left, pp. 21–3; Cohen, 'Independent Labour Party and Standing
     Orders', pp. 207–12.
4   Indeed, Williams, *Labour and Russia*, p. 158, argues that this difference over the
     Soviet Union 'was enough almost in itself to drive many ILP members into exile
     from the Labour party'.

5 For more on Labour intellectuals at this time see R. Dare, 'Instinct and Organisation: Intellectuals and British Labour after 1931', *Historical Journal*, 26, 3 (1983), pp. 677–97.

6 M. I. Cole, *Growing up into Revolution* (1949), p. 148. For Cole in these years see N. Riddell, '"The Age of Cole"? G. D. H. Cole and the British Labour Movement, 1929–33', *Historical Journal*, 38, 4 (1995), pp. 933–57.

7 'Annual Report of the SSIP for the year ending 31 March 1932', Nuffield College, Oxford, Cole papers, GDHC/D4/4/1/1–6; also in Modern Records Centre (MRC), University of Warwick, TUC archive, MSS.126/EB/SS/1/12.

8 'Aims and Methods of the SSIP', n.d., Cole papers, GDHC/D4/2/3/1–2; also in TUC archive, MSS.292/756.1/3. See also Cole, *Growing up into Revolution*, p. 145.

9 For Bevin's trade union commitments see A. Bullock, *Life and Times of Ernest Bevin: Volume One Trade Union Leader 1881 to 1940* (1960), p. 505.

10 'Rules of the SSIP', n.d., Cole papers, GDHC/D4/2/1; also in TUC archive, MSS.292/756.1/3.

11 The authoritative account of the crisis is P. A. Williamson, *National Crisis and National Government: British Politics, the Economy and Empire, 1926–1932* (Cambridge, 1992), chs. 8, 9 and 10.

12 See A. Thorpe, *The British General Election of 1931* (Oxford, 1991) ch. 6 and pp. 159–61.

13 A. Thorpe, 'Arthur Henderson and the British Political Crisis of 1931', *Historical Journal*, 31, 1 (1988), pp. 117–39.

14 Bullock, *Bevin i*, chs. 13–16.

15 Ibid., ch. 17.

16 Ibid., p. 480.

17 Williamson, *National Crisis*, pp. 312–14, 376–9, quoting NEC minutes, 26 and 27 August 1931.

18 Williamson, *National Crisis*, p. 376.

19 See B. Donoughue and G. W. Jones, *Herbert Morrison: Portrait of a Politician* (1973), ch. 11, for discussion of this contentious issue.

20 *The Times*, 8 September 1931, quoted in Williamson, *National Crisis*, p. 384.

21 For Dalton see H. Dalton, 'Draft Report to the Main Committee', NEC Sub-committee on International Policy, September 1931, Bodleian Library, Oxford, Cripps papers (not catalogued at time of use), which stated that capitalism was 'swiftly approaching a complete breakdown'; for Morrison see *Labour Party Annual Conference Report* (1931), p. 177 [hereafter cited as *LPACR*, year], where he argued it was necessary for the party to think in terms of 'changing fundamentally the economic order'.

22 This was chaired by William Graham, the former President of the Board of Trade. The Cripps papers contain much relevant material concerning the work of this committee.

23 Williamson, *National Crisis*, pp. 427–33, comments on these developments.

24 *LPACR*, 1931, pp. 179, 182, 184, 187–8, 195, 204, 217.

25 'The Election Issue – Capitalism versus Socialism', incorrectly dated in handlist as c. December 1931, Cole papers, GDHC/D4/5/3/1–5.

26 See P. Clarke, *The Cripps Version: The Life of Sir Stafford Cripps* (2002), pp. 3–51.

27 Cripps to MacDonald, 28 August 1931, copy in Cripps papers.

28 Cripps to Graham, 1 September 1931, copy in Cripps papers.

29 *LPACR*, 1931, p. 205. For Cripps's immediate response to the events of August 1931 see S. Burgess, *Stafford Cripps: A Political Life* (1999), pp. 66–8.

30 Dowse, *Left in the Centre*, pp. 152–73.

31 *New Leader*, 28 August 1931.

32 *LPACR*, 1931, p. 190.

33 See Williamson, *National Crisis*, p. 432.

34 Ibid., p. 382.

35 Brockway in *House of Commons Debates*, 5th series [hereafter 5 HC Debs], vol. 256, cols. 458–67, 11 September 1931, quoted in Williamson, *National Crisis,* pp. 382–3.

36 Middlemas, *The Clydesiders*, p. 261; Williamson, *National Crisis*, p. 383.

37 Finance and Trade Policy Committee minutes, 9, 17, 18 September 1931; E. A. Radice, 'Memorandum on Banking Policy', 23 September 1931, all Cripps papers. Finance and Trade Policy Committee minutes, 21 September 1931, Bodleian Library, Oxford, Addison papers, Ms. Addison dep.c.204.331.

38 See Dalton diary, 7 October 1931, British Library of Political and Economic Science (BLPES), Dalton papers, 1/14.

39 For the general election see Thorpe, *General Election*, chs. 7 to 10.

40 For the rest of this paragraph see Pimlott, *Labour and the Left*, pp. 17–18

41 D. E. McHenry, *The Labour Party in Transition* (1938), p. 141, aptly describes the PLP's role after October 1931 as 'futile and unreal'.

42 *LPACR*, 1932, p. 67; Pimlott, *Labour and the Left*, pp. 18–19.

43 Pimlott, *Labour and the Left*, p. 36.

44 Pimlott, *Dalton*, p. 204, discusses this aspect of the debates. See Webb diary, 7 March 1932, BLPES, Passfield papers, for Morrison's jealousy of Cripps for similar reasons [N. and J. MacKenzie (eds.) *The Diary of Beatrice Webb Diary: volume iv 1924–43: The Wheel of Life* (1985), p. 283].

45 Donoughue and Jones, *Morrison*, p. 185.

46 H. Dalton, *The Fateful Years: Memoirs 1931–45* (1957), pp. 23–4; Pimlott, *Dalton*, p. 212. For a full discussion of the NEC's attempt to develop a new Labour programme see Durbin, *New Jerusalems*, ch. 4.

47 NEC minutes, 7 October 1931.

48 ILP NAC minutes, 7 November 1931; Jupp, *Radical Left*, p. 24. For Maxton's views see *Daily Herald*, 16 November 1931, quoted in Dowse, *Left in the Centre*, p. 177.

49 ILP NAC minutes, 7 November 1931.

50 Buchanan and Kirkwood were both nominated by trade unions.

51 A. F. Brockway, *Inside the Left* (1942), p. 238; Dowse, *Left in the Centre*, p. 177; Williamson, *National Crisis*, p. 464.

52 *New Leader*, 29 January 1932.

53 ILP NAC minutes, 20–21 February 1932; Jupp, *Radical Left*, p. 34.

54 Dowse, *Left in the Centre*, p. 6. For further discussion of the ILP's structure, identifying the same features, see Howell, *MacDonald's Party*, pp. 242–6.

55 See G. Cohen, 'From Insufferable Petty Bourgeois to Trusted Communist: Jack Gaster, the RPC and the Communist Party', in J. McIlroy et al (eds.), *Party People* (2001), pp. 190–209.

56 Dowse, *Left in the Centre*, pp. 180–1.

57 Jupp, *Radical Left*, p. 34.

58 Chairman's address to 1932 ILP Annual Conference, p. 10, quoted in Dowse, *Left in the Centre*, p. 182. Cohen, 'Independent Labour Party and Standing Orders', pp. 219–20, stresses that in practice Maxton and Brockway's stance owed at least as much to frustration at the on-going dispute over Standing Orders as it did to a commitment to a 'revolutionary policy'.

59 *The Times*, 28 March 1932, quoted in Williamson, *National Crisis*, p. 467.
60 *New Leader*, 8 June 1932; *New Leader*, 1 July 1932, quoted in Dowse, *Left in the Centre*, p. 183; Jupp, *Radical Left*, p. 34.
61 Brockway speech, Special ILP Conference Report, quoted in Williamson, *National Crisis*, p. 467.
62 Dowse, *Left in the Centre*, p. 184; Jupp, *Radical Left*, p. 85.
63 Cole in *New Statesman and Nation*, 14 November 1931, Cripps in *Labour Magazine*, January 1932 and Brailsford in *New Leader*, 6 November 1931.
64 See, for example, *New Leader*, 25 March 1932.
65 Dalton diary, 11 January 1932, Dalton papers, 1/14 [B. Pimlott (ed.), *The Political Diary of Hugh Dalton, 1918–1940, 1945–1960* (1986), p. 169].
66 'Suggestions on Future Work', November 1931, Cole papers, GDHC/D4/5/6/1–2. See also 'Rules of the SSIP', Cole papers, GHHC/D4/2/1; also in TUC archive, MSS.292/756.1/3.
67 Bullock, *Bevin i*, p. 501.
68 'Notes on the Easton Lodge weekend', 16–17 April 1932, Cole papers, GDHC/D1/67/2/1–7.
69 Cole to Henderson, 2 June 1932, Cole papers, GDHC/D1/69/27/1–4, for a list of members of the group.
70 Bevin to Cole, 12 May 1932, Cole papers, D1/69/30; also in TUC archive, MSS.126/EB/SS/1/6.
71 This is apparent from Cole to Bevin, 8 and 13 July 1932, Cole papers, GDHC/D1/69/48 and GDHC/D1/69/50.
72 House of Commons Group minutes, 13 May 1932, Cole papers, GDHC/D1/66/2/1–4; also in TUC archive, MSS.126/EB/SS/1/11 and Addison papers, Ms. Addison dep. c.205.4–7. See also Pimlott, *Dalton*, p. 207; and Williamson, *National Crisis*, pp. 463–4. For Cole's perspective see Cole, 'Answers to questions for discussion at Easton Lodge', April 1932, wrongly dated in Cole papers as December 1931, Cole papers, GDHC/D4/5/2/1–7.
73 House of Commons Group minutes, 13 May 1932, Cole papers, GDHC/D1/66/2/1–4; also in TUC archive, MSS.126/EB/SS/1/11 and Addison papers, Ms. Addison dep. c.205.4–7. See also Pimlott, *Dalton*, pp. 207–8; and Williamson, *National Crisis*, pp. 464–5.
74 Morrison to Cole, 16 March and 28 April 1932, Cole papers, GDHC/D1/69/13 and GDHC/D1/69/28.
75 Morrison to Cole, 9 May 1932, Cole papers, GDHC/D1/69/29.
76 'A Labour Programme of Action', first draft, n.d., revised draft, 30 May 1932, Cole papers, GDHC/D1/68/1/1–3 and GDHC/D1/68/2/1–4; also in TUC archive, MSS.126/EB/SS//1/5 and MSS.126/EB/SS/1/8.
77 See Dalton's retrospective comments on the group: Dalton diary, 8 October 1932, Dalton papers, 1/14 [Pimlott (ed.), *Political Diary*, pp. 168–9].
78 Lathan to Cole, 14 June 1932, Cole papers, GDHC/D1/69/38.
79 NEC minutes, 22 June 1932; Williamson, *National Crisis*, p. 464.
80 For the approaches made by Cole and Wise to Dalton see Dalton to Pethick-Lawrence, 15 May 1932, Trinity College, Cambridge, Pethick-Lawrence papers, PL1, 181; and Dalton to Cole, 30 May 1932, Cole papers, GDHC/D4/8/1/1–2.
81 Dalton to Pethick-Lawrence, 15 May 1932, Pethick-Lawrence papers, P-L1-181.
82 Durbin, *New Jerusalems*, pp. 204–7. See also Dalton, *Fateful Years*, pp. 23–4; and Pimlott, *Dalton*, pp. 222–3.
83 Cole to the SSIP Executive Committee, 7 July 1932, handwritten and typescript versions, Cole papers, GDHC/D4/3/2/1–7 and GDHC/D4/3/1/1–3.

Wise discussed the letter with Trevelyan: Wise to Trevelyan, 17 July 1932, Robinson Library, University of Newcastle-upon-Tyne, Trevelyan papers, CPT 145, 31–3. See also draft letter to ILP, n.d. but July 1932, Cole papers, GDHC/D4/6/4/1–2; Cole to Lansbury, 15 July 1932, Cole papers, GDHC/D4/8/5/1–2.

84   Wise in *New Leader*, 5 August 1932, quoted in Pimlott, *Labour and the Left*, p. 44.

85   *New Clarion*, 13 August 1932.

86   Ibid., 20 August 1932.

87   *Daily Herald*, 22 August 1932.

88   Wise to Trevelyan, 3 September 1932, Trevelyan papers, CPT 145, 39–41.

89   Cole to Catlin, 10 September 1932, Cole papers, GDHC/D4/8/17/1–4.

90   Durbin, *New Jerusalems*, p. 81.

91   See, for instance, NFRB Report of first AGM, 29 May 1932, Cole papers, GDHC/D1/51/1/1–2, for NFRB membership; and NFRB, 'Redraft of Memo on Plan of Research', 11 July 1932, Cole papers, GDHC/D1/59/10/1–10, for the scope of its research at this point.

92   Cole to Bevin, 18 September 1932, Cole papers, GDHC/D4/8/22/1–3.

93   Cole to C. T. Cramp, 20 September 1932, Cole papers, GDHC/D4/8/26/1–3.

94   Cole to Bevin, 18 September 1932, Cole papers, GDHC/D4/8/22/1–3.

95   Horrabin to Cole, 18 September 1932, Cole papers, GDHC/D4/8/19.

96   Cole to Bevin, 18 September 1932, Cole papers, GDHC/D4/8/22/1–3. Dare, 'Socialist League', pp. 124–6, wrongly dates this letter as 18 July 1932 and suggests that there were two sets of negotiations between the SSIP and the ILP affiliationists – one in July and then another in September.

97   See Cole to Bevin, 24 September 1932, TUC archive, MSS.126/TG/61195/temp. 44. Cole subsequently asked Bevin to become vice-chairman of the NFRB but he refused: Cole to Bevin, 24 September 1932, TUC archive, MSS.126/TG/61195/temp. 44; Bevin to Cole, 29 September 1932, TUC archive, MSS.126/TG/61195/temp. 44; also in Cole papers, GDHC/D4/8/37; Cole to Bevin, 2 October 1932, TUC archive, MSS.126/TG/61195/temp. 44.

98   See Cole to Cripps, Pritt, Attlee, Pugh with addendum to Cripps, 19 September 1932, Cole papers, GDHC/D4/8/21/1–6.

99   Cole added a paragraph to Cripps's letter: Cole to Cripps, Pritt, Attlee, Pugh with addendum to Cripps, 19 September 1932, Cole papers, GDHC/D4/8/21/1–6.

100   *Daily Herald*, 26 September 1932.

101   G. D. H. Cole, *A History of the Labour Party from 1914* (1948), p. 284. See also Cole to Bevin, 18 September 1932, Cole papers, GDHC/D4/8/22/1–3, for Cole trying to persuade Bevin to join the executive to make sure that the Socialist League would not be a political body like the old ILP.

102   *New Clarion*, 8 October 1932; *Daily Herald*, 7 November 1932.

103   Wise to Trevelyan, 3 September 1932, Trevelyan papers, CPT 145 39–41.

104   Indeed, Riddell, 'Age of Cole', p. 956, states that his gradual withdrawal from the Socialist League between 1932 and 1934 'had more to do with the fact that he was no longer in charge of his own organisation than with any fundamental disagreement over policy'.

105   Cole to Cramp, 20 September 1932, Cole papers, GDHC/D4/8/26/1–3.

106   Bevin to Cole, 24 September 1932, Cole papers, GDHC/D4/8/33/1–2; also in TUC archive, MSS.126/TG/61195/temp. 44. See also Pimlott, *Labour and the Left*, p. 46. Interestingly, on 5–6 November the SSIP as a whole met to discuss its Executive's decision to amalgamate with the ILP Affiliation Committee and form the Socialist League. At the meeting a resolution moved by Elvin asking

for further negotiations between the SSIP and the Socialist League was defeated by 64 votes to 45. A resolution moved by Cripps supporting the Executive's decision and accepting the rules and constitution was approved by 67 votes to 42. Not only did this show how divided the SSIP was as a whole, but also meant that since a two-thirds majority had not been reached that it could not become official policy. The SSIP then took a straight vote on dissolution, which was carried by 70 to 27 – though obviously with some abstentions. In any case, this did not affect the existence of the Socialist League. See *Daily Herald*, 7 and 8 November 1932.

107 Bevin to Cole, 24 September 1932, Cole papers, GDHC/D4/8/33/1–2; also in TUC archive, MSS.126/TG/61195/temp. 44. F. L. Stevens (editor of *New Clarion*) to Cole, 26 September 1932, Cole papers, GDHC/D4/8/35. See Bullock, *Bevin i*, p. 505, for details about the *New Clarion*.
108 *Daily Herald*, 3 October 1932; Pimlott, *Labour and the Left*, p. 48.
109 *Forward*, 8 October 1932.
110 *LPACR*, 1932, pp. 182–5, 188–94.
111 Ibid., pp. 201, 216–17. See the detailed discussion of this debate in Durbin, *New Jerusalems*, pp. 85–6, 89, 207–8; and Pimlott, *Labour and the Left*, p. 62.
112 *LPACR*, 1932, pp. 204.
113 Ibid., pp. 204–5.
114 Ibid., pp. 205–6.
115 Dalton diary, 8 October 1932, Dalton papers, 1/14 [Pimlott (ed.), *Political Diary*, pp. 168–9]. See also Dalton, *Fateful Years*, p. 24.
116 Radice to Henderson, 10 October 1932, Labour History Archive and Study Centre (LHASC), Manchester, Labour Party Archive (LPA), uncatalogued papers in file marked 'Socialist League and Scottish Socialist Party'. In the same file see Radice to Shepherd, 11 October 1932; and 'Constitution of the Socialist League' (with another copy marked 'NEC 26 October 1932').
117 National Agent [Shepherd] to Henderson, 15 October 1932, uncatalogued papers in file marked 'Socialist League and Scottish Socialist Party', LPA.
118 Henderson to Shepherd, 17 October 1932, uncatalogued papers in file marked 'Socialist League and Scottish Socialist Party', LPA.
119 Shepherd to Radice, 3 November 1932, uncatalogued papers in file marked 'Socialist League and Scottish Socialist Party', LPA.
120 *New Clarion*, 7 January 1933.
121 Ibid., 17 December 1932, for the North East conference; ibid., 7 January 1933, for the Wales conference; ibid., 28 January 1933, for the conferences in Lancashire and Yorkshire.
122 M. Cole, *The Story of Fabian Socialism* (1961), p. 230. See *Daily Herald*, 6 October 1932, for Radice's appointment.
123 ILP NAC minutes, 12 December 1932. See also Dowse, *Left in the Centre*, p. 185.
124 J. Paton, *Left Turn: The Autobiography of John Paton* (1936), p. 398.
125 Dowse, *Left in the Centre*, p. 185.
126 *New Clarion*, 15 October 1932.
127 Socialist League Gateshead branch Executive Committee minutes, Tyne and Wear Archives, Newcastle, PO/SL1/1.
128 *New Clarion*, 7 January 1933.
129 See ibid., 11, 18, 25 February 1933; 4, 18, 25 March 1933; 8 April 1933; 6 May 1933.
130 *LPACR*, 1933, p. 102. This was the number of members for which the Socialist League paid affiliation fees in 1933.

131 See the information in Barker to Cripps, 5 April 1937, Cripps papers.
132 *New Clarion*, 8 October 1932 and 12 November 1932. See also Pimlott, *Labour and the Left*, pp. 49–50.
133 Gateshead branch Executive Committee minutes, 3 November 1932, PO/SL1/1.
134 Ibid., 8 December 1932.
135 Ibid., 21 January 1933.
136 Durbin, *New Jerusalems*, p. 212.
137 By this point the House of Commons Group – renamed the Friday Group which met at the Labour party conference at Leicester and again on 21 October 1932 and 11 November 1932 – had become inactive. The relevant agendas and minutes of the Group are in the Cole papers.
138 The authoritative account is Toye, *Planned Economy*, chs. 2 and 3.
139 See Socialist League, *Annual Conference Report 1933*, p. 8.
140 In addition to Toye, *Planned Economy*, see Williams, *Labour and Russia*, chs. 11 and 14.
141 Labour party, *Socialism and the Condition of the People* (1933), p. 6.
142 Socialist League, *Annual Conference Report 1933*, p. 8.
143 See Durbin, *New Jerusalems*, pp. 87–90.
144 Socialist League, *Annual Conference Report 1933*, p. 9.
145 Here the Socialist League analysis drew on Laski's thinking on the constitution: see H. J. Laski, *The Crisis and the Constitution* (1932); and H. J. Laski, *Democracy in Crisis* (1933). For a recent discussion see W. Frame, 'Sir Stafford Cripps and his Friends: the Socialist League, the National government and the Reform of the House of Lords 1931–1935', *Parliamentary History*, 24, 3 (2005), pp. 316–31.
146 At this point the International Bureau called itself the Left International Committee.
147 *New Leader*, 18 February 1933. See also Jupp, *Radical Left*, p. 44.
148 *LPACR*, 1933, p. 16.
149 The best account of the CPGB in the 1920s and 1930s is A. Thorpe, *The British Communist Party and Moscow 1923–43* (Manchester, 2000), which uses recently released material from the Russian Centre for the Preservation and Study of Contemporary Historical Documents – formerly The Archive of Marxism-Leninism – in Moscow and argues that the CPGB was not as tightly controlled by Moscow as other scholars have contended. For particular detail on the united front in early 1933 see pp. 199–200.
150 ILP NAC minutes, 4–5 March 1933.
151 Dowse, *Left in the Centre*, p. 186; Jupp, *Radical Left*, p. 47.
152 For the LSI position see *LPACR*, 1933, pp. 8–9. For CPGB-ILP co-operation see Dowse, *Left in the Centre*, p. 186.
153 *New Leader*, 28 April 1933. See also Pimlott, *Labour and the Left*, p. 89.
154 G. D. H. Cole, *The People's Front* (1937), p. 42.
155 Cripps to Brockway, 7 April 1933, Cripps papers.
156 Socialist League, *Annual Conference Report 1933*, p. 1. See also Pimlott, *Labour and the Left*, p. 89.
157 Appendix IX, *LPACR*, 1933, pp. 277–8.
158 R. S. Cripps, 'Can Socialism come by Constitutional Means?' in C. Addison et al., *Problems of a Socialist Government* (1933), pp. 35–66. For interpretation of the NJC document as an attack on the Socialist League see, for example, *The Times*, 25 March 1933.
159 The clearest exposition of these views were given by Laski and Brailsford: Laski,

'Democracy Under Fire', *New Clarion*, 27 May 1933; Brailsford, *Property or Peace?*, pp. 55, 27–35.

160 *New Clarion*, 13 May 1933. See also Pimlott, *Labour and the Left*, pp. 51–2.
161 Dalton diary, 12 May 1933, Dalton papers, 15/1 [Pimlott (ed.), *Political Diary*, pp. 175–6]. They had seen the article the day before it was published. Earlier in May, following a talk with Cripps, Dalton concluded that he had 'no judgement at all' and that it 'may become a duty to prevent him from holding any influence or position in the party': Dalton diary, 4 May 1933, Dalton papers, 15/1. See also Dalton, *Fateful Years*, pp. 41–3.
162 Citrine, 'Labour Policy and Practical Politics', *New Clarion*, 24 June 1933.
163 *Manchester Guardian*, 6 June 1933. For further coverage and comment on the dispute see *The Times*, 6 June 1933; *Daily Telegraph*, 6 June 1933; *News Chronicle*, 8 June 1933; *Observer*, 11 June 1933.
164 *Manchester Guardian*, 6 June 1933.
165 Cripps, 'What I want for Labour', *News Chronicle*, 22 June 1933; Laski, 'The Labour Party and Democracy', *New Clarion*, 17 June 1933; Wise, 'Free Speech and Free Press', *New Clarion*, 15 July 1933.
166 W. Citrine, *Men and Work* (1964), pp. 293–301.
167 Dalton diary, 14–16 July 1933, Dalton papers, 1/15 [Pimlott (ed.), *Political Diary*, p. 178].
168 For the Socialist League's changing membership see Pimlott, *Labour and the Left*, p. 51 and the useful table on p. 47.
169 Pethick-Lawrence to Cripps, 28 September 1932, Pethick-Lawrence papers, P-L5, 43.
170 Socialist League, *Annual Conference Report 1933*, p. 15.
171 'Report of the National Council for 1933–1934' in Socialist League, *Final Agenda: Second Annual Conference 1934* (1934), p. 3.
172 Cripps to Beatrice Webb, 24 December 1932, Passfield papers, II, 4, J1.
173 'Report of the National Council for 1933–1934', p. 3.
174 Socialist League, *Annual Conference Report 1933*, p. 4.
175 *New Clarion*, 29 July 1933; 'Report of the National Council for 1933–1934', p. 4.
176 Socialist League, *Annual Conference Report 1933*, p. 4
177 *New Clarion*, 12 August 1933. See also ibid., 18 November 1933.
178 Ibid., 22 July 1933.
179 *LPACR*, 1933, pp. 156–7.
180 Ibid., pp. 159–60.
181 Ibid., p. 166.
182 'Report of the NEC', *LPACR*, 1934, pp. 6–7.
183 For the development of the Labour party's foreign policy in the 1920s see H. R. Winkler, *Paths Not Taken: British Labour and International Policy in the 1920s* (Chapel Hill, 1994).
184 A. Henderson, *Labour's Foreign Policy* (1933), esp. pp. 19–22.
185 Socialist League, *Annual Conference Report 1933*, pp. 2, 13.
186 See M. Ceadel, *Semi-Detached Idealists: The British Peace Movement and International Relations, 1854–1945* (Oxford, 2000), esp. pp. 244–6, 264. Ceadel classifies them as 'socialist pacificists', and provides much useful analysis of earlier and wider traditions of this type of 'war resistance' – see also ibid., pp. 50, 146–7, 173–4, 176, 181, 241, 290–1, 295–7, 307–9, 314.
187 Socialist League, *Annual Conference Report 1933*, p. 12.
188 See also Williams, *Labour and Russia*, pp. 161, 232

189 *LPACR*, 1933, pp. 185–7, for Trevelyan's speech, pp. 187–8, for Elvin's supporting remarks.

190 For Dalton's acceptance see ibid., p. 188. For Henderson's remarks also welcoming the resolution see ibid., pp. 188–91.

191 Dalton diary, 29 September–6 October 1933, Dalton papers, 1/15 [Pimlott (ed.), *Political Diary*, p. 180] suggests that the NEC accepted the Socialist League resolution for public relations reasons. This view was reiterated in Dalton's memoirs: Dalton, *Fateful Years*, pp. 44–5.

192 Brockway, *Inside the Left*, p. 248.

193 Jupp, *Radical Left*, pp. 40, 47.

194 ILP NAC minutes, 8 October 1932. See also Jupp, *Radical Left*, p. 39; and Cohen thesis, p. 158.

195 Jupp, *Radical Left*, p. 48.

196 *New Leader*, 21 March 1933; Brockway, *Inside the Left*, p. 248. See also Jupp, *Radical Left*, p. 47; Dowse, *Left in the Centre*, p. 191; and Cohen thesis, p. 160. J. McNair, *James Maxton: The Beloved Rebel* (1955), p. 235, claimed that the RPC controlled the votes of half the delegates at the conference.

197 *New Leader*, 5 May 1933. See also Jupp, *Radical Left*, p. 47; and Dowse, *Left in the Centre*, p. 191.

198 Jupp, *Radical Left*, p. 47; Dowse, *Left in the Centre*, p. 188.

199 *New Leader*, 19 May 1933.

200 Brockway, *Inside the Left*, p. 249.

201 *New Leader*, 25 August 1933.

202 Brockway, *Inside the Left*, p. 250.

203 Ibid., p. 281.

204 Ibid., pp. 255–6.

205 Ibid., p. 253.

206 Ibid., p. 252.

207 ILP NAC minutes, 10–11 February 1934. See also *New Leader*, 16 February 1934.

208 *New Leader*, 6 April 1934; Brockway, *Inside the Left*, pp. 251–2.

209 Jupp, *Radical Left*, p. 39. For discussion of the Comintern Affiliation Committee see Cohen thesis, pp. 162–4.

210 ILP NAC minutes, 13 May 1934. Seven of the 32 ILP branches in Lancashire joined the ISP. The best account of the ISP is G. Cohen, 'The Independent Socialist Party' in K. Gildart, D. Howell and N. Kirk (eds.), *Dictionary of Labour Biography Volume XI* (2003), pp. 231–38. The ISP had emerged out of Sandham's Unity Group – see Cohen thesis, pp. 172–180.

211 *New Leader*, 16 February 1934.

212 ILP NAC documents, letter of 15 February 1934. See also Jupp, *Radical Left*, p. 49.

213 ILP NAC minutes, 9–10 June 1934.

214 See the analysis in Blaazer, *Popular Front*, ch. 6.

215 *New Clarion*, 23 September 1933. See also Cripps's speech at Bristol, reported in *The Times*, 8 May 1933; and his comments to the Birmingham branch of the Socialist League when he argued that a 'parliamentary form' of fascism was a greater danger in Britain than the type advocated by Mosley: *Birmingham Post*, 23 October 1933.

216 *Manchester Guardian*, 8 January 1934; *The Times*, 8 January 1934. Cripps subsequently explained that he was not referring to the Crown but using 'a well-known phrase' to describe 'court circles and the officials and other people who surround the King at Buckingham Palace': *The Times*, 8 January 1934.

217 Dalton diary, 19 January 1934, Dalton papers, 1/15 [Pimlott (ed.), *Political Diary*, pp. 181–2].
218 Dalton diary, 24 January 1934, Dalton papers, 1/15 [Pimlott (ed.), *Political Diary*, p. 183]. See also Webb diary, 4 February 1934, Passfield papers.
219 Webb diary, 4 July 1933, Passfield papers.
220 Dalton diary, 24 January 1934, Dalton papers, 1/15 [Pimlott (ed.), *Political Diary*, p. 183]. For Susan Lawrence's support of Cripps and the Socialist League see Webb diary, 4 February 1934, Passfield papers. For the wording of the resolution see *Daily Herald*, 25 January 1934; and *LPACR*, 1934, p. 9.
221 J. T. Murphy, *Fascism: The Socialist Answer* (1934), pp. 8–15.
222 Socialist League, *Forward to Socialism* (1934), p. 4; R. S. Cripps, *The Choice for Britain* (1934), p. 4. See also General Secretary of the Socialist League (Henry) to Middleton, 29 May 1934, copy in Cripps papers.
223 Socialist League, *Forward to Socialism*, pp. 6–14; 'Conference declares for "Forward to Socialism"', *Socialist Leaguer*, Special Conference Number, June–July 1934.
224 *The Times*, 21 May 1934.
225 For the policy-making process, see NEC minutes, 27, 28 February, 28 June 1934; TUC General Council minutes, 28 June 1934.
226 *War and Peace*, *LPACR*, 1934, Appendix II, pp. 242–5. See also Dalton, *Fateful Years*, pp. 53–5.
227 See 'Amendments to For Socialism and Peace tabled by the Socialist League', enclosed in Barber to Middleton, 18 August 1934, copy in Cripps papers.
228 *Socialist Leaguer*, June–July 1934.
229 Murphy, 'What will Congress do about fascism?', *Socialist Leaguer*, August–September 1934.
230 *Socialist Leaguer*, September–October 1934.
231 *LPACR*, 1934, pp. 148–9; 'Parliamentary Problems and Procedure', *LPACR*, 1934, Appendix VIII, pp. 261–3
232 Mellor, 'Southport and After', *Socialist Leaguer*, October–November 1934.
233 *LPACR*, 1934, pp. 158–160.
234 Ibid., pp. 160–1, for Dalton's speech; ibid., pp. 161–2, for Mellor's support of Cripps; and ibid., pp. 163–5, for Morrison's criticism of the Socialist League amendment. Dalton was on strong ground. At the Socialist League conference some of the branch delegates said they had expected 'a more detailed statement of policy with less rhetoric': 'Conference declares for "Forward to Socialism"', *Socialist Leaguer*, Special Conference Number, June–July 1934.
235 *LPACR*, 1934, p. 165.
236 The NEC wanted to provide 'net reasonable maintainable revenue': NEC Report, 'Public Ownership and Compensation', Appendix III, ibid., pp. 247–50.
237 *LPACR*, 1934, pp. 191–2, for Mitchison; ibid, pp. 197–9 for Morrison.
238 See Williams, *Labour and Russia*, pp. 234–5.
239 Attlee spoke strongly in favour of the type of sanctionist League of Nations policy contained in *War and Peace* and explicitly against the Socialist League's 'mass resistance' policy, arguing that: 'We cannot wash our hands of responsibility for [the sake of] Socialist workers and comrades in other countries': *LPACR*, 1934, pp. 170–1. See K. Harris, *Attlee* (1982), p. 118, for more on Attlee's position at this point.
240 *LPACR*, 1934, pp. 152–8.
241 Ibid., pp. 174–5, for Mellor's speech; ibid., pp. 175–8, for amendments and voting.

Chapter 2

1   Barber, 'Head Office Notes', *Socialist Leaguer*, October–November 1934.
2   Mellor, 'Southport and After', *Socialist Leaguer*, October–November 1934. See also Cripps, 'The Fight Goes On', *Socialist Leaguer*, October–November 1934. On the Socialist League's new stance see R. Groves, *Trades Councils in the Fight for Socialism* (1935).
3   Socialist League, Special National Conference, November 25 1934, Cambridge University Library, Needham papers, K15; 'On the Basis of the Class Struggle: The League's New Tasks', *Socialist Leaguer*, 15 December 1934. Dare, 'Socialist League', pp. 32–3; Pimlott, *Labour and the Left*, pp. 54–6; and Seyd, 'Factionalism within the Labour Party', pp. 218–19, discuss this change of emphasis within the Socialist League.
4   Cripps, '1931 – and 1934', *Socialist Leaguer*, 15 January 1935.
5   'The Socialist League: Cambridge branch: Memorandum of Future Activities and Organisation, December 1934', Needham papers, K15.
6   'Notes from Areas', *Socialist Leaguer*, 15 January 1935.
7   Murphy, 'League Doings', *Socialist Leaguer*, 15 February 1935.
8   'What the SL is Doing', *Socialist Leaguer*, March–April 1935.
9   Murphy, 'The Year in Review', *Socialist Leaguer*, May 1935.
10 *LPACR*, 1935, p. 102.
11 The general election had to take place before November 1936.
12 Dalton diary, 'Note on 1934', Dalton papers, 1/16.
13 See, for instance, Horrabin, 'Class Rule and War', *Socialist Leaguer*, 15 December 1934; 'The Price will be paid in Blood: Labour must resist war', *Socialist Leaguer*, March–April 1935.
14 'On the Basis of the Class Struggle: The League's New Tasks', *Socialist Leaguer*, 15 December 1934.
15 See, for instance, 'What is the Socialist League', n.d. but c. late 1934 or early 1935, Needham papers, K15.
16 *New Leader*, 8 March 1935.
17 Ibid., 15 March 1935.
18 Ibid., For further examples of the ILP stance see editorial, *New Leader*, 12 April 1935; and editorial, *New Leader*, 26 April 1935.
19 ILP Inner Executive minutes, 15 April 1935.
20 ILP NAC minutes, 19 April 1935. For this incident see also Cohen thesis, pp. 166–7.
21 *New Leader*, 26 April 1935.
22 Ibid., 3 May 1935.
23 Brockway, *Inside the Left*, p. 257.
24 *New Leader*, 8 March 1935.
25 Ibid., 26 April 1935, for Maxton's speech at the ILP conference. See also editorial, *New Leader*, 26 April 1935.
26 *New Leader*, 2 March 1935.
27 See M. Ceadel, 'The First British Referendum: The Peace Ballot, 1934–5', *English Historical Review*, 95, 377 (1980), pp. 810–39.
28 For an analysis of Baldwin's actions see Cowling, *Impact of Hitler*, pp. 62, 84–94; and P. A. Williamson, *Stanley Baldwin* (Cambridge, 1999), ch. 10, esp. pp. 303–5, 311–12, 321–3.
29 Reported in NEC minutes, 19 September 1935.
30 *Trades Union Congress Annual Report*, 1935 [herafter *TUCAR*, year], pp. 345–50, 366–71.

31 Quoted in Cowling, *Impact of Hitler*, p. 89. J. F. Naylor, *Labour's International Policy: The Labour Party in the 1930s* (1969), pp. 91–111, describes in detail the Labour party's advocacy of a sanctions policy.

32 M. Ceadel, *Pacifism in Britain 1914–45* (Oxford, 1980), ch. 1, distinguishes between pacifism – the conviction that war is always wrong – and *pacificism* – the view that the preservation of peace should be an absolute priority but underpinned by the recognition that war might sometimes be necessary. He explains how pacifism was accepted within the *pacificist* Labour party in 1920s and, crucially, how prominent pacifists were able to follow the official party line – see pp. 75, 77, 80–3.

33 See Ceadel, *Pacifism*, pp. 197–8.

34 Ibid., pp. 188–91.

35 For Lansbury's position at this point see J. Shepherd, *George Lansbury: At the Heart of Old Labour* (Oxford, 2002), ch. 16, esp. pp. 315–28.

36 See Pimlott, *Labour and the Left*, pp. 89–91; Dare, 'Socialist League', pp. 378–87; Seyd, 'Factionalism', p. 212; Cowling, *Impact of Hitler*, pp. 82, 84, 215; Naylor, *Labour's International Policy*, pp. 93–4, 103–4; Blaazer, *Popular Front*, pp. 166–7, 174. In his wider survey Ceadel, *Semi-Detached Idealists*, pp. 322–4, briefly discusses the position of Cripps and Brailsford at the time of the Abyssinian crisis.

37 *Socialist Leaguer*, May 1935.

38 Brailsford, 'Facing the Next War', ibid.

39 R. S. Cripps, *Fight Now Against War* (1935), pp. 2–3, for Cripps's remarks, and pp. 7–8, for mass resistance resolutions. Resolutions also given in 'Special Supplement, Bristol Annual Conference, 1935', *Socialist Leaguer*, July-August 1935. See also Chairman's speech to the Socialist League Annual Conference, June 1935, draft in Cripps papers.

40 J. T. Murphy, *New Horizons* (1940), p. 314.

41 Ibid., chs. 8–17; Murphy, 'Why I have joined the Socialist League', *New Clarion*, 15 April 1933. See also R. Darlington, *The Political Trajectory of J. T. Murphy* (Liverpool, 1998), chs. 1–7.

42 Murphy, *New Horizons*, p. 313. The editorial in the *Socialist Leaguer* also stated that it had been 'an amazingly unanimous conference', see 'Notes and Comments', *Socialist Leaguer*, July-August 1935. See also Darlington, *Murphy*, pp. 237–9.

43 Cripps, *Fight Now Against War*, pp. 6–7. See also *Daily Herald*, 11 June 1935.

44 Murphy to Middleton, 17 June 1935, copy in Cripps papers. See also 'Notes and Comments', *Socialist Leaguer*, June 1935.

45 Murphy to Middleton, 31 July 1935, copy in Cripps papers. See also 'What the "SL" is Doing', *Socialist Leaguer*, July–August 1935.

46 For the details surrounding Henderson's resignation and his replacement by Middleton see Pimlott, *Labour and the Left*, p. 71.

47 Middleton to Murphy, 2 August 1935, copy in Cripps papers.

48 Dalton diary, 'beginning of Sept', but certainly 3, 4 September 1935, Dalton papers, 1/16. See also Dalton, *Fateful Years*, p. 66.

49 Alfred Wall (Secretary, London Trades Council) to Murphy, 9 September 1935, copy in Cripps papers. See also Murphy's reply reiterating the Socialist League's line of 'mass resistance': Murphy to Wall, 10 September 1935, copy in Cripps papers.

50 Murphy to Cripps, 9 September 1935, Cripps papers. See also Wall to Citrine, 13 September 1935, enclosing reply to Murphy, 13 September 1935, TUC archive, MSS.292/756.1/3.

51 Murphy to Socialist League branches, 13 September 1935, copy in Cripps papers.
52 'War or Socialism', *Socialist*, September 1935.
53 Mellor to Cripps, 11 September 1935, Cripps papers. Cripps recognised that there was 'no real divergence' between them, Cripps to Mellor, 12 September 1935, copy in Cripps papers.
54 For Mitchison see *Manchester Guardian*, 17 September 1935; for Horrabin see Murphy to Cripps, 10 September 1935, Cripps papers; Lionel Elvin confirmed his support for the Cripps-Mellor line, interview with the author, 12 October 2000; for Wilkinson see Wilkinson to Cripps, 19 September 1935, Cripps papers; for Dodds see Dodds to Cripps, 17 September 1935, Cripps papers.
55 B. Castle, *Fighting All the Way* (1993), p. 68.
56 Betts to editor, *New Statesman and Nation*, 14 September 1935. See also Betts, 'International Notes', *Socialist*, September 1935
57 *Forward*, 31 August 1935. K. Martin, *Harold Laski: A Biographical Memoir* (1953), p. 99, recognised that Laski was in support of the Cripps-Mellor line. However, I. Kramnick and B. Sheerman, *Harold Laski: A Life on the Left* (1993), p. 347, argue that Laski supported sanctions.
58 Borrett to Cripps, 20 September 1935; Borrett to Cripps, 24 September 1935, both Cripps papers.
59 Naomi Mitchison to Cripps, 19 September 1935, Cripps papers.
60 See Socialist League Executive Committee minutes, 25 February 1937, Cripps papers, for discussion of this point.
61 Murphy, *New Horizons*, p. 316.
62 Murphy to Cripps, 17 September 1935, Cripps papers.
63 Trevelyan to Bellerby, 19 April 1933, copy in Trevelyan papers, CPT 147/27. See also Trevelyan to M. K. Trevelyan, 28 February 1934, Trevelyan papers, CPT Ex 128/21.
64 C. P. Trevelyan, *Soviet Russia: A Description for British Workers* (1935). There is unfortunately no discussion of Trevelyan's political trajectory after 1931 in A. J. A. Morris, *C. P. Trevelyan 1870–1958: Portrait of a Radical* (Belfast, 1977).
65 'Special Supplement, Bristol Annual Conference, 1935', *Socialist Leaguer*, July–August 1935.
66 Trevelyan to Cripps, 12 September 1935, Cripps papers.
67 Trevelyan to Cripps, 15 September 1935, Cripps papers. Disingenuously he added that he had 'always recognised the necessity for force as a police measure in the last resort'.
68 Trevelyan to Cripps, 19 September 1935, Cripps papers; copy in Trevelyan papers, 149. Those with the outlook associated with Trevelyan have sometimes been labelled fellow travellers. For a discussion of the term fellow travellers – which came into common usage in Europe and the United States in the 1930s – see D. Caute, *The Fellow Travellers: A Postscript to the Enlightenment* (1973), pp. 1–7.
69 Pritt to Cripps, 8 October 1935, Cripps papers. See also D. N. Pritt, *The Autobiography of D. N. Pritt Part One: From Right to Left* (1965), p. 99. Here Pritt wrongly dates the Abyssinian crisis as summer 1936.
70 Pritt, *Right to Left*, pp. 36–9.
71 Ibid., pp. 39–40.
72 Mellor to Cripps, 11 September 1935, Cripps papers.
73 M. Foot, *Aneurin Bevan: A Biography Volume One 1897–1945* (1962), p. 211. M. Jones, *Michael Foot* (1994), p. 39, explains how Foot looked to Bevan as a mentor.

74 Bevan to Wise, quoted in Foot, *Bevan i*, p. 156.
75 *Daily Herald*, 23 September 1935.
76 Ibid., 30 September 1935.
77 See his articles on the Abyssinian crisis, *Reynolds Illustrated News*, 25 August, 1, 8 September 1935.
78 Ibid., 15 September 1935.
79 Ibid., 22 September 1935.
80 Ibid., 29 September 1935.
81 Leventhal, *Last Dissenter*, ch. 9. The fullest expression of Brailsford's views was given in H. N. Brailsford, *After the Peace* (1920).
82 Leventhal, *Last Dissenter*, pp. 231–5.
83 See ibid., pp. 240–2.
84 See, for instance, *New Statesman and Nation*, 29 September 1934; 'The United Front at Southport', *New Statesman and Nation*, 6 October 1934.
85 *New Statesman and Nation*, 31 August 1935; 'For League or Empire', *New Statesman and Nation*, 7 September 1935.
86 *New Statesman and Nation*, 14 September 1935. See also *New Statesman and Nation*, 21 September 1935.
87 Martin to Cripps, 23 September 1935, Cripps papers. See also K. Martin, *Editor: A Second Volume of Autobiography 1931–45* (1968), pp. 166–72.
88 Martin to Zilliacus, '1.30am Saturday night', n. d. but September 1935, University of Sussex, Martin papers, 15/5.
89 Martin to Zilliacus, 2 October 1935, Martin papers, 15/5.
90 *Daily Herald*, 16 September 1935; *Daily Worker*, 16 September 1935; *Manchester Guardian*, 16 September 1935.
91 Martin to Zilliacus, '1.30am Saturday night', n. d. but September 1935, Martin papers, 15/5. See also his description of the conference: Critic, 'A London Diary', *New Statesman*, 21 September 1935.
92 Murphy to Cripps, 18 September 1935, Cripps papers. See also *Daily Worker*, 17 September 1935, for a brief report of the divided Socialist League conference at Leeds; and *Manchester Guardian*, 17 September 1935, for reports on the conferences at Manchester and Sheffield. The account of the conferences in 'What the League is Doing', *Socialist*, November 1935, exaggerates the extent of support for the official Socialist League line among the delegates.
93 Murphy to Cripps, 18 September 1935, Cripps papers.
94 CPGB Central Committee minutes, 6 October 1935, LHASC, Communist Party Archive (CPA).
95 *Sunday Referee*, 15 September 1935.
96 Cripps to Parmoor, 20 September 1935, copy in Cripps papers (also quoted in E. Estorick, *Stafford Cripps: A Biography* (1949), p. 141). For Cripps's actual resignation, see Cripps to Middleton, 15 September 1935, copy in Cripps papers.
97 See, for instance, *Daily Herald*, 19, 20, 21, 23 September 1935; *Manchester Guardian*, 19, 21 September 1935; *The Times*, 20, 21 September 1935.
98 See Borrett to Cripps, 20 September 1935, Cripps papers, for details of the Executive Committee's discussion. For Wilkinson's decision to withdraw see Wilkinson to Cripps, 19 September 1935, Cripps papers; and *Daily Herald*, 23 September 1935. For a report of Elvin's withdrawal see *Daily Worker*, 1 October 1935.
99 Statement from the National Council to all branches and members, 22 September 1935, Needham papers, K16.

100 Webb diary, 2 September 1935, Passfield papers [MacKenzie and MacKenzie (eds.), *Webb Diary iv*, p. 357].

101 Unnamed draft, p. 38A, n.d., but c. September 1935, Cripps papers.

102 Ibid., p. 50.

103 Ibid., p. 40 A1–A3. Cripps to Trevelyan, 16 September 135, copy in Cripps papers.

104 Betts, 'International Notes', *Socialist*, November 1935.

105 Editorial, *New Leader*, 19 July 1935.

106 Ibid., 5 July 1935.

107 Ibid., 19 July 1935. For Brockway's role in formulating this policy see Brockway, *Inside the Left*, p. 325.

108 *New Leader*, 16 August 1935.

109 Brockway, *Inside the Left*, p. 325.

110 'We Must Stop the War', *New Leader*, 23 August 1935; 'Workers, Beware!', *New Leader*, 6 September 1935.

111 Brockway, 'In the Melting Pot', *New Leader*, 16 August 1935.

112 'Don't Trust Government', *New Leader*, 30 August 1935.

113 McGovern, 'Three Questions to Communists', *New Leader*, 27 September 1935.

114 Brockway, *Inside the Left*, p. 326.

115 Ibid.

116 For further discussion of the ILP's structure see Cohen thesis, p. 21.

117 Brockway, *Inside the Left*, p. 326. The account in McNair, *Maxton*, p. 252, draws heavily on Brockway's account.

118 'ILP Call: Resolution adopted by the Inner Executive of the ILP', *New Leader*, 13 September 1935. The inference that the 'two rival dictators' concerned were Selassie and Mussolini is made clear in *New Leader*, 10 April 1936, p. 1.

119 *New Leader*, 20 September 1935; *The Times*, 19 September 1935.

120 'A Letter to You' from James Maxton and Fenner Brockway, *New Leader*, 27 September 1935.

121 Editorial, *New Leader*, 20 September 1935.

122 *New Leader*, 20 September 1935. Indeed, a later editorial argued that in contrast to the failure of the Socialist League to urge working-class action, the ILP 'has not diverted from its advocacy of a general strike against a threatened war under a capitalist government and of social revolution should war take place': editorial, *New Leader*, 27 September 1935.

123 Martin aptly described how it 'was in a sense academic because the big card vote was known to have decided the issue before the debate began': Martin to Zilliacus, 2 October 1935, Martin papers, 15/5.

124 Dalton to Martin, 24 September 1935, Martin papers, 11/4.

125 *LPACR*, 1935, pp. 153–6. For Cripps's actual speech see 5 *HC Debs*, vol. 299, cols. 149–50, 11 March 1935.

126 Webb diary, 1 October 1935, Passfield papers.

127 *LPACR*, 1935, pp. 156–8.

128 Trevelyan to M. K. Trevelyan, 1 October 1935, Trevelyan papers, CPT Ex 129/80.

129 *LPACR*, 1935, p. 162.

130 Ibid., pp. 170–2.

131 Ibid., pp. 175–7.

132 Ibid., p. 178, reports Bevin as using the term '*taking* your conscience', but this conflicts with many other accounts. See, for instance, A. Olivier Bell (ed.), *The Diary of Virginia Woolf: volume iv 1931–5* (1983), p. 345; Dalton, *Fateful Years*,

p. 69; and Citrine, *Men and Work*, p. 352. J. Shepherd, 'Labour and the Trade Unions: George Lansbury, Ernest Bevin and the Leadership Crisis of 1935', in C. Wrigley and J. Shepherd (eds.), *On the Move* (1991), pp. 204–30, analyses the personal dynamics of the confrontation between Bevin and Lansbury.

133 *LPACR*, 1935, pp. 177–80. A. J. P. Taylor, *English History 1914–45* (Oxford, 1965), p. 382 note 1, perceptively remarks that 'Bevin played loyalty both ways. Lansbury was denounced for remaining on the party executive when he disagreed with its policy; Cripps was denounced for resigning from it for the same reason'.

134 *LPACR*, 1935, p. 193. The importance of these events in 1935 was first and most forcefully brought out in the influential political polemic 'Cato', *Guilty Men* (1940), pp. 31–4. Its co-authors – Michael Foot, Peter Howard and Frank Owen – were writing in summer 1940 with the defeat at Dunkirk in mind and attached particular weight to Bevin's dismissal of Lansbury as they sought to absolve the Labour party of any responsibility for the supposed failure to recognise earlier the imperative of resisting Hitler.

Chapter 3

1 C. P. Trevelyan to M K. Trevelyan, 1 October 1935, Trevelyan papers, CPT ex, 129, 82.
2 Murphy to Cripps, 17 September 1935, Cripps papers.
3 Murphy, *New Horizons*, p. 317.
4 Pritt to Cripps, 8 October 1935, Cripps papers.
5 *Reynolds Illustrated News*, 24 November, 1 December 1935.
6 'Readers' Letters on the War', *Daily Herald*, 15 October 1935, in Needham papers, K20.
7 'What the League is Doing', *Socialist*, November 1935.
8 Socialist League circular, 11 October 1935, reported in *Bristol Evening World*, 12 November 1935.
9 See T. Stannage, *Baldwin Thwarts the Opposition: The British General Election of 1935* (1980), pp. 123–7.
10 Murphy, *New Horizons*, p. 317.
11 Cripps, 'Your Enemy is at Home!', *Socialist*, November 1935.
12 *Bristol Evening World*, 12 November 1935. See also Pimlott, *Labour and the Left*, p. 91.
13 C. L. Mowat, *Britain Between the Wars*, pp. 553–4. For the course of the election campaign see Stannage, *Baldwin*, chs. 5 and 6.
14 For details see Pimlott, *Labour and the Left*, pp. 74–5.
15 *Western Daily Press*, 16 December 1935.
16 *5 HC Debs*, vol. 307, cols. 2062–2070, 19 December 1935.
17 Pritt, 'Autobiography: first uncut version', BLPES, Pritt papers, 3/10.
18 Brailsford, 'Which sort of League?', *New Statesman and Nation*, 11 January 1936.
19 Editorial, *New Leader*, 4 October 1935.
20 'An Open Letter to Ernest Bevin from Jennie Lee', *New Leader*, 11 October 1935.
21 Editorial, *New Leader*, 18 October 1935. See also *New Leader*, 1 November 1935.
22 *New Leader*, 18 October 1935.
23 Ibid., 1 November 1935.
24 Ibid., 6 December 1935.
25 Ibid., 27 December 1935.
26 Editorial, ibid. Another editorial early in the New Year struck the same

conditional note: 'If they [the workers] had the will they could by their own action . . . in their own countries . . . prevent imperialist adventures and stop the rival imperialisms of capitalist powers from developing into an extended war.': *New Leader*, 10 January 1936.

27 *Daily Herald*, 7 August 1935.

28 *Daily Worker*, 26 October 1935.

29 Pollitt to Middleton, 25 November 1935, in 'NEC Report', *LPACR*, 1936, p. 50; another copy in Cripps papers. See also Thorpe, *Communist Party*, ch. 9, esp. pp. 225–7.

30 *Daily Herald*, 22 May 1934; ibid., 10 June 1935; What the SL is Doing', *Socialist Leaguer*, April 1935.

31 Strachey to Cripps, 20 September 1934, Cripps papers; Cripps to Strachey, 16 October 1934, copy in Cripps papers.

32 Cripps to Strachey, 16 October 1934, copy in Cripps papers.

33 Special Branch informant, 301/MP/3780, 126a in SF.464/6, vol. 2, 30 November 1934, National Archives, London, PRO/KV2/668.

34 See Middleton to Murphy, 1 July 1935, with enclosure, copy in Cripps papers. See also Brockway to ILP NAC, 12 April 1935, copy in Socialist League file, LP/SL/35/1, LPA. Lionel Elvin confirmed this view of the meetings, interview with the author, 12 October 2000.

35 See the correspondence, running from May 1935 to August 1935, in the Socialist League file, LP/SL/35, LPA.

36 Cripps to Parmoor, 28 February 1936, Cripps papers (also quoted in Estorick, *Cripps*, p. 149).

37 Murphy to Middleton, 15 January 1936, copy in Cripps papers. See also draft of Murphy to Middleton, n.d., but early 1936, copy in Cripps papers. Earlier Mellor had urged the NEC to 'take the application seriously and . . . not allow the past to obliterate the present', especially in light of the current 'world situation': Editor, 'Matters of Moment', *Socialist*, January 1936.

38 Middleton to Murphy, 17 January 1936, copy in Cripps papers.

39 Bevin to Cole, 31 December 1935, TUC archive, MSS.126/TG/61195/temp 44.

40 Middleton to Pollitt, 27 January 1936, copy in Cripps papers. See also *Daily Herald* and *The Times*, 30 January 1936. And see Pollitt's reply suggesting that the social democratic parties were at fault for not uniting with the Communists in Germany in 1932, Pollitt to Middleton, 30 January 1936, copy in Cripps papers; *Daily Herald*, 31 January 1936.

41 Murphy to Middleton, 5 February 1936, copy in Cripps papers; also in Socialist League file, LPA, LP/SL/35/16. See also *Daily Herald*, 5 February 1936; *The Times*, 7 February 1936. Pimlott, *Labour and the Left*, pp. 92–3; Seyd, 'Socialist League', p. 213; Dare, 'Socialist League', p. 403; Blaazer, *Popular Front*, pp. 159, 169, discuss the Socialist League's support for CPGB affiliation at this juncture.

42 Middleton to Murphy, 6 February 1936, copy in Cripps papers (also in Socialist League file, LPA, LP/SL/35/17).

43 Pritt, *From Right to Left*, p. 97. See also reports of Cripps – *Daily Telegraph*, 13 February 1936; *Warrington Guardian*, 14 February 1936; *East London Observer*, 29 February 1936.

44 Webb diary, 2 May 1936, Passfield papers.

45 Bullock, *Bevin i*, pp. 129, 589.

46 CPGB to Middleton and to Citrine, 14 March 1936, LHASC, CPA, Pollitt papers, POLL/14/07.

47 CPGB to Murphy, 14 March 1936, Pollitt papers, CP/IND/POLL/14/07. The

CPGB reported to Moscow that it had proposed united action between the Labour party, the TUC, the ILP and the Socialist League: London CP to Moscow, 15 March 1936, National Archives, HW/17/21, Government Code and Cypher School: Decrypts of Communist International (Comintern) messages.

48   Mellor, 'A Word to Those Who Seek For Peace', *Socialist*, March 1936.

49   Socialist League Executive Committee minutes, 19 March 1936. See Murphy to Pollitt, 16 March 1936, Pollitt papers, CP/IND/POLL/14/07, for the Socialist League's decision to consider the CPGB letter; and see Murphy to Pollitt, 23 March 1936, Pollitt papers, CP/IND/POLL/14/07, for the Socialist League conveying its decision to the CPGB.

50   Editor, 'Some matters of moment', *Socialist*, April 1936.

51   Editorial, *New Leader*, 1 November 1935.

52   Maxton, 'Why Parliament Needs a Strong ILP Group', *New Leader*, 8 November 1935.

53   *New Leader*, 1 November 1935.

54   ILP NAC minutes, 30 November–1 December 1935, discusses the resignations.

55   *New Leader*, 8 November 1935. See also Jupp, *Radical Left*, p. 69.

56   See, for instance, C. K. C. Cullen, 'The War Crisis', *The RPC Bulletin*, October 1935, cited in Cohen thesis, p. 169.

57   ILP Inner Executive minutes, 24 October 1935. Indeed, on this basis the Inner Executive deleted Cullen from the list of approved ILP speakers.

58   J. Gaster and H. Vernon, 'The War Situation – And the League', *The RPC Bulletin*, October 1935, cited in Cohen thesis, p. 168. Brockway also noted the divisions within the RPC: Brockway, *Inside the Left*, p. 326.

59   Cohen thesis, p. 171, citing *The RPC Bulletin*, November 1935. For further analysis of the debates within the RPC see Cohen thesis, p. 298.

60   *New Leader*, 10 January 1936.

61   Ibid., 7 February 1936.

62   Editorial, ibid., 6 December 1935.

63   Ibid., 13 December 1935. See also ibid., 20 December 1935.

64   *New Leader*, 6 March 1936; editorial, ibid., 10 April 1936.

65   Editorial, *New Leader*, 7 February 1936; editorial, ibid., 28 February 1936.

66   *New Leader*, 10 April 1936, p. 1. These were the terms in which it was explained to *New Leader* readers for the first time. See also the discussion of the debate in G. J. Brown, *Maxton* (Edinburgh, 1986), pp. 278–9.

67   For details on James see S. Howe, 'Cyril Lionel Robert James', Oxford DNB online. For discussion of the development of Trotskyism see J. Callaghan, *British Trotskyism: Theory and Practice* (Oxford, 1984), introduction and ch. 1.

68   For further discussion see Cohen thesis, pp. 180–5.

69   Brockway, *Inside the Left*, p. 326.

70   *New Leader*, 17 April 1936; *The Times*, 13 April 1936.

71   Brockway, *Inside the Left*, p. 326.

72   *New Leader*, 17 April 1936; *The Times*, 13 April 1936.

73   *New Leader*, 17 April 1936; *The Times*, 13 April 1936.

74   Brockway, *Inside the Left*, p. 327.

75   *New Leader*, 17 April 1936; *The Times*, 13 April 1936. See also McNair, *Maxton*, p. 252.

76   Brockway, *Inside the Left*, p. 327.

77   *New Leader*, 17 April 1936.

78   ILP NAC minutes, 12 April 1936. See also McNair, *Maxton*, p. 253.

79 Brockway, *Inside the Left*, p. 327.
80 *New Leader*, 17 April 1936. See also McNair, *Maxton*, p. 254.
81 Brockway, *Inside the Left*, p. 328.
82 CPGB Politburo minutes, 16 April 1936.
83 Brockway, 'The ILP Decides', *New Leader*, 17 April 1936.
84 *New Leader*, 1 May 1936.
85 For further details see Cohen thesis, pp. 163–4, 166.
86 *Controversy*, May 1936.
87 *New Leader*, 29 May 1936.
88 C. L. R. James to editor, *New Leader*, 5 June 1936.
89 *New Leader*, 10 July 1936.
90 ILP Executive Committee minutes, 23 May 1936.
91 *New Leader*, 10 July 1936. See also the conciliatory tone in editorial, *New Leader*, 3 July 1936, which argued that the 'party must now turn all its energies to positive and important tasks which are before it'. The Executive Committee's statement, which was endorsed at the 1937 conference, was very much a compromise. Superficially it appeared to endorse ' working-class sanctions' by stating that in 'the event of an attack by an imperialist government on a subject people, it will be the duty of the British working class to take all possible action in support of the subject people, including organised action to refuse war materials to the imperialist government'. In reality, however, this policy was undermined by the discretionary powers given to the NAC not to follow such a course if British imperialism stood to benefit, or if the leadership of the subject people were not of a 'character which will eventually make for the emancipation of the working and peasant populations'. The resolution was published as *Through the Class Struggle to Socialism* (1937).
92 *New Leader*, 10 July 1936.
93 Brockway, 'The ILP Decides', *New Leader*, 17 April 1936. For the conference resolution see *New Leader*, 6 March 1936.
94 See R. Toye, 'The Labour Party and the Economics of Rearmament, 1935–39', *Twentieth Century British History*, 12, 3 (2001), pp. 303–26, for a discussion of the range of views on rearmament in the Labour party at this time.
95 Dalton diary, 2, 3, 4 March 1936, Dalton papers. See also Dalton, *Fateful Years*, pp. 87–8.
96 Attlee, 'Millions for the Scrap Heap', *Daily Herald*, 4 February 1936.
97 Dalton diary, 19 February 1936, Dalton papers.
98 *The Times*, 12 March 1936.
99 For Bevan see *New Leader*, 20 September 1935.
100 Cripps, 'Your Enemy is at Home!', *Socialist*, November 1935.
101 Murphy to NCL, 3 March 1936, copy in Cripps papers.
102 Dalton noted this at the time: Dalton diary, 12 March 1936, Dalton papers [Pimlott (ed.), *Political Diary*, p. 198].
103 Trevelyan to M. Philips Price, 16 March 1936, Trevelyan papers, CPT 69, 86–7.
104 *Reynolds News*, 15 March 1936.
105 Cripps, 'Fight War Now!, *Socialist*, April 1936.
106 Ibid. See also Mellor's supporting comments: Editor, 'Some Matters of Moment', *Socialist*, April 1936.
107 'What the League is Doing: Anti-war Fight wins Support', *Socialist*, May 1936.
108 Ibid.
109 Trevelyan to M. Philips Price, 11 December 1935, Trevelyan papers, CPT 69, 82–3.

110 *Reynolds Illustrated News*, 23 February 1936.
111 'Labour and the Arms Race', *New Statesman and Nation*, 22 February 1936.
112 *Daily Herald*, 2 June 1936; *The Times*, 2 June 1936.
113 Editorial, *New Leader*, 13 March 1936. The ILP pitted itself firmly against the pro-rearmament views of Bevin, Citrine and Dalton: Brockway, 'Don't Shout but Think this May Day', *New Leader*, 1 May 1936.
114 *New Leader*, 13 March 1936.
115 Editorial, ibid., 3 April 1936.
116 *New Leader*, 27 March 1936.
117 Ibid., 8 May 1936.
118 Cripps, 'Weld the Workers together', *Socialist*, March 1936. See also Betts's criticism of the popular fronts in Spain and France: 'International Notes', *Socialist*, March and April 1936.
119 *Imprecorr*, 30 May 1936, quoted in Jupp, *Radical Left*, p. 79.
120 Pritt endorsed the CPGB application for affiliation from November 1935, arguing that 'it would have at least brought all the enthusiasm, devotion and political education of the Communists into the centre of the political struggle': Pritt, *From Right to Left*, p. 97. For Trevelyan's support see Trevelyan to Rothstein, 9 October 1935, Trevelyan papers, CPT 149/21.
121 Brockway, 'The World this Week', *New Leader*, 6 March 1936. See also ibid., 20 March 1936.
122 J. Lee, 'The World this Week', *New Leader*, 1 May 1936.
123 Brockway, 'The World this Week', *New Leader*, 10 April 1936. See also ibid., 13 March 1936.
124 Editorial, *New Leader*, 8 May 1936. See also Brockway, 'The World this Week', *New Leader*, 22 May 1936.
125 J. Maurin, 'What Now in Spain', *New Leader*, 28 February 1936.
126 Brockway, 'The World this Week', *New Leader*, 6 March 1936.
127 Ibid., 15 May 1936.
128 Brockway, *Inside the Left*, p. 289.
129 *New Leader*, 5 June 1936.
130 The NAC reiterated this in a resolution for the annual conference: ibid., 6 March 1936
131 *New Leader*, 17 April 1936.
132 Editorial, ibid., 15 May 1936; ibid., 12 June 1936.
133 *New Leader*, 10 July 1936.
134 Ibid., 24 July 1936.
135 Ibid.
136 Cripps, 'Fight War Now!', *Socialist*, April 1936.
137 Cripps to Zilliacus, 18 April 1936, copy in Cripps papers.
138 NCL, *Labour and the Defence of Peace* (1936). This was published on 5 May.
139 Cripps, 'National Unity a Delusion', *Socialist*, June 1936.
140 Editor, 'Matters of Moment', *Socialist*, June 1936.
141 *Daily Worker*, 4 June 1936.
142 Socialist League National Council minutes, 1 June 1936. For the conference's acceptance of Mellor as the new chairman see *Daily Herald*, 2 June 1936; *The Times*, 2 June 1936.
143 *Daily Herald*, 2 June 1936; *The Times*, 2 June 1936.
144 Socialist League Executive Committee minutes, 11 June 1936; Murphy to Middleton, 18 June 1936, Cripps papers.
145 Reported in *Daily Herald*, 27 June 1936.

146 Ibid., 15 July 1936.
147 Reported in ibid., 16 July 1936.
148 For AEU support for a united front see *The Times*, 6 June 1936; for MFGB support see *Daily Herald*, 24 June 1936.
149 Trade Unionist, 'Wage Fights Ahead', *Socialist*, July–August 1936.
150 Socialist League Executive Committee minutes, 11 June 1936.
151 K. Morgan, *Against Fascism and War: Ruptures and Continuities in British Communist Politics 1935–41* (Manchester, 1989), p. 62. Branson, *Communist Party*, does not consider the CPGB's attitude to rearmament.
152 Dalton diary, 27 July 1936, Dalton papers [Pimlott (ed.), *Political Diary*, p. 200]. See also Dalton, *Fateful Years*, p. 90.
153 PLP Statement of 24 July, reported in *Daily Herald*, 25 July 1936.
154 Mellor, 'Here is a Popular Front! Smash the Unemployment Regulations – And the Act. End Any Means Test', *Socialist*, July–August 1936. In the title of his article Mellor confusingly referred to united working-class action as a popular front.
155 Socialist League Executive Committee minutes, 30 July 1936.
156 Murphy to Branch Secretaries and Area Committees, 4 August 1936, Cripps papers.
157 Murphy to NEC, 4 August 1936, copy in Cripps papers.
158 Middleton to Murphy, 12 August 1936, Cripps papers.
159 J. V. Delahaye to editor, *New Statesman and Nation*, 4 July 1936.
160 Bevan, 'in an interview', 'Problems of Labour Policy', *Labour Monthly*, June 1936, pp. 340–4, at pp. 342–4.
161 Brailsford, 'Lessons of the Great Betrayal', *Reynolds News*, 5 July 1936.
162 Brailsford, 'Austria is not Worth a War!', *Reynolds News*, 19 July 1936.
163 Cripps, 'A Short Programme of Action', *Socialist*, July–August 1936.
164 Socialist League Executive Committee minutes, 9 July 1936.
165 Ibid., 23 July 1936.

Chapter 4

1 For a fuller description of Spanish politics see Buchanan, *Labour Movement*, pp. 25–8, and H. Thomas, *The Spanish Civil War* (1961).
2 Socialist League Executive Committee minutes, 30 July 1936; Murphy to 'all members', 4 August 1936, copy in Cripps papers.
3 Buchanan, *Labour Movement*, pp. 37–65.
4 Ibid., *passim*.
5 Ibid., p. 30, stresses how little was known about Spain in Britain.
6 Brailsford, 'Can Britain Stay Neutral? Europe's fate linked with the Spanish Civil War', *Reynolds News*, 2 August 1936.
7 Brailsford, 'Mussolini puts up a New Bluff', *Reynolds News*, 9 August 1936; Brailsford, 'Must Europe Play the Coward', *Reynolds News*, 16 August 1936, noting 'the arrival of 25 bomber planes in Seville'; and Brailsford, 'Buying Peace and Losing Honour', *Reynolds News*, 23 August 1936, noting that 'pilots, drawn from the regular air forces of Italy and Germany, are actually fighting in General Franco's advance from Seville'.
8 Brailsford, 'Can Britain Stay Neutral? Europe's fate linked with the Spanish Civil War', *Reynolds News*, 2 August 1936.
9 Brailsford, 'What Road will Spain Tread?', *Reynolds News*, 6 September 1936.
10 Brailsford, 'Can Britain Stay Neutral? Europe's fate linked with the Spanish Civil War', *Reynolds News*, 2 August 1936.

11   Brailsford, 'When Hitler will Strike', *Reynolds News*, 30 August 1936.
12   Brailsford, 'Can Britain Stay Neutral? Europe's fate linked with the Spanish Civil War', *Reynolds News*, 2 August 1936.
13   *New Statesman and Nation*, 1 and 15 August 1936.
14   Brailsford, 'Buying Peace and Losing Honour', *Reynolds News*, 23 August 1936.
15   Brailsford, 'Must Europe Play the Coward', *Reynolds News*, 16 August 1936.
16   Socialist League Special Executive Committee minutes, 18 August 1936.
17   'There can be no Neutrality', *Socialist*, September 1936. Mellor also stressed that the Spanish Civil War was part of an international class war: Editor, 'Matters of Moment', *Socialist*, September 1936.
18   Groves, 'TS outline SL history', n.d., MRC, University of Warwick, Groves papers, MSS 172/SL/1/5, pp. 13–14. See also R. Groves, 'The Socialist League', *Revolutionary History*, 1, 1 (1988), p. 13.
19   TUC Documents 1, Labour Movement Conference, verbatim report, 28 August 1936, p. 42, quoted in Buchanan, *Labour Movement*, pp. 47–8.
20   *Daily Herald*, 27 February 1939, quoted in Buchanan, *Labour Movement*, p. 14.
21   Editor, 'Matters of Moment', *Socialist*, September 1936.
22   *Daily Herald*, 31 August 1936; *The Times*, 31 August 1936; *News Chronicle*, 31 August 1936.
23   Murphy, 'What the League is Doing', *Socialist*, September 1936.
24   'Non-intervention', *New Statesman and Nation*, 8 August 1936.
25   'Not our Concern', *New Statesman and Nation*, 29 August 1936. See also Martin, *Editor*, pp. 210–13.
26   *Daily Herald*, 20 August 1936.
27   Pritt, *Right to Left*, pp. 114–16.
28   *Daily Herald*, 2 September 1936.
29   'There can be no Neutrality', *Socialist*, September 1936.
30   Groves, 'TS outline SL history', n.d., MSS 172/SL/1/5, pp. 13–14, Groves papers. Groves had originally written that while the workers were fighting with the Liberal government, he hoped the workers would 'smash the militarists so that they and their fellows may rule Spain'. However, the committee inserted the word 'afterwards'. Groves had also written that the 'defeat of the militarists is a necessary part of the struggle to win full economic and political power for the Spanish workers and peasants' but the committee changed 'necessary' to 'a necessary preliminary'. See also Groves, 'Socialist League', p. 13.
31   Murphy, *New Horizons*, pp. 118–19. See also Darlington, *Murphy*, pp. 240–2.
32   Socialist League Executive Committee minutes, 10 September 1936.
33   Socialist League National Council minutes, 20 September 1936. See also *Daily Herald*, 21 September 1936. Blaazer, *Popular Front*, pp. 174–5, mentions Murphy's resignation from the Socialist League but without the use of the Socialist League's committee minutes.
34   Murphy, *New Horizons*, pp. 118–19.
35   See also Blaazer, *Popular Front*, pp. 177–9.
36   Brailsford, 'Workers will yet save Spain', *Reynolds News*, 26 July 1936.
37   Brailsford to Cripps, 31 July 1936, Cripps papers.
38   Brailsford, 'Can Britain Stay Neutral? Europe's fate linked with the Spanish Civil War', *Reynolds News*, 2 August 1936. See also H. N. Brailsford, *Towards a New League* (1936), esp. pp. 60–3.
39   Brailsford, 'Must Europe Play the Coward', *Reynolds News*, 16 August 1936.
40   Note on Brailsford to Cripps, 31 July 1936, Cripps papers.
41   Tawney to Woolf, 15 August 1936, University of Sussex, Woolf papers, D6.

42   Socialist League National Council minutes, 20 September 1936.
43   Editorial, *New Leader*, 31 July 1936. See also ibid., 7 August 1936.
44   Ibid., 31 July 1936.
45   Brockway, 'Spain's Struggle is Ours', *New Leader*, 14 August 1936.
46   *New Leader*, 28 August 1936; Brockway, *Inside the Left*, p. 294.
47   J. McNair, 'What I Saw in Spain', *New Leader*, 4 September 1936. See also *New Leader*, 4 September 1936, for further details of the ILP contribution.
48   *New Leader*, 21 August 1936.
49   Ibid., 25 September 1936. See also Brockway, 'Fascists Execute Joaquin Maurin', ibid.; and Brockway, *Inside the Left*, p. 290.
50   Brockway, 'Nazis behind Spanish Fascists', *New Leader*, 31 July 1936.
51   Editorial, *New Leader*, 7 August 1936.
52   Brockway, 'Why Sanctions Against Spain?', *New Leader*, 7 August 1936.
53   *New Leader*, 7 August 1936.
54   J. Lee, 'Open Letter to a Labour Party Member', ibid., 14 August 1936.
55   Brockway, 'Nazis behind Spanish Fascists', *New Leader*, 31 July 1936.
56   Brockway, 'Spain's Struggle is Ours', *New Leader*, 14 August 1936.
57   Editorial, *New Leader*, 14 August 1936.
58   Ibid. Brockway's points were reiterated in ibid., 21 August 1936. See also Brockway, 'British Planes Still Go', *New Leader*, 11 September 1936; and Pollitt's comments in *Daily Worker*, 6 August 1936. The ILP also criticised the Labour party for arguing that the on-going struggle in Spain was about 'democracy'. This is brought out clearly in editorial, *New Leader*, 28 August 1936.
59   *New Leader*, 28 August 1936.
60   Editorial, ibid.
61   *New Leader*, 4 September 1936.
62   For a reiteration of ILP policy (and its stance towards the Communists and the Labour party) see editorial, ibid., 18 September 1936.
63   *New Leader*, 4 September 1936.
64   Ibid., 11 September 1936.
65   Ibid., 18 September 1936.
66   H. N. Brailsford, 'Federal Union in Europe?', *Reynolds News*, 28 June 1936. See also his statement that the new constitution had seemed to mark 'a great advance towards democracy and civil liberty': Brailsford, 'When Hitler will Strike', *Reynolds News*, 30 August 1936.
67   *New Leader*, 19 June 1936. See also 'Russia's New Constitution: towards socialist democracy', ibid., 26 June 1936.
68   'Trotsky and the Soviet Trial: demand for investigation by the working class', *New Leader*, 28 August 1936.
69   Brockway, 'Doubts caused by the Moscow trial', *New Leader*, 28 August 1936.
70   Ibid. In his autobiography Brockway recalled his reaction to the first wave of trials: 'My personal knowledge of the prisoners undoubtedly influenced my judgment . . . . But the greatest impression was made on my mind not so much by the fact that the leading prisoners were the trusted colleagues of Lenin and proven revolutionaries . . . as by the huge proportions of the purge': Brockway, *Inside the Left*, p. 258.
71   *New Leader*, 4 September 1936.
72   Socialist League Executive Committee minutes, 10 September 1936, Cripps papers. See also ibid., 17 September 1936.
73   Socialist League National Council minutes, 20 September 1936, Cripps papers.

74 R. Groves, *The Balham Group* (1974), pp. 36–7, 54–60; Thorpe, *Communist Party*, pp. 197–8.
75 'Information on Trotskyism in Britain', by N. Raylock, 1937, CPA, Moscow 1995 microfilm reel, 495/100/1024.
76 CPGB Central Committee minutes, 10 October 1936.
77 Brailsford, 'When Hitler will Strike', *Reynolds News*, 30 August 1936. Brailsford evidently reiterated the same sentiments in a public speech in London in late September 1936: see special branch informant, 320/FRS/2500, 29 September 1936, National Archives, KV2/686.
78 D. N. Pritt, *The Zinoviev trial* (1936). Pritt had expressed his views as soon as the trials were over: 'Lawyer's view of Moscow trial', *News Chronicle*, 27 August 1936; 'D. N. Pritt KC says the Moscow Trial was Fair', *News Chronicle*, 3 September 1936. See also his autobiography – *From Right to Left*, pp. 108–14.
79 'The Moscow Trial: Brailsford replies to his critics', *Reynolds News*, 13 September 1936.
80 'Comments', *New Statesman and Nation*, 13 June 1936. See also ibid., 5 September 1936.
81 Ibid., 22 August 1936. See also ibid., 29 August 1936.
82 Ibid., 29 August 1936. See also ibid., 22 August 1936.
83 Ibid., 5 September 1936.
84 For the Left Book Club see S. Samuels, 'The Left Book Club', *Journal of Contemporary History*, 1, 2 (1966), pp. 65–86; and J. Lewis, *The Left Book Club: An Historical Record* (1970). For Strachey's support of the purges see H. Thomas, *John Strachey* (1973), p. 164.
85 H. J. Laski, 'A London Diary', *New Statesman and Nation*, 20 June 1936.
86 Laski to Pollitt, 21 August 1936, CPA, 1995 microfilm reel 1.
87 H. J. Laski, *Law and Justice in Soviet Russia* (1935).
88 Laski to Pollitt, 21 August 1936, CPA, 1995 microfilm reel 1.
89 The fullest account of these responses is P. Corthorn, 'Labour, the Left, and the Stalinist Purges of the late 1930s', *Historical Journal*, 48, 1 (2005), pp. 62–85, at pp. 185–7.
90 *Daily Herald*, 28 August 1936. Citrine expressed similar views about the trials to Stanley Baldwin when they met on 7 November 1936 – see Citrine, *Men and Work*, p. 323. For an in-depth discussion of Citrine's views of the Soviet Union see J. Davis, '"Altered Images": The Labour Party and the Soviet Union in the 1930s' (unpublished De Montfort University Ph.D., 2002).
91 Editorial, *Daily Herald*, 24 August 1936. Subsequent editorials drew further comparisons between Stalin's regime and those of Hitler and Mussolini: see, for instance, ibid., 2 September 1936.
92 Ibid., 24 August 1936.
93 Ibid., 25 August 1936.
94 *TUCAR*, pp. 359–67.
95 Ibid., pp. 367–70.
96 Cripps, 'Unity Now For Action! No Truce with Baldwin. Advance!', *Socialist*, October 1936. See also Cripps's comments in other speeches in the weeks before the Labour party conference: *Bristol Evening World*, 21 September 1936.
97 Groves, 'Menace to Unions', *Socialist*, October 1936. Groves had earlier analysed Germany's war economy: see 'Prelude to War 1: Germany's War Machine', *Socialist*, July–August 1936.
98 Foot, *Bevan i*, p. 219. See also J. Campbell, *Nye Bevan and the Mirage of British Socialism* (1987), p. 73.

99   Bevan, 'If We Desert our Comrades', *Socialist*, October 1936.
100 Socialist League Executive Committee minutes, 10 September 1936; resolution enclosed in McCarthy to Morrison, 17 September 1936, copy in Cripps papers.
101 Socialist League Executive Committee minutes, 17 September 1936.
102 McCarthy to Morrison, 17 September 1936, copy in Cripps papers.
103 Morrison to McCarthy, 17 September 1936, Cripps papers.
104 McCarthy, 'What the League is Doing', *Socialist*, October 1936.
105 McCarthy to NCL Secretary, 19 August 1936, copy in Cripps papers; and Middleton to McCarthy, 20 August 1936, Cripps papers.
106 Socialist League Special Executive Committee minutes, 24 August 1936. These points were conveyed to the NCL the following day: see McCarthy to NCL Secretary, 25 August 1936, copy in Cripps papers.
107 Socialist League Executive Committee minutes, 10 September 1936.
108 Ibid., 1 October 1936.
109 Betts, 'International Notes', *Socialist*, September 1936.
110 Pimlott's claim that negotiations for the actual Unity Campaign began in summer 1936 overstates the Socialist League's position at this point: Pimlott, *Labour and the Left*, p. 94.
111 Socialist League Executive Committee minutes, 11 June 1936.
112 Socialist League Special Executive Committee minutes, 24 August 1936.
113 Socialist League Executive Committee minutes, 10 September 1936.
114 Brockway to Cripps, 23 September 1936, Cripps papers.
115 Cripps to Brockway, 25 September 1936, copy in Cripps papers.
116 *LPACR*, 1936, pp. 169–72. The NCL's statement supporting non-intervention in the Spanish Civil War can be seen at ibid., pp. 28–31.
117 Ibid., pp. 172–3.
118 Ibid., pp. 173–5.
119 Ibid., pp. 177–8.
120 Ibid., pp. 179–80.
121 Ibid., pp. 182–207, for the debate.
122 Ibid., pp. 250–1.
123 Ibid., p. 254.
124 Ibid., p. 257.
125 Zilliacus to Cripps, 18 September 1936, Cripps papers. For earlier correspondence over Spain see Zilliacus to Cripps, 26 August 1936, Cripps papers.
126 *LPACR*, 1936, pp. 212–13 and 213–15 respectively.
127 The following year Cole aptly commented on the 'revulsion of feeling which swept over the conference . . . after the speeches of the Spanish delegates': Cole, *Peoples Front*, p. 298.
128 *LPACR*, p. 258.
129 Ibid., p. 262.

Chapter 5

1   See J. Stevenson and C. Cook, *Britain in the Depression: Society and Politics 1929–39* (1994, 2nd edition), pp. 205–9; and Ellen Wilkinson's own account: E. Wilkinson, *The Town that was Murdered* (1939).
2   Brockway, *Inside the Left*, pp. 270–1. See also Aplin, 'The Means Test Must Go', *New Leader*, 2 October 1936, which discusses ILP-CPGB co-operation.
3   Foot, *Bevan i*, pp. 159–69.
4   Jupp, *Radical Left*, p. 36.
5   Socialist League Executive Committee minutes, 1 October 1936

6   Ibid., 15 October 1936.
7   Reporting letter from the Socialist League to the Labour party, 17 October 1936, National Archives, KV2/668.
8   See also Pimlott, *Labour and the Left*, p. 93.
9   McCarthy to all Socialist League members, 13 October 1936, Cripps papers, emphasis in original.
10 Socialist League Executive Committee minutes, 5 November 1936.
11 Socialist League National Council minutes, 7–8 November 1936.
12 McCarthy, 'What the League is Doing: For the Workers and Spain', *Socialist*, November 1936.
13 Socialist League Executive Committee minutes, 5 November 1936.
14 Quoted in Foot, *Bevan i*, p. 238. See also editorial, *New Leader*, 13 November 1936.
15 Bevan, 'Challenge of the Hunger March: Banners of United Front Point Road to Victory', *Socialist*, November 1936. Similarly, Mellor noted how the hunger marchers had 'proved the value of unity': Mellor, 'Edinburgh – and After', *Socialist*, November 1936.
16 McCarthy, 'What the League is Doing', *Socialist*, December 1936–January 1937.
17 Socialist League Executive Committee minutes, 19 November 1936.
18 See T. Kushner and N. Valman (eds.), *Remembering Cable Street: Fascism and Anti-Fascism in Britain* (2000).
19 Socialist League Executive Committee minutes, 24 September 1936.
20 Ibid., 15 October 1936.
21 Campbell, 'What the League is Doing: East End Campaign Launched', *Socialist*, November 1936.
22 Ibid. See also *New Leader*, 30 October 1936. Groves gave a report of the conference to the Socialist League Executive Committee on 5 November 1936 – see Executive Committee minutes, 5 November 1936. See also Pimlott, *Labour and the Left*, p. 93.
23 McCarthy, 'What the League is Doing', *Socialist*, December 1936–January 1937.
24 R. Groves, *East End Crisis! Socialism, the Jews and Fascism* (1936), esp. pp. 3–6, Groves papers, MSS.172/RG/4/33.
25 Editorial, *New Leader*, 16 October 1936.
26 Editor, 'Matters of Moment', *Socialist*, November 1936. For discussion of ILP-Socialist League-CPGB collaboration see Brockway, *Inside the Left*, pp. 270–2.
27 Socialist League Executive Committee minutes, 22 October 1936.
28 Ibid., 5 November 1936.
29 CPGB Central Committee minutes, 10 October 1936; Brockway, *Inside the Left*, p. 264; McNair, *Maxton*, p. 262; Foot, *Bevan*, p. 243; Pollitt to Page Arnot, 29 October 1936, CPA, transcriptions of microfilm, 495/14/220. Parts of the latter are in 'extracts from letters of Harry Pollitt, Oct 29 to Nov 6', CPA, 1995 microfilm reel 1, 495/12/80.
30 CPGB Central Committee minutes, 10 October 1936.
31 Ibid.
32 Brailsford, 'How to Re-build the Movement', *New Leader*, 13 November 1936.
33 Ibid.
34 Murphy, *New Horizons*, pp. 318–19. Interestingly Murphy still continued to cause some concern. The London Area Committee informed the Executive Committee that they believed Murphy had been making use of confidential material acquired while he was general secretary in order to circulate popular

front material to Socialist League members. The Executive Committee discussed the matter on 22 October and agreed that Mellor should write to Murphy. Murphy, however, was adamant that he had not taken any lists of members from Head Office: Socialist League Executive Committee minutes, 22 October 1936; Socialist League Executive Committee minutes, 29 October 1936.

35 'Answers to Pollitt to questions by Secretariat of ECCI', 5 January 1937, CPA, 1995 microfilm reel, 495/18/1149.

36 Pollitt to Page Arnot, 29 October 1936, CPA, transcriptions of microfilm, 495/14/220.

37 CPGB Central Committee minutes, 10 October 1936.

38 Castle, *Fighting All the Way*, pp. 76–7.

39 Pollitt to Page Arnot, 29 October 1936, CPA, transcriptions of microfilm, 495/14/220. Pollitt remarked that Cripps 'did not go as far as Mellor'. Brockway, *Inside the Left*, p. 265, states that Cripps 'was obviously lost when William Mellor put the Marxist case against the Popular Front; he acknowledged that he had not thought out the subject'.

40 CPGB Politburo minutes, 13 November 1936.

41 Pollitt to Page Arnot, 6 November 1936, CPA, 1995 microfilm reel 1, 495/12/80.

42 See the drafts and redrafts – 'Proposals of the Communist Party for a National Unity Campaign', 29 October 1936, Pollitt papers, CP/IN/POLL/14/15; also in LHASC, CPA, Dutt papers, CP/IND/DUTT/16/07; 'Basis of Unity Campaign' by Socialist League, 4 November 1936, Dutt papers, CP/IND/DUTT/16/09.

43 CPGB Politburo minutes, 13 November 1936. See also K. Morgan, *Harry Pollitt* (Manchester, 1993), p. 91.

44 McCarthy to branch secretaries, 30 October 1936, copy in Cripps papers.

45 Socialist League Executive Committee minutes, 5 November 1936.

46 Socialist League National Council minutes, 7–8 November 1936.

47 Ibid.

48 Groves, 'The Socialist Left in the 1930s', n.d., Groves papers, MSS.172/SL/1/3.

49 Groves, 'A Documentary History of the SL, 1932–37', n.d., Groves papers, MSS.172/SL/1/15/3. See also Groves, 'Socialist League', p. 14.

50 Socialist League National Council minutes, 7–8 November 1936.

51 See, for instance, 'Formulation of Point no. 3 in Section "The Fight for Peace"', 11 November 1936, Dutt papers, CP/IND/DUTT/16/09.

52 Socialist League Executive Committee minutes, 12 November 1936.

53 Ibid.

54 'Agreed CP-SL document', Dutt papers, CP/IND/DUTT/16/09.

55 Thorpe, *Communist Party*, pp. 235–6.

56 Socialist League Emergency Executive Committee minutes, 20 November 1936.

57 See Barker to Groves, 24 November 1936, Groves papers.

58 Socialist League Executive Committee minutes, 26 November 1936.

59 Barker to Groves, 24 November 1936, Groves papers.

60 See, for instance, Mellor to Brockway, with attachment, 20 November 1936, copy in Cripps papers.

61 Socialist League Executive Committee minutes, 26 November 1936.

62 CPGB Politburo minutes, 13 November 1936.

63 For the fine detail of the ILP's stance see 'The unity campaign negotiations:

decisions of the ILP executive committee, 24 November 1936', Cripps papers;
also in Dutt papers, CP/IND/DUTT/16/09.

64 Brockway to Cripps, 3 December 1936 (2 letters), Cripps papers; copies in
Groves papers, MSS.172/SL/1/4/6; Pollitt papers, CP/IND/POLL/14/15; and
Dutt papers, CP/IND/DUTT/16/09; 'Basis of the Unity Campaign:
Amendments proposed by the ILP', n.d. but 1, 2 or 3 December 1936, Cripps
papers. For CPGB discussion of the changing ILP stance see: CPGB Politburo
minutes, 27 November 1936.

65 For the Socialist League position on Spain in October 1936 see 'Draft
Resolution on Spain, prepared by J. F. Horrabin', Cripps papers.

66 Buchanan, *Labour Movement*, pp. 70–1.

67 Ibid., p. 74.

68 Ibid., p. 84.

69 'What some ILP branches are Doing', *New Leader*, 23 October 1936. This co-
operation later produced a series of joint meetings: 'Brockway in North East',
New Leader, 4 December 1936.

70 *Daily Herald*, 21 November 1936. The letter was signed by Cripps and Mellor
from the Socialist League; Pollitt and Gallacher from the CPGB; and Brockway
and Maxton from the ILP. See also *New Leader*, 27 November 1936.

71 Brockway, 'The World this Week', *New Leader*, 9 October 1936.

72 Jennie Lee, 'Labour Party Commits Suicide', *New Leader*, 16 October 1936.

73 *New Leader*, 16 October 1936.

74 Ibid., 23 October 1936.

75 Brockway, 'The World this Week', ibid., 23 October 1936.

76 Brockway, 'From Brussels to Barcelona', *New Leader*, 13 November 1936. See
also editorial, *New Leader*, 6 November 1936. Brockway later reflected that at
this point he was 'apprehensive . . . about the effect of the Russian aid' fearing
that 'Russia would not sell arms to Spain without demanding control of the use
of the arms': Brockway, *Inside the Left*, pp. 265–6.

77 Pimlott, *Labour and the Left*, chs. 11–13. See also Dare, 'Socialist League',
pp. 393, 403–4. M. Worley, *Labour Inside the Gate: A History of the British
Labour Party between the Wars* (2005), esp. pp. 189–92 and more generally ch.
4, casts important light on the activities of the constituency parties at this
time.

78 Pimlott, *Labour and the Left*, p. 112.

79 National Council Annual Party Conference resolutions, n.d. but May 1936,
Cripps papers. See also *Daily Herald*, 1 June 1936; *The Times*, 1 June 1936.

80 See Pimlott, *Labour and the Left*, pp. 122–3.

81 Greene, 'The Constituency Parties', *Socialist*, December 1936–January 1937.
See also Pimlott, *Labour and the Left*, pp. 126–8; and Dare, 'Socialist League',
pp. 409–11.

82 Socialist League Executive Committee minutes, 15 October 1936.

83 'Resolution drafted by Stafford Cripps', Cripps papers.

84 Editor, 'Matters of Moment', *Socialist*, December 1936–January 1937.

85 Socialist League Executive Committee minutes, 10 December 1936; see also
Greene's memorandum – 'Individual Membership of the Labour Party: Personal
and Confidential to the Members of the Socialist League Executive', n.d., but
early December 1936, Cripps papers.

86 Socialist League Executive Committee minutes, 3 December 1936; 'Basis of
Unity Campaign: Accepted by the EC of the Socialist League', Cripps papers;
also in Dutt papers, CP/IND/DUTT/16/0; and Pollitt papers, CP/IND/POLL/

14/15, which notes that this draft was also accepted by the Executive Committees of both the CPGB and the ILP.

87   Unity Campaign Committee minutes, 9 December 1936, Cripps papers.

88   Socialist League Executive Committee minutes, 3 December 1936.

89   Ibid., 10 December 1936.

90   Mellor, 'Get Together, Comrades!', *Socialist*, December 1936–January 1937.

91   Socialist League Executive Committee minutes, 17 December 1936.

92   Socialist League Special Executive Committee minutes, 21 December 1936. See also the report of the London aggregate meeting in *Daily Herald*, 21 December 1936.

93   *Daily Herald*, 19 December 1936; *News Chronicle*, 19 December 1936.

94   Mellor to all branch secretaries, 19 December 1936, Cripps papers.

95   Socialist League Executive Committee minutes, 21 December 1936. *Daily Herald*, *The Times*, 22 December 1936, reports the Socialist League meeting. These points were communicated to the branches the following day: see McCarthy to branch secretaries, 22 December 1936, Cripps papers.

96   Minute: 11 November 1936, Dalton papers, 3/1/4–5 [Pimlott (ed.), *Political Diary*, pp. 210–12].

97   *Daily Herald*, 19 December 1936.

98   Ibid., 2, 4 and 13 January 1937.

99   Pollitt reported in CPGB Central Committee minutes, 16 January 1937.

100 Socialist League Executive Committee minutes, 5 January 1937.

101 NEC minutes, 8 January 1937; *Daily Herald*, 9 January 1937.

102 *Daily Herald*, 14 January 1937.

103 Unity Campaign Committee minutes, 16 December 1936, Cripps papers.

104 Brockway, 'Report of Unity Campaign Committee', 16 December 1936, Ruskin College, Oxford, Middleton papers, JSM/ILP/26.

105 Brockway, 'How can we get Unity?', *New Leader*, 4 December 1936. See also Brockway's dismissive views of 'neo-Trotskyites' in his report on the International Revolutionary Socialist Congress held at Brussels in early November: 'From Brussels to Barcelona', *New Leader*, 13 November 1936. In his autobiography Brockway echoed these sentiments stating: 'I have often been called a Trotskyist. Much of my criticism of Russia's policy was similar to Trotsky's, but my conclusions were reached quite independently . . . . Trotsky's dealing with his followers convinced me that, despite his advocacy of "proletarian democracy", he had the same instinct for personal power as Stalin and that were he head of the Russian state he would treat dissentients from his policy with a ruthlessness similar to Stalin's': Brockway, *Inside the Left*, p. 263.

106 See the information contained in circular of 5 December 1936, ILP NAC Documents. See also Jupp, *Radical Left*, p. 70.

107 For further discussion of Trotskyist activity within the ILP see Cohen thesis, p. 187.

108 'Information on Trotskyism in Britain', by N. Raylock, 1937, CPA, Moscow 1995 microfilm reel, 495/100/1024.

109 Brockway to Mellor, 28 December 1936, copy in Cripps papers.

110 Brockway, 'The World this Week', *New Leader*, 1 January 1937. Brockway had already criticised the Soviet representative in Barcelona for 'denouncing the workers party as in effect pro-fascist and supporters of Hitler and Mussolini': ibid., 18 December 1936.

111 Brockway, *Inside the Left*, p. 300, discusses the problems this caused.

112 Brockway, 'The World this Week', *New Leader*, 8 January 1937.

113 CPGB Central Committee minutes, 16 January 1937.
114 *New Leader*, 25 December 1936.
115 Brockway, *Inside the Left*, p. 267.
116 *New Leader*, 15 January 1937.
117 Socialist League Executive Committee minutes, 15 and 29 October 1936.
118 Sgt. Hodge, 301/AFAW/87, 26 October 1936, National Archives, KV2/668; *New Leader*, 23 October 1936. See also the brief report in McCarthy, 'What the League is Doing: for the workers and Spain', *Socialist*, November 1936.
119 Socialist League Executive Committee minutes, 5 January 1937.
120 Ibid., 14 January 1937.
121 Groves to all branches, 13 January 1937, copy in Cripps papers.
122 Pimlott, *Labour and the Left*, does not consider Groves's opposition to the Unity Campaign. Dare, 'Socialist League', pp. 417–23, gives the impression that Groves's objection to the campaign was entirely based on Cripps and Mellor's disregard for Socialist League procedure.
123 Groves, 'A Documentary History of the SL, 1932–37', Groves papers, MSS.172/SL/1/15/3; Groves, 'Socialist League', p. 13. See also Groves's similar comments in Groves, 'The Socialist Left in the 1930s', Groves papers, MSS.172/SL/1/3.
124 See the notes in Needham papers, no title or date, but January 1937 because of references to voting at special conference, K19, for brief coverage of arguments made in favour of the Unity Campaign. These concerned the local importance of the ILP and the way in which the energy and commitment of CPGB members outweighed their numerical significance.
125 For this speculation see *Morning Post*, 19 January 1936.
126 For coverage of Cripps's speech see *Daily Herald*, 18 January 1937; and *News Chronicle*, 18 January 1937.
127 Socialist League Executive Committee minutes, 21 January 1937.
128 Campbell to Comrade, 18 January 1937; Campbell to secretaries of all London branches, 18 January 1937, all Cripps papers.
129 Mellor and McCarthy to all branches and members, 19 January 1937, Needham papers, K18.

Chapter 6

1 *Tribune*, 22 January 1937. He stated frankly that he had 'never seen any reason why men like . . . Harry Pollitt [and] James Maxton . . . should not stand as Labour candidates and work with the party in the House of Commons'.
2 *Daily Worker*, 19 January 1937; *News Chronicle*, 25 January 1937.
3 New Statesman and Nation', 23 January 1937.
4 'Unity Manifesto', Cripps papers.
5 *Tribune*, 29 January 1937. See also *Daily Herald*, 25 January 1937.
6 Editorial, *New Leader*, 15 January 1937.
7 Edwards, 'Why We Go', *New Leader*, 15 January 1937; Brockway, *Inside the Left*, pp. 297–8.
8 Editorial, *New Leader*, 22 January 1937.
9 Buchanan, *Labour Movement*, p. 78, notes that the TUC 'refused even to involve itself with fund-raising on behalf of the dependents of volunteers'. See also ibid., p. 85.
10 *Daily Herald*, 25 January 1937; *Manchester Guardian*, 25 January 1937. See also Cripps's unpublished article: 'New Masses', dated 9 May 1937, Cripps papers.
11 Campbell to Comrade, 18 January 1937; Campbell to secretaries of all London branches, 18 January 1937, both Cripps papers. See the reports in

Daily Herald, 18 January 1937; *News Chronicle*, 18 January 1937; *The Times*, 18 January 1937.

12 McCarthy to Secretary of London Area Committee (Campbell), 19 January 1937, copy in Cripps papers.

13 Strachey made the same criticisms a few days later: 'Trotskyism', *Daily Worker*, 22 January 1937.

14 Thorpe, *Communist Party*, pp. 236–7.

15 CPGB Secretariat to all party organisations, 20 January 1937, Dutt papers, CP/IND/DUTT/29/10. See also 'Information on Trotskyism in Britain', by N. Raylock, 1937, Moscow 1995 microfilm reel, 495/100/1024.

16 Socialist League Executive Committee minutes, 21 January 1937. It would seem very likely that Groves was the person who opposed the final decision.

17 Socialist League Executive Committee minutes, 21 January 1937.

18 H. A. Studer to Cripps, 25 January 1937, Cripps papers.

19 Cripps to comrade (Studer), 27 January 1937, copy in Cripps papers.

20 Middleton to McCarthy, 21 January 1937, LP/SL/35/30; McCarthy to Middleton, 22 January 1937, LP/SL/35/31–32; Middleton to McCarthy, 23 January 1937, LP/SL/35/33; McCarthy to Middleton, 23 January 1937, LP/SL/35/34; McCarthy to Middleton, 25 January 1937, LP/SL/35/35; Middleton to McCarthy, 25 January 1937, LP/SL/35/36, all LPA, Socialist League file.

21 *Daily Herald*, 22 January 1937.

22 *Daily Worker*, 27 January 1937.

23 Cole to Middleton, TUC archive, MSS.126/TG/2000 box 9, dep. 5/5/2000. For an earlier draft of the letter see Addison to Middleton, n.d. but January 1937, Cole papers, GDHC/D5/2/28/1. Cole also secured Leonard Woolf's signature: see Cole to Woolf, 25 January 1937, Cole papers, GDHC/D5/2/29. *News Chronicle*, 25 January 1937, comments on this letter.

24 Cole to Bevin, 25 January 1937, TUC archive, MSS.126/TG/2000, box 9, dep. 5/5/2000.

25 Bevin to Cole, 27 January 1937, TUC archive, MSS.126/TG/2000, box 9, dep. 5/5/00; also quoted in Bullock, *Bevin i*, p. 596, but misdated as 25 January 1937. See also Cole to Bevin, 1 February 1937, TUC archive, MSS.126/TG/2000, box 9, dep. 5/5/00; and Bevin to Cole, 2 February 1937, TUC archive, MSS.126/TG/2000, box 9, dep. 5/5/00. At the annual festival of the TGWU in Bristol Bevin reiterated some of these feelings publicly. He stated: 'I saw Mosley come into the Movement and I see no difference in the tactics of Mosley and Cripps': *Daily Herald*, 15 February 1937.

26 'Copy of Declaration received from the Labour party, 27/1/37', Cripps papers. See also Middleton to McCarthy, 27 January 1937, Cripps papers.

27 *Daily Herald*, 28 January 1937.

28 Socialist League Executive Committee minutes, 4 February 1937.

29 Ibid., 28 January 1937; McCarthy to all members of the National Council, 29 January 1937, Cripps papers; Socialist League Executive Committee minutes, 4 February 1937.

30 Socialist League press statement, 28 January 1937, LPA, Socialist League file, LP/SL/35/40; another copy in Cripps papers and in Needham papers, K18; McCarthy to Middleton, 29 January 1937, Socialist League file, LPA, LP/SL/35/39; another copy in Cripps papers.

31 Dodds to Cripps, 28 January 1937, Cripps papers. Dodds's continuing involvement on the Gateshead City Council during her time in the Socialist

League is apparent from the Gateshead County Borough Council minutes, 1931 to 1937, Newcastle, Tyne and Wear Archives, GB/CA/186–191.

32 Preface to Gateshead branch Executive Committee minutes, PO/SL1/1.

33 See Pimlott, *Labour and the Left*, p. 225.

34 Mellor, 'Our Message to Labour Party Members', *Socialist Broadsheet*, February 1937.

35 Socialist League Executive Committee minutes, 4 February 1937.

36 Ibid., 28 January 1937.

37 Ibid., 5 January 1937.

38 McCarthy to all branches, 29 January 1937, Cripps papers. Cripps's East Bristol Divisional Labour Party had already passed such a resolution: Rogers to Middleton, 28 January 1937, copy in Cripps papers.

39 'The Moscow Trial', *New Leader*, 29 January 1937.

40 *New Leader*, 29 January 1937.

41 CPGB Secretariat to Mellor, 28 January 1937, Cripps papers. For more discussion of the CPGB attitude to the ILP at this point see 'Information on Trotskyism in Britain', by N. Raylock, 1937, CPA, Moscow 1995 microfilm reel, 495/100/1024.

42 CPGB Politburo minutes, 28 January 1937.

43 *New Leader*, 12 February 1937.

44 Ibid., 19 February 1937.

45 Ibid., 2 April 1937. Before the conference Brockway had written that there was 'some uncertainty due to doubts about the facts of internal developments there' and that the party was 'right not to be dogmatic until these doubts are cleared up': Brockway, 'Why the ILP is Confident', *New Leader*, 26 March 1937.

46 CPGB Politburo minutes, 28 January 1937.

47 M. Foot, 'The Road to Ruin' in E. Thomas (ed.), *Tribune 21* (1958), pp. 7–8.

48 Brockway, *Inside the Left*, p. 265.

49 *New Leader*, 4 December 1936. See also J. M. Stuart, 'The Soviet experiment in English revolutionary thought and politics 1928–41' (University of Cambridge Ph.D., 1991), p. 150.

50 See in particular Brailsford, 'Moscow trial must not shake our faith in Russia', *Reynolds News*, 7 February 1937, where he explained that the trials had left him 'bewildered, doubtful and miserable'.

51 Foot, 'Road to Ruin', p. 7.

52 'Will Stalin Explain', *New Statesman and Nation*, 30 January 1937.

53 Editorial, *Daily Herald*, 23 January 1937. For more detail on the response of the NEC-TUC grouping at this juncture see Corthorn, 'Labour and the Purges', pp. 197–8.

54 Editorial, *Daily Herald*, 28 January 1937.

55 Brockway, 'My Interview with Gorkin', *New Leader*, 19 February 1937.

56 *New Leader*, 2 April 1937.

57 Brockway, *Inside the Left*, pp. 300–1. McNair told the participants at the 1937 ILP Summer School about these meetings: *New Leader*, 6 August 1937.

58 'We are Proud of POUM: McNair answers the charges against the Spanish Workers Party', *New Leader*, 12 March 1937. Significantly, he denied it was Trotskyist: McNair, 'Charge Against Spanish Workers Party', *New Leader*, 2 January 1937.

59 Brockway, 'Unity Wanted in Spain', *New Leader*, 12 February 1937. See also *New Leader*, 5 February 1937, which called the attacks on the POUM 'disgraceful'.

60 Brockway, 'A Look Round the World', *New Leader*, 19 March 1937.
61 *New Leader*, 19 February 1937. See also editorial, ibid., 19 March 1937.
62 *New Leader*, 2 April 1937.
63 Ibid., 1 January 1937.
64 Ibid., 2 April 1937.
65 Ibid. This was Brockway's most favourable response to a popular front. Indeed, editorial, ibid., 5 March 1937, dismisses it as a way of putting 'socialism on the shelf'.
66 Editorial, *New Leader*, 2 April 1937.
67 Ibid.
68 Brockway, review of C. L. R. James, *World Revolution 1917–36*, *New Leader*, 16 April 1937.
69 *Daily Herald*, 1 February 1937; Foot, *Bevan i*, pp. 247–8.
70 *Western Daily Press*, 15 February 1937. See also *Daily Herald*, 15 February 1937.
71 *Daily Herald*, 22 February 1937.
72 Mellor and McCarthy to branch secretaries and Head Office members, 27 February 1937, Cripps papers.
73 *Socialist*, July–August 1936. See also Groves, 'The Labour Party and the Young Workers', *Socialist*, June 1936.
74 Mitchison to editor, *New Statesman and Nation*, 23 January 1937.
75 T. Willis, *Whatever Happened to Tom Mix?* (1970), p. 150. For youth support of the Unity Campaign see also McNair, *Maxton*, p. 262.
76 Socialist League Executive Committee minutes, 28 January 1937.
77 Ibid., 4 February 1937.
78 'Constitution of the Socialist League', 1932, LPA, uncatalogued papers in box marked 'Communist Party and the Popular Front'.
79 Socialist League Executive Committee minutes, 4 February 1937.
80 Ibid.
81 Ibid., 18 February 1937.
82 Ibid., 25 February 1937.
83 *Socialist Broadsheet*, February 1937.
84 Socialist League Executive Committee minutes, 18 February 1937.
85 Dodds to Cripps, 28 January 1937, Cripps papers, for Shildon; Socialist League Executive Committee minutes, 21 January 1937, for Miles Platting.
86 Socialist League Executive Committee minutes, 4 February 1937.
87 Mellor and McCarthy to branch secretaries and Head Office members, 27 February 1937, Cripps papers.
88 See, for instance, *News Chronicle*, 20 February 1937; *Manchester Guardian*, 22 February 1937; *The Times*, 22 February 1937.
89 Attlee told Laski that he would 'do all that is in my power' to oppose the disaffiliation of individual members. He said he was 'against heresy hunting, but the heretics seem to seek martyrdom': Attlee to Laski, 22 February 1937, Laski papers, DLA/13i, Brynmor Jones Library, University of Hull.
90 Speaking in Bristol on 27 February, Greenwood stressed that the Labour party should 'not seek alliances with forces that for years have been stabbing us in the back': *Daily Herald*, 1 March 1937.
91 *Daily Herald*, 22 February 1937 – Cripps at Glasgow where he said that so far as his membership of the Labour party was concerned, he was 'hanging by the skin of my teeth, but I propose to hang on as long as I can'.
92 Mellor to Middleton, 2 February 1937, LP/SL/35/46; Secretary's Department to Mellor, 3 February 1937, LP/SL/35/47, both LPA, Socialist League file.

93 *Daily Herald*, 25 February 1937. Cripps's speech on the Gresford Mining Disaster in the House of Commons on 23 February undoubtedly made the NEC reluctant to expel him: see Pimlott, *Labour and the Left*, p. 103; and Clarke, *Cripps Version*, p. 66.

94 NEC, 'The Labour Party and the "Unity Campaign"', n.d., but February 1937, LPA, uncatalogued papers in box marked 'Communist Party and the Popular Front'.

95 G. R. Strauss, unpublished autobiography, p. 68, Churchill College, Cambridge, Strauss papers.

96 Strauss, 'Make it a Waterloo: Unity Spells Victory in Fight for Power in London', *Tribune*, 12 February 1937. See also *New Leader*, 5 February 1937.

97 Morrison to Cripps, 15 February 1937; Cripps to Morrison, 17 February 1937. See also Cripps to Morrison, 16 February 1937, all Cripps papers.

98 Socialist League Executive Committee minutes, 18 February 1937.

99 Extracts of the letter are quoted in Mellor and McCarthy to branch secretaries and head office members, 27 February 1937, Cripps papers.

100 Mellor and McCarthy to branch secretaries and Head Office members, 27 February 1937, Cripps papers.

101 Socialist League Executive Committee minutes, 25 February 1937.

102 Ibid., 18 February 1937.

103 Ibid., 25 February 1937.

104 Ibid., 11 March 1937.

105 See Buchanan, *Labour Movement*, pp. 86–91.

106 Ibid., pp. 95–6. See also C. Fleay and M. L. Sanders, 'The Labour Spain Committee: Labour Party Policy and the Spanish Civil War', *Historical Journal*, 28, 1 (1985), pp. 187–97.

107 Editorial, *New Leader*, 19 February 1937.

108 Socialist League Executive Committee minutes, 25 February 1937.

109 Ibid., 11 March 1937. See also Mellor to McCarthy, 11 March 1937, copy in Cripps papers.

110 'National Unity Committee's Statement on Armaments, 6 March 1937', Cripps papers. Also printed in 'Fight Now Against War Plan – Unity Campaign's Call', *Tribune*, 5 March 1937. For further reiteration of the same arguments see *New Leader*, 12 March 1937; Bevan, 'Giant Strides to the Next War: We must Oppose Arms Plan Root and Branch', *Tribune*, 19 February 1937; Laski, 'A Policy for Labour: Win Peace, Bread, Security by Unity in Action', *Tribune*, 26 February 1937; Cripps, 'Arms for What? Beware Menace of the National Front', *Tribune*, 12 March 1937.

111 Strauss, unpublished autobiography, p. 68, Strauss papers.

112 Provisional Committee of Constituency Labour Parties minutes, 21 March 1937, Cripps papers; St John Reade to Hill, 13 March 1937, copy in Cripps papers.

113 Socialist League National Council minutes, 13–14 March 1937.

114 Editorial, *New Leader*, 12 March 1937, which argued that the 'Labour victory in London was in large part due to the united working-class support given to the Labour party'.

115 Strauss, 'Laying the Red Bogey: London's Answer to all this talk of Disruptive Forces', *Tribune*, 12 March 1937.

116 *Daily Herald*, 18 March 1937.

117 Ibid., 17 March 1937. See also Strauss, unpublished autobiography, p. 64, Strauss papers.

118 NEC minutes, 24 March 1937. Middleton to McCarthy, 25 March 1937, LPA, Socialist League file, LP/SL/35/49; also in Cripps papers.
119 Middleton to Mellor, 25 March 1937, LPA, Socialist League file, LP/SL/35/48.
120 *Daily Herald*, 25 March 1937.
121 Dalton, *Fateful Years*, p. 125.
122 Ibid., p. 129.
123 Labour party, *Labour's Immediate Programme* (1937).
124 McCarthy to Middleton, 30 March 1937, LPA, Socialist League file, LP/SL/35/50; also in Cripps papers.
125 *Daily Herald*, 30 March 1937; 'Unions for Unity: Swift Rebuffs to Inquisition of Transport House', *Tribune*, 2 April 1937.
126 Lansbury, 'Suppression No Remedy: Tolerance is the Real Mark of a Movement's Confidence', *Tribune*, 2 April 1937.
127 Barker to McCarthy, 7 April 1937, Cripps papers.
128 It has not been possible to find a copy of the Socialist League National Council minutes for 4 April 1937. Nevertheless, some sense of the different views expressed and the decision reached by the National Council can be derived from Rogers to Cripps, 5 April 1937; Barker to Cripps, 5 April 1937; Cripps to Rogers, 6 April 1937; and Barker to Cripps, 7 April 1937, all Cripps papers. See also *News Chronicle*, 10 April 1937.
129 McCarthy to Middleton, 10 April 1937, LPA, Socialist League file, LP/SL/35/51; copy in Cripps papers.
130 Barker to Cripps, 5 April 1937, Cripps papers.
131 Cripps to Rogers, 6 April 1937, copy in Cripps papers.
132 Middleton to McCarthy, 12 April 1937, LPA, Socialist League file, LP/SL/35/52.
133 NEC, 'The Labour Party and the So-Called "Unity Campaign"', April 1937, LPA, uncatalogued papers in box marked 'Communist Party and the Popular Front'.
134 *Daily Herald*, 10 April 1937.
135 Ibid., 12 April 1937.
136 Ibid., 16 April 1937.
137 *Tribune*, 16 April 1937.
138 Editorial, *New Leader*, 16 April 1937, arguing that these 'assertions in relation to the Unity Campaign are miles from the truth'. See also ibid., 23 April 1937.
139 *Daily Herald*, 19 April 1937.
140 'Proposals for next steps in Unity Campaign drawn up by Harry Pollitt and submitted for the Committee's consideration', 27 April 1937, Dutt papers, CP/IND/DUTT/16/09.
141 Pimlott, *Labour and the Left*, p. 104.
142 Brockway, *Inside the Left*, p. 268. For Pollitt's attempts to influence Cripps see ibid., p. 265; and Pimlott, *Labour and the Left*, pp. 94–5.
143 Laski to Cripps, 25 February 1937, Cripps papers. Clarke, *Cripps Version*, pp. 55–6, comments on Cripps's relationship with Laski.
144 Webb diary, 6 and 18 April 1937, Passfield papers.
145 Barker to Cripps, 5 April 1937; Rogers to Cripps, 5 April 1937, both Cripps papers.
146 Rogers to Cripps, 5 April 1937, Cripps papers.
147 See Socialist League Executive Committee minutes, 28 January 1937.
148 Barker to Cripps, 5 April 1937, Cripps papers, emphasis in original. Indeed, on 22 April the Borough Labour party endorsed the NEC's decision of

24 March and expressed its commitment to operating any subsequent expulsions: Barker to Cripps, 23 April 1937, Cripps papers.

149 Cripps to Rogers, 6 April 1937, copy in Cripps papers.

150 Barker to Cripps, 11 April 1937; Rogers to Cripps, 12 April 1937, both Cripps papers.

151 Rogers to Cripps, 12 April 1937, Cripps papers. Rogers had developed a plan for the League, which he discussed with Barker who then advanced the idea as her own to the Executive Committee. The idea was that at a date nearer to the Socialist League conference, the ILP and the CPGB would issue a statement asking the Socialist League to dissolve 'in order to demonstrate their sincerity for the campaign and to maintain contact with the Labour party'. At such short notice, it was argued that the National Council would waive its recommendation to the Socialist League annual conference and allow an open vote on the issue. See Barker to Cripps, 7 April 1937; Barker to McCarthy, 7 April 1937; and Rogers to Cripps, 7 April 1937, all Cripps papers.

152 See Cripps to Parmoor, 12 April 1937, copy in Cripps papers.

153 On the voting see the report of *Daily Telegraph*, 22 April 1937. McNair, *Maxton*, p. 264, also states that Mellor was reluctant to dissolve the Socialist League.

154 'National Council Report', p. 12, in Socialist League, *Report of National Council and Final Agenda of the Annual Conference*, (1937).

155 Socialist League National Council minutes, 18 April 1937. *Tribune*, 23 April 1937, comments on the confidential National Council decision and the confidential branch circular.

156 *LPACR*, 1935, p. 102; ibid., 1936, p. 130.

157 These were the figures leaked to the *Daily Herald*, 17 May 1937.

158 'National Council Report', p. 8.

159 Socialist League National Council minutes, 13–14 March 1937.

160 McCarthy to all branch secretaries, 16 March 1937, Cripps papers.

161 *Daily Herald*, 17 May 1937.

162 Socialist League National Council minutes, 18 April 1937.

163 See 'Proposals for next steps in Unity Campaign drawn up by Harry Pollitt and submitted for the Committee's consideration', 27 April 1937, Dutt papers, CP/IND/DUTT/16/09; and Horrabin to Cripps, 25 April 1937, Cripps papers.

164 'National Council Report', p. 8.

165 Calculations based on a comparison of the figures given in Mellor and McCarthy to branch secretaries and Head Office members, 27 February 1937, Cripps papers.

166 See Pimlott, *Labour and the Left*, ch. 16.

167 *Daily Herald*, 26 April 1937.

168 Andrew Campbell, 'How to Oppose Transport House', *New Leader*, 16 April 1937.

169 Frederick Adams, 'A New Socialist Party?', *New Leader*, 23 October 1936. In early 1937 Pollitt had noted his impression that after the Labour party conference 'the ILP policy was: leave the Labour Party and set up a new revolutionary organisation. Also certain leading members of the Socialist League gave us the impression that they would not be opposed to creating a new party as a result of the amalgamation of the ILP, the Socialist League and the Communist Party': Report on the British Situation given by Pollitt to the Secretariat of the ECCI', 4 January 1937, 1995 microfilm reel, 495/18/1149.

170 Cripps to Campbell, 28 April 1937, copy in Cripps papers.

171 Groves, 'A Documentary History of the SL 1932–37, pp. 18–19, Groves papers, MSS.172/SL/1/15/3.; Groves, 'Socialist League', p. 14.

172 MIIc. CX/22542/v, 86a in SF.464/41, 4 May 1937, National Archives, KV2/668.

173 *New Leader*, 30 April 1937.

174 Brockway, 'The Spirit of May Day', ibid.

175 *New Leader*, 30 April 1937.

176 'Final Agenda', p. 24, in Socialist League, *Report of National Council and Final Agenda of the Annual Conference 1937* (1937).

177 *Daily Herald*, 17 May 1937.

178 Cripps, draft of speech for Socialist League annual conference, May 1937, Cripps papers. This seems to be an almost verbatim draft of Cripps's speech. Cripps later told the editor of the *News Chronicle* that: 'I took the precaution of making my speech entirely from written notes so that I might have a record of what I said': Cripps to Barry, 17 May 1937, copy in Cripps papers.

179 Cripps, draft of speech for Socialist League annual conference, May 1937.

180 Ibid.

181 Ibid.

182 Barker to Cripps, 22 April 1937, Cripps papers.

183 Cripps, 'New Masses' (unpublished article), 9 May 1937, Cripps papers.

184 Cripps, draft of speech for Socialist League annual conference, May 1937. Cripps had adumbrated many of his arguments in an unpublished article entitled 'New Masses', 9 May 1937, Cripps papers. See also Cripps to Ponsonby, 12 May 1937, Bodleian Library, Oxford, Ponsonby papers, Ms.Eng.hist.c.679, for Cripps's determination to 'go on fighting inside the party as long as ever I can'.

185 Socialist League, *Report of National Council and Final Agenda of the Annual Conference 1937*, pp. 25–6. See also *Daily Herald*, 15 May 1937.

186 Socialist League, *Report of National Council and Final Agenda of the Annual Conference 1937*, pp. 25–6. See also *Daily Herald*, 15 May 1937.

187 *Daily Herald*, 17 May 1937. Also quoted in Castle, *Fighting All the Way*, p. 86.

188 *News Chronicle*, 17 May 1937.

189 Socialist League Emergency National Council minutes, 16 May 1937, Groves papers, MSS/SL/1/4/4.

190 Mitchison and McCarthy to branch secretaries, 26 May 1937, Needham papers, K19.

Chapter 7

1 *Daily Herald*, 27 May 1937. The NEC statement can be found in the 'Report of the NEC, 1936–7', *LPACR*, 1937, p. 27.

2 *The Times*, 7 June 1937; *Tribune*, 11 June 1937.

3 Cripps to Elvin, 9 June 1937, copy in Cripps papers.

4 Elvin to Cripps, 7 June 1937; Elvin to Cripps, 11 June 1937, both Cripps papers.

5 National Unity Campaign Committee to all local unity committees, 5 June 1937, Cripps papers. This was signed by the former Socialist Leaguers Cripps, Mellor and Mitchison; by Brockway and Maxton for the ILP; and by Dutt, Gallacher and Pollitt for the CPGB. The contents of the letter are described in No. XL, with SHS U.F., 5 June 1937, National Archives, KV2/668. See also Central Committee CPGB statement, 7 June 1937, Cripps papers.

6 Cripps, 'Unity is Now the Issue: why the Socialist League came to its decision to dissolve', *Tribune*, 21 May 1937.
7 This was certainly how Brockway saw it: Brockway, *Inside the Left*, p. 269. Pimlott, *Labour and the Left*, p. 105, emphasises this explanation.
8 *Daily Herald*, 1 June 1937.
9 CPGB Secretariat to 'all party organisations', 5 June 1937, Dutt papers, LP/IND/DUTT/29/10.
10 Cripps to Elvin, 9 June 1937, copy in Cripps papers.
11 CPGB Secretariat to 'all party organisations', 5 June 1937, Dutt papers, LP/IND/DUTT/29/10.
12 Cripps to Elvin, 9 June 1937, copy in Cripps papers.
13 See, for instance, J. R. Campbell, 'Is the ILP for Winning the War or Aiding Franco', *Daily Worker*, 22 May 1937; and Pollitt's criticism of the ILP and the POUM at the CPGB annual congress: *Daily Worker*, 31 May 1937.
14 *New Leader*, 21 May 1937. See also Brockway, *Inside the Left*, p. 302.
15 McNair, 'Barcelona Diary', *New Leader*, 21 May 1937. See also 'An Open Letter to Palme Dutt from John McNair', *New Leader*, 4 June 1937, in which he asserted that the Communists were responsible for the disunity in Spain.
16 Brockway, 'Background to Barcelona', *New Leader*, 21 May 1937. He reiterated this argument on many occasions – see, for instance, editorial, *New Leader*, 2 July 1937. McNair gave the same interpretation of events when he spoke at the ILP summer school, arguing that the Soviet aim in Spain was simply the 'restoration of republican capitalist democracy': *New Leader*, 6 August 1937.
17 Brockway, 'The Test of Spain: the workers were on the wrong sides of the barricades', *New Leader*, 28 May 1937. McNair had informed Brockway about 'the ruthless suppression of POUM and its friends': Brockway, *Inside the Left*, p. 305.
18 Maxton to Strauss, 4 June 1937, copy in Cripps papers.
19 Aplin to members of the National Unity Campaign Committee, 24 May 1937, Dutt papers, CP/IND/DUTT/16/09; also in Cripps papers.
20 Rogers to Cripps, 8 June 1937, Cripps papers.
21 Barker to Cripps, 30 May 1937; Rogers to Cripps, 30 May 1937, both Cripps papers.
22 These concerns were expressed in CPGB Secretariat to 'all party organisations', 15 June 1937, Dutt papers, CP/IND/DUTT/29/10.
23 McCarthy to Middleton, 9 June 1937, LP/SL/35/58; 'A Call to the Socialist Left', June 1937, LP/SL/60i, both LPA, Socialist League file.
24 Editorial, *New Leader*, 11 June 1937.
25 *New Leader*, 18 June 1937.
26 *Daily Herald*, 7 June 1937; 'Cripps's speech at the Hull Rally for New Unity Campaign', *Tribune*, 11 June 1937. See also CC. Hull 99a in 460/Hull/1 vol. 2, 6 June 1937, National Archives, KV2/668.
27 'Unity Drive's New Phase', *Tribune*, 18 June 1937. See also 91a, OF.81/1, vol. 2, 12 June 1937, National Archives, KV2/668.
28 'Unity Drive's New Phase', *Tribune*, 18 June 1937.
29 C.C. Cardiff 178a in 460/Cardiff 3/1, vol. 4, 19 June 1937, National Archives, KV2/668.
30 'Labour Unity Campaign: those million new voters', *Tribune*, 9 July 1937. See also C.C.Newcastle 223a in 460/N'tle/1, vol. 4, 4 July 1937 National Archives, KV2/668.
31 'After Unity Sunday', *Tribune*, 23 July 1937.

32 *New Leader*, 25 June 1937.
33 Editorial, ibid., 2 July 1937.
34 Brockway made this point even before the committee had reported: 'A Socialist World Roundabout', *New Leader*, 9 April 1937. Martin took the same line: Critic, 'A London Diary', *New Statesman and Nation*, 22 May 1937.
35 Editorial, 'Spain and the USSR', *New Leader*, 2 July 1937.
36 Editorial, *New Leader*, 2 July 1937. The ILP Guild of Youth expressed its criticism of the Young Communist League for supporting Soviet action: Audrey Brockway, 'What is Unity', *New Leader*, 2 July 1937.
37 Brockway, 'Mass Arrests of Revolutionary Socialists by Spanish Government', *New Leader*, 2 July 1937.
38 Brockway, 'What I Saw in Spain', *New Leader*, 9 July 1937.
39 'What Brockway said about the International Brigade', *New Leader*, 23 July 1937.
40 Brockway, *Inside the Left*, p. 317.
41 *New Leader*, 23 July 1937.
42 Ibid., 30 July 1937.
43 Ibid., 13 August 1937.
44 Maxton, 'These are my Impressions', ibid., 3 September 1937. There was a personal element: he recorded that each day 'I was in Valencia the Communist party denounced me as a Trotskyist and a fascist.'
45 CPGB Politburo minutes, 6 August 1937.
46 Pollitt reported in CPGB Central Committee minutes, 6 August 1937. At another Central Committee meeting on 10 September Cornforth stressed the need to 'expose the rottenness of the policy of Brockway'.
47 For coverage of this incident see E. Hyams, *The New Statesman: The History of the First Fifty Years 1913–1963* (1963), pp. 198–9; and C. H. Rolph, *Kingsley: The Life, Letters and Diaries of Kingsley Martin* (1973), esp. p. 227.
48 Martin, *Editor*, pp. 211, 214–15.
49 Leventhal, *Last Dissenter*, pp. 254–5.
50 CPGB Central Committee minutes, 16 January 1937. See also 'Information on Trotskyism in Britain' by N. Raylock, 1937, CPA, 1995 microfilm reel 1, for Brailsford's support of the International Brigade in Spain.
51 Brockway, 'Background to Barcelona', *New Leader*, 21 May 1937.
52 Eric Blair (George Orwell) to Brailsford, 10 December 1937, LHASC, LPA, Brailsford papers, HND/3/4; Eric Blair to Brailsford, 18 December 1937, Brailsford papers, HND/3/5i–iii.
53 Brailsford, 'Russia's darkest hour', *Reynolds News*, 20 June 1937. See also Brailsford, 'The Russian Tragedy: I stand by my charges', *Reynolds News*, 27 June 1937, for condemnation of Stalin's rule as a 'bloody tyranny'.
54 Beatrice Webb diary, 25 July 1937, Passfield papers.
55 Brailsford to editor, *New Statesman and Nation*, 17 July 1937. This was in response to: Dutt to editor, *New Statesman and Nation*, 10 July 1937. For the on-going debate see Dutt to editor, *New Statesman and Nation*, 24 July 1937; and Brailsford to editor, *New Statesman and Nation*, 31 July 1937.
56 Mellor to Cripps, 24 July 1937, Cripps papers.
57 Entwhistle to Cripps (with attached statement), 23 August 1937, Cripps papers.
58 *The Times*, 8, 10, 23 July 1937.
59 Pollitt to Page Arnot, 27 Oct. 1937, CPA, transcriptions of microfilm, 495/14/243.

60 See Pimlott, *Labour and the Left*, pp. 128–9.
61 NEC minutes, 3 June 1937.
62 See Pimlott, *Labour and the Left*, pp. 130–1.
63 Greene to Cripps, 22 July 1937, Cripps papers.
64 Ibid.
65 Ibid., 30 July 1937.
66 Ibid., 30 September 1937.
67 Report of Constituency Parties meeting, 3, 5 October 1937, Cripps papers.
68 Laski, 'The Answer of the Ostrich: Labour Executive's Plan to Stem Drive for Unity', *Tribune*, 27 August 1937.
69 C.C. M'ter, 525a in 460/M'ter/1, vol. 12, 4 September 1937, National Archives, KV2/668.
70 *Daily Herald*, 7 September 1937; this meeting was also noted in 6 September 1937, National Archives, KV2/668.
71 Cripps to Middleton, 5 September 1937, copy in Cripps papers; Middleton to Cripps, 8 September 1937, Cripps papers.
72 For Cripps see Cripps to Middleton, 9 September 1937, copy in Cripps papers; for Laski see *Tribune*, 10 September 1937; for Strauss see Strauss to editor, *Tribune*, 17 September 1937, and Strauss to Cripps, n.d., Cripps papers; for Horrabin see Horrabin to editor, *Tribune*, 24 September 1937.
73 *LPACR*, 1937, pp. 156–8.
74 Ibid., pp. 158–9.
75 Ibid., pp. 160–1.
76 Ibid., pp. 161–4.
77 Cripps, 'Labour's Grave Step: Decision that Menaces Future Power of Workers', *Tribune*, 17 September 1937.
78 *LPACR*, 1937, p. 164.
79 *Tribune*, 8 October 1937.
80 The conference had agreed that in the future it would meet in May but that there would be insufficient time to organise a conference for May 1938.
81 *LPACR*, 1937, pp. 140–55. See also the discussion in Pimlott, *Labour and the Left*, pp. 134–7.
82 *LPACR*, 1937, p. 151.
83 *Labour Organiser*, October 1937, quoted in Pimlott, *Labour and the Left*, p. 226. See also *The Times*, 7 October 1937, for an analysis of the voting patterns at the Labour party conference.
84 Report of Constituency Parties meeting, 3, 5 October 1937, Cripps papers.
85 Cripps, 'A Chance to be Seized', *Tribune*, 22 October 1937.
86 Dalton, *Fateful Years*, p. 133.
87 *LPACR*, pp. 208–9. For others on the Labour left see, for instance, Laski, 'Labour and the Arms Vote: Why We Must Fight Government's War Preparations', *Tribune*, 30 July 1937; and *Tribune*, 22 October 1937.
88 Statement given in *Tribune*, 29 October 1937.
89 See, for instance, Cripps to Laski, 12 October 1937, copy in Cripps papers. Discussing the new NEC, Laski commented to Cripps that 'the sooner the big questions are raised the better': Laski to Cripps, 13 October 1937, Cripps papers. *Tribune*, 8 October 1937, comments on the 'compact representation of the Left' on the NEC. For subsequent attempts to exert this left-wing influence on the NEC, note Cripps's plans to raise the issue of Mellor's candidature at Stockport: Cripps to George [Dallas], 12 October 1937, copy in Cripps papers.
90 This donation is clear from Morrison to Cripps, 11 October 1937, Cripps

papers. Morrison had earlier encouraged Cripps to adopt a conciliatory position: Morrison to Cripps, 15 June 1937; Cripps to Morrison, 16 June 1937; Morrison to Cripps, 17 June 1937, all Cripps papers.

91   *Tribune*, 22 October 1937; ibid., 5 November 1937. The campaign was launched at the Manchester Free Trade Hall on 14 November 1937: ibid., 19 November 1937. Cripps spoke at a large meeting organised by the Labour Spain Campaign Committee at the Albert Hall on 19 December: Cripps, 'Our Spanish Colleagues', ibid., 23 December 1937, is a verbatim report of his speech criticising non-intervention. For further details of the involvement of Cripps and Wilkinson see Spain Campaign Committee minutes, 1, 4, 24 November 1937, all Cripps papers.

92   *Tribune*, 3 December 1937. See also Cripps, 'An Appeal to our Youth', ibid.

93   'Cripps's Speech at the Hull Rally for New Unity Campaign', *Tribune*, 11 June 1937.

94   *LPACR*, 1937, pp. 181–3, for Attlee's speech; pp. 185–6, for Morrison's remarks and the unanimous acceptance. *Labour's Immediate Programme* is reproduced in Appendix X, pp. 277–9.

95   Editorial, *New Leader*, 30 July 1937.

96   Brockway, 'How Unity', *New Leader*, 28 August 1937.

97   *New Leader*, 6 August 1937.

98   Maxton, 'Duty of Socialists', *New Leader*, 30 July 1937. Brockway later described the Labour party's direction in international policy as marking a 'complete betrayal': editorial, *New Leader*, 10 September 1937. For Stephen's criticism of support for rearmament see: Stephen, 'The War Danger', *New Leader*, 26 November 1937.

99   Brockway, 'Should We Make War on Germany?', *New Leader*, 24 September 1937.

100 *The Times*, 5 November 1937. See also editorial, 'The Communists and Unity', *New Leader*, 12 November 1937, for discussion of the breakdown of relations. For the CPGB perspective see CPGB Politburo minutes, 29 October 1937; and CPGB Central Committee minutes, 30 October 1937.

101 McGovern, 'Government Wants Amnesty for Anti-Fascist prisoners but Communists have Prevented it', *New Leader*, 10 December 1937.

102 McNair, 'They Called this Man a Fascist Spy', *New Leader*, 17 December 1937.

103 'What's Wrong with Russia?', *New Leader*, 17 December 1937.

104 Maxton, 'I Put it to Stalin', *New Leader*, 17 December 1937.

105 Brockway, 'Must We Pass through Dictatorship?', *New Leader*, 14 January 1938. Brockway reiterated the same point time and again. See, for instance, 'International Notes', *New Leader*, 18 March 1938, when he added that the 'question mark over Russia is whether the socialist economic basis beneath will succeed in expressing itself politically, or whether the bureaucracy will destroy the socialist basis first'.

106 *New Leader*, 4 March 1938.

107 Betts, 'Women in Russia No. 1', *Tribune*, 15 October 1937; Betts, 'Women in Russia No. 2', *Tribune*, 22 October 1937; Betts, 'Women in Russia No. 3', *Tribune*, 29 October 1937; Betts, 'Women in Russia, No 4', *Tribune*, 5 November 1937; Betts, 'Russia Goes Gay with Sport, Play and Dancing', *Tribune*, 19 November 1937.

108 Betts, 'Women in Russia', *Tribune*, 26 November 1937.

109 Editorial, *Tribune*, 12 November 1937.

110 S. Webb and B. Webb, *Soviet Communism: a new civilisation?* (1935), 2 vols; S. Webb and B. Webb, *Soviet Communism: a new civilisation* (1937), 2 vols.

111 Editorial, *Tribune*, 12 November 1937.

112 *Tribune*, 12 November 1937.

113 'Notes on the News', ibid., 17 December 1937.

114 'We Ask Stalin', *Tribune*, 23 December 1937.

115 For examples of the Labour left's public statements on Spain see Laski, 'Spain, Mr Eden and Labour', *Tribune*, 29 October 1937; 'Sir Stafford Cripps indicts Cabinet's Peace Proposal', *Tribune*, 12 November 1937.

116 *Tribune*, 25 February 1938.

117 For instances of co-operation see CPGB Politburo minutes, 14–15 October 1937; Pollitt to Cripps, 28 January 1938, Cripps papers; Cripps to Pollitt, 31 January 1938, copy in Cripps papers; Pollitt to Cripps, 16 February 1938, Cripps papers; Cripps to Pollitt, 18 February 1938, copy in Cripps papers.

118 'People and Politics: in which Harold Laski gives his own personal views on topics of the week', *Daily Herald*, 24 January 1938.

119 *Political Quarterly*, January–March 1938, quoted in M. Newman, *Harold Laski: a political biography* (1993), p. 194.

120 Kramnick and Sheerman, *Laski*, ch. 15, provides useful background on Laski's activities in the late 1930s but does not specifically consider his views of the purges.

121 See, for instance, editorial, 'Changes in Russia', *New Leader*, 28 January 1938, which commented that 'until the last few weeks he [Laski] has appeared to countenance all that has happened in Soviet Russia'.

122 'Harold Laski Writes an Open Letter to Youth', *Tribune*, 7 January 1938.

123 CPGB Central Committee minutes, 30 October 1937.

124 Pollitt to Page Arnot, 27 October 1937, CPA, transcriptions of microfilm, 495/14/243.

125 For instance, Brockway's editorial spoke frankly of 'the distrust into which the Stalin bureaucracy has fallen': *New Leader*, 4 March 1938.

126 'Stalin – Stop! A Powerful Appeal to Moscow from the ILP MPs', *New Leader*, 11 March 1938.

127 Brockway, 'International Notes', *New Leader*, 18 March 1938, which states that 'my general conclusion is that there were undoubtedly "oppositions" which contrived in secret against the Stalin bureaucracy, but that the charges of acting as agents of Britain, Germany, Japan and other powers were not proved'.

128 'Conference Supplement', *New Leader*, 22 April 1938. See also Brockway, 'Issues at the ILP Conference', *New Leader*, 15 April 1938, for a clear indication of the more critical attitude towards the Soviet Union.

129 'Fact or Frame up? Afterthoughts on events before Soviet Trials by a Special Correspondent', *Tribune*, 11 March 1938.

130 Indeed, Martin explicitly stated that there was 'nothing fresh to be said about the Soviet trials': Critic, 'A London Diary', *New Statesman and Nation*, 5 March 1938.

131 Ibid., 26 March 1938. See also ibid., 5 March 1938; 'Comments', *New Statesman and Nation*, 12 March 1938; and Critic, 'A London Diary', *New Statesman and Nation,* 4 June 1938.

132 Brailsford, 'Russia's New Purge: are all these men guilty?', *Reynolds News*, 6 March 1938; Brailsford, 'Tyranny over Russia', *Reynolds News*, 13 March 1938.

133 R. Pearce, *Patrick Gordon Walker: political diaries 1932–71* (1991), p. 75.

134 Laski, 'Whither Liberty?', *Tribune*, 11 March 1938.

135 Ibid., 18 March 1938. Laski was also highly critical of the Nazi attacks on the Jews, and later wrote that in contrast 'one of the most remarkable experiences

of the Soviet Union is the proof it has accumulated that the growth of socialism reduces racial antagonism to infinitesimal proportions': Laski, '5m people face living death', *Tribune*, 15 July 1938.

136 Editorial, *Daily Herald*, 14 March 1938.

137 Dalton to Martin, 26 July 1937, Martin papers 11/4; copy in Dalton papers, 5/2/33.

Chapter 8

1 Editorial, *New Leader*, 10 September 1937.

2 Brockway, 'Should We Make War on Germany?', *New Leader*, 24 September 1937. Brockway similarly argued that the 'fact that Britain possesses one-third of the world is as much a menace to peace as the fact that Germany wants to possess a little more of the world': editorial, *New Leader*, 5 November 1937.

3 *Tribune*, 11 February 1938.

4 For the Labour left see: 'Sir Stafford Cripps indicts Cabinet's Peace Proposal', ibid., 12 November 1937, which argued that Chamberlain saw Hitler as 'a pillar of defence against Bolshevism'; and editorial, *Tribune*, 18 February 1938, which stated that were 'the Soviet Union to be conquered by its capitalist and fascist enemies, victory [for socialism] would be buried for generations to come'. For the ILP see Brockway, 'Fight Fascism and War', *New Leader*, 26 November 1937; and editorial, *New Leader*, 3 December 1937.

5 Laski, '1937–1914', *Tribune*, 19 November 1937.

6 *New Leader*, 28 January 1938. See also editorial, ibid., 21 January 1938; *New Leader*, 4 February 1938; and *New Leader*, 18 February 1938. Brockway recalled these events in his autobiography: Brockway, *Inside the Left*, pp. 328–9.

7 *Tribune*, 21 January 1938; 'Notes on the News', ibid., 28 January 1938; *Tribune*, 4 February 1938.

8 'Notes on the News', *Tribune*, 21 January 1938.

9 McNair, 'Workers of the World Unite', *New Leader*, 25 February 1938.

10 *New Leader*, 18 February 1938.

11 The particular issue at stake was Chamberlain's willingness to conciliate Italy, but it also involved a clash of personalities and rival jurisdictions.

12 Brockway, 'Eden, Chamberlain and the Workers', *New Leader*, 25 February 1938.

13 Other interpretations of the Labour left's action are, of course, possible. The central argument of Blaazer, *Popular Front*, is that the Labour left's support of the popular front was consistent with its membership of a 'progressive tradition'.

14 Cripps, editorial, 'Now is our Time', *Tribune*, 25 February 1938.

15 Cripps, editorial, *Tribune*, 18 March 1938. Meanwhile, *Tribune* was still thinking in terms of an alternative Labour government which it argued would 'resist by all means, in concert with its allies, such action as the seizure of Austria by the German Nazis': *Tribune*, 25 February 1938.

16 Cripps to Levens, 23 March 1938, copy in Cripps papers.

17 Cripps to Bennett, 23 March 1938, copy in Cripps papers.

18 'Spain Fights On', *Tribune*, 1 April 1938.

19 Cripps, 'Peace Fronts', *Tribune*, 14 April 1938.

20 *Tribune*, 8 April 1938; Cripps, 'Peace Fronts', ibid., 14 April 1938.

21 'Labour and the Peace Front', *Tribune*, 22 April 1938; Cripps to Bennett, 23 March 1938, copy in Cripps papers.

22 Cripps, 'Peace Fronts', *Tribune*, 14 April 1938.

23 Cripps, 'At Queen's Hall', *Tribune*, 29 April 1938.
24 Cripps to John Gollan, 15 March 1938, copy in Cripps papers.
25 Martin to Cripps, 18 March 1938, Cripps papers.
26 Laski, 'Whither Liberty?, *Tribune*, 18 February 1938.
27 Pollitt reported in CPGB Central Committee minutes, 6 August 1937.
28 Cole, *People's Front*, p. 14.
29 Ibid., pp. 15, 130, 135–7, quotation at p. 15.
30 Ibid., pp. 172–3.
31 Ibid., p. 5. He also sent Cripps a copy: Cole to Cripps, 2 July 1937, Cripps papers.
32 Cole, *People's Front*, p. 342.
33 Ibid., p. 20.
34 For the receipt of this see Middleton to Cripps, 29 April 1938, Cripps papers.
35 'The International Situation', 5 May 1938, Cripps papers. See also R. Eatwell, 'The Labour Party and the Popular Front Movement in Great Britain in the 1930s', (University of Oxford D.Phil, 1975).
36 Despite the Labour left's concern for Spain, few of its members went as far as Brailsford in suggesting that the Labour party should 'defiantly procure arms of one sort or another and export them' to Spain: Brailsford to Cripps, 17 May 1938, Cripps papers; Cripps to Brailsford, 30 May 1938, copy in Cripps papers. For the genesis of this idea see Brailsford to Cripps, 11 April 1938, Cripps papers.
37 See, for instance, 'Labour and the Peace Front', *Tribune*, 22 April 1938.
38 Trevelyan to Cripps, 26 March 1938, Cripps papers.
39 Trevelyan to Pritt, 26 March 1938, copy in Cripps papers.
40 Cripps to Trevelyan, 28 March 1938, copy in Cripps papers.
41 Labour Party, *Labour and the Popular Front* (1938), esp. pp. 4–6. In ways that demonstrate the continuous reshaping of the Left, Cripps's proposal did gain the public support of L. A. Fenn who had resigned from the Socialist League in October 1936 because of his support for the popular front: L. A. Fenn to editor, *Tribune*, 6 May 1938.
42 Cripps to Miss Forsyth, 16 May 1938, copy in Cripps papers.
43 Cripps, 'At Queen's Hall', *Tribune*, 29 April 1938; 'Spain fights on', *Tribune*, 1 April 1938.
44 'Labour and Arms', *Tribune*, 20 May 1938. During the summer there were further calls for a special conference: Cripps, 'Labour's Choice: Why I Support Call for a Special Conference of Action', *Tribune*, 22 July 1938; Laski, 'Critical Months Ahead for Labour', *Tribune*, 29 July 1938; Laski, 'Why not a Special Conference', *Tribune*, 5 August 1938.
45 Brailsford and J. Pole to editor, *Tribune*, 27 May 1938; Brailsford and J. Pole to editor, *Tribune*, 8 July 1938.
46 Cole, *People's Front*, pp. 336–7.
47 Cole, 'Dilution? British Labour must not be fooled a second time', *Tribune*, 1 April 1938.
48 Brailsford to Cripps, 11 April 1938, Cripps papers.
49 'Labour and Arms', *Tribune*, 20 May 1938, emphasis added.
50 Mellor, 'Spain 1936–1938', *Tribune*, 15 July 1938. This article repeated – almost word for word but under Mellor's own name – the points made in 'Labour and Arms', *Tribune*, 20 May 1938.
51 Mike [Foot] to Cripps, n.d. but July 1938, Cripps papers.
52 Barbara Castle later wrote that she and Mellor were 'never enthusiastic about

the popular front': Castle, *Fighting All the Way*, p. 87. Mellor's views had not changed since the previous summer when he had reviewed Cole's *The People's Front*: *Tribune*, 27 August 1937.

53   Strauss, unpublished autobiography, p. 68, Strauss papers.

54   'Heads of Arrangements between the Left Book Club and The Tribune', 24 July 1938, Cripps papers.

55   Mike [Foot] to Cripps, n.d. but July 1938, Cripps papers.

56   Strauss, unpublished autobiography, p. 68, Strauss papers.

57   Mike [Foot] to Cripps, n.d. but July 1938, Cripps papers.

58   Addendum, ibid. See Cripps's reply: Cripps to Foot, 25 July 1938, quoted in Jones, Foot, pp. 62–3. See also Clarke, *Cripps Version*, p. 75.

59   Strauss, unpublished autobiography, p. 68, Strauss papers.

60   'Left Book Club and Tribune: a statement', *Tribune*, 16 September 1938. This was a week earlier than originally planned: 'Heads of Arrangements between the Left Book Club and The Tribune', 24 July 1938, Cripps papers.

61   Brockway, 'Sack the Lot', *New Leader*, 4 March 1938; Brockway, 'How to Stop War', *New Leader*, 11 March 1938.

62   *New Leader*, 18 March 1938.

63   Brockway, 'International Notes', *New Leader*, 18 March 1938. Indeed, it was in the context of preventing Germany and Italy from helping Franco that Brockway advocated refusing to make, handle or transport their supplies: Brockway, 'A Programme of Action Against Fascism and War', *New Leader*, 25 March 1938; Brockway, 'Two Things To Do', *New Leader*, 1 April 1938; editorial, *New Leader*, 8 April 1938.

64   *New Leader*, 22 April 1938.

65   Conference Supplement, ibid.

66   Brockway, 'Sack the Lot', *New Leader*, 4 March 1938; *New Leader*, 25 March 1938 respectively.

67   Conference Supplement, *New Leader*, 22 April 1938.

68   Editorial, *New Leader*, 6 May 1938.

69   'Peace Alliance Supplement', *New Leader*, 13 May 1938.

70   Editorial, *New Leader*, 3 June 1938.

71   The *New Leader* for 1938 and 1939 contains many articles on the theme, indicating a much greater level of interest than earlier in the decade.

72   Editorial, *New Leader*, 20 May 1938.

73   *New Leader*, 13 May 1938; ibid., 27 May 1938.

74   McNair, 'Anti-fascist Prisoners', *New Leader*, 3 June 1938.

75   Editorial, *New Leader*, 22 July 1938.

76   Ibid.

77   'Save Spanish Working-class Revolutionaries: an appeal from the ILP to other sections of the working class' signed by Maxton, Brockway and McNair, *New Leader*, 29 July 1938.

78   McNair, 'POUM Trial: the whole story', *New Leader*, 11 November 1938; *New Leader*, 4 November 1938.

79   *New Leader*, 12 August 1938.

80   Brockway, *Inside the Left*, p. 274.

81   Brockway, 'Issues at the ILP Conference', *New Leader*, 8 April 1938.

82   Conference Supplement, *New Leader*, 22 April 1938.

83   Editorial, *New Leader*, 1 April 1938.

84   Conference Supplement, *New Leader*, 22 April 1938.

85   Editorial, *New Leader*, 20 May 1938.

86 *New Leader*, 17 June 1938.
87 'Notes on interview between representatives of the Labour party and representatives of the ILP held on 14 June 1938', LHASC, LPA, J. S. Middleton papers, JSM/ILP/31.
88 Editorial, *New Leader*, 15 July 1938. Brockway reiterated his view that the 'guiding principle . . . must be the need for contact with the mass movement and at the same time the need for freedom to maintain the revolutionary socialist policy of the party'.
89 Printed in editorial, *New Leader*, 29 July 1938.
90 *New Leader*, 5 August 1938. See also ILP NAC minutes, 29 July 1938.
91 This is very clear in Cripps to Colonel Jarrett-Kerr, 12 October 1938, copy in Cripps papers.
92 L. G. Shaw, *The British Political Elite and the Soviet Union 1937–39* (2003), ch. 4, esp. pp. 76–7, 80–1, reveals the extent to which Dalton, Attlee, and other Labour figures publicly endorsed the Soviet Union as a prospective strategic ally after April 1938.
93 Laski, 'Why not a Special Conference', *Tribune*, 5 August 1938.
94 Strachey, 'What Must Socialists Do if War Comes?', *Tribune*, 16 September 1938, in which he wrote: 'I am convinced that the victory of the USSR, fighting in a war in alliance with the Western democracies, against a fascist coalition would be of paramount importance.'
95 *New Statesman and Nation*, 27 August 1938.
96 Strauss, unpublished autobiography, p. 68, Strauss papers.
97 'Chamberlain has Sold You', *Tribune*, 23 September 1938.
98 'Britain's Freedom is now at Stake', *Tribune*, 30 September 1938.
99 Strachey, 'Advice to a Future Socialist', *Tribune*, 30 September 1938.
100 'Victor Gollancz says In Peace or War this is the Policy of the Club', *Tribune*, 30 September 1938. For Labour left support of such a stance see Cripps, 'Premier is Gambling with our Lives', *Tribune*, 7 October 1938; Bevan, 'Call a Labour Party Conference at Once', *Tribune*, 7 October 1938; and Strauss, 'A Positive Policy for Labour', *Tribune*, 14 October 1938.
101 Martin expressed his views in a letter to the *News Chronicle*: Martin, *Editor*, p. 256. He later admitted that 'in my excoriating analysis of Chamberlain's behaviour, I had really been attacking myself': Martin, *Editor*, p. 256.
102 Jamaica diary, 28 September 1938, Cripps papers.
103 Clarke, *Cripps Version*, pp. 76–8. See also C. Cooke, *The Life of Richard Stafford Cripps* (1957), p. 225.
104 Jamaica diary, 28 September 1938, Cripps papers.
105 Ibid., 30 September 1938.
106 Dalton diary, 6 October 1938, quoted in Dalton, *Fateful Years*, pp. 200–1. For valuable accounts of these events see Pimlott, *Labour and the Left*, p. 166; Clarke, *Cripps Version*, p. 78.
107 Cripps, 'Premier is Gambling with our Lives', *Tribune*, 7 October 1938.
108 Pimlott, *Labour and the Left*, p. 166.
109 For Oxford see: *Tribune*, 21 October 1938; and A. D. Lindsay, 'This Defeat Teaches Us How to Win', *Tribune*, 4 November 1938. For Bridgwater see *Tribune*, 11 November 1938; and 'Victor Gollancz shows the vital importance of the Bridgwater result, describes the work being done by the LBC', LBC Section, *Tribune*, 25 November 1938. Cripps was prevented by other commitments from campaigning on behalf of Bartlett: Cripps to Vernon Bartlett, November 1938, copy in Cripps papers.

110 Cripps, 'Who Wants War', *Tribune*, 25 November 1938. This conviction about the use of force was matched by a growing awareness of the nature of the internal Nazi regime. As news of Kristallnacht emerged, Cripps wrote of the 'government-organised pogrom of the Jews' which was 'so typical of a sadistic outlook': Cripps, 'German Pogroms are Part of World-wide Terror', *Tribune*, 18 November 1938.

111 Cripps, 'Who Wants War', *Tribune*, 25 November 1938.

112 Dodds to Cripps, 7 November 1938; Cripps papers; Cripps to Dodds, 10 November 1938, copy in Cripps papers.

113 Editorial, *New Leader*, 12 August 1938. The International Bureau had issued a statement on 4 August embracing this position: *New Leader*, 5 August 1938.

114 'Stop War', *New Leader*, 2 September 1938. Editorial, *New Leader*, 9 September 1938 made the same points, criticising the lack of democracy in the British Empire.

115 Ibid., 16 September 1938.

116 See, for instance, ibid., 23 September 1938.

117 Ibid., 23 September 1938.

118 Ibid., 30 September 1938.

119 Ibid.

120 Ibid., 23 September 1938.

121 Ibid., 30 September 1938.

122 Ibid., 7 October 1938.

123 Brockway, *Inside the Left*, p. 332.

124 Ibid.

125 See Brown, *Maxton*, p. 285.

126 Maxton's speech is repeated in McNair, *Maxton*, pp. 273–6.

127 Brockway, *Inside the Left*, p. 332.

128 Ibid, p. 333; McNair, *Maxton*, p. 277; *New Leader*, 14 October 1938.

129 *New Leader*, 14 October 1938. See also the account in Brockway, *Inside the Left*, p. 335, which is repeated, like many other passages, almost word for word in McNair, *Maxton*, p. 277. Brown, *Maxton*, pp. 292–5, also discusses these events.

130 Editorial, *New Leader*, 14 October 1938.

131 Ibid., 30 December 1938. The lecture was reproduced as a pamphlet *Pacifism and the Left Wing* (1938).

132 *New Leader*, 23 September 1938. See also 'Capitalist Peace Means War Unless . . . ', ibid., 7 October 1938; editorial, *New Leader*, 14 October 1938.

133 'Bartlett as a War Patriot', *New Leader*, 16 December 1938.

134 *New Leader*, 21 October 1938.

135 'National Register is a Step to Fascism', ibid., 2 December 1938.

136 *New Leader*, 4 November 1938. This was attended by Brockway, McNair and Tom Reed, the NAC representative for the Midlands.

137 Ibid., 10 February 1939.

138 Ibid., 24 February 1939.

139 Ibid., 10 March 1939. See also Brown, *Maxton*, p. 296.

140 *New Leader*, 31 March 1939.

141 Ibid., 14 April 1939.

142 Ibid. 13 January 1939.

143 Ibid., 14 April 1939.

144 Ibid.

145 Ibid.

146 Brockway, *Inside the Left*, p. 333.

147 Ibid., p. 334.
148 *New Leader*, 14 April 1939.
149 Ibid.
150 Quoted in Brockway, *Inside the Left*, p. 334.
151 For the outlines of this whole episode see Pimlott, *Labour and the Left*, ch. 18; and Clarke, *Cripps Version*, pp. 80–3.
152 Cripps Memorandum, 9 January 1939, Cripps papers.
153 Cripps, 'Make Labour Strong', *Tribune*, 2 December 1938.
154 Cripps to Shepherd, 25 November 1938. Shepherd argued that he should not have given such advice to the constituency: Shepherd to Cripps, 19 December 1938. For the drawn-out dispute see: Cripps to Shepherd, 21 December 1938; Shepherd to Cripps, 23 December 1938; Cripps to Shepherd, 30 December 1938; Shepherd to Cripps, 10 January 1939; Cripps to Shepherd, 11 January 1939; Shepherd to Cripps, 13 January 1939, copies and originals in Cripps papers.
155 Naomi Mitchison to Cripps, 8th [n.d. but December 1938], quotation from enclosed letter: Mitchison to Bella, n.d., Cripps papers.
156 Rogers to Cripps, 19 November 1938, Cripps papers.
157 Cripps, 'What's Mr Churchill After? Who Will Lead Youth?', *Tribune*, 6 January 1939; Bevan, 'Our Reply to Anderson', *Tribune*, 9 December 1938, which argued strongly against incorporating 'the machinery of the Labour movement into the recruiting mechanism of the state'.
158 Cripps, 'What's Mr Churchill After? Who Will Lead Youth?', *Tribune*, 6 January 1939.
159 Cripps Memorandum, 9 January 1939, Cripps papers, which asserted that the basis of co-operation 'must be wide enough to contribute effective increase in opposition power but not so wide as to bring in elements so discordant that combined working with them is impossible'. Crucially it made clear that a 'minimal progressive programme' would involve the removal of the means test, the improvement of education and the national control of transport and the Bank of England.
160 Cripps to Middleton, 9 January 1939, copy in Cripps papers. From local experience Rogers had envisaged a Labour alliance just with Liberals and Communists: Rogers to Cripps, 19 November 1938, Cripps papers.
161 Cripps Memorandum, 9 January 1939, Cripps papers.
162 NEC minutes, 13 January 1939.
163 'Notes taken by RSC on the discussion on his memorandum on the Popular Front by the NEC', January 1939, Cripps papers.
164 Cripps to Middleton, 9 January 1939, copy in Cripps papers.
165 Cripps to comrade, January 1939, Cripps papers.
166 P. Strauss, *Cripps – Rebel and Advocate* (1943), p. 113, quoted in Pimlott, *Labour and the Left*, p. 172.
167 Cripps to Middleton, 15 January 1939, copy in Cripps papers.
168 Cripps to Director General of the BBC, 14 January 1939, copy in Cripps papers.
169 Middleton to Cripps, 16 January 1939, Cripps papers; Cripps to Middleton, 17 January 1939, copy in Cripps papers.
170 Dalton, *Fateful Years*, p. 213; Pimlott, *Labour and the Left*, p. 173.
171 NEC minutes, 18 January 1939; Middleton to Cripps, 19 January 1939, Cripps papers.
172 'Statement on the Memorandum issued by Sir Stafford Cripps and on his

attitude to the party during recent years', NEC minutes, 24 January 1939; Organisation Sub-committee minutes, 18 January 1939, Cripps papers.

173 NEC minutes, 25 January 1939.

174 Shepherd to Cripps, 26 January 1939, Cripps papers.

175 Cripps to Middleton, 28 January 1939, copy in Cripps papers.

176 'The Petition', Cripps papers.

177 Cripps, 'Plan for the Monster Petition Campaign', n.d. but January 1939, Cripps papers. The support of the *Manchester Guardian*, *News Chronicle* and *Reynolds News* was subsequently confirmed: Cripps, 'Unity Marches On', *Tribune*, 3 February 1939.

178 'The Speech delivered by Sir Stafford Cripps MP when launching "The Petition" at Newcastle on Feb 5th 1939', Cripps papers.

179 Naomi Mitchison to Cripps, 18th [n.d. but January 1939], Cripps papers; G. D. H. Cole to Cripps, 29 January 1939, Cripps papers.

180 Trevelyan to Cripps, 27 January 1939, Cripps papers.

181 Trevelyan to Cripps, 2 March 1939, Cripps papers.

182 Rogers to Cripps, 26 January 1939, Cripps papers. Rogers told Cripps that he was 'wholeheartedly' behind him 'in view of the very serious national and international situation'. The previous evening the Bristol East General Council had passed a resolution expressing its 'profound dissatisfaction with the treatment meted out to Sir Stafford Cripps'.

183 Wilfred Roberts to Cripps, 18 January 1939; Acland to Cripps, 24 January 1939, both Cripps papers.

184 Wilfred Roberts to Cripps, 18 January 1939, Cripps papers.

185 Gollancz, 'They Met in Unity – for Spain', LBC section, *Tribune*, 3 February 1939. Other speakers included Vernon Bartlett, Ted Willis and the Communist Isobel Brown.

186 'Notes on Policy Conference No. 11', 26 January [1939], Trinity College, Cambridge, Layton papers. The participants included L. J. Cadbury, Walter Layton, Gerald Barry, R. J. Cruikshank, Vernon Bartlett and A. J. Cummings. See also 'Notes on Policy Conference No. 13', n.d., Layton papers.

187 Cripps to Acland, 26 January 1939; Cripps to Roberts, 19 January 1939, copies of both in Cripps papers.

188 G. D. H. Cole to Cripps, 29 January 1939, Cripps papers.

189 Cripps, 'Plan for the Monster Petition Campaign', n.d. but January 1939, Cripps papers. See also Cripps, 'On with the Struggle', *Tribune*, 27 January 1939.

190 Cripps to Ian McColl, 15 March 1939, copy in Cripps papers.

191 Keynes to Cripps, 9 February 1939, Cripps papers; Cripps to Keynes, 10 February 1939, copy in Cripps papers.

192 See Violet Bonham Carter to Cripps, 27 February [1939], Cripps papers, where she states that after a speech in Trafalgar Square she had collected 3,000 signatures.

193 Cripps, 'Plan for Plenty', *Tribune*, 3 March 1939.

194 Cripps to Middleton, 14 February 1939; Middleton to Cripps, 17 February 1939; Cripps to Middleton, 17 February 1939, copies and originals in Cripps papers.

195 Middleton to Cripps, 2 February 1939; Cripps to Middleton, 23 February 1939; Middleton to Cripps, 24 February 1939, copies and originals in Cripps papers.

196 Shepherd to colleague, 1 March 1939, Cripps papers.

197 G. D. H. Cole to Cripps, 29 January 1939, Cripps papers.
198 Foot, *Bevan i*, p. 288; Pimlott, *Labour and the Left*, p. 175.
199 Bevan, 'They've had it', *Tribune*, 10 February 1939.
200 Pritt, *From Right to Left*, p. 103.
201 Strauss, *Advocate and Rebel*, p. 116, cited in Pimlott, *Labour and Left*, p. 175.
202 NEC minutes, 22 February 1939.
203 Cripps to Laski, 14 March 1939, copy in Cripps papers.
204 'Notes on Policy Conference No. 12', n.d., Layton papers. See also 'Notes on Policy Conference No. 11', 26 January [1939]; and 'Notes on Policy Conference No. 13', n.d., which states that 'Cripps had so much rank and file support that Labour headquarters was rattled in spite of its bold front', both Layton papers.
205 Pimlott, *Labour and the Left*, p. 177.
206 'The Labour party and the "Popular Front" Campaign: Declaration by the National Executive Committee', March 1939, Cripps papers.
207 Tawney to Cripps, 14 March 1939, Cripps papers.
208 Pimlott, *Labour and the Left*, pp. 177–8.
209 Trevelyan to Cripps, 14 March 1939, Cripps papers.
210 NEC minutes, 22 March 1939. The figures were 134 and 134.
211 Pimlott, *Labour and the Left*, p. 178.
212 Strauss and Bevan, 'We Challenge Expulsion', *Tribune*, 6 April 1939.
213 The first public sign of a change of stance came in Chamberlain's speech to the Birmingham Conservative Association on 17 March 1939.
214 Cripps to Middleton, 21 March 1939 (wrongly dated 1937), copy in Cripps papers.
215 Middleton to Cripps, 23 March 1939, Cripps papers.
216 Pimlott, *Labour and the Left*, p. 179.
217 Hill to Rees, 'Monday', c. mid April 1939, copy in Cripps papers.
218 Gwendoline Hill (candidate Bristol West) and Lyall Wilkes (candidate Newcastle Central) to 'fellow candidate', 29 March 1939, enclosing 'Labour candidates' to NEC [Middleton], 4 April 1939, Cripps papers.
219 'Your World in Brief', *Tribune*, 14 April 1939. See also ibid., 31 March 1939; and H. J. Hartshorn, 'Peace is Yours – if you'll take it', *Tribune*, 31 March 1939, which also claimed that an alliance with the Soviet Union would make 'a large part of our colossal rearmament unnecessary'.
220 Cripps, 'Dismiss Chamberlain', *Tribune*, 5 May 1939.
221 Meanwhile Cripps appealed directly to the Petition Committees to mobilise opposition to conscription: Cripps to Petition Campaign Committees, 28 April 1939, Cripps papers.
222 Foot, *Bevan i*, p. 295.
223 Cripps to Laski, 14 March 1939, copy in Cripps papers. For Brailsford's reaction see Leventhal, *Last Dissenter*, p. 266.
224 Pimlott, *Labour and the Left*, p. 179.
225 'Statement for submission to the Conference of the Petition Committees', n. d. but May 1939, Cripps papers.
226 G. H. Oliver (chair of Organisation Sub-committee) to Cripps, 27 April 1939; Cripps to G. H. Oliver, 28 April 1939; R. J. Windle (Secretary of the Standing Orders Committee) to Cripps, n.d. but May 1939, copies and originals in Cripps papers. In the final issue of *Tribune* before the conference, Bevan asserted their 'right to press it [the popular front] upon the party', stressing that they did 'not . . . seek to form the Popular Front' but rather wanted 'the Labour party to lead it': Bevan, 'An Open Letter to Conference Delegates', *Tribune*, 26 May 1939.

227 *LPACR*, 1939, p. 220.
228 1,227,000 to 1,083,000.
229 He dryly asserted 'the right of any member of the party to communicate in any way that he or she wishes and at any time that he or she considers necessary any suggestion or argument in favour of changing the policy or tactics of the party': *LPACR*, 1939, pp. 226–29, at p. 227.
230 Ibid., pp. 229–232, at p. 232.
231 It received only 248,000 votes.
232 Cripps, Strauss, Bevan, Young, Robert Bruce to Middleton, 30 May 1939, copy in Cripps papers.
233 Middleton to Cripps, 1 June 1939, Cripps papers.
234 Brailsford to Cripps, 1 June 1939, Cripps papers.
235 Cripps to Brailsford, 5 June 1939, copy in Cripps papers.
236 Cripps to Laski, 5 June 1939, copy in Cripps papers.
237 Cripps, 'Why We Want to Get Back', *Tribune*, 9 June 1939. Pollitt also urged this course on Cripps who he had already decided on his strategy: Pollitt to Cripps, 9 June 1939, Cripps papers; Cripps to Pollitt, 9 June 1939, copy in Cripps papers.
238 'Chairman's Address, delivered by Sir Stafford Cripps, to the conference of Delegates from Petition Committees held at the Alliance Hall, London on Sunday 11 June 1939', Cripps papers.
239 'Resolution Passed by the Conference of Petition Committees held in London on Sunday June 11 1939', Cripps papers.
240 Laski to Cripps, 27 June 1939, Cripps papers.
241 Ibid.
242 Middleton to Cripps, 29 June 1939, Cripps papers.
243 Bob [R. J. Watson] to Cripps, 8 June 1939, Cripps papers.
244 Statement for submission to the Conference of the Petition Committees', n. d. but May 1939, Cripps papers.
245 Statement on 'The Tribune' for Left News, Cripps papers.
246 Gollancz to Cripps, 25 July 1939, Cripps papers.
247 Statement on 'The Tribune' for Left News, Cripps papers.
248 Indeed, the *Tribune* Board wanted Gollancz to remain a member: Gollancz to Cripps, 25 July 1939. See also Gollancz to Cripps, 5 July 1939; and Cripps to Gollancz, 7 July 1939, originals and copies in Cripps papers.
249 He was not re-admitted to the party until the closing stages of the Second World War. Bevan, on the other hand, was allowed to re-join in November 1939.
250 Churchill to Cripps, 8 July 1939, Cripps papers.
251 Baldwin to Cripps, 1 June 1939, Cripps papers.
252 News and Comments of the Week', *Tribune*, 2 June 1939; ibid., 9 June 1939; Cripps, 'Our Fuehrer', *Tribune*, 30 June 1939; Strauss, 'Beware of Halifax', *Tribune*, 7 July 1939; Cripps, 'The Way to a New Britain', *Tribune*, 28 July 1939.
253 For earlier examples of this trend see: Cripps, 'Our Safety Depends on Alliance with Russia', *Tribune*, 12 May 1939.
254 *New Leader*, 20 January 1939.
255 McNair, 'Spanish Tragedy', ibid., 10 March 1939. See also McNair, 'The Workers of Catalonia Unity Need Our Aid', *New Leader*, 10 February 1939; and 'Direct Action Alone Can Save Spain!', *New Leader*, 24 February 1939.
256 Brockway, 'How to Stop Hitler Without War', *New Leader*, 24 March 1939.

257 *New Leader*, 7 April 1939.
258 Ibid., 14 April 1939.
259 Brockway, 'ILP Call to World Workers', ibid., 31 March 1939.
260 *New Leader*, 14 April 1939.
261 Indeed, the *New Leader* had recently described how it saw the events surrounding the POUM trial as 'the rallying centre for anti-Stalinism': *New Leader*, 13 January 1939.
262 *New Leader*, 5 May 1939.
263 Ibid., 12 May 1939.
264 Ibid., 4 November 1938.
265 Ibid., 2 December 1938. Importantly, it did add that each party should 'maintain its own policy on other issues where agreement has not been reached'.
266 See ibid., 2 September 1938, for affirmation of this policy.
267 For an analysis of ILP rank and file debate in *Controversy* see Cohen thesis, pp. 258–9.
268 *New Leader*, 10 February 1939.
269 Ibid., 14 April 1939.
270 C. A. Smith, 'Our Task Now', ibid., 14 April 1939.
271 Brockway, 'The ILP Conference', *New Leader*, 7 April 1939. The ILP had earlier argued that the Cripps's expulsion showed that there was 'not room within the wide scope of the Labour party to advocate views contrary to those of the Executive, a dangerous precedent has been established which will be fatal to the democratic vitality of the Labour party': 'Cripps: Good and Bad', *New Leader*, 3 February 1939. See also Brockway, 'Where is Stafford Cripps Going?', *New Leader*, 10 February 1939. At no point, of course, did the ILP cease to be critical of the popular front.
272 *New Leader*, 14 April 1939.
273 Ibid.
274 Ibid., 12 May 1939. See ibid., 5 May 1939, for the ILP's May Day statement opposing conscription.
275 C. A. Smith, 'Why Socialists Resist Conscription', 'Conscription Supplement', ibid., 12 May 1939. The ILP also had the support of its youth section: 'Guild of Youth says Conscription must be Smashed', *New Leader*, 9 June 1939.
276 *New Leader*, 30 June 1939. The ILP also called on the support of Groves, who was an executive member of the No Conscription League: Groves, 'Conscripting the Whole Nation', ibid., 14 July 1939.
277 *New Leader*, 14 July 1939.
278 Ibid., 28 April 1939. It appears that he was encouraged to do this by the Pattern Makers Union, of which he was chairman, because it was only prepared to endorse parliamentary candidates who were in the Labour party.
279 Ibid. See also Jupp, *Radical Left*, p. 95.
280 Middleton to Brockway, 3 July 1939, copy in Middleton papers, JSM/ILP/37. Also reported in *New Leader*, 14 July 1939.
281 Brockway, *Inside the Left*, pp. 274–5.
282 See, for instance, their comments in *Daily Herald*, 25 July 1939.
283 For an attempt to downplay the significance of the events see *New Leader*, 21 July 1939. The conference also endorsed arrangements for the election of a new Divisional Council which was prepared to carry out party decisions.
284 'The ILP and the Labour Party', ibid., 11 August 1939. See also Brockway, *Inside the Left*, p. 275.
285 In fact, the ILP never re-affiliated to the Labour party. Instead it played an

increasingly marginal part in British politics, particularly after 1946 when Maxton died and Brockway re-joined the Labour party.

Conclusion

1   Buchanan, 'Death of Bob Smillie', p. 441, makes similar points about the ILP.
2   P. Graves, *Labour Women* (Cambridge, 1994).
3   This contrasts with Jones, *Russia Complex*, ch. 3, which contends that more critical attitudes to the Soviet Union only developed on the Left after the Nazi-Soviet Pact.
4   Morrison speaking in October 1937: *LPACR*, 1937, p. 164.
5   See Orwell, 'Review of Eugene Lyons, *Assignment in Utopia*', in *New English Weekly*, 8 June 1938, in G. Orwell, *Orwell and Politics* (2001), pp. 31–4. See also Orwell, 'Why I join the ILP', *New Leader*, 24 June 1938.
6   For Pritt's account of these events see Pritt, *Right to Left*, pp. 190, 195–211, 216–26.
7   *Tribune*, 25 August 1939.
8   Jones, *Russia Complex*, p. 45, citing 5 HC Debs, vol. 351, cols., 55–60, 24 August 1939.
9   *Tribune*, 8 December 1939, quoted in Jones, *Russia Complex*, p. 48.
10 Jones, *Russia Complex*, p. 48.
11 5 HC Debs, vol. 351, cols., 37–43, 24 August 1939, quoted in Jones, *Russia Complex*, p. 37.
12 *New Leader*, 1 March 1940, quoted in Jones, *Russia Complex*, p. 37.
13 Cohen thesis, p. 331, footnote 3.
14 *New Republic*, 13 September 1939, quoted in Leventhal, *Last Dissenter*, p. 267.
15 *Reynolds News*, 3 December 1939, quoted in Leventhal, *Last Dissenter*, p. 269.
16 *New Statesman and Nation*, 6 January 1940, quoted in Jones, *Russia Complex*, p. 47.
17 See the discussion in S. Brooke, *Labour's War: The Labour Party During the Second World War* (Oxford, 1992), pp. 273–4.
18 Kramnick and Sheerman, *Laski*, p. 426; Brooke, *Labour's War*, p. 272.
19 See Corthorn, 'Stalinist Purges'.
20 *TUCAR*, 1939, pp. 302–6, quoted in Jones, *Russia Complex*, p. 35.
21 *Daily Herald*, 30 November 1939, quoted in Jones, *Russia Complex*, p. 36.
22 A more detailed examination is needed but for the outlines see Jones, *Russia Complex*, chs. 3–11; A. Thorpe, 'Stalinism and British Politics', *History*, 83, 272 (1998), pp. 608–27; and K. O. Morgan, *Labour in Power 1945–51* (Oxford, 1984), ch. 6 and pp. 320–1.

BIBLIOGRAPHY

PRIMARY SOURCES

National Archives material
Security Service file on H. N. Brailsford, KV2/686
Security Service file on Stafford Cripps, KV2/668
Government Code and Cypher School: Decrypts of Communist International (Comintern) messages, HW/17/21

Party and Organisational papers
CPGB Central Committee minutes, CPA, LHASC
CPGB Politburo minutes, CPA, LHASC
CPGB 'microfilms from Moscow', 1930s, CPA, LHASC
Gateshead City Borough Council minutes, 1931 to 1937, Tyne and Wear Archives Service, Newcastle-Upon-Tyne
ILP archives, BLPES and microform
Labour party NEC minutes, microform
Socialist League Executive Committee minutes, 1936–7, Cripps papers
Socialist League National Council minutes, 1936–7, Cripps papers
Socialist League and Scottish Socialist Society file, LPA, LHASC
Socialist League file, LPA, LHASC
Socialist League Gateshead branch Executive Committee minutes, Tyne and Wear Archives Service, Newcastle-Upon-Tyne
TUC archive, MRC, University of Warwick
TUC General Council minutes, microform

Personal papers
Christopher Addison papers, Bodleian Library, Oxford
Clement Attlee papers, Bodleian Library, Oxford and Churchill College, Cambridge
Ernest Bevin papers, Churchill College, Cambridge
H. N. Brailsford papers, LPA, LHASC
A. Fenner Brockway papers, Churchill College, Cambridge
Walter Citrine papers, BLPES
G. D. H. Cole papers, Nuffield College, Oxford
Stafford Cripps papers, Bodleian Library, Oxford (in possession of Professor Peter Clarke at time of consultation)
Hugh Dalton papers, BLPES
R. Palme Dutt papers, CPA, LHASC
Reg Groves papers, MRC, University of Warwick
George Lansbury papers, BLPES
Harold Laski papers, Brynmor Jones Library, University of Hull

Walter Layton papers, Trinity College, Cambridge
Kingsley Martin papers, University of Sussex
James Middleton papers, Ruskin College, Oxford and LPA, LHASC
J. T. Murphy papers, LPA, LHASC
Joseph Needham papers, Cambridge University Library
Passfield papers, BLPES
F. W. Pethick-Lawrence papers, Trinity College, Cambridge
Harry Pollitt papers, CPA, LHASC
Arthur Ponsonby papers, Bodleian Library, Oxford
D. N. Pritt papers, BLPES
George Strauss papers, Churchill College, Cambridge
Charles Trevelyan papers, Robinson Library, University of Newcastle-Upon-Tyne
Leonard Woolf papers, University of Sussex

Labour party publications
Labour Party Annual Conference Reports (LPACR)
Democracy versus Dictatorship (1933)
Socialism and the Condition of the People (1933)
For Socialism and Peace (1934)
Labour and the Defence of Peace (1936)
Labour's Immediate Programme (1937)
The Labour Party and the so-called 'Unity Campaign' (1937)
Labour and the Popular Front (1938)

Other organisational publications
ILP, *Through the Class Struggle to Socialism* (1937)
Parliamentary Debates: House of Commons [*HC Debs*]
Socialist League, *First Annual Conference Report* (1933)
——*Final Agenda: Second Annual Conference* (1934)
——*Forward to Socialism* (1934)
——*Report of National Council and Final Agenda of the Annual Conference* (1937)
Trades Union Congress, *Trades Union Congress Annual Reports (TUCAR)*

Newspapers and journals
Controversy
Daily Herald
Daily Worker
Forward
Labour Magazine
Labour Monthly
Manchester Guardian
New Clarion
New Leader
New Statesman and Nation
News Chronicle
Reynolds Illustrated News (*Reynolds News* after 1 March 1936)
Socialist Broadsheet
Socialist Leaguer
The Socialist
The Times
Tribune

Press cuttings from a range of other contemporary newspapers: Cripps papers, Bodleian Library, Oxford

Contemporary publications of individuals
Brailsford, H. N., *Property or Peace?* (1934)
——*Spain's Challenge to Labour* (1936)
——*Towards a New League* (1936)
'Cato', *Guilty Men* (1940)
Cole, G. D. H., *The Socialist Control of Industry* (1932)
——*The People's Front* (1937)
Cripps, Richard Stafford, *The Choice for Britain* (1934)
——*Fight Now Against War* (1935)
——*'National' Fascism in Britain* (1935)
——'Can Socialism come by Constitutional Means?' in Addison, C. et al., *Problems of a Socialist Government* (1933), pp. 35–66
Cripps, Richard Stafford *et al*, *Problems of a Socialist Transition* (1934)
Dutt, R. Palme, *Fascism and Social Revolution* (1935)
Groves, Reg, *Trades Councils in the Fight for Socialism* (1935)
——*East End Crisis: Socialism, the Jews and Fascism* (1936)
Henderson, Arthur, *Labour's Foreign Policy* (1933)
Hobson, J. A., *Imperialism* (1902)
Horrabin, J. Frank, *The Break with Imperialism* (1934)
Laski, Harold J., *The Crisis and the Constitution: 1931 and After* (1932)
——*Nationalism and the Future of Civilisation* (1932)
——*Democracy in Crisis* (1933)
——*The Labour Party and the Constitution* (1933)
——'The Economic Foundation of Peace', in Woolf, Leonard (ed.), *The Intelligent Man's Way to Prevent War* (1933), pp. 499–547
——*Law and Justice in Soviet Russia* (1935)
Mitchison, G. Richard, *The First Workers' Government or New Times for Henry Dubb* (1934)
Murphy, J. T., *Fascism: The Socialist Answer* (1934)
Orwell, George, *Homage to Catalonia* (1938)
——*Orwell and Politics* (reprinted essay collection, 2001)
Pritt, D. N., *The Zinoviev Trial* (1936)
Trevelyan, Charles, *Mass Resistance to War* (1934)
——*Soviet Russia: A Description for British Workers* (1935)
Wilkinson, Ellen, *The Town that was Murdered* (1939)

Autobiographies/memoirs
Brockway, A. Fenner, *Inside the Left* (1942)
Castle, Barbara, *Fighting all the Way* (1993)
Citrine, Walter, *Men and Work* (1964)
Cole, Margaret, *Growing up into Revolution* (1948)
Dalton, Hugh, *Call Back Yesterday: Memoirs 1887–1931* (1953)
——*The Fateful Years: Memoirs 1931–45* (1957)
Martin, Kingsley, *Editor: A Second Volume of Autobiography 1931–45* (1968)
Murphy, J. T., *New Horizons* (1940)
Paton, John, *Left Turn: The Autobiography of John Paton* (1936)
Pritt, D. N., *The Autobiography of D. N. Pritt Part One: From Right to Left* (1965)
Willis, Ted, *Whatever Happened to Tom Mix?* (1970)

Oral evidence
Lionel Elvin, interview with the author, 12 October 2000

SECONDARY SOURCES
Published works
Bell, A. Olivier (ed.), *The Diary of Virginia Woolf: volume iv 1931–5* (1983)
Birn, David, *The League of Nations Union* (New York, 1981)
Blaazer, David, *The Popular Front and the Progressive Tradition: Socialists, Liberals and the Quest for Unity, 1884–1939* (Cambridge, 1992)
Bornstein, Sam, and Richardson, Al, *Against the Stream: A History of the Trotskyist Movement in Britain 1924–38* (1986)
Branson, Noreen, *History of the Communist Party of Great Britain 1927–41* (1985)
Brooke, Stephen, *Labour's War: the Labour Party during the Second World War* (Oxford, 1992)
Brown, Gordon J., *Maxton* (Edinburgh, 1986)
Buchanan, Tom, *The Spanish Civil War and the British Labour Movement* (Cambridge, 1992)
—— 'The Death of Bob Smillie, the Spanish Civil War and the Eclipse of the Independent Labour Party', *Historical Journal*, 40, 2 (1997), pp. 435–61
Bullock, Alan, *Life and Times of Ernest Bevin: Volume One Trade Union Leader 1881 to 1940* (1960)
Burgess, Simon, *Stafford Cripps: A Political Life* (1999)
Callaghan, John, *British Trotskyism: Theory and Practice* (Oxford, 1984)
Campbell, John, *Nye Bevan and the Mirage of British Socialism* (1987)
Caute, David, *The Fellow Travellers: A Postscript to the Enlightenment* (1973)
Ceadel, Martin, *Pacifism in Great Britain 1914–45: The Defining of a Faith* (Oxford, 1980)
—— 'The First British Referendum: The Peace Ballot, 1934–5', *English Historical Review*, 95, 377 (1980), pp. 810–39
—— *Semi-Detached Idealists: The British Peace Movement and International Relations, 1854–1945* (Oxford, 2000)
Clarke, Peter F., *The Cripps Version: The Life of Sir Stafford Cripps* (2002)
Cohen, Gidon, 'The Independent Labour Party, Disaffiliation, Revolution and Standing Orders', *History*, 86, 2 (2001), pp. 200–21
—— 'From Insufferable Petty Bourgeois to Trusted Communist: Jack Gaster, the RPC and the Communist Party', in McIlroy, J. et al (eds.), *Party People* (2001), pp. 190–209
—— 'The Independent Socialist Party' in Gildart, K., Howell, D., and Kirk, N. (eds.), *Dictionary of Labour Biography volume XI* (2003), pp. 231–8
Cole, G. D. H., *A History of the Labour Party from 1914* (1948)
Cole, Margaret, *The Story of Fabian Socialism* (1961)
Cooke, Colin Arthur, *The Life of Richard Stafford Cripps* (1957)
Corthorn, Paul, 'The Labour Party and the League of Nations: The Socialist League's Role in the Sanctions Crisis of 1935', *Twentieth Century British History*, 13, 1 (2002), pp. 62–85
—— 'Labour, the Left, and the Stalinist Purges of the late 1930s', *Historical Journal*, 48, 1 (2005), pp. 179–207
Cowling, Maurice, *The Impact of Hitler: British Politics and Policy 1933–40* (Cambridge, 1975)
Dare, Robert, 'Instinct and Organisation: Intellectuals and British Labour after 1931', *Historical Journal*, 26, 3 (1983), pp. 677–97
Darlington, Ralph, *The Political Trajectory of J. T. Murphy* (Liverpool, 1998)
Donoughue, Bernard and Jones, G. W., *Herbert Morrison: Portrait of a Politician* (1973)
Dowse, R. E., *Left in the Centre: The ILP 1893–1940* (1966)

Durbin, Elizabeth, *New Jerusalems: The Labour Party and the Economics of Democratic Socialism* (1985)
Estorick, Eric, *Stafford Cripps: A Biography* (1949)
Fleay, C., and Sanders, M. L., 'The Labour Spain Committee: Labour Party Policy and the Spanish Civil War', *Historical Journal*, 28, 1 (1985), pp. 187–97
Foot, Michael, 'The Road to Ruin' in Thomas, E. (ed.), *Tribune 21* (1958)
——*Aneurin Bevan: A Biography Volume One 1897 to 1945* (1962)
Frame, William, 'Sir Stafford Cripps and his Friends: the Socialist League, the National government and the Reform of the House of Lords 1931–1935', *Parliamentary History*, 24, 3 (2005), pp. 316–31
Graves, Pamela, *Labour Women* (Cambridge, 1994)
Groves, Reg, *The Balham Group* (1974)
——'The Socialist League', *Revolutionary History*, 1, 1 (1988)
Harris, Kenneth, *Attlee* (1982)
Howe, Stephen, 'Cyril Lionel Robert James', Oxford DNB online (2004)
Howell, David, *MacDonald's Party: Labour Identities and Crisis 1922–31* (Oxford, 2002)
Hyams, E., *The New Statesman: The History of the First Fifty Years 1913–1963* (1963)
Jones, Bill, *The Russia Complex: The British Labour Party and the Soviet Union* (Manchester, 1987)
Jones, Mervyn, *Michael Foot* (1994)
Jupp, James, *The Radical Left in Britain 1931–41* (1982)
Kramnick, I., and Sheerman, Barry, *Harold Laski: A Life on the Left* (1993)
Kushner, Tony, and Valman, Nadia (eds.), *Remembering Cable Street: Fascism and Anti-Fascism in Britain* (2000)
Leventhal, Fred, *The Last Dissenter: H. N. Brailsford and his World* (Oxford, 1985)
Lewis, J., *The Left Book Club: An Historical Record* (1970)
McHenry, Dean, *The Labour Party in Transition* (1938)
MacKenzie, Norman and MacKenzie, Jeanne (eds.) *The Diary of Beatrice Webb: volume four – 1924–43: The Wheel of Life* (1985)
McNair, John, *James Maxton: The Beloved Rebel* (1955)
Marquand, David, *Ramsay MacDonald* (1977)
Martin, Kingsley, *Harold Laski 1893–1950: A Biographical Memoir* (1953)
Middlemas, R. K., *The Clydesiders: A Left Wing Struggle for Parliamentary Power* (1965)
Morgan, Kevin, *Against Fascism and War: Ruptures and Continuities in British Communist Politics 1935–41* (Manchester, 1989)
——*Harry Pollitt* (Manchester, 1993)
Morgan, K. O., *Labour in Power 1945–51* (Oxford, 1984)
Morris, A. J. A., *C. P. Trevelyan 1870–1958: Portrait of a Radical* (Belfast, 1977)
Mowat, C. L., *Britain Between the Wars 1918–40* (1955)
Naylor, John F., *Labour's International Policy: The Labour Party in the 1930s* (1969)
Newman, Michael, *Harold Laski: A Political Biography* (1993)
Pearce, Robert (ed.), *Patrick Gordon Walker: Political Diaries 1932–71* (1991)
Pelling, Henry, *A Short History of the Labour Party* (1961)
Pimlott, Ben, 'The Socialist League – Intellectuals and the Labour Left in the 1930s', *Journal of Contemporary History*, 6, 3 (1971), pp. 12–39
——*Labour and the Left in the 1930s* (Cambridge, 1977)
——*Hugh Dalton* (1985)
——(ed.) *The Political Diary of Hugh Dalton* (1986)
Riddell, Neil, '"The Age of Cole"? G. D. H. Cole and the British Labour Movement, 1929–33', *Historical Journal*, 38, 4 (1995), pp. 933–57
——*Labour in Crisis: The Second Labour Government 1929–31* (Manchester, 1999)

Rolph, C. H., *Kingsley: The Life, Letters and Diaries of Kingsley Martin* (1973)

Samuels, S., 'The Left Book Club', *Journal of Contemporary History*, 1, 2 (1966), pp. 65–86

Seyd, Patrick, 'Factionalism Within the Labour Party: The Socialist League 1932–1937', in Briggs, Asa and Saville, John (eds.) *Essays in Labour History 1918–1939* (1977), pp. 204–31

Shackleton, Richard, 'Trade Unions and the Slump', in Pimlott, Ben and Cook, Chris, *Trade Unions in British Politics* (1982), pp. 120–48

Shaw, Louise Grace, *The British Political Elite and the Soviet Union 1937–39* (2003)

Shepherd, John, 'Labour and the Trade Unions: George Lansbury, Ernest Bevin and the Leadership Crisis of 1935', in Wrigley, Chris and Shepherd, John (eds.) *On the Move* (1991), pp. 204–30

——*George Lansbury: At the Heart of Old Labour* (Oxford, 2002)

Stannage, Tom, *Baldwin Thwarts the Opposition: The British General Election of 1935* (1980)

Stevenson, John, and Cook, Chris, *Britain in the Depression: Society and Politics 1929–39* (1994, 2nd Edition)

Taylor, A. J. P., *English History 1914–45* (Oxford, 1965)

Thomas, Hugh, *The Spanish Civil War* (1961)

——*John Strachey* (1973)

Thorpe, Andrew, 'Arthur Henderson and the British Political Crisis of 1931', *Historical Journal*, 31, 1 (1988), pp. 117–39

——*The British General Election of 1931* (Oxford, 1991)

——*A History of the British Labour Party* (1997)

——'Stalinism and British Politics', *History*, 83, 272 (1998), pp. 608–27

——*The British Communist Party and Moscow*, 1920–43 (Manchester, 2000)

Toye, Richard, 'The Labour Party and the Economics of Rearmament, 1935–39', *Twentieth Century British History*, 12, 3 (2001), pp. 303–26

——*The Labour Party and the Planned Economy 1931–51* (Woodbridge, 2003)

Williams, Andrew J., 'The Labour Party's Attitude to the Soviet Union 1927–35: an overview with specific reference to Unemployment Policy and Peace', *Journal of Contemporary History*, 22, 1 (1987), pp. 71–90

——*Labour and Russia: The Attitude of the Labour Party to the USSR, 1924–34* (Manchester, 1989)

Williams, Francis, *Ernest Bevin: Portrait of a Great Englishman* (1952)

Williamson, Philip, *National Crisis and National Government: British Politics, the Economy and Empire, 1926–32* (Cambridge, 1992)

——*Stanley Baldwin* (Cambridge, 1999)

Winkler, Henry, *Paths Not Taken: British Labour and International Policy in the 1920s* (Chapel Hill, 1994)

Worley, Matthew, *Labour Inside the Gate: A History of the British Labour Party between the Wars* (2005)

Unpublished theses

Cohen, Gidon, 'The Independent Labour Party, 1932–39' (University of York D. Phil., 2000)

Dare, Robert, 'The Socialist League 1932–37' (University of Oxford D. Phil., 1973)

Davis, Jonathan Shaw, 'Altered Images: The British Labour Party and the Soviet Union in the 1930s' (De Montfort University Ph.D., 2002)

Eatwell, Roger, 'The Labour Party and the Popular Front Movement in Britain in the 1930s', (University of Oxford D. Phil., 1975)

Stuart, Jill Marie, 'The Soviet Experiment in English Revolutionary Thought and Politics 1928–41' (University of Cambridge Ph.D., 1991)

INDEX

Abyssinia, 44, 72, 79
Acland, Richard, 200–1
Addison, Christopher, 13, 15, 19, 132
Alexander, A. V., 181
Allighan, Garry, 128, 131, 141–2, 144, 154
Amery, Leo, 5, 192
Anti-Stalinism, 6, 8, 86, 97, 99, 106, 113, 125, 129, 137, 163, 177–9, 188, 213–16
Aplin, John, 68, 120, 161, 180, 187, 190, 194, 196, 197, 208
Atholl, Duchess of, 181
Attlee, Clement, 10–11, 15–16, 19, 21, 24, 36, 39, 45, 48, 61–2, 73, 81, 104–5, 117–18, 143, 189, 203, 216
Austria, 35, 38, 181–3, 187
Baldwin, Stanley, 45, 61–2, 76, 105, 179, 206
Balham Group, 98, 128
Ballantine, William, 209
Barber, Donald, 30, 144–5, 154, 162
Barker, Deborah, 116, 134–5, 149, 151–2, 157, 162
Bartlett, Vernon, 193, 195, 198
Bennett, Arnold, 128
Betts, Barbara, 2, 31, 49, 54, 89, 103, 107, 113, 115–16, 120, 149, 158, 163, 174, 185, 213
Bevan, Aneurin, 2–3, 44, 50–1, 73, 75, 83, 101–4, 107–8, 111, 114, 119, 140, 171, 198, 201–3, 205, 214
Bevin, Ernest, 4, 11, 13, 16, 19, 22–3, 45, 48, 58–9, 61, 63, 66–7, 73, 87, 100, 104, 117, 122, 132, 170–1, 216
Blaazer, David, 3
Blair, Eric; see Orwell, George
Bonham Carter, Violet, 201
Borrett, Constance, 30, 49, 108, 114, 116, 133–5, 145, 147, 149
Brailsford, H. N., 2–3, 11, 14, 21–3, 30–2, 46, 51–2, 61, 63, 74, 76, 84, 87–9, 93–4, 97–8, 110–12, 114, 116,
127, 138, 158–9, 165–6, 177–8, 182, 184, 187, 205, 213–15
British Union of Fascists, 108–9
Brockway, Audrey, 180
Brockway, Fenner, 2, 10–11, 15, 17–18, 28, 33–5, 43–4, 55–6, 60, 64, 68–72, 78–9, 94–7, 103, 111–12, 116–18, 120, 124–5, 136, 138–40, 146, 150, 155, 161, 163–5, 172–3, 175–7, 180, 188–90, 193–7, 207, 209–10, 214
Buchanan, George, 17, 56, 68, 70, 164, 176, 210
Buchanan, Tom, 4, 87, 117
Bukharin, Nikolai, 176–7
Campbell, Andrew, 109, 128, 131, 133, 141, 145, 154–5
Campbell, J. R., 120, 155
Carmichael, James, 70–1, 137, 189–90, 208
Castle, Barbara; see Betts, Barbara
Ceadel, Martin, 45
Chamberlain, Neville, 5, 105, 179–81, 183–4, 191–2, 194–6, 198–9, 203, 206, 214
Chelmsford, Bishop of, 181
Churchill, Winston, 5, 135, 169, 181, 192, 198–9, 206
Citrine, Walter, 4, 13, 16, 29–30, 36, 45, 48, 73, 87, 99–101, 104, 117, 135, 171, 216
Clarke, Peter, 192
Cole, G. D. H., 2, 11, 14, 19–23, 26, 28, 30, 37, 66, 132, 183–5, 200–2
Cole, Margaret, 19
Comintern/Communist International, 27–8, 33–5, 44, 46–7, 55, 64–6, 69, 77, 81, 92, 95, 98, 113, 115, 125, 131–2, 140, 173, 176, 188, 212
Communist Party of Great Britain, 4–5, 7–9, 18, 27–8, 33–6, 42, 44, 47, 49, 53, 60, 64–9, 71, 77–83, 86, 92, 95,

98–100, 103–10, 165–6, 169–70, 172–3, 175–7, 183–4, 188–9, 212–14; see also Unity Campaign
Conscription,   74, 76, 80, 179, 195–8, 204, 208–10
Constituency parties movement,   118–20, 147, 154, 159, 166–8, 170–1
Cripps, John,   186
Cripps, R. Stafford,   2, 5, 8, 11, 14–16, 19, 22–5, 28–31, 36–8, 41–2, 46–54, 57–62, 64–6, 73, 75–7, 79–81, 84–5, 89–90, 93, 100, 103–5, 107, 111, 113–15, 119–20, 122, 125–32, 136–9, 141, 143–4, 146–7, 149–63, 166–72, 177, 181–6, 189, 192–3, 197–207, 213–14
Cullen, C. K.,   18, 68
Cummings, A. J.,   181
Czechoslovakia,   190–3, 203, 216
Dallas, George,   189
Dalton, Hugh,   4, 13, 16–17, 19–21, 23–4, 26, 29–30, 36, 39, 42, 45, 48, 57–8, 62, 65–6, 73, 82, 104–5, 122, 132–3, 148, 150, 167, 171, 178, 192, 199, 202, 204, 216
De Asua, Jimenev,   105
De Azcarate, Pablo,   105
De Palencia, Isabel,   105
Del Vayo, Alvarez,   105
Delahaye, Jim,   83, 85, 94, 112
Dodds, Ruth,   25, 31, 49, 134, 193
Dollan, Pat,   18, 23
Dowse, R. E.,   17
Durbin, Evan,   17, 21, 148
Dutt, Rajani Palme,   53, 98, 111, 120, 125, 166, 176
Eden, Anthony,   5, 62, 87, 89–90, 180–1, 192
Edwards, Bob,   72, 130, 180, 193, 207–8
Elvin, Lionel,   30, 49, 53–4, 65, 116, 146, 160
Entwhistle, Robert,   163
Evans, Glynn,   25
Fenn, L. Anderson,   93–4, 112
Foot, Michael,   51, 101, 107, 137–8, 185–6, 204
Franco, Francisco,   1, 86, 88–91, 95, 101, 104, 173, 181, 187–8, 200, 204
Gaitskell, Hugh,   17, 21
Gaster, Jack,   18, 33, 43, 68
General elections,   15, 61–2, 68
Germany,   27, 29, 32, 34, 38, 42, 67, 74, 181–3, 187, 190–1, 211, 213–16; see also Hitler, Adolf
Gollancz, Victor,   2, 99, 154, 181, 186, 206
Gorkin, Julian,   138
Graves, Pamela,   213
Greene, Ben,   119–20, 159, 167–8, 170
Greenwood, Arthur,   16, 31, 62, 104–5, 117, 135, 143

Grenfell, David,   181
Groves, Reg,   80–2, 89–91, 97–8, 101–2, 106–10, 114–16, 120–2, 126–35, 138, 141–7, 149, 152–8, 162, 172, 188, 195, 214
Hartshorn, H. J.,   186, 191, 214
Hawkins, A. H.,   43
Henderson, Arthur,   10, 12, 16–17, 24, 32–3, 35–6, 38–9, 44–5, 47, 118
Hill, Gwen,   203–4
Hitler, Adolf,   1, 6, 9, 27, 29, 32, 38, 42, 51, 55, 67, 74–5, 88, 90, 98, 101, 131, 138, 173, 178, 190–2, 203, 207, 213, 216
Hoare, Samuel,   45, 62; see also Hoare-Laval pact
Hoare-Laval pact,   62, 64
Hobson, J. A.,   3, 10–11
Home Counties Labour Association,   119, 146, 185
Horrabin, J. Frank,   11, 19, 21–3, 30, 38, 46, 49, 102, 109, 114, 135, 138, 142, 146–7, 152–3, 168, 194–5
House of Commons Group,   19–20, 22
Howell, David,   6
Hunger marches,   106–8, 121, 134, 169; see also National Unemployed Workers' Movement
Hunter, Ernest,   141
Huntz, Jack,   187, 193
Independent Labour Party,   1–8
    affiliation committee   20–3
    CPGB   33–5, 44, 68, 161, 172, 188–9, 212, (see also Unity Campaign)
    crisis of 1931   14–15
    early rise of Hitler   34
    Labour party   10–11, 17, 18, 20, 35, 68–9, 172–3, 189–90, 207–11, 213
    League of Nations   43, 55–6, 68
    Marxist Group   69–70, 124
    mass/war resistance   55–7, 63–4, 69–72, 179–81, 186–7, 193–4, 207, 209–10, 212–13
    national conferences   18, 43–4, 69–71, 140, 177, 187, 189–90, 196–7, 207–8
    National government   43
    Non-intervention   95–6, 117–18
    popular front   78–9, 140, 187–8, 190, 195, 206, (see also Unity Campaign)
    POUM   94–5, 125, 138–40, 155, 161, 164–5, 173–4, 188–9, 214
    rearmament   60, 63, 76–7, 111, 130, 146–7, 172–3, 180, 187, 189, 195, 210
    RPC   18, 33, 35, 43–4, 56, 68
    Socialist League   28, 35, 57, 76–7, 103–4, (see also Unity Campaign)
    Soviet foreign policy   43–4, 55–6, 68–9, 95–6, 117–18, (see also Independent

Labour Party, POUM; and Unity Campaign)
Soviet purges 97, 136–7, 163–4, 173–4, 176–7, 188, 214
structure 1–3, 17–18, 25, 56, 69–71
united front/workers front 28, 33–5, 68–9, 78–9, 95–6, 187, 195, 206–7, (see also Unity Campaign)
'working-class sanctions' 55–6, 68–72, 213
Independent Socialist Party, 35
International Bureau, 27, 55, 70, 78–9, 94, 97, 164, 174, 188, 193, 195, 196, 207
International Federation of Trade Unions, 180
Italy, 40, 44; see also Mussolini, Benito
James, C. L. R., 69–72, 124, 140
Japan, 32, 180
Jay, Douglas, 17
Joad, C. E. M., 194
Johnson, George, 194, 197
Jowett, Fred, 10, 209
Jupp, James, 5
Kamenev, Lev, 96
Keynes, John Maynard, 201
Kirkwood, David, 17, 23, 30
Kirov, Sergei, 96
Labour and Socialist International, 27–8, 44, 55, 180
Labour party; annual conferences 23–4, 33, 38–9, 57–9, 104–5, 168–71
CPGB, (see Labour party, popular front; Labour party, united front; Labour party, Unity Campaign)
crisis of 1931 3–4, 12–14
Daily Herald 67
economic policies 26, 38
ILP 189–90, 210
League of Nations 32, 38–9, 45, 57, 59, 79
League of Youth 141
NEC 4–5, 7–9, 13, 15–17, 19–20, 23–7, 31–3, 35–9, 41–5, 47–8, 53–4, 57–62, 64–7, 73, 75, 79–83, 102, 104, 107–8, 110, 118–19, 122–4, 129, 132–5, 141, 143–4, 147–51, 155–7, 159–62, 167–71, 178–9, 183–4, 186, 189–90, 198–9, 201–5, 212–13
NJC/NCL 4, 7, 16, 28–9, 39, 73–4, 79, 81–2, 86–7, 89–91, 94, 100–3, 105, 130, 146
Non-intervention 87, 104–5, 117
PLP 2, 11, 13, 15–17, 19, 24, 36, 45, 53, 73–4, 82, 119, 171–2
popular front 184, 197–9, 201–5
rearmament 82, 104, 171
Socialist League 29–30, 36, 39, 42, 47, 57–9, 66–7, 75, 122–3, 132–3, 143, 147–50, 159–60

Soviet purges 99–100, 138, 178
Spain Campaign Committee 171–2
united front 28–9, 66, 104–5, (see also Labour party, Unity Campaign)
Unity Campaign 132–3, 143, 147–50, 159–60, 168–71
Labour Spain Committee, 146, 184–5
Labour Unity Committee, 160–3, 166, 168–71
Lansbury, George, 13, 16–17, 19, 24, 36, 45–6, 49, 54, 57–9, 61, 103, 129, 132, 148–9
Laski, Harold J., 2, 15, 19, 21, 35–6, 49, 91, 99, 129, 150, 159, 161, 163, 168–71, 175–8, 180, 182–3, 191, 199, 205, 214–15
Lawther, Will, 202
Lee, Jennie, 44, 63, 68, 78, 96, 118, 139–40, 177, 187, 208, 213
Left Book Club, 2, 99, 154, 159, 176, 186, 191–2, 200, 205–6
Lenin, Vladimir, 44, 47, 69
Lindsay, A. D., 192–3
Lloyd George, Megan, 181
London County Council, 102, 143–4, 147–8, 169
McCarthy, Margaret, 31, 93, 147, 153, 162
MacDonald, J. Ramsay, 3, 9–15, 45, 59
McGovern, John, 17, 34, 56, 68, 70–2, 79, 96, 139, 164, 173, 176, 180, 190, 194, 196–7, 210, 215
McNair, John, 94, 96, 139, 161, 164, 173, 180, 188, 194, 197, 207
Maisky, Ivan, 50, 54, 165–6
Marchbank, John, 180
Maurin, Joaquin, 78–9, 94
Maxton, James, 2, 10–11, 15, 17–18, 33–5, 44, 56–7, 60, 68–9, 71–2, 94, 96, 103, 111, 129–30, 137, 139, 141, 155, 160–1, 163–5, 172–3, 176, 179, 188–90, 194, 196–7, 208–9, 213–14
Mellor, William, 2, 11, 19, 23, 26, 30, 37, 39, 41–2, 46–50, 53, 57–8, 62, 65, 67, 75–7, 79–82, 84–5, 90, 92, 94, 102–5, 107–16, 119–28, 130–1, 133–7, 140, 142–6, 148–9, 152–3, 156, 159–60, 163, 167–9, 174, 177, 185–6, 204, 213–14
Middleton, Jim, 47, 65, 83, 133, 183, 197–9, 210
Mitchison, G. R., 19, 21, 39, 46, 49, 53, 65, 108, 114, 116, 120, 123, 136, 142, 145–6, 152, 158, 161
Mitchison, Naomi, 49, 198, 200
Morris, William, 9
Morrison, Herbert, 4, 13, 16–17, 20, 39, 62, 73, 81, 90, 102, 144, 147–8, 169, 192, 203

Munich agreement, 5, 179, 191– 2, 194–8, 203, 207–8
Murphy, J. T., 31, 36, 38, 42, 46–50, 53, 60–2, 67, 76, 81–3, 91–3, 112, 128
Mussolini, Benito, 1, 7, 37, 40, 44–6, 48–52, 56, 58, 75, 88, 90, 173, 178
National government, 3–4, 7, 9, 12–15, 32–3, 35–7, 39, 43, 45–6, 48, 50, 52–4, 57–8, 60–5, 70, 73–6, 79–80, 82, 86–8, 90, 92, 95–6, 100–1, 103–4, 111, 113, 115, 117, 130, 146–7, 165, 171, 179–80, 184–7, 189, 191, 193–5, 197–8, 200–1, 203, 208, 210, 213
National Unemployed Workers' Movement, 15, 33, 106–8
Nazi-Soviet pact, 8, 211, 213–16
Needham, Joseph, 61
Negrin, Juan, 164
New Fabian Research Bureau, 21
Nicolson, Harold, 181
Nin, Andres, 164, 173
Noel-Baker, Philip, 181
Orwell, George, 2, 6, 161, 164–5, 194, 214–15
Pacifism (including pacifist organisations), 13, 23, 45–6, 49, 54, 57–9, 179, 193–6, 209
Page Arnot, Robin, 166
Paton, John, 17–18, 25, 34
Patterson, Ernie, 137, 187, 190, 196, 208, 210, 214
Pelling, Henry, 4
Pethick-Lawrence, Frederick, 23, 30
Petition Campaign/Cripps Memorandum, 197–205
Pimlott, Ben, 4–5, 118–19, 150
Pole, Joseph, 184
Pollitt, Harry, 33, 47, 64, 77–8, 95, 98–9, 103, 111–13, 115–16, 125, 129–30, 139, 141–2, 150, 155, 160, 163, 165–6, 169, 176, 183, 188
Popular front, 5, 7–8, 77–9, 181–8, 192–3, 197–205, 213; see also Independent Labour Party, popular front; Socialist League, popular front; and Unity Campaign
POUM, 8, 78–9, 87, 94–5, 103, 118, 125–6, 129, 138–40, 142, 145–6, 155, 161, 164–5, 169, 174–5, 187–9, 207, 214
Pritt, D. N., 11, 19, 50, 61–2, 91, 98, 132, 170–1, 181, 183, 199, 202, 214
Pugh, Arthur, 23, 30
Purkis, Stuart, 98, 138
Radek, Karl, 136
Radice, E. A., 11, 15, 25, 30
Roberts, Wilfred, 181, 200–1
Salter, Alfred, 23, 30, 194–5
Sandham, Elijah, 34–5

Sankey, Lord, 12
Scottish Socialist Party, 23
Shepherd, George, 24, 198
Show Trials; see Soviet Union, purges
Sinclair, Archibald, 5, 181
Smith, C. A., 70, 72, 187, 190, 196, 209–10, 215
Snowden, Philip, 10–13
Socialist League, 1–8
    constitutional policies 27, 29, 31
    CPGB 28, 64–5, 67, 103, (see also Unity Campaign)
    dissolution 123–4, 135, 147–58
    early rise of Hitler 29–30, 32–3
    economic policies 25–7, 37
    formation 20–3
    ILP 103–4, (see also Unity Campaign)
    Labour Party 23–4, 31, 33, 36, 38–41, 47–8, 53–4, 57–9, 61–2, 65–7, 79, 133–5
    League of Nations 32–3, 43, 46–54, 58, 60–3, 212
    mass/war resistance 32–3, 38–9, 42, 46–53, 57–61, 212–13
    national conferences 28, 31–3, 37, 41, 46–7, 80–1, 127, 156–8
    National government 35–7
    Non-intervention 87–91, 100–5, 117
    popular front 77–8, 83–5, 91–4, 111–12, 145–6, 157
    POUM 103, 125–6, 142
    rearmament 53, 60, 73–7, 80–2, 100–1, 111, 130, 146–7
    Soviet foreign policy 39, 43, 46–7, 49–50, 54–5, 58, 67, (see also Unity Campaign)
    Soviet purges 97–9, 137–8, 142, (see also Unity Campaign)
    structure 1–3, 23–5, 30–1, 37, 41–2
    united front 28, 64–7, 77–8, 80–5, 91–4, 100, 104–5, 107–10, (see also Unity Campaign)
    'working-class sanctions' 48, 58
Socialist Left Federation, 162–3, 172
Society for Socialist Inquiry and Propaganda, 11–12, 14–15, 19, 20, 21
Sokolnikov, Grigory, 136
Southall, Joseph, 72
Soviet Union, 34, (see also Stalin, Joseph)
    constitution (1936) 97
    entry into League of Nations 39
    Nazi-Soviet pact 211, 213–16
    purges 96–7, 136, 163, (see also Independent Labour Party, Soviet purges and Socialist League, Soviet purges)
Spain, 86–7, 200, 204, (see also Franco, Francisco)
    Non-intervention 87, 89

Spanish Civil War; see Spain
Spurrell, Kate, 193
St John Reade, R., 119
Stalin, Joseph, 1, 47, 69, 96, 99, 100, 124, 132, 136, 138, 159, 163, 165–6, 173–6, 207, 213–16; see also anti-Stalinism; and Stalinism
Stalinism, 137, 188, 215–16
Stephen, Campbell, 55, 68, 71, 79, 164, 176, 190, 194, 210
Stephenson, Tom, 196
Strachey, John, 64–5, 99, 124, 191
Strauss, G. R., 144, 147–8, 155, 159–61, 163, 168–70, 175, 202–3, 205
Tawney, R. H., 19, 28, 94, 202–3
Thomas, J. H., 12
Trade Unions (including specific unions), 11, 16, 81, 104–5, 148, 166, 170, 180, 204, 209
Trades Union Congress; annual meeting 38, 45, 59, 100–1, 103, 166, 168, 216
    General Council 4–5, 7, 9, 12–13, 15–16, 19, 23, 28, 35–6, 42–3, 45, 47–8, 57–60, 65, 67, 74–6, 79–82, 104, 122–3, 150, 167, 171, 178–80, 208, 212, 215–16
Treaty of Versailles, 42, 51, 67, 74
Trevelyan, Charles, 2, 14, 23–4, 33, 50, 54, 58, 60, 74, 76, 91, 104, 181, 184, 200, 202–3
Tribune, 1
    alliance with Soviet Union 191
    mass/war resistance 180
    popular front 185–6

rearmament 184
Soviet purges 137–8, 174–5, 177, 191, (see also Unity Campaign)
Trotsky, Leon, 69, 96–8, 136, 138, 140, 163–4, 169, 173–4, 214; see also Trotskyism
Trotskyism, 6, 69–70, 98, 124, 131, 136–7, 140, 142, 163, 187, 208, 214
United front, 4–5, 7–8, 27–8, 33–5, 44, 60, 64–9, 77–9, 81–3; see also Independent Labour Party, united front; Socialist League, united front; and Unity Campaign
Unity Campaign, 111–62
University Labour Federation, 135
Wallhead, Richard, 17, 34
Webb, Beatrice, 10, 14, 36, 57, 67, 150, 166, 174–5
Webb, Sidney, 10, 14, 150, 174–5
Wheatley, John, 10
Wicks, Harry, 98, 128, 138
Wilkes, Lyall, 203–4
Wilkinson, Ellen, 2, 49, 54, 107, 171–2, 181, 183, 199, 201–2, 213
Williams, Andrew J., 6, 11
Willis, Ted, 141
Wimbush, Arthur, 128
Wise, E. Frank, 10–11, 14–16, 18–24, 28–30, 37
XYZ Club, 17
Yagoda, Genrikh, 176
Young, E. P., 200, 202–3, 205
Zilliacus, Konni, 52, 105
Zinoviev, Grigori, 96, 98